חומש קורן מקראות הדורות
THE KOREN MIKRAOT HADOROT

פרשת תרומה
PARASHAT TERUMA

ירושלים
KOREN

THE ROHR FAMILY EDITION

חומש קורן מקראות הדורות

THE KOREN MIKRAOT HADOROT

THE ZAHAVA AND MOSHAEL STRAUS EDITION OF SEFER SHEMOT

פרשת תרומה עם מפרשים

PARASHAT TERUMA WITH COMMENTARIES

TORAH TRANSLATION BY
Rabbi Lord Jonathan Sacks שליט״א
FROM THE MAGERMAN EDITION OF THE KOREN TANAKH

EDITOR IN CHIEF
Rabbi Shai Finkelstein

COMMENTARIES COLLECTED AND ABRIDGED BY
Rabbi David Fuchs

COMMENTARIES TRANSLATED BY
Rabbi Jonathan Mishkin

MANAGING EDITOR
Rabbi Yedidya Naveh

•

KOREN PUBLISHERS JERUSALEM

The Koren Mikraot HaDorot, The Rohr Edition
Volume 19: Parashat Teruma
First Edition, 2021

Koren Publishers Jerusalem Ltd.
POB 4044, Jerusalem 9104001, ISRAEL
POB 8531, New Milford, CT 06776, USA

www.korenpub.com

The Tanakh translation is excerpted from the Magerman Edition of The Koren Tanakh.

The creation of this work was made possible with the generous support of the Jewish Book Trust Inc.

Printed in ISRAEL

ISBN 978 965 7760 74 1

KMDTR01

The Rohr Family Edition of
The Koren Mikraot HaDorot
pays tribute to the memory of

Mr. Sami Rohr ז״ל
ר׳ שמואל ב״ר יהושע אליהו ז״ל

who served his Maker with joy
and whose far-reaching vision, warm open hand, love of Torah,
and love for every Jew were catalysts for the revival and growth of
vibrant Jewish life in the former Soviet Union
and in countless communities the world over

and to the memory of his beloved wife

Mrs. Charlotte Rohr (née Kastner) ע״ה
שרה בת ר׳ יקותיאל יהודה ע״ה

who survived the fires of the Shoah to become
the elegant and gracious matriarch,
first in Colombia and later in the United States,
of three generations of a family
nurtured by her love and unstinting devotion.
She found grace in the eyes of all those whose lives she touched.

Together they merited to see all their children
build lives enriched by faithful commitment
to the spreading of Torah and *Ahavat Yisrael*.

Dedicated with love by
The Rohr Family
NEW YORK, USA

עֲטֶרֶת זְקֵנִים בְּנֵי בָנִים
(משלי יז, ו)

Grandchildren
are the crowning glory of the aged
(Proverbs 17:6)

May the learning and traditions of our people
be strengthened by our future generations.
In honor of our wonderful grandchildren

Zahava and Moshael Straus

CONTENTS

FOR THE COMPLETE RASHI AND HAFTAROT
TURN TO THE OTHER END OF THIS VOLUME.

PUBLISHER'S PREFACE

The genius of Jewish commentary on the Torah is one of huge and critical import. Jewish life and law for millennia have been directed by our interpretations of the Torah, and each generation has looked to its rabbinic leadership for a deeper understanding of its teachings, its laws, its stories.

For centuries, *Mikraot Gedolot* have been a core part of understanding the Ḥumash; the words of Rashi, Ibn Ezra, Ramban, Rashbam, Ralbag, and other classic commentators illuminate and help us understand the Torah. But traditional editions of *Mikraot Gedolot* present only a slice in time and a small selection of the corpus of Jewish commentators. Almost every generation has produced rabbinic scholars who speak to their times, from Philo and Onkelos two thousand years ago, to Rabbi Joseph B. Soloveitchik, Rabbi Aharon Kotler, the Lubavitcher Rebbe, and Nehama Leibowitz in ours.

The Koren Mikraot HaDorot – Scriptures or Interpretations for the Generations – brings two millennia of Torah commentary into the hands and homes of Jews around the world. Readers will be able not only to encounter the classic commentators, but to gain a much broader sense of the issues that scholars grappled with in their time and the inspiration they drew from the ancient texts. We see, for example, how Philo speaks to an assimilating Greek Jewish audience in first-century Alexandria, and how similar yet different it is from Rabbi Samson Raphael Hirsch's approach to an equally assimilating nineteenth-century German readership; how the perspectives of Rabbi Soloveitchik and Rabbi Kotler differ in a post-Holocaust world; how Rav Se'adya Gaon interpreted the Torah for the Jews of Babylonia. It is an exciting journey through Jewish history via the unchanging words of the Torah.

The text of the Torah features the exceptional new translation of Rabbi Lord Jonathan Sacks, together with the celebrated and meticulously accurate Koren Hebrew text. Of course, with the exception of Rashi – for whom we present an entirely new translation in full – the commentaries are selected. We offer this anthology not to limit our reader's exploration but rather as a gateway for further learning of Torah and its commentaries on a broader and deeper level than space here permits. We discuss below how to use this book.

We must thank **Pamela and George Rohr** of New York, who recognized the unique value of *The Koren Mikraot HaDorot* and its ability to communicate historical breadth and context to the reader. For my colleagues here at Koren, we thank you; for the many generations of users who will find this a continuing source of new learning, we are forever in your debt.

We also are indebted to **Zahava and Moshael Straus**, true leaders of this Jewish generation in so many fields, who have invested not only in *Parashat Teruma* but the entire book of Shemot. Together, we were thus able to launch this innovative and unique project.

We are honored to acknowledge and thank **Debra and David Magerman**, whose support for the Koren Ḥumash with Rabbi Sacks's exemplary translation and commentary laid the foundation for the core English text of this work.

Finally, I must personally thank **Rabbi Marvin Hier**, with whom I had a special breakfast some years ago at the King David Hotel. During the meal, he raised the problem that so few people knew the writings of Rabbi Joseph B. Soloveitchik and Rabbi Aharon Kotler on the Torah; and I, who had just read some of Philo's work, had the same reaction. From that conversation came the seed for this project.

HOW TO USE *THE KOREN MIKRAOT HADOROT*

The Koren Mikraot HaDorot will be a fifty-five-volume edition of the Ḥumash (one for each *parasha* plus a companion volume). Each of the fifty-four volumes of the *parashot* can be read from right to left (Hebrew opening side), and left to right (English opening side).

Opening from the Hebrew side offers:

▸ the full Torah text, the translation of Rabbi Sacks, and the full commentary of Rashi in both Hebrew and the new English translation

▸ all *haftarot* associated with the *parasha* of the volume, including Rosh Ḥodesh and special readings, both in Hebrew and English

Opening from the English side presents four sections:

▸ THE TIME OF THE SAGES – includes commentaries from the Second Temple period and the talmudic period

▸ THE CLASSIC COMMENTATORS – quotes selected explanations by Rashi as well as most of the commentators found in traditional *Mikraot Gedolot*

▸ CONFRONTING MODERNITY – selects commentaries from the eighteenth century to the close of the twentieth century

▸ THE BIBLICAL IMAGINATION – features essays surveying some of the broader conceptual ideas as a supplement to the linear, text-based commentary

The first three of these sections each feature the relevant verses, in Hebrew and English, on the page alongside their respective commentaries, in chronological order, providing the reader with a single window onto the text without excessive page turning.

In addition to being a valuable resource in a Jewish home or synagogue library, we conceived of these volumes as a weekly accompaniment in the synagogue. There is scope for the reader to study each *parasha* on a weekly basis in preparation for the reading on Shabbat. One may select a particular group of commentators for study that week, or perhaps alternate between ancient and modern viewpoints. Some readers may choose to delve into the text through verse-by-verse interpretation, while others may prefer a conceptual perspective on the *parasha* as a whole. The broad array of options for learning means this is a series which can be returned to year after year, always presenting new insights and new approaches to understanding the text.

ACKNOWLEDGMENTS

The creation of this book was possible only thanks to the small but exceptional team here at Koren Jerusalem. We are grateful to:

▸ Rabbi Tzvi Hersh Weinreb, שליט״א, who conceptualized the structure of the project and provides both moral and halakhic leadership at Koren

▸ Rabbi Shai Finkelstein, whose encyclopedic knowledge of Torah and its interpreters is equaled only by his community leadership, formerly in Memphis and today in Jerusalem

▸ Rabbi David Fuchs, whose deep expertise in the midrashim and commentaries built a volume that is both comprehensive and concise

▸ Rabbi Yedidya Naveh, whose knowledge, organizational skills, and superb leadership brought the disparate elements together

▸ Rabbi Jonathan Mishkin, translator of the commentaries, who crafted a fluent, accurate, and eloquent English translation

Our design, editing, typesetting, and proofreading staff, including Tani Bayer, Esther Be'er, Tomi Mager, and Carolyn Budow Ben David, enabled an attractive, user-friendly, and accurate edition of these works.

> "One silver basin" (Numbers 7:13) was brought as a symbol of the Torah, which has been likened to wine, as the verse states: "And drink of the wine which I have mingled" (Proverbs 9:5). Because it is customary to drink wine in a basin – as we see in the verse "that drink wine in basins" (Amos 6:6) – he therefore brought a basin. "Of seventy shekels, after the shekel of the sanctuary" (Numbers 7:13). Why? Because just as the numerical value of "wine" [*yayin*] is seventy, so there are seventy modes of expounding the Torah. (Bemidbar Rabba 13:16)

Each generation produces exceptional rabbinic, intellectual leadership. It has been our purpose to enable all Jews to taste the wine of those generations, in the hope of expanding the breadth and depth of their knowledge. Torah is our greatest treasure, and we need the wisdom of those generations to better understand this bountiful gift from God. We hope that we at Koren can deepen that understanding for all who seek it.

Matthew Miller, Publisher
Jerusalem, 5781 (2021)

EDITOR'S INTRODUCTION

Over the course of millennia, the Jewish people have watched while the surrounding society and its values have changed unceasingly. For the Jews, the steadfast response to an evolving world has always been the study of Torah, specifically engagement with the weekly *parasha*. Devotees of Jewish learning have always looked to the weekly Torah portion for spiritual and intellectual guidance through life's challenges. And in every generation, commentaries on the Ḥumash have debated the precise interpretation of the verses therein. These scholars have continuously asked what message God is trying to convey to Israel and the world through the Torah's narratives and laws. Their explanations have struggled to identify the correct ways to apply its lessons to our daily lives.

Throughout, all these authors have approached the Torah text from their own unique perspectives, shaped in no small measure by the eras and environments they lived in. Naturally, the pantheon of commentaries present widely different styles in their writings. Occasionally the commentators will subject a particular verse to piercing scrutiny as a self-contained unit. At other times they present interpretations that seem to stray from the straightforward meaning of the text. Ultimately, all commentaries demand that a verse provide readers with theological meaning and direction for communal and social life.

Recognition of the wisdom embedded in the vast literature of commentary on the Torah spanning the various eras of Jewish history planted the seeds of the project whose fruit you now hold. We have called this publication ***Mikraot HaDorot*** – Readings of the Generations. This window into the world of Torah commentaries is not simply an upgrade of the classical *Mikraot Gedolot* collections, which give readers merely a handful of familiar

interpretations. *The Koren Mikraot HaDorot* instead presents a plethora of exegetical contributions, with more than forty scholars spanning Jewish teachings from the past two thousand years represented on its pages.

Each volume of the *Koren Mikraot HaDorot* series can be opened from both the right (Hebrew) side and left (English) side. The Hebrew opening side includes the Hebrew and a new English text of the *parasha*, translated by Rabbi Lord Jonathan Sacks, with a full, new translation of Rashi and the *haftarot*. The English opening side contains the bulk of the commentaries, and is divided into four parts: The first, **THE TIME OF THE SAGES**, comprises commentaries from antiquity – ranging from Philo to the Yalkut Shimoni. These figures lived mainly in the land of Israel, Egypt, and Babylonia. The second, **THE CLASSIC COMMENTATORS**, contains interpretations from the Middle Ages – starting from Rav Se'adya Gaon and Rashi and continuing through time to the work of Rabbi Shlomo Efrayim of Luntschitz, author of the *Keli Yakar*. The authors included here represent the rich traditions of both Sephardic (Spanish and North African) and Ashkenazic (central and eastern European) schools of exegesis. The third section, **CONFRONTING MODERNITY**, offers the work of both Old World and New World scholars who lived between the eighteenth and twentieth centuries. Before each of these three sections we include a time line that specifies the chronological relationships between the commentators and the places they lived.

In the final section, **THE BIBLICAL IMAGINATION**, we provide three in-depth investigations of particular ideas through the writings of the various commentaries. There are several goals to these essays. First, we aim to reveal common threads weaving across the generations of Torah scholarship. Second, we hope to illustrate how the various authors were influenced by their lives and times, and that the lessons they transmitted to their communities reflected their environments. Finally, each essay highlights for the reader some central issues that the commentaries have grappled with. We trust that this tool will facilitate the reader's understanding of the words of the commentaries themselves.

Three principles have governed the decision making in our work on *The Koren Mikraot HaDorot*:

- Chronological order: We have striven to sketch out the historical development of Torah exegesis, an enterprise that has occupied innumerable communities of Jews in far-flung lands for centuries.

- Economy of selection: In compiling the excerpts used in this work, we have gone through the authors' works and isolated those sections which most directly address the particular question, issue, or difficulty that confronted the scholar.
- Objectivity of presentation: This book presents ideas of the commentaries authentically, never censoring them or smoothing them over in light of our own positions or perspectives. We always strove to faithfully transmit the legal, conceptual, social, and ethical messages of the commentators.

The modern world constantly challenges us as individuals, as a society, and as communal leaders, teachers, and parents. The values and culture of the society that surrounds us force thinking Jews to seriously consider and reconsider their ideas and priorities on a regular basis as we struggle to find the correct path through life. Furthermore, we constantly must ask ourselves what teachings we wish to transmit to future generations. It is our hope that the *Koren Mikraot HaDorot* project will help guide its readers as they grapple with these very real problems. The world of Torah commentary is wide and deep beyond measure. It contains innumerable answers to the questions that face the individual, the family, the generation, and indeed all of humanity.

Rabbi Shai Finkelstein, Editor-in-Chief
Jerusalem, 5781 (2021)

A NOTE ON THE TRANSLATION

The terse writing style prevalent in Jewish scholarship over most of history can be difficult for the modern reader to decipher. Since our goal in the *Koren Mikraot HaDorot* series is to make thousands of years of Torah commentary accessible to a modern, English-speaking audience, we have opted for a relatively loose translation style that accurately presents the content of the Hebrew commentary while not necessarily mirroring its exact syntax. We have also resorted occasionally to paraphrase in instances where a literal translation would be opaque in English. As any student of Torah exegesis will recognize, draconian insistence on a word-for-word translation would result in an English text that was unreadable and that preserved neither the clarity nor the majesty of the original Hebrew.

Many of the commentaries' discussions focus on the meanings of words and phrases that are ambiguous in the Hebrew text of the *parasha*. The beautiful new translation of the Torah by Rabbi Lord Jonathan Sacks that we include here often dispels these ambiguities in the interest of clarity, necessarily coming down on one side or the other of a disagreement between commentators. The reader of the commentaries should therefore view the Torah translation presented here as one possible reading of the often-cryptic Hebrew original. In a similar vein, the significance of certain interpretations may seem unclear, or their points obvious, until one encounters another commentary with a starkly different read of the same verse. These contrasts, and the realization that themes and meanings we thought to be clear are actually ambiguous and multifaceted, are the essence of *The Koren Mikraot HaDorot*.

We have, as far as possible, allowed each text to speak for itself, and have left editorial comments to a minimum. Nevertheless, the commentaries often

assume the reader's knowledge of other biblical episodes, midrashim, or Hebrew grammar beyond what might be expected from the English-speaking public today. To ensure clarity, we have therefore interpolated brief editor's notes where we deemed it necessary, setting them off from the original text in square brackets.

Throughout Jewish history, the text of the Tanakh has been viewed as the apogee of the Hebrew language. For many commentators, especially those of the Middle Ages, it served as a fountain of language from which they drew numerous idioms and phrases. The result is that the Hebrew text of many commentaries is shot through with snippets of biblical prose or poetry to such an extent that almost every sentence can be viewed as a quote or allusion. Marking and citing all of these would make for a cluttered translation and would hinder rather than enhance the reader's understanding. We have therefore opted to cite only those quotes which are brought by the author as explicit evidence to further the point being made, and not those that supply only a turn of phrase.

The Hebrew side of this volume contains a complete and unabridged translation of Rashi's commentary. For those who wish to follow the *parasha* on the English side of the book, we have also reprinted many of Rashi's explanations alongside those of the other classic commentators. This will allow the reader to compare Rashi's interpretation to those of Rashbam, Ibn Ezra, and others, as well as appreciate how Rashi's commentary often serves to define the issues that will be addressed by later exegetes.

The text of the commentaries is of course abridged. We have not included ellipses to mark every point where text has been omitted, to maintain a clutter-free translation. However, we have included ellipses at points where the subject of discussion would otherwise appear to have changed abruptly and inexplicably, to save the reader confusion. We have also not adhered strictly to the original heading, or s.v. (*dibbur hamatḥil*) of every text, changing it in instances where it would help to focus the reader on those words that are the actual subject of discussion, and adding it to texts that did not originally have it.

Most of the commentaries that we quote in this series were originally organized by chapter and verse. Therefore, anyone who wishes to consult the original Hebrew text of a given commentary can simply open to the verse in question. However, not all sources are organized this way. The midrashim in particular are often ordered loosely; an important interpretation of a verse in Exodus might be found in a midrash on Deuteronomy. For the reader's

convenience in locating the original Hebrew source, we have provided citations for those works not organized sequentially, as well as for commentaries originally composed on verses other than the one under discussion. These citations can be found outside of the final punctuation at the end of the excerpt in question.

Our translation has generally relied upon the Hebrew text found in the Bar-Ilan Responsa Project and the online compendia Sefaria and AlHatorah.org, as well as the standard printed editions of commentaries not found in any of these. The Responsa Project contains more than one edition of several midrashim (Midrash Tanḥuma, Midrash Rabba, and Avot Derabbi Natan). For these works, our citations should be understood as referring to the standard editions published in Vilna and Warsaw unless otherwise indicated. Aside from this, please note:

- Text from Mekhilta Derabbi Shimon is understood to be from the Epstein-Melamed edition unless otherwise indicated.
- Excerpts from Ibn Ezra are almost always taken from his Long Commentary on Exodus, and we have marked those instances where we quote from his Short Commentary.
- Passages from Philo are quoted with permission from *Torah from Alexandria: Philo as a Biblical Commentator,* edited by Rabbi Michael Leo Samuel (New York: Kodesh Press, 2015).
- Selected commentaries of Rabbi Joseph B. Soloveitchik are printed with permission from *Chumash Mesoras HaRav,* edited by Dr. Arnold Lustiger (New York: OU Press and Ohr Publishing Inc., 2017).
- The commentaries of the Lubavitcher Rebbe are quoted from *The Torah, with an Interpolated Translation and Commentary Based on the Works of the Lubavitcher Rebbe,* edited by Rabbi Chaim Nochum Cunin and Rabbi Moshe Yaakov Wisnefsky (New York: Kehot Publication Society, 2017).
- The commentaries of Nehama Leibowitz are quoted, with generous permission, from *Studies in Shemot (Exodus),* translated by Aryeh Newman (Jerusalem: World Zionist Organization Department for Torah Education and Culture in the Diaspora, 1981).

While we have thus done our best to aid the reader in finding and consulting the original Hebrew text of the commentaries we have translated, we emphasize that this is not a critical edition, and the scope and readership of the series

do not permit us to fully cite every allusion and internal reference that authors make to midrashim and other commentaries. Still, we have made a supreme effort to provide citations of talmudic passages, and of course biblical verses, quoted or referred to in the material included here.

Yedidya Naveh, Managing Editor
Jerusalem, 5781 (2021)

1ST CENTURY BCE

PHILO, 25 BCE – 50 CE

1ST CENTURY CE

TARGUM ONKELOS, 35 – 120

2ND CENTURY

3RD CENTURY

MISHNA AND TOSEFTA, 3RD CENTURY

HALAKHIC MIDRASHIM, 3RD CENTURY
(MEKHILTA, SIFRA, SIFREI)

TARGUM YERUSHALMI, 3RD – 4TH CENTURY

4TH CENTURY

TALMUD YERUSHALMI, 3RD – 5TH CENTURY

TALMUD BAVLI, 3RD – 6TH CENTURY

5TH CENTURY

MIDRASH TANḤUMA, 5TH CENTURY

PESIKTA DERAV KAHANA,
5TH – 6TH CENTURY

6TH CENTURY

7TH CENTURY

8TH CENTURY

MIDRASH RABBA, 5TH – 12TH CENTURY

9TH CENTURY

PESIKTA RABBATI, 9TH CENTURY

10TH CENTURY

11TH CENTURY

MIDRASH LEKAḤ TOV, 11TH CENTURY

12TH CENTURY

13TH CENTURY

YALKUT SHIMONI, 13TH CENTURY

פרשת תרומה
PARASHAT TERUMA

THE **TIME** OF THE **SAGES**

כה א ב וַיְדַבֵּר יְהוָה אֶל־מֹשֶׁה לֵּאמֹר: דַּבֵּר אֶל־בְּנֵי יִשְׂרָאֵל וְיִקְחוּ־ יח
לִי תְּרוּמָה מֵאֵת כָּל־אִישׁ אֲשֶׁר יִדְּבֶנּוּ לִבּוֹ תִּקְחוּ אֶת־

CHAPTER 25, VERSE 1

TANḤUMA

לֵאמֹר – *Saying:* When exactly did God describe to Moshe these plans for the Tabernacle? On the day of Yom Kippur itself. This is so even though the chapters relating to the Tabernacle appear in the Torah before the incident of the golden calf. [According to tradition, the golden calf was made in the month of Tamuz, months before Israel's first Yom Kippur.] For Rabbi Yehuda son of Rabbi Shalum taught: Events in the Torah are not always recorded in chronological order. On Yom Kippur, the people atoned for that sin, and only then did the Holy One, blessed be He, say to Moshe: *They shall make Me a Sanctuary and I will dwell in their midst* (25:8). The construction of the Tabernacle would be a sign to all the surrounding nations that the crime of the golden calf had been forgiven. And this is why the structure was called *the Tabernacle of testimony* (38:21), for its construction would be a testament to the whole world that the Holy One, blessed be He, dwells among Israel. Said the Holy One, blessed be He, to Moshe: Let the people donate gold to atone for the gold that was used to fashion the statue of the calf, of which the verse states: *So all the people took the gold rings from their ears and brought them to Aharon* (32:3). Because the Israelites employed gold to commit their sin, they had to donate the same metal in order to repent.

VERSE 2

BARAITA DIMLEKHET HAMISHKAN

וְיִקְחוּ־לִי תְּרוּמָה – *Take an offering for Me:* Rabbi Yehuda Hanasi taught: There are ten kinds of donations [*terumot*]: (1) *teruma* [an unspecified amount of produce given by a farmer to the priests]; (2) *terumat maaser* [a portion of the Levites' tithe also] given to the priests; (3) *ḥalla* [a portion of a baker's dough] given to the priests; (4) *bikkurim* [first fruits of the year that are brought to the Temple and] given to the priests.... (9) *terumat shekalim* [see 38:26–27] for the sockets in the Tabernacle's construction; (10) *terumat hamishkan* comprised the voluntary donations for the building of the Tabernacle, the oil for the candelabrum, the ingredients for the incense, the priestly vestments, and the garments of the High Priest. (1)

TARGUM YERUSHALMI

אֲשֶׁר יִדְּבֶנּוּ לִבּוֹ – *Whose heart moves them to give:* Take My offering from all those whose heart moves them to give, but do not force anybody to donate.

TALMUD YERUSHALMI

וְיִקְחוּ־לִי תְּרוּמָה – *Take an offering for Me:* [The word "offering" appears three times in verses 2–3.] Rabbi Ḥagai taught in the name of Rabbi Shmuel bar Naḥman: This passage describes three different kinds of donations: Contributions for the Tabernacle's sockets [see 38:26–27], contributions of *shekalim* [see 30:11–16], and contributions for the Tabernacle. (Shekalim 1:1)

25 1 2 The Lord spoke to Moshe, saying, "Tell the Israelites to take
an offering for Me; take My offering from all whose heart

TANḤUMA

וְיִקְחוּ־לִי תְּרוּמָה – *Take an offering for Me:* Whenever the Torah uses the term "for Me," it bears implications for both this world and the next. For example, when the verse states: *The land shall not be sold for ever: for the land is Mine* (Leviticus 25:23) – it means the land of Israel is His in this world and in the next world. And when our verse states: *Take an offering for Me*, it means that the offering will be valued in both this world and the World to Come. (Teruma 3) וְיִקְחוּ־לִי – *Take for Me:* Said the Holy One, blessed be He: Do not mock this instruction and say: "Is then God a priest who requires feeding?" Rather, I am informing you that if you give the priests only one percent of your produce [as a tithe – the Sages require the donation of two percent], I will consider you to have cheated not them, but Me. תְּרוּמָה – *An offering:* Said the Holy One, blessed be He, to Israel: I am not bothering the nations of the world to donate their money, just you. For when the prophet declares: *The just shall live by his faith* (Habakkuk 2:4), he means that in the next world, the Holy One, blessed be He, will judge each person along with the other members of his faith. The Holy One, blessed be He, will say to Israel: Each one of you Israelites owes your faith to Me. I redeemed you from Egypt; ought you not offer donations to Me? Hence the verse states, *Tell the Israelites to take an offering for Me.* (Teruma 4)

SHEMOT RABBA

וְיִקְחוּ־לִי תְּרוּמָה – *Take an offering for Me:* The verse states: *I sleep, but my heart wakes* (Song of Songs 5:2). Here the congregation of Israel admits that they are asleep due to the sin of the golden calf, but the Holy One, blessed be He, is knocking at my door to wake me up, saying: *Take an offering for Me.* (Teruma 33:3) מֵאֵת כָּל־אִישׁ – *From all:* [Literally, "from each man."] When the Holy One, blessed be He, issued His instructions for the Tabernacle to Moshe, the prophet responded: "Master of the Universe! Will Israel really be able to complete this project?" God retorted: "Each single Israelite could build the Tabernacle himself, as the verse states, *Take My offering from each man whose heart moves them to give.*" (33:8)

LEKAḤ TOV

תִּקְחוּ אֶת־תְּרוּמָתִי – *Take My offering:* Once a person has committed to make donations for the Tabernacle's construction, you may take his pledge by force [if he balks].

YALKUT SHIMONI

וְיִקְחוּ־לִי תְּרוּמָה – *Take an offering for Me:* Of course, God owns the entire world, as the verse states: *The earth is the Lord's, and the fulness thereof* (Psalms 24:1). Why then does He then require human beings to donate materials to Him? It is because Israel wanted the Divine Presence to dwell among them, like a parent longing for his children to live close by. So God instructed the people: *Take an offering for Me.* [to build a Tabernacle for Him]. Now we can construct an argument against the nations from the way that God treats Israel. The Tabernacle was meant to glorify the Jewish people and to provide them means of atonement, and even so God speaks as if the project was for His benefit. And so if the nations of the world persecute and rob Israel– what will their fates be? (Teruma 363)

ג תְּרוּמָתִי׃ וְזֹאת הַתְּרוּמָה אֲשֶׁר תִּקְחוּ מֵאִתָּם זָהָב וָכֶסֶף
ד ה וּנְחֹשֶׁת׃ וּתְכֵלֶת וְאַרְגָּמָן וְתוֹלַעַת שָׁנִי וְשֵׁשׁ וְעִזִּים׃ וְעֹרֹת
ו אֵילִם מְאָדָּמִים וְעֹרֹת תְּחָשִׁים וַעֲצֵי שִׁטִּים׃ שֶׁמֶן לַמָּאֹר
ז בְּשָׂמִים לְשֶׁמֶן הַמִּשְׁחָה וְלִקְטֹרֶת הַסַּמִּים׃ אַבְנֵי־שֹׁהַם
ח וְאַבְנֵי מִלֻּאִים לָאֵפֹד וְלַחֹשֶׁן׃ וְעָשׂוּ לִי מִקְדָּשׁ וְשָׁכַנְתִּי

VERSE 3

TANḤUMA

וְזֹאת הַתְּרוּמָה – *These are the offerings:* The Holy One, blessed be He, said to the Israelites: It is not your own possessions that I expect you to donate; rather it is the valuables that I gave you at the seashore [looted from the drowned Egyptians]. (Teruma 5)

SHEMOT RABBA

וְזֹאת הַתְּרוּמָה – *These are the offerings:* Rabbi Tavyumei taught: When the hour arrived for the patriarch Yaakov to depart from this world, he summoned his sons to him and said: You should know that in the future, the Holy One, blessed be He, will ask your descendants to construct a Tabernacle for Him. And so you must make sure that you have all the materials ready to build it. This is what Yaakov meant when he said: *Behold, I die: but God shall be with you* (Genesis 48:21) – he meant that *They shall make Me a Sanctuary and I will dwell in their midst* (25:8), for it is then that God would descend from heaven and let His presence exist among them. And although Yaakov's progeny were urged to prepare for that calling, only some of them heeded his advice, while others forgot about the mission. Thus, when Moshe arrived and began to prepare the Tabernacle, some Israelites donated materials that they procured recently, while others brought the goods that they had kept ready for just such an occasion. (Teruma 33:8)

VERSE 4

TANḤUMA

וּתְכֵלֶת וְאַרְגָּמָן – *Sky-blue, purple:* This refers to sky-blue that has been dyed with blood [of a snail], as a remembrance of the sign that the ancient patriarchs established. **וְתוֹלַעַת שָׁנִי** – *And scarlet wool:* [Literally, "scarlet worm." The dye was obtained from such an animal.] As a later verse states: *Fear not, you worm Yaakov, O men of Israel; I will help you, says the Lord* (Isaiah 41:14). (Teruma 5)

VERSE 5

TANḤUMA

וְעֹרֹת אֵילִם – *Rams' hides:* The rams' hides evoked the merit of Yaakov, about whom the Torah states: *And she [Rivka] put the skins of the kids of the goats upon his hands* (Genesis 27:16). Said the Holy One, blessed be He: The skies and the heavens above cannot contain Me, and yet My Divine Presence will inhabit a space enclosed by sheepskins. **וְעֹרֹת תְּחָשִׁים** – *And fine leather:* [The word *taḥash* appears to name an unidentified animal.] Rabbi Yehuda and

3 moves them to give. These are the offerings you shall receive
4 from them: gold, silver and bronze; sky-blue, purple, and scar-
5 let wool; linen and goats' hair; rams' hides dyed red and fine
6 leather; acacia wood; oil for the lamps; spices for the anoint-
7 ing oil and the fragrant incense; and rock crystal together with
8 other precious stones for the ephod and breast piece. They

TANHUMA *(cont.)*

Rabbi Neḥemya offered different identities for the *taḥash*. Rabbi Yehuda argued that it was a pure [i.e., kosher] beast that lives in the wilderness and boasts a single horn sprouting from its forehead. Its fur is of six different colors and was used to prepare the coverings for the Tabernacle. According to Rabbi Neḥemya, however, the *taḥash* was a miraculous creature that God created for the singular purpose of donating its hides to the Tabernacle. After serving that function, the species disappeared from the world. (Teruma 6)

VERSE 6

TANHUMA

שֶׁמֶן לַמָּאֹר – *Oil for the lamps:* The gold in the Tabernacle symbolized the kingdom of Babylon, of which it is written: *Ruler over them all; you are this head of gold* (Daniel 2:38). The silver corresponds to the kingdom of Persia, about which it is stated: *I will weigh out ten thousand talents of silver* (Esther 3:9). The bronze evokes the kingdom of Greece, which is the most inferior of all. The rams' hides died red suggest the kingdom of Edom [in rabbinic literature a reference to Rome], about which the verse states: *And the first came out red* (Genesis 25:25). By all this, the Holy One, blessed be He, assured Israel: Although you may witness the rise of these kingdoms and their prideful dominion over you, I will issue salvation from your servitude. For after all of these materials are listed, the verse mentions *oil for the lamps* – a reference to the Messiah, of who it is stated: *There will I make the horn of David to shoot up: I have set up a lamp for My anointed* (Psalms 132:17). (Teruma 7)

LEKAḤ TOV

בְּשָׂמִים לְשֶׁמֶן הַמִּשְׁחָה – *Spices for the anointing oil:* This oil would be used to anoint the High Priest. **וְלִקְטֹרֶת הַסַּמִּים** – *And the fragrant incense:* As a later verse states: *I will accept you with your sweet savor* (Ezekiel 20:41).

VERSE 7

LEKAḤ TOV

וְאַבְנֵי מִלֻּאִים – *Other precious stones:* The verse refers to rubies, as a later text states, *And I will make your windows of rubies* (Isaiah 54:12).

VERSE 8

PHILO

וְעָשׂוּ לִי מִקְדָּשׁ – *They shall make Me a Sanctuary:* Had the Israelites already occupied their ancestral land, they would have had to set up a magnificent temple.... However, such a

ט בְּתוֹכָם׃ כְּכֹל אֲשֶׁר אֲנִי מַרְאֶה אוֹתְךָ אֵת תַּבְנִית הַמִּשְׁכָּן
י וְאֵת תַּבְנִית כָּל־כֵּלָיו וְכֵן תַּעֲשׂוּ׃ וְעָשׂוּ אֲרוֹן
עֲצֵי שִׁטִּים אַמָּתַיִם וָחֵצִי אָרְכּוֹ וְאַמָּה וָחֵצִי רָחְבּוֹ וְאַמָּה

PHILO *(cont.)*

building project would have to wait for later. For the present moment, they were still wandering in the desert and they were far from any kind of settled habitation. Nevertheless, it still suited them to have a portable sanctuary, so that during their journeys, military expeditions, and encampments they might bring their sacrifices to it and perform all their other religious duties, not lacking anything that city dwellers should have. It was determined, therefore, to fashion a tabernacle, a work of the highest sanctity.

TARGUM ONKELOS

וְעָשׂוּ לִי מִקְדָּשׁ – *They shall make Me a Sanctuary:* The shall make a sanctuary before Me, and I will permeate it with My Presence.

MEKHILTA DERABBI YISHMAEL

וְעָשׂוּ לִי מִקְדָּשׁ – *They shall make Me a Sanctuary:* How are we meant to understand this? Does not a different verse state: *Do not I fill heaven and earth? says the Lord* (Jeremiah 23:24)? Why then would God command Israel to construct a sanctuary for Him? In order to reward them for their efforts. (Massekhta Defisha 16)

SHEMOT RABBA

וְעָשׂוּ לִי מִקְדָּשׁ – *They shall make Me a Sanctuary:* Said the Holy One, blessed be He, to Israel: Once I have sold you My Torah, it is as if I have I sold Myself along with it. A parable will explain this point: A tale is told of a king who had a lone daughter, who wedded another king. When the new husband wished to take his bride and return to his own kingdom, the father-in-law confronted him. "You know that your wife is my only child," he said, "and I cannot part with her. On the other hand, I cannot ask you to leave her with me for she is your rightful wife. Please do me a favor and make sure that wherever you live, you set apart a guest room so that I might come and visit you, for I cannot sever my bond with my daughter." So did the Holy One, blessed be He, say to Israel: "Yes, I have given you My Torah. But I cannot be long apart from it. So wherever you go, build a sanctuary for Me so that I may come and visit. Hence the Torah commands: *They shall make Me a Sanctuary.* (Teruma 33:1)

וְעָשׂוּ לִי מִקְדָּשׁ – *They shall make Me a Sanctuary:* Said the Holy One, blessed be He, to Israel: You are My sheep and I am your shepherd, as the prophet declares: *But you my flock, the flock of my pasture, are men, and I am your God* (Ezekiel 34:31). You should therefore construct a hut for the shepherd so that He may come and tend you. This is the sense of the verse, *They shall make Me a Sanctuary and I will dwell in their midst.* (Teruma 34:3)

9 shall make Me a Sanctuary and I will dwell in their midst. Form
the Tabernacle and form all of its furnishings following the pat-
10 terns that I show you. Make an Ark of acacia wood,
two and a half cubits long, a cubit and a half wide, and a cubit

VERSE 9

TALMUD BAVLI

וְכֵן תַּעֲשׂוּ – *Form:* [Literally, "and so shall you make it."] In future generations, you must fashion any later Tabernacle or Temple in the same way as described here. Rava objected: We know that all the Tabernacle accoutrements constructed by Moshe were consecrated by being anointed, while all such items constructed later were dedicated simply by their use. Why should that be? Should we not say that the phrase *And so shall you make it* equates the items of all eras? No, it was different in Moshe's time, for a subsequent verse states: *And it came to pass on the day that Moshe had finished setting up the Tabernacle, and had anointed it, and sanctified it, and all its instruments* (Numbers 7:1), emphasizing that only those original utensils were sanctified by anointing, but those of later generations were not. (Shevuot 15a)

LEKAḤ TOV

כְּכֹל אֲשֶׁר אֲנִי מַרְאֶה אוֹתְךָ – *Following the patterns that I show you:* This verse teaches us that the Holy One, blessed be He, showed Moshe all the plans for the Tabernacle. God presented the schematics to Moshe in figures of fire.

VERSE 10

SHEMOT RABBA

וְעָשׂוּ אֲרוֹן עֲצֵי שִׁטִּים – *Make an Ark of acacia wood:* Just as when the world was created the Torah preceded everything else [according to rabbinic tradition God composed the Torah before forming the rest of the universe], so too when the Tabernacle was constructed the Ark [that housed the Torah] was mentioned before all its other furniture. When God began the work of creation, He made the light first, as the verse states: *God said, "Let there be light." And there was light* (Genesis 1:3). Similarly, when the Tabernacle was built, Moshe first crafted the Ark that held the Torah, which is compared to light: *For the commandment is a lamp; and Torah is light* (Proverbs 6:23). Another interpretation: Why is it that the instructions for building the Tabernacle consistently speak in the second person singular [*ve'asita*], but the commandment to build the Ark uses the third-person plural form [*ve'asu*]? Rabbi Yehuda bar Shalum taught: the Holy One, blessed be He, said to Moshe: Let the entire community come and participate in the creation of the Ark, so that they will all deserve to receive the Torah. (Teruma 34:2)

YALKUT SHIMONI

וְעָשׂוּ אֲרוֹן עֲצֵי שִׁטִּים – *Make an Ark of acacia wood:* Said God to Israel: You have prepared a home for Me, now build one for the Torah that will accompany Me. For the Torah is My delight, which I enjoyed for thousands of years before the world even existed. As the verse states concerning the Torah: *Then I was by Him, as a foster child* (Proverbs 8:30). (Teruma 368)

יא וָחֵצִי קֹמָתוֹ: וְצִפִּיתָ אֹתוֹ זָהָב טָהוֹר מִבַּיִת וּמִחוּץ תְּצַפֶּנּוּ
יב וְעָשִׂיתָ עָלָיו זֵר זָהָב סָבִיב: וְיָצַקְתָּ לּוֹ אַרְבַּע טַבְּעֹת זָהָב
וְנָתַתָּה עַל אַרְבַּע פַּעֲמֹתָיו וּשְׁתֵּי טַבָּעֹת עַל־צַלְעוֹ הָאֶחָת
יג וּשְׁתֵּי טַבָּעֹת עַל־צַלְעוֹ הַשֵּׁנִית: וְעָשִׂיתָ בַדֵּי עֲצֵי שִׁטִּים
יד וְצִפִּיתָ אֹתָם זָהָב: וְהֵבֵאתָ אֶת־הַבַּדִּים בַּטַּבָּעֹת עַל צַלְעֹת
טו הָאָרֹן לָשֵׂאת אֶת־הָאָרֹן בָּהֶם: בְּטַבְּעֹת הָאָרֹן יִהְיוּ הַבַּדִּים
טז לֹא יָסֻרוּ מִמֶּנּוּ: וְנָתַתָּ אֶל־הָאָרֹן אֵת הָעֵדֻת אֲשֶׁר אֶתֵּן
יז אֵלֶיךָ: וְעָשִׂיתָ כַפֹּרֶת זָהָב טָהוֹר אַמָּתַיִם וָחֵצִי אָרְכָּהּ וְאַמָּה שני
יח וָחֵצִי רָחְבָּהּ: וְעָשִׂיתָ שְׁנַיִם כְּרֻבִים זָהָב מִקְשָׁה תַּעֲשֶׂה

VERSE 11

TALMUD YERUSHALMI

וְצִפִּיתָ אֹתוֹ זָהָב טָהוֹר – *Overlay it with pure gold:* How exactly did Betzalel [the artisan mentioned in 31:2] construct the Ark? Rabbi Ḥanina ben Gamliel taught: He fashioned three separate chests – two of gold and one of wood. The smaller gold box was fitted into the wood container and both items were inserted into the larger gold chest. Thus was the wood box covered in gold *inside and out*. What do we learn from the additional word "overlay" [the Hebrew verb appears twice in the verse]? It teaches that even the top edge of the Ark was to be overlaid with gold [since neither the inner nor the outer box covered it by itself]. Rabbi Shimon ben Lakish teaches: Actually, the Ark comprised a single chest which was simply overlaid with gold. If so, what do we learn from the additional word "overlay"? Rabbi Pinḥas explains: Even the gaps between the planks were to be filled in with gold. (Shekalim 6:1)

TALMUD BAVLI

זֵר זָהָב – *A gold rim:* [The word *zer* can also mean "crown."] Rabbi Yoḥanan taught: Three "crowns" are mentioned in the Tabernacle: that of the altar, that of the Ark, and that of the table. The crown of the altar [which represents the priesthood] was bestowed upon Aharon. The crown of the table [symbolizing wealth and power] was given to King David. But the crown of the Ark [i.e., Torah learning] is available to everybody – whoever wishes to come and claim it may do so. And lest you argue that the crown of the Torah is inferior to the other two, note that the verse states of the Torah: *By me kings reign, and princes decree justice* (Proverbs 8:15). Rabbi Yoḥanan noted. The word is spelled the same as the word *zar* [meaning "alien"], but tradition demands that the word be read *zer* ["crown"]. This teaches that for those who deserve the reward for studying Torah [by applying themselves], the commandments will be a crown. But to those who do not treat the Torah with respect, the commandments will seem alien.... The Torah commands that when constructing the Ark, we must *overlay it with pure gold, inside and out*. Rava explained: One can only be a true Torah scholar if his inner character matches his outer presentation of himself. (Yoma 72b)

11 and a half high. Overlay it with pure gold, inside and out, and
12 around it make a gold rim. Cast four gold rings for it and place
them on its four corners, two rings on one side and two on the
13 other. Make staves of acacia wood and overlay them with gold;
14 place these staves in the rings on the sides of the Ark so that
15 the Ark may be carried. The staves must stay in the rings of the
16 Ark; they must not be removed. Inside the Ark, place the tab-
17 lets of the Covenant that I will give you. Make an Ark cover SHENI
of pure gold, two and a half cubits long and a cubit and a half
18 wide. Make two cherubim of beaten gold and place them at the

VERSE 13

LEKAḤ TOV

וְעָשִׂיתָ בַדֵּי עֲצֵי שִׁטִּים – *Make staves of acacia wood:* These symbolize those who support students of Torah. **וְצִפִּיתָ אֹתָם זָהָב** – *And overlay them with gold:* In the future, the Holy One, blessed be He, will create shade [protection] for those who study Torah and for those who assist them, as the verse states: *For wisdom is a defense* (Ecclesiastes 7:12), and *She is a tree of life to those who lay hold on her* (Proverbs 3:18).

VERSE 14

LEKAḤ TOV

אֶת־הַבַּדִּים בַּטַּבָּעֹת עַל צַלְעֹת הָאָרֹן – *Place these staves in the rings on the sides of the Ark:* We learn from this that wherever a Torah scholar lives, his neighbors are commanded to work to sustain him [as the staves supported the Ark]. **לָשֵׂאת אֶת־הָאָרֹן בָּהֶם** – *So that the Ark may be carried:* Whoever occupies himself with the study of Torah is lifted higher and higher.

VERSE 17

TALMUD YERUSHALMI

וְעָשִׂיתָ כַפֹּרֶת זָהָב טָהוֹר – *Make an Ark cover of pure gold:* Rabbi Abba bar Aḥa taught: It is difficult to fathom the character of the Israelite people. When they were asked for gold to make an idolatrous calf, they donated willingly, yet when they were asked to donate gold for the Tabernacle they similarly opened their purses. Rabbi Yosef ben Ḥanina taught: This is exactly the meaning of the teaching claiming that the gold of the Ark's cover atoned for the gold of the calf. (Shekalim 1:1)

VERSE 18

PHILO

כְּרֻבִים – *Cherubim:* Some people say that these cherubim are the symbols of the two hemispheres, placed opposite to and facing one another. However, I myself must say that what we have here are the two most ancient and supreme powers of the divine God: His creative and divine power, by which He is called "God," and governing power, by which He is called "the Lord," as He governs with justice and firmness.

יט אֹתָם מִשְּׁנֵי קְצוֹת הַכַּפֹּרֶת׃ וַעֲשֵׂה כְּרוּב אֶחָד מִקָּצָה מִזֶּה
וּכְרוּב־אֶחָד מִקָּצָה מִזֶּה מִן־הַכַּפֹּרֶת תַּעֲשׂוּ אֶת־הַכְּרֻבִים
כ עַל־שְׁנֵי קְצוֹתָיו׃ וְהָיוּ הַכְּרֻבִים פֹּרְשֵׂי כְנָפַיִם לְמַעְלָה סֹכְכִים
בְּכַנְפֵיהֶם עַל־הַכַּפֹּרֶת וּפְנֵיהֶם אִישׁ אֶל־אָחִיו אֶל־הַכַּפֹּרֶת
כא יִהְיוּ פְּנֵי הַכְּרֻבִים׃ וְנָתַתָּ אֶת־הַכַּפֹּרֶת עַל־הָאָרֹן מִלְמָעְלָה

MEKHILTA DERABBI YISHMAEL

וְעָשִׂיתָ שְׁנַיִם כְּרֻבִים זָהָב – *Make two cherubim of beaten gold:* Why does the Torah state: *Make yourselves no silver gods, no golden gods* (20:20)? For once the verse commanded Israel to *make two cherubim of beaten gold,* the people might have decided to go further and make four. Hence the warning: Should you add another two cherubim to those which I have sanctioned, I will consider them to be idols of gold. Why then does the text also need to forbid *silver gods*? We find that when gold was unavailable to fashion accoutrements for the Temple, silver was substituted as the material of choice. Hence we might have thought that silver could also be employed to create the cherubim. Therefore the verse prohibits silver gods, teaching: If you deviate from the mandated gold, I will consider the cherubim to be gods of silver. Furthermore, the verse emphasizes that even though the Torah commands that golden cherubim be created for the Temple, we must not think it is also permitted to install such images within synagogues and study halls. (Massekhta Devaḥodesh 10)

VERSE 19

BEMIDBAR RABBA

כְּרוּב אֶחָד מִקָּצָה מִזֶּה – *One cherub at one end:* Rabbi Natan taught: The construction of the Ark of the Covenant was as precious to God as that of His celestial throne of glory. For the verse *The place, Lord, that You made for Your dwelling, the sanctuary, Lord, that Your hands established* (15:17) teaches that the location of the Temple lies directly below the position of the heavenly sanctuary, and the Ark under God's throne of glory. God commanded that the Ark cover be made with cherubim to symbolize the angels that hover above God's throne [see Isaiah 6:2]. The two cherubim were precious to God, for they represented the earth and the sky, and just as He dwells between those two realms, God manifests Himself between the two cherubim. And just as the heavens open their storehouses to benefit the earth, as the verse states: *The Lord shall open to you His good treasure, the heaven, to give the rain to your land in its season* (Deuteronomy 28:12), similarly does the Divine Presence issue its blessing from between the two cherubim. The two cherubim stood facing each other directly, as the verse states: *They should face one another, and look toward the cover* (Exodus 25:20), focusing on the spot directly beneath the throne of glory, which sits under God Himself, as the verse states: *Out of Zion, the perfection of beauty, God has shone forth* (Psalms 50:2). (Bemidbar 4:13)

19 two ends of the cover: one cherub at one end and one at the
other; the cherubim shall be made of one piece with the cover.
20 These cherubim should have wings spread upward, sheltering
the cover. They should face one another, and look toward the
21 cover. Place the cover on top of the Ark, and inside the Ark

VERSE 20

TALMUD BAVLI

וּפְנֵיהֶם אִישׁ אֶל־אָחִיו – *They should face one another:* Rabbi Levi taught: There is a tradition that the space occupied by the Ark of the Covenant and the cherubim should not be included when calculating the measurements of the Holy of Holies in which it rested. [That is, miraculously the Ark occupied no space at all.] This point is also taught in a *baraita*, which states: When they brought the Ark that Moshe crafted into the Holy of Holies in the Temple, there were ten cubits of empty space on every side of it. [This was so even though that chamber in the Temple was twenty cubits by twenty cubits.]… How did the cherubim stand? Rabbi Yoḥanan and Rabbi Elazar offered differing approaches. One scholar claims that the cherubim's faces were turned one toward the other [as described in our verse], while the other believes that the cherubim's faces were turned toward the interior of the Temple [that is, they both faced straight ahead]. But according to the position that the faces were turned one toward the other, does the verse not state [concerning the larger cherubim that King Shlomo constructed in the Holy of Holies] *and their faces were inward* [II Chronicles 3:13; i.e., toward the interior of the building? The Gemara assumes that both Shlomo's and Moshe's cherubim must have been similarly oriented.] That text presents no difficulty: The cherubim faced each other at times when the Jewish people were fulfilling the will of God [thereby reflecting the affection between God and the nation]. But when Israel did not obey God's will, the cherubim looked away from each other. And according to the Sage who says that the cherubim were placed with their faces toward the interior of the building, how does he explain the verse stating that they should face each other? He would argue that the cherubim were angled slightly sideways [such that they faced both each other as well as the adjacent chamber]. It was taught: Onkelos the convert said: The cherubim were fashioned *in the form of children* (II Chronicles 3:10), and their faces were angled sideways like a student taking leave of his teacher. (Bava Batra 99a)

VERSE 21

TARGUM YERUSHALMI

אֶת־הָעֵדֻת – *The tablets of the Covenant:* [Literally, simply "the testimony." The Targum interprets this to mean:] The tablets of the testimony.

TALMUD YERUSHALMI

אֶת־הָעֵדֻת – *The tablets of the Covenant:* [Literally, simply "the testimony."] According to Rabbi Yehuda, the first Torah scroll was not placed inside the Ark, but kept outside it, as the verse states: *Take this book of the Torah, and put it next to of the ark of the covenant* (Deuteronomy 31:26). According to Rabbi Yehuda, a small case was constructed and placed outside the

כב וְאֶל־הָאָרֹן תִּתֵּן אֶת־הָעֵדֻת אֲשֶׁר אֶתֵּן אֵלֶיךָ׃ וְנוֹעַדְתִּי
לְךָ שָׁם וְדִבַּרְתִּי אִתְּךָ מֵעַל הַכַּפֹּרֶת מִבֵּין שְׁנֵי הַכְּרֻבִים
אֲשֶׁר עַל־אֲרוֹן הָעֵדֻת אֵת כָּל־אֲשֶׁר אֲצַוֶּה אוֹתְךָ אֶל־בְּנֵי
יִשְׂרָאֵל׃
כג וְעָשִׂיתָ שֻׁלְחָן עֲצֵי שִׁטִּים אַמָּתַיִם אָרְכּוֹ וְאַמָּה רָחְבּוֹ וְאַמָּה

TALMUD YERUSHALMI *(cont.)*

Ark, and the Torah scroll was placed inside it. However, according to Rabbi Meir, the Torah scroll was kept inside the Ark, for the verse states, *Place the cover on top of the Ark, and inside the Ark place the testimony that I will give you.* [Rabbi Meir understands the "testimony" to be the Torah scroll.] Now even though the text first states: *Place the cover on top of the Ark,* and only then directs: *Inside the Ark place the testimony that I will give you* [when surely the testimony must have been inserted before the cover was placed atop] that is no matter, since events in the Torah are not always recorded in chronological order. (Shekalim 6:1)

VERSE 22

TARGUM ONKELOS

וְנוֹעַדְתִּי לְךָ שָׁם – *There I will meet you:* I will deliver My statements to you and speak with you.

SIFRA

מֵעַל הַכַּפֹּרֶת – *From above the cover:* A later verse states: *And the Lord called to Moshe, and spoke to him out of the Tent of Meeting* (Leviticus 1:1) suggesting that God's voice emanated from the entire structure of the Tabernacle. However, our verse specifies the voice emerged from *between the two cherubim.* Such is the understanding of Rabbi Akiva. Rabbi Shimon ben Azzai added: I do not mean to contradict the words of my teacher, but only to expand upon them. The Almighty, about whom the verse states: *Do not I fill heaven and earth?* (Jeremiah 23:24), so loved Israel that He compressed His glory to [dwell among them,] appearing as if He were speaking above the Ark's cover and from between the two cherubim. (Vayikra 1:1)

TALMUD BAVLI

וְנוֹעַדְתִּי לְךָ שָׁם – *There I will meet you:* A certain man used to boast: When love was strong between my wife and myself, we were so close that we could have made our bed on the edge of a sword blade. However, now that we have grown apart, even a bed sixty cubits wide is insufficient for us. Rav Huna responded: Indeed, the Torah alludes to such a fluctuation in a relationship. For when the verse states: *There, from above the cover, I will meet you and speak with you,* it reflects the early days of Israel's devotion to God [when the Divine Presence could commune with the people in such a small space]. But subsequently, even when Shlomo built an enormous Temple, as the verse states: *And the House which King Shlomo built for the Lord, its length was sixty cubits, and its breadth was twenty cubits, and*

22 **place the tablets of the Covenant that I will give you. There,**
from above the cover, between the two cherubim, above the
Ark of the Testimony, I will meet with you and speak with you,
and give you all My commands to the Israelites.
23 **Make a table of acacia wood, two cubits long, a cubit wide, and**

TALMUD BAVLI *(cont.)*

its height was thirty cubits (I Kings 6:2), God still said: *The heaven is My throne, and the earth is My footstool: where is the house that you would build for Me?* (Isaiah 66:1). (Sanhedrin 7a)

מֵעַל הַכַּפֹּרֶת – *From above the cover:* A sukka that is not at least ten handbreadths high is invalid. How do we know this is so? The Ark of the Covenant was itself nine handbreadths high, and the Ark cover was one handbreadth thick, for a total height of ten handbreadths. And it is written: *There, from above the cover I will meet with you and speak with you* [teaching that the Divine Presence will never descend lower than this]. Rabbi Yosei taught: The Divine Presence never actually descended below to earth, and Moshe and Eliyahu never actually ascended to heaven, for the verse states: *The heavens are the heavens of the Lord, and the earth He gave to the children of man* (Psalms 115:16). But can it be true that God never came down to earth, when a verse clearly states: *And the Lord descended on Mount Sinai* (19:20)? Actually, God did come down, but He stopped ten handbreadths short of the top of the hill. And on the other hand, how can we claim that neither Moshe nor Eliyahu ever went up to the heavens, when the verses clearly state: *And Moshe went up to God* (19:3), and *Eliyahu went up by a storm of wind into heaven* (II Kings 2:11)? Actually, both men did go up, but they each stopped short ten handbreadths from heaven.... Now, how do we know that the cover itself had a height of one handbreadth? Rabbi Ḥanina taught: For all the furniture that Moshe crafted for the Tabernacle, the Torah specified their lengths, widths, and heights. However, for the Ark cover, while the Torah did give its length and width, it did not state its height. So we must infer from the smallest dimension mentioned in connection with any of the Tabernacle vessels, as the verse states with regard to the showbread table: *Make a frame a handbreadth wide all around* (25:25). Just as there, the frame measured one handbreadth, so too here, the thickness of the Ark cover measured a single handbreadth. (Sukka 4b)

VERSE 23

TALMUD BAVLI

וְעָשִׂיתָ שֻׁלְחָן – *Make a table:* Rav Ashi said: Ravin bar Ḥanina told me that the table in the Temple was jointed [and could be taken apart]. For if the parts of the table were permanently fixed, how could a cubit be immersed in a cubit? [The Gemara has just argued that a ritual bath must be a square cubit. In the event that the table became impure, it would not fit whole into a ritual bath for purification. The Gemara responds:] Where exactly is the difficulty? Perhaps the table could fit in Shlomo's Sea [a large brass basin which supplied water to the Temple courtyard; see I Kings 7:23–26]. For Rabbi Ḥiyya taught: The Sea that Shlomo constructed was large enough to hold the contents of one hundred and fifty standard ritual baths. (Pesaḥim 109b)

כד וָחֵצִי קֹמָתוֹ: וְצִפִּיתָ אֹתוֹ זָהָב טָהוֹר וְעָשִׂיתָ לּוֹ זֵר זָהָב
כה סָבִיב: וְעָשִׂיתָ לּוֹ מִסְגֶּרֶת טֹפַח סָבִיב וְעָשִׂיתָ זֵר־זָהָב
כו לְמִסְגַּרְתּוֹ סָבִיב: וְעָשִׂיתָ לּוֹ אַרְבַּע טַבְּעֹת זָהָב וְנָתַתָּ אֶת־
כז הַטַּבָּעֹת עַל אַרְבַּע הַפֵּאֹת אֲשֶׁר לְאַרְבַּע רַגְלָיו: לְעֻמַּת
הַמִּסְגֶּרֶת תִּהְיֶיןָ הַטַּבָּעֹת לְבָתִּים לְבַדִּים לָשֵׂאת אֶת־
כח הַשֻּׁלְחָן: וְעָשִׂיתָ אֶת־הַבַּדִּים עֲצֵי שִׁטִּים וְצִפִּיתָ אֹתָם זָהָב
כט וְנִשָּׂא־בָם אֶת־הַשֻּׁלְחָן: וְעָשִׂיתָ קְּעָרֹתָיו וְכַפֹּתָיו וּקְשׂוֹתָיו
ל וּמְנַקִּיֹּתָיו אֲשֶׁר יֻסַּךְ בָּהֵן זָהָב טָהוֹר תַּעֲשֶׂה אֹתָם: וְנָתַתָּ
עַל־הַשֻּׁלְחָן לֶחֶם פָּנִים לְפָנַי תָּמִיד:

LEKAḤ TOV

וְעָשִׂיתָ שֻׁלְחָן – *Make a table:* Both the table that held the showbread and the sacrificial altar are called "tables" [in Ezekiel 41:22]. However, the offerings that are raised to the altar are burned entirely, whereas the bread that is placed on the table is fed to the priests. Still, even the table gives its part to God in the incense burned in its receptacles.

VERSE 25

TOSEFTA

וְעָשִׂיתָ לּוֹ מִסְגֶּרֶת טֹפַח סָבִיב – *Make a frame a handbreadth wide all around:* The table had four golden attachments from which extended four branches on top like brackets, and these supported the loaves, which resembled the keel of a ship, so that they would not wobble. Rabbi Yehuda taught: There were no attachments there; rather, the border of the table was simply raised a handbreadth, as the verse states: *Make a frame a handbreadth wide all around.* Said the Rabbis to him: The frame was only at the legs of the table. (Menaḥot 11:3)

VERSE 28

LEKAḤ TOV

וְעָשִׂיתָ אֶת־הַבַּדִּים עֲצֵי שִׁטִּים – *Make the staves of acacia wood:* The staves were necessary to transport the table, which was taken out of the Temple on festivals and displayed before the pilgrims to Jerusalem. A pronouncement was made at that time: See how beloved you are of God! For He performs the following miracle for you: The loaves of bread are as fresh when they are removed from the table at the end of the week as they were when they were first put there at its start.

VERSE 29

SIFREI ZUTA

אֲשֶׁר יֻסַּךְ בָּהֵן – *For pouring libations:* We learn from this phrase that anything that fell into these receptacles was immediately consecrated, and that their contents became unfit if they came into contact with impurity. (Bemidbar 7:13)

24 a cubit and a half high. Overlay it with pure gold and around it
25 make a gold rim. Make a frame a handbreadth wide all around,
26 and around the frame also make a gold rim. Make for it four
gold rings, and place the rings on the four corners where the
27 four legs are. The rings should be attached next to the frame
28 as holders for staves to carry the table. Make the staves of acacia wood and overlay them with gold; by these the table shall
29 be carried. You must also make, out of pure gold, its bowls,
30 spoons, pitchers, and jars for pouring libations. On this table
the showbread must be placed before Me at all times.

TALMUD BAVLI

קְעָרֹתָיו וְכַפֹּתָיו וּקְשׂוֹתָיו וּמְנַקִּיֹּתָיו – *Its bowls, spoons, pitchers, and jars:* [The meaning of these terms is unclear. The Gemara interprets:] *Ke'arotav* are the molds [in which the loaves of bread were baked]; *kappotav* are the receptacles that held the incense; *kesotav* were four panels [of gold that supported the loaves and prevented them from falling]; *menakkiyyotav* are the rods [which rested on notches in the panels and bore the weight of the loaves]. The clause *asher yussakh bahen* [translated here as "for pouring libations," but which might also mean "for covering it"], indicates that the bread is to be covered by the rods. (Menaḥot 97a)

VERSE 30

MISHNA

וְנָתַתָּ עַל־הַשֻּׁלְחָן לֶחֶם פָּנִים – *On this table the showbread must be placed:* There were two tables just inside the Temple's entrance hall next to the building's doors. One was made of marble and the other of gold. On the table of marble, the priests placed the new showbread that had just been baked, before it was brought into the Sanctuary. When the old showbread was removed from the table, it was placed on the table of gold before being removed from the Sanctuary altogether. [The reason the old loaves were placed on the gold table rather than the marble one is] that one may elevate a thing to a higher level of sanctity but one may not downgrade it. [Since the bread had sat on the ceremonial gold table all week, it would be disrespectful to the loaves to place them on a marble or a silver table upon their removal.] And there was one main table of gold within the Sanctuary upon which the showbread was always found. [The mishna now describes how the priests ensured that there were loaves continuously on the table.] Four priests would enter the chamber, two men holding two arrangements of the new showbread in their hands, and two different priests carried the two bowls of frankincense in their hands. Meanwhile, four other priests preceded them in entering the Sanctuary, two men to remove the two arrangements of the old showbread from the table, and two men to take away the two bowls of frankincense. The emptyhanded priests would draw the old showbread from the table, and simultaneously the second team of priests would place the new showbread in the vacated berths, so that the table was never without loaves upon it, as the verse states, *On this table the showbread must be placed before Me at all times*. The priests who carried the old showbread loaves came out of the Sanctuary and placed them on the table of gold that was in the Entrance

לא וְעָשִׂיתָ מְנֹרַת זָהָב טָהוֹר מִקְשָׁה תֵּיעָשֶׂה הַמְּנוֹרָה יְרֵכָהּ
לב וְקָנָהּ גְּבִיעֶיהָ כַּפְתֹּרֶיהָ וּפְרָחֶיהָ מִמֶּנָּה יִהְיוּ: וְשִׁשָּׁה קָנִים
יֹצְאִים מִצִּדֶּיהָ שְׁלֹשָׁה ׀ קְנֵי מְנֹרָה מִצִּדָּהּ הָאֶחָד וּשְׁלֹשָׁה
לג קְנֵי מְנֹרָה מִצִּדָּהּ הַשֵּׁנִי: שְׁלֹשָׁה גְּבִעִים מְשֻׁקָּדִים בַּקָּנֶה
הָאֶחָד כַּפְתֹּר וָפֶרַח וּשְׁלֹשָׁה גְבִעִים מְשֻׁקָּדִים בַּקָּנֶה
הָאֶחָד כַּפְתֹּר וָפָרַח כֵּן לְשֵׁשֶׁת הַקָּנִים הַיֹּצְאִים מִן־הַמְּנֹרָה:

MISHNA *(cont.)*

Hall. The priests then burned on the altar the frankincense that was in the table's bowls. The old loaves were subsequently distributed to the priests. (Menaḥot 11:7)

TALMUD YERUSHALMI

תָּמִיד – *At all times:* The students asked Rabbi Ila: If, through some error, new loaves have not been placed on the table on the Sabbath, and subsequently bread becomes available during the week, should it be placed on the table as usual until the next Sabbath? He answered: The verse states: *On this table the showbread must be placed before Me at all times,* meaning that showbread should be placed there even if it is disqualified [unable to fill the full duration of seven days]. (Shekalim 6:3)

VERSE 31

TALMUD BAVLI

וְעָשִׂיתָ מְנֹרַת זָהָב טָהוֹר – *Make a candelabrum of pure gold:* Rav Pappa, son of Rav Ḥanin, taught a *baraita* before Rav Yosef: The candelabrum had to be fashioned from a solid block of metal, and it had to be made of gold. Nevertheless, if one made it out of silver, it is acceptable. If one fashioned it from tin, or from lead, or from other types of metal, Rabbi Yehuda Hanasi deems it unfit, while Rabbi Yosei son of Rabbi Yehuda deems it fit. If one crafted it from wood, or bone, or glass, all agree that it is unfit. Rav Yosef said to Rav Pappa: I suggest that you abandon your *baraita* in view of my *baraita*: If Temple service vessels are fashioned from wood, Rabbi Yehuda Hanasi deems them unfit, while Rabbi Yosei son of Rabbi Yehuda, accepts them as fit. [According to this *baraita*, the two rabbis' dispute was with regard to a candelabrum fashioned from wood, not from metal as in Rav Pappa's *baraita*]. Said Rav Pappa to Rav Yosef: On the contrary! You would do better to abandon your *baraita* in view of mine. Rav Yosef responded: No, I think not, for it is taught in a third *baraita*: If the one who is fashioning the candelabrum has no gold, he may bring even one made of silver, of copper, of iron, of tin, or of lead. But Rabbi Yosei son of Rabbi Yehuda deems it valid even if it was fashioned from wood. It is evident from this *baraita* that the dispute pertains only to a candelabrum fashioned from wood, and Rabbi Yehuda Hanasi therefore must agree that the utensil may be crafted from other types of metal. (Menaḥot 28b)

31 Make a candelabrum of pure gold. Its base and shaft, cups,
knobs, and flowers shall be hammered from a single piece.
32 Six branches shall extend from its sides, three on one side,
33 three on the other. On each branch there shall be three finely
crafted cups, each with a knob and a flower. All six branches

YALKUT SHIMONI

וְעָשִׂיתָ מְנֹרַת זָהָב טָהוֹר – *Make a candelabrum of pure gold:* The prophet's vision of *a candelabrum of pure gold* (Zechariah 4:2) represents the community of Israel.... Similarly, when God instructed Moshe to *make a candelabrum of pure gold* – that item also symbolized the nation of Israel. *Its base* signified the Nasi [the president of the Sanhedrin]; the *shaft* represented the *Av Beit Din* [the Nasi's deputy]; its *cups* symbolized the Sages; its *knobs* were the Torah students; *and* its *flowers* symbolized the nation's young people. Thus when the verse concludes: They *shall be hammered from a single piece,* it suggests the sentiment of the verse praising Israel: *You are all fair, my love; there is no blemish in you* (Song of Songs 4:7). (Zephaniah 567)

VERSE 32

BARAITA DIMLEKHET HAMISHKAN

וְשִׁשָּׁה קָנִים יֹצְאִים מִצִּדֶּיהָ – *Six branches shall extend from its sides:* How did Betzalel fashion the candelabrum? He started with a block of gold flattened like a board. From that he crafted the utensil's base on its bottom, and moving upward he carved its cups, its knobs, and its flowers. The artisan then drew out two branches on either side of the candelabrum, followed by an additional two arms on either side of the object. Betzalel thereby fulfilled the description *Six branches shall extend from its sides.* (10)

VERSE 33

BARAITA DIMLEKHET HAMISHKAN

שְׁלֹשָׁה גְבִעִים מְשֻׁקָּדִים – *Three finely crafted cups:* [From the Hebrew phrasing] it is unclear whether it is the cups themselves that should be finely designed, or rather the knobs and flowers. This is one of five phrases in the Torah that cannot be definitively parsed. The other examples appear in the following verses: *If you act well, will you not be uplifted* [Genesis 4:7, which might also be translated: "If you bear it well]; *They hamstrung oxen. Cursed be their anger, for it is most fierce* [Genesis 49:6–7, which might also mean: "They hamstrung a cursed ox; their anger was fierce"]; *Battle against Amalek. Tomorrow I will stand* [Exodus 17:9, which could also be parsed to mean: "Battle against Amalek tomorrow. I will stand..."]; and *You shall sleep with your fathers; and this people will rise up and go astray* [Deuteronomy 31:16, which could actually mean: "You shall sleep with your fathers and rise up; and this people will go astray." In this second interpretation the Talmud sees a prophecy of the resurrection of the dead – see Sanhedrin 90b]. (10)

לד וּבַמְּנֹרָה אַרְבָּעָה גְבִעִים מְשֻׁקָּדִים כַּפְתֹּרֶיהָ וּפְרָחֶיהָ׃
לה וְכַפְתֹּר תַּחַת שְׁנֵי הַקָּנִים מִמֶּנָּה וְכַפְתֹּר תַּחַת שְׁנֵי הַקָּנִים
מִמֶּנָּה וְכַפְתֹּר תַּחַת־שְׁנֵי הַקָּנִים מִמֶּנָּה לְשֵׁשֶׁת הַקָּנִים
לו הַיֹּצְאִים מִן־הַמְּנֹרָה׃ כַּפְתֹּרֵיהֶם וּקְנֹתָם מִמֶּנָּה יִהְיוּ כֻּלָּהּ
לז מִקְשָׁה אַחַת זָהָב טָהוֹר׃ וְעָשִׂיתָ אֶת־נֵרֹתֶיהָ שִׁבְעָה
לח וְהֶעֱלָה אֶת־נֵרֹתֶיהָ וְהֵאִיר עַל־עֵבֶר פָּנֶיהָ׃ וּמַלְקָחֶיהָ
לט וּמַחְתֹּתֶיהָ זָהָב טָהוֹר׃ כִּכָּר זָהָב טָהוֹר יַעֲשֶׂה אֹתָהּ אֵת
מ כָּל־הַכֵּלִים הָאֵלֶּה׃ וּרְאֵה וַעֲשֵׂה בְּתַבְנִיתָם אֲשֶׁר־אַתָּה

VERSE 34

TARGUM ONKELOS

כַּפְתֹּרֶיהָ וּפְרָחֶיהָ – *A knob and a flower:* The shaft of the candelabrum shall have four cups decorated with the forms of apples and lilies.

VERSE 37

SIFREI BEMIDBAR

וְהֵאִיר עַל־עֵבֶר פָּנֶיהָ – *So that they light the space in front of it:* When the Torah states: *So that they light the space in front of it,* we might think that each of the lamps was oriented straight forward and was not angled to either side. Hence, a subsequent verse states: *When you light the lamps, the seven lamps shall give light toward the body of the candelabrum* (Numbers 8:2), meaning that three lamps on the west side of the candelabrum faced east toward the middle flame, and the three lamps on the east side of the candelabrum faced west toward that same center lamp. Thus all the candles were focused on the middle lamp. Hence Rabbi Natan said that the middle flame was the most honored of all the lamps. (Behaalotekha 59)

VERSE 39

TALMUD YERUSHALMI

כִּכָּר זָהָב טָהוֹר – *A talent of pure gold:* Rav Yehuda taught in the name of Asi: Shlomo took one thousand talents of gold and cast them into the furnace, refining that mass down to a single talent. He thereby fulfilled the instruction to use *a talent of pure gold* in fashioning the Temple's utensils. But have we not learned in a *baraita*: Rabbi Yosei son of Rav Yehuda taught: It once happened that the candelabrum that was used in the Temple was found to be heavier than that made by Moshe in the wilderness by the weight a single gold dinar. Thereupon it was cast into the furnace eighty times [to purify it] but its mass was not reduced even one bit. Now that is certainly surprising, since we see ourselves that gold inserted into a furnace always emerges as a lesser quantity. The explanation is that before gold is fully refined, its mass will in fact be reduced by heat, but once it is completely pure it will not be lessened no matter how many times it is put into the furnace. (Shekalim 6:3)

34 extending from the candelabrum shall be like this. The shaft of
the candelabrum shall have four finely crafted cups, each with
35 a knob and a flower. For the six branches that extend from the
candelabrum, there must be a knob at the base of each pair of
36 branches. The knobs and their branches shall be of one piece
with it, the whole of it a single, hammered piece of pure gold.
37 Make its seven lamps and mount them so that they light the
38 39 space in front of it. Make its tongs and pans of pure gold. All
40 these items shall be made from a talent of pure gold. Take care
to make them according to that design that is shown to you on

TALMUD BAVLI

כִּכַּר זָהָב טָהוֹר – *A talent of pure gold:* The candelabrum and its lamps must be produced together from the same talent of gold, but its tongs [used to remove and replace wicks] and its pans [used to clean out the ashes from the lamps], were not fashioned from that same gold talent. Rabbi Neḥemya disputes this, saying: Only the frame of the candelabrum was produced from that single talent of gold; neither its lamps nor its tongs and pans were produced from that same gold talent. Now, what is the point of contention between the two positions? The disputants disagree how to interpret this verse, as is taught in the following *baraita*: [Rendering the word order of the Hebrew verse in English translations yields: "From a talent of pure gold shall it be made – all these items."] The verse states that the candelabrum must be made *from a talent of pure gold,* which teaches only that the frame of the candelabrum should be produced from the gold talent. How do we know that the utensil's lamps should also be crafted out of that block? The verse [in the Hebrew] ends with the phrase "all these items," which indicates that not only the frame, but also its subsidiary parts should be fashioned from the same talent of gold. In that case, might we also not include the candelabrum's tongs and its pans in the same talent? No, for the verse literally begins: "Out of a talent of pure gold shall it be made," [the word "it" – *otah* – emphasizes that only it should be made in this way, to the exclusion of some other accoutrements]. But Rabbi Yehoshua ben Korḥa states: Only the frame of the candelabrum was produced from the one talent of gold, whereas its tongs, its pans, and its lamps were not. How then does that Sage explain the words *all these items*? Rabbi Yehoshua ben Korḥa would argue that the phrase teaches only that all the vessels associated with the candelabrum were made of gold [but not that they were fashioned from the same gold piece used to fashion the candelabrum itself]. (Menaḥot 88b)

VERSE 40

PHILO

בְּתַבְנִיתָם – *According to that design:* Here the term "design" indicates the incorporeal heaven, the archetype of the sense-perceptible, for it is a visible pattern and impression and measure. Moshe testifies to these things by saying "take care" [literally, "and see"], thereby admonishing us to keep the vision of the soul sleepless and ever wakeful in order to see incorporeal forms, since, if it were merely a question of seeing the sense-perceptible with the eyes of the body, it is clear that no divine command would be needed for this.

כו א מָרְאֶה בָּהָר׃ וְאֶת־הַמִּשְׁכָּן תַּעֲשֶׂה עֶשֶׂר יט שלישי
יְרִיעֹת שֵׁשׁ מָשְׁזָר וּתְכֵלֶת וְאַרְגָּמָן וְתֹלַעַת שָׁנִי כְּרֻבִים
ב מַעֲשֵׂה חֹשֵׁב תַּעֲשֶׂה אֹתָם׃ אֹרֶךְ ׀ הַיְרִיעָה הָאַחַת שְׁמֹנֶה
וְעֶשְׂרִים בָּאַמָּה וְרֹחַב אַרְבַּע בָּאַמָּה הַיְרִיעָה הָאֶחָת מִדָּה
ג אַחַת לְכָל־הַיְרִיעֹת׃ חֲמֵשׁ הַיְרִיעֹת תִּהְיֶיןָ חֹבְרֹת אִשָּׁה
ד אֶל־אֲחֹתָהּ וְחָמֵשׁ יְרִיעֹת חֹבְרֹת אִשָּׁה אֶל־אֲחֹתָהּ׃ וְעָשִׂיתָ
לֻלְאֹת תְּכֵלֶת עַל שְׂפַת הַיְרִיעָה הָאֶחָת מִקָּצָה בַּחֹבָרֶת

SIFREI BEMIDBAR

אֲשֶׁר־אַתָּה מָרְאֶה בָּהָר – *That is shown to you on the mountain:* The verse *According to the vision that the Lord had shown Moshe, so he made the candelabrum* (Numbers 8:4) demonstrates Moshe's adherence to God's wishes – he produced the Tabernacle exactly as instructed by God. Rabbi Natan replied: That text cannot merely mean that, for the Torah states earlier: *Take care to make them according to that design that is shown to you* [and we can assume that Moshe followed the instructions loyally]. Rather, the later verse teaches that the Holy One, blessed be He, showed Moshe images of the Tabernacle's furniture and candelabrum fully constructed, and Moshe made exact replicas of those. (Behaalotekha 61)

TALMUD BAVLI

אֲשֶׁר־אַתָּה מָרְאֶה בָּהָר – *That is shown to you on the mountain:* It was taught: An ark of fire, a table of fire, and a candelabrum of fire all descended from heaven. Moshe studied these and made replicas of them using earthly materials. This is what the Torah means when it states, *Take care to make them according to that design that is shown to you on the mountain.* But as for the Tabernacle as a whole, the verse states: *So shall you set up the Tabernacle, according to the plan you were shown on the mountain* (26:30) – should we not also suggest that a Tabernacle of fire was brought down from heaven for Moshe to copy? The two cited verses differ: In the first one, Moshe is instructed to follow their "design" [*tavnitam*, indicating that he was shown an actual image], whereas the subsequent verse employs the word "plan" [*kemishpato*, which implies that Moshe was given instructions without an accompanying model to observe]. (Menaḥot 29a)

CHAPTER 26, VERSE 1

TANḤUMA

תַּעֲשֶׂה עֶשֶׂר יְרִיעֹת – *Make it with ten sheets:* One verse states: *The Almighty…is excellent in power* (Job 37:23), and another: *Behold, God is exalted by His power?* (Job 36:22). What is the relationship between these two texts [between "power" and "His power"]? When God bestows His beneficence upon Israel, He provides for them according to His own abilities, but when He makes demands of His people, He only asks what He knows they can give. Behold the verse *As for the Tabernacle itself, make it with ten sheets* [a manageable demand]. On the other hand, when God provides to Israel in kind, He creates supernatural wonders – for in the future

26 1 **the mountain.** **As for the Tabernacle itself, make it** SHELISHI
with ten sheets of finely spun linen and sky-blue, purple, and
scarlet wool, with a design of cherubim worked into them.
2 **Each sheet shall be twenty-eight cubits long and four cubits**
3 **wide; all the sheets should be the same size. Five of the sheets**
4 **should be sewn together; the other five likewise. Make loops**
of sky-blue wool on the upper edge of the end sheet in the first

TANḤUMA *(cont.)*

the Holy One, blessed be He, will grace every righteous person with a canopy made from the clouds of glory, as the verse states: *And the Lord will create upon every dwelling place of Mount Zion, and upon her assemblies, a cloud and smoke by day, and the shining of a flaming fire by night: for upon all the glory shall there be a canopy* (Isaiah 4:5). Similarly, when God commands: *Bring you pure oil from crushed olives for light, to kindle the lamp, every night* (Exodus 27:20), He asks only what it is in their power to give. But when God Himself brightened the sky for Israel, He did so according to His own ability, as the verse states: *The Lord went ahead of them by day in a column of cloud to guide them, and at night in a column of fire to give them light, so that they might travel day and night* (13:21). Furthermore, when God asks Israel to *bring the best first fruits of your land to the House of the Lord your God.* (23:19), His demands are modest. But, when He similarly provides for Israel, He arranges that *by the stream upon its bank, on this side and on that side, shall grow all trees for food, whose leaf shall not wither, neither shall its fruit fail: it shall bring forth new fruit every month* (Ezekiel 47:12). (Pinḥas 14)

BEMIDBAR RABBA

וּתְכֵלֶת וְאַרְגָּמָן וְתֹלַעַת שָׁנִי – *And sky-blue, purple, and scarlet wool:* The verse *Blow upon my garden* (Song of Songs 4:16) refers to the Tabernacle. For the term "my garden" [*ganni*]? The term echoes "my bridal chamber" [*genuni*; the Tabernacle was a place of communion between God and Israel]. And just as a bridal chamber is festooned with all manner of colors, so was the Tabernacle decorated with a range of hues, as the verse states: *Finely spun linen and sky-blue, purple, and scarlet wool.* (Naso, 13:2)

VERSE 3

TARGUM ONKELOS

חֹבְרֹת – *Sewn:* Five of the sheets should be clasped together.

LEKAḤ TOV

חֹבְרֹת – *Sewn:* These should be attached with a needle and thread, and not with loops or clasps.

VERSE 4

BARAITA DIMLEKHET HAMISHKAN

וְעָשִׂיתָ לֻלְאֹת – *Make loops:* How was the Tabernacle covered? The craftsmen fashioned ten sheets. Two sets of five sheets were combined to create two large curtains, as the verse states: *Five of the sheets should be sewn together* (26:3). The two sets were in turn attached to each other with a row of sky-blue loops, as the verse states: *Make loops of sky-blue wool*

וְכֵ֤ן תַּעֲשֶׂה֙ בִּשְׂפַ֣ת הַיְרִיעָ֔ה הַקִּיצוֹנָ֖ה בַּמַּחְבֶּ֥רֶת הַשֵּׁנִֽית׃
ה חֲמִשִּׁ֣ים לֻלָאֹ֗ת תַּעֲשֶׂה֮ בַּיְרִיעָ֣ה הָאֶחָת֒ וַחֲמִשִּׁ֣ים לֻלָאֹ֗ת
תַּעֲשֶׂה֙ בִּקְצֵ֣ה הַיְרִיעָ֔ה אֲשֶׁ֖ר בַּמַּחְבֶּ֣רֶת הַשֵּׁנִ֑ית מַקְבִּילֹת֙
ו הַלֻּ֣לָאֹ֔ת אִשָּׁ֖ה אֶל־אֲחֹתָֽהּ׃ וְעָשִׂ֕יתָ חֲמִשִּׁ֖ים קַרְסֵ֣י זָהָ֑ב
וְחִבַּרְתָּ֨ אֶת־הַיְרִיעֹ֜ת אִשָּׁ֤ה אֶל־אֲחֹתָהּ֙ בַּקְּרָסִ֔ים וְהָיָ֥ה
ז הַמִּשְׁכָּ֖ן אֶחָֽד׃ וְעָשִׂ֙יתָ֙ יְרִיעֹ֣ת עִזִּ֔ים לְאֹ֖הֶל עַל־הַמִּשְׁכָּ֑ן
ח עַשְׁתֵּֽי־עֶשְׂרֵ֥ה יְרִיעֹ֖ת תַּעֲשֶׂ֥ה אֹתָֽם׃ אֹ֣רֶךְ ׀ הַיְרִיעָ֣ה הָאַחַ֗ת
שְׁלֹשִׁים֙ בָּֽאַמָּ֔ה וְרֹ֙חַב֙ אַרְבַּ֣ע בָּֽאַמָּ֔ה הַיְרִיעָ֖ה הָאֶחָ֑ת מִדָּ֣ה
ט אַחַ֔ת לְעַשְׁתֵּ֥י עֶשְׂרֵ֖ה יְרִיעֹֽת׃ וְחִבַּרְתָּ֞ אֶת־חֲמֵ֤שׁ הַיְרִיעֹת֙
לְבָ֔ד וְאֶת־שֵׁ֥שׁ הַיְרִיעֹ֖ת לְבָ֑ד וְכָפַלְתָּ֙ אֶת־הַיְרִיעָ֣ה הַשִּׁשִּׁ֔ית

BARAITA DIMLEKHET HAMISHKAN *(cont.)*

on the upper edge. Fifty gold clasps were inserted into the loops, as the verse states: *And make fifty gold clasps* (26:6). Once placed in the loops, the gold clasps shone like the stars in the night sky. The length of each sheet was twenty-eight cubits. (2)

VERSE 6

PHILO

וְהָיָה הַמִּשְׁכָּן אֶחָד – *So that the Tabernacle becomes one whole:* The verse stresses that the Tabernacle's function is to create oneness. Although the earth is distinct from water, as water is from air, and air from fire, and fire from all those things – they are nevertheless adapted for a single purpose. The Tabernacle's oneness consists in the fact that this project brought together many disparate parts for a united singular purpose.

PESIKTA DERAV KAHANA

וְהָיָה הַמִּשְׁכָּן אֶחָד – *So that the Tabernacle becomes one whole:* Rabbi Yudan quoting Rabbi Levi Taḥlifa of Caesarea and Reish Lakish each interpreted this command differently. One said: By joining them all together, Moshe was in effect joining each of them individually. The other said: The phrase *So that the Tabernacle becomes one whole* means that it should be measured and anointed [see Numbers 7:1] as a single unit. (1)

VERSE 7

TANḤUMA

וְעָשִׂיתָ יְרִיעֹת עִזִּים לְאֹהֶל – *Make sheets of goats' hair as a tent:* A verse states: *I have loved you, says the Lord. Yet you say, In what way have You loved us?* (Malachi 1:2). Said the Holy One, blessed be He, to Israel: See how I adore you! Consider: from the earth to the heavens is a five hundred-year journey, and between the first heaven and the next lies the same distance, and so it goes between each level of the heavens. But I have put

set, and likewise on the upper edge of the outermost sheet
5 in the second set. Make fifty loops on each sheet on one side
and fifty on the upper edge of the corresponding sheets in the
6 other set, with the loops opposite one another. And make fifty
gold clasps. With the clasps, join the sheets together so that the
7 Tabernacle becomes one whole. Make sheets of goats' hair as
8 a tent over the Tabernacle; make eleven of these sheets. Each
sheet shall be thirty cubits long and four cubits wide, all eleven
9 sheets the same size. Join five of the sheets by themselves, and
the other six by themselves. Fold the sixth sheet over the front

TANHUMA *(cont.)*

all that aside and say to you: *Make sheets of goats' hair as a tent* – that will suffice for Me to come and dwell amongst you. (Teruma 9)

וְעָשִׂיתָ יְרִיעֹת עִזִּים – *Make sheets of goats' hair:* Rabbi Yaakov son of Rabbi Asi taught: What is meant by the verse *Lord, I love the habitation of Your house, and the place where Your glory dwells* (Psalms 26:8)? God considers Israel's construction of the Tabernacle to be on par with to His own creation of the world. For regarding the universe, the verse states: *God stretches out the heavens like a sheet* (Psalms 104:2). This is echoed in the verse, *Make sheets of goats' hair.* (Pekudei 2)

YALKUT SHIMONI

וְעָשִׂיתָ יְרִיעֹת עִזִּים לְאֹהֶל – *Make sheets of goats' hair as a tent:* Our Sages taught: The bottom layer sheets were composed of *finely spun linen and sky-blue, purple and scarlet wool* (26:1), whereas the upper sheets were made out of simple goats' hair. Yet it required greater skill and craftsmanship to produce the upper curtains than the lower ones. For with regard to the lower layer, the verse states: *Every skilled woman spun with her own hands, and brought what she had spun* (35:25). But when describing the upper sheets' production, the verse states: *All the women whose hearts inspired them used their skill to spin the goats' hair* (35:26). ["Inspiration" is superior to mere "skill."] On this, Rabbi Ḥiyya taught: The wool was washed while still on the goats and spun directly from the goats [which is not an easy task]. (370)

VERSE 9

TARGUM YERUSHALMI

וְחִבַּרְתָּ אֶת־חֲמֵשׁ הַיְרִיעֹת לְבָד – *Join five of the sheets by themselves:* Join five of the sheets by themselves, corresponding to the five books of the Torah; and the other six sheets by themselves, corresponding to the six tractates of the Mishna.

LEKAḤ TOV

וְחִבַּרְתָּ אֶת־חֲמֵשׁ הַיְרִיעֹת – *Join five sheets:* Connect five of the sheets by sewing them together. **וְכָפַלְתָּ אֶת־הַיְרִיעָה הַשִּׁשִּׁית** – *Fold the sixth sheet:* This was done such that two cubits overlapped the end of the structure. **אֶל־מוּל פְּנֵי הָאֹהֶל** – *Over the front of the Tent:* This refers to the material at the border of the sheets that lay at the entrance to the

י אֶל־מוּל פְּנֵי הָאֹהֶל׃ וְעָשִׂיתָ חֲמִשִּׁים לֻלָאֹת עַל שְׂפַת
הַיְרִיעָה הָאֶחָת הַקִּיצֹנָה בַּחֹבָרֶת וַחֲמִשִּׁים לֻלָאֹת עַל שְׂפַת
יא הַיְרִיעָה הַחֹבֶרֶת הַשֵּׁנִית׃ וְעָשִׂיתָ קַרְסֵי נְחֹשֶׁת חֲמִשִּׁים
וְהֵבֵאתָ אֶת־הַקְּרָסִים בַּלֻּלָאֹת וְחִבַּרְתָּ אֶת־הָאֹהֶל וְהָיָה
יב אֶחָד׃ וְסֶרַח הָעֹדֵף בִּירִיעֹת הָאֹהֶל חֲצִי הַיְרִיעָה הָעֹדֶפֶת
יג תִּסְרַח עַל אֲחֹרֵי הַמִּשְׁכָּן׃ וְהָאַמָּה מִזֶּה וְהָאַמָּה מִזֶּה בָּעֹדֵף
בְּאֹרֶךְ יְרִיעֹת הָאֹהֶל יִהְיֶה סָרוּחַ עַל־צִדֵּי הַמִּשְׁכָּן מִזֶּה

LEKAḤ TOV *(cont.)*

Tabernacle. The final sheet was folded down in the middle so that the final two cubits of material [out of its breadth of four] descended like a scarf upon a person's forehead.

VERSE 10

LEKAḤ TOV

וְעָשִׂיתָ חֲמִשִּׁים לֻלָאֹת – *Make fifty loops:* Align the seams so that the fifty bronze clasps on the upper layer [described in the next verse] lie directly on top of the fifty gold clasps of the lower level [mentioned in 26:6].

VERSE 11

BARAITA DIMLEKHET HAMISHKAN

וְעָשִׂיתָ קַרְסֵי נְחֹשֶׁת חֲמִשִּׁים – *Make, also, fifty bronze clasps:* Eleven sheets of goats' hair were fashioned, each one thirty cubits long, as the verse states: *Make sheets of goats' hair* (26:7). These were combined into two sets to create two large curtains, one of five sheets and one of six sheets, as the verse states: *Join five of the sheets by themselves* (26:9). Each of the two large curtains was fixed with fifty loops, and the two rows of loops were attached to each other using fifty bronze clasps, as the verses state: *Make fifty loops* (26:10), and *Make, also, fifty bronze clasps.* The total length of all the sheets was forty-four cubits, as there were eleven sheets, and the verse states: *Each sheet shall be…four cubits wide* (26:8). Now, thirty out of the forty-four cubits of material stretched across the top of the Tabernacle to serve as its roof, and ten cubits descended down the back [western] side of the structure. This left the width of a single sheet of four cubits which came down in front of the Tabernacle, as the verse states: *Fold the sixth sheet over the front of the Tent* (26:9). However, Rabbi Yosei held that half of the eleventh sheet descended over the front of tent structure, and the other half [the remaining two cubits] came down the back, as the verse states: *As for the additional length of the tent sheets, the extra half sheet is to hang down at the rear of the Tabernacle* (26:12). (3)

VERSE 12

TARGUM YERUSHALMI

תִּסְרַח – *Is to hang down:* Is to hang down at an incline at the rear of the Tabernacle.

10 of the Tent. Make fifty loops on the edge of the end sheet of one
11 set, and fifty on the edge of the end sheet of the other. Make,
also, fifty bronze clasps. Put the clasps through the loops, join-
12 ing the tent together so that it becomes one whole. As for the
additional length of the tent sheets, the extra half sheet is to
13 hang down at the rear of the Tabernacle. The extra cubit at either end of each of the tent sheets should hang over the sides

VERSE 13

TALMUD BAVLI

וְהָאַמָּה מִזֶּה וְהָאַמָּה מִזֶּה – *The extra cubit at either end:* [The Gemara understands this verse as referring to the dimensions of the Tabernacle from east to west, i.e., from front to back, elaborating on the previous verse.] The verse states: *The extra cubit at either end of each of the tent sheets should hang over the sides of the Tabernacle to cover it on both sides.* In the view of Rabbi Yehuda, these extra cubits covered the sockets [the base of the Tabernacle's rear wall]. However, Rabbi Neḥemya maintains that the extra material covered the cubit of the beams [left exposed by the first layer. That is, according to Rabbi Yehuda, there was more available material down the western side than Rabbi Neḥemya believes there to have been, as will be explained below.] For consider: Once the width of the sets of sheets was laid across the length of the Tabernacle, all the sheets combined added to a length of forty-four cubits. Subtract thirty for the length of the roof [that covered the open space of the Tabernacle's interior], and fourteen cubits remain. Subtract two for the folding of the sixth curtain, as the verse states, *Fold the sixth sheet over the front of the Tent* (26:9), and twelve remain [covering the entirety of the Tabernacle's ten-cubit height, with two cubits left trailing at the bottom]. Granted, according to the opinion of Rabbi Yehuda [who maintains that the beams narrowed to a fingerbreadth at the top, and therefore the tops of the boards did not take up any of the width of the curtains], we can understand the verse *As for the additional length of the tent sheets, the extra half sheet is to hang down at the rear of the Tabernacle* [26:12; this refers to the extra two cubits left trailing on the ground behind the Tabernacle]. However, according to Rabbi Neḥemya [who maintains that material was necessary for the width of the curtains to cover the thickness at the top of the beams], what is the meaning of that verse? [According to his understanding, there was no material left to sit on the desert floor behind the structure.] Rabbi Neḥemya understands the verse to mean that the layer of goats' hair simply hung down further than the others [i.e., further than the inner layer of curtains.] On this point, the school of Rabbi Yishmael taught: To what was the Tabernacle similar? To a woman walking in the marketplace with her skirts flowing after her. (Shabbat 98b)

LEKAḤ TOV

וְהָאַמָּה מִזֶּה וְהָאַמָּה מִזֶּה – *The extra cubit at either end:* Because the inner layer of sheets had a width of twenty-eight cubits, while the outer curtains of goats' hair ran for thirty cubits, there were two additional cubits to cover the sides of the Tabernacle. [This text describes the dimension of the sheets extending from the north wall to the south wall.]

יד וּמִזֶּה לְכַסֹּתוֹ׃ וְעָשִׂיתָ מִכְסֶה לָאֹהֶל עֹרֹת אֵילִם מְאָדָּמִים
וּמִכְסֵה עֹרֹת תְּחָשִׁים מִלְמָעְלָה׃
טו וְעָשִׂיתָ אֶת־הַקְּרָשִׁים לַמִּשְׁכָּן עֲצֵי שִׁטִּים עֹמְדִים׃ רביעי

VERSE 14

BARAITA DIMLEKHET HAMISHKAN

וְעָשִׂיתָ מִכְסֶה לָאֹהֶל עֹרֹת אֵילִם – *Make a covering for the tent from rams' hides:* A single curtain of hide was prepared measuring thirty cubits by twenty-eight cubits, and that was used to cover the tent, as the verse states" *Make a covering for the tent.* [According to this view, the length of this third covering equaled the length of the structure, such that it did not descend down the rear, western side. Its width was the same as the first layer of sheets, so it too covered the majority of the boards' heights on the northern and southern walls.] The top of this layer comprised two different types of materials [i.e., the rams' hides and the "fine leather" covering were stitched together to form one outermost layer] – this is the opinion of Rabbi Neḥemya. Rabbi Yehuda however, believes that there were two separate coverings [above the goats' hair sheets]: the lower one was composed of rams' hides dyed red, while the upper one was made out of fine leather. (3)

TALMUD BAVLI

וְעָשִׂיתָ מִכְסֶה לָאֹהֶל – *Make a covering for the tent:* The next verse states: *Make the upright boards for the Tabernacle* (26:15), and from the language of that verse, we understand that only the curtains themselves are properly called the "Tabernacle" [see 26:1], while the supporting beams are not. However, consider the verse *Make a covering for the tent from rams' hides* – does that verse not also imply that these coverings were not themselves part of the "tent"? If so, however, what about the dilemma raised by Rabbi Elazar: What is the ruling with regard to the hide of an impure animal that shelters a corpse? Can it become ritually impure as a tent would? [Impurity from a corpse is transmitted to anyone in the same enclosure, or "tent."] If the covering of the Tabernacle is not considered a "tent," it follows the hide of a pure animal that covered the Tabernacle cannot become ritually impure in this manner. And if this is so for the hide of a pure animal, surely there was no need for Rabbi Elazar to ask concerning that of an impure animal [of which the same should be true *a fortiori.* The Gemara responds:] The verse subsequently restores the status of hides as "tents" by treating the tent and its covering as the same in a later verse: *And they shall bear the curtains of the Tabernacle, and the Tent of Meeting, its covering, and the covering of fine leather that is above upon it* (Numbers 4:25).... [The phrase *or taḥash* is translated here as "fine leather." However, the Gemara understands the word *taḥash* as referring to a species of animal:] The *taḥash* was similar to the species of wild animals called *tela ilan* in that it was multicolored. Rav Yosef said: If so, that is the reason that the Targum translates the word *taḥash* as *sasegona*, because that animal would rejoice [*sas*] in its many colors [*gevanim*]. (Shabbat 28a)

14 of the Tabernacle to cover it on both sides. Make a covering for
the tent from rams' hides dyed red. Above it make a covering
of fine leather.
15 Make the upright boards for the Tabernacle of acacia wood. REVI'I

VERSE 15

TALMUD BAVLI

אֶת־הַקְּרָשִׁים – *The boards:* A later verse states: *This is the law: when a person dies in a tent, whoever enters that tent and whoever is in it shall remain impure for seven days* (Numbers 19:14). An earlier verse, however, states: *He spread the Tent over the Tabernacle and placed the covering over the Tent* (Exodus 40:19). We can learn from this pairing that just as in the Tabernacle a covering of linen constitutes a tent, similarly any covering of linen can be termed a tent. We might have thought that just as boards were used in construction of the Tabernacle, so must boards be a necessary component of a tent [that is subject to impurity]. Hence the verse emphasizes: *Make the upright boards for the Tabernacle* – meaning that the covering is referred to as Tabernacle, but the boards themselves are not called a Tabernacle [and hence not properly part of the tent]. (Shabbat 28a) **עֹמְדִים** – *Upright:* Ḥizkiya taught in the name of Rabbi Yirmeya, who himself was quoting Rabbi Shimon bar Yoḥai: In order to fulfill one's obligation of taking up the four species on the festival of Sukkot, one must hold them in the same orientation in which they grow [with the stems pointed downward and the tops upward], as in the verse *Make the upright boards.* For it is taught in a *baraita*: When the verse speaks of "upright boards," it means that the boards should stand in the manner that they grew. Another interpretation: The term "upright" [*omedim*] means that that boards held up their coverings. Another interpretation: We might have feared that because the Tabernacle is lost, so is any hope of retrieving the boards. Therefore the verse uses the term "upright" [*omedim*], meaning that the boards will stand [i.e., exist or survive] forever. (Sukka 45b)

TANḤUMA

וְעָשִׂיתָ אֶת הַקְּרָשִׁים – *Make the boards:* Where did the Israelites procure the boards to construct the Tabernacle? The patriarch Yaakov planted trees when he went down to Egypt, telling his sons: My children, you will one day be redeemed from this land, and then the Holy One, blessed be He, will command you to build Him a Tabernacle. Thus you ought to plant trees now, so that by the time God instructs you to build His dwelling the wood will be ready for the project. Immediately, Yaakov's sons set about planting the trees they would need for the timber. Furthermore, those trees that the family planted sang a song before the Holy One, blessed be He, as the verse states: *Then the trees of the wood sang for joy* (Psalms 96:12). When did they do so? As they were fashioned into the boards for the Tabernacle. The Holy One, blessed be He, directed Moshe to craft the Tabernacle, saying: *Make the upright boards for the Tabernacle of acacia wood.* He employed the definite article to indicate that the wood used for the construction came from trees that were already known – those that the nation's ancestor had prepared for the very purpose.

טז עֶשֶׂר אַמּוֹת אֹרֶךְ הַקָּרֶשׁ וְאַמָּה וַחֲצִי הָאַמָּה רֹחַב
יז הַקֶּרֶשׁ הָאֶחָד׃ שְׁתֵּי יָדוֹת לַקֶּרֶשׁ הָאֶחָד מְשֻׁלָּבֹת אִשָּׁה
יח אֶל־אֲחֹתָהּ כֵּן תַּעֲשֶׂה לְכֹל קַרְשֵׁי הַמִּשְׁכָּן׃ וְעָשִׂיתָ אֶת־
הַקְּרָשִׁים לַמִּשְׁכָּן עֶשְׂרִים קֶרֶשׁ לִפְאַת נֶגְבָּה תֵימָנָה׃
יט וְאַרְבָּעִים אַדְנֵי־כֶסֶף תַּעֲשֶׂה תַּחַת עֶשְׂרִים הַקָּרֶשׁ שְׁנֵי
אֲדָנִים תַּחַת־הַקֶּרֶשׁ הָאֶחָד לִשְׁתֵּי יְדֹתָיו וּשְׁנֵי אֲדָנִים

SHEMOT RABBA

עֲצֵי שִׁטִּים – *Acacia wood:* Why was Israel required to use acacia wood in the construction of the Tabernacle? The Holy One, blessed be He, thereby taught the world not to use fruit-bearing trees when building houses. For if the King of Kings who rules the entire world, commanded that wood for His house be taken from trees that do not produce fruit [thus minimizing waste], should not human beings be similarly discriminatory? Another interpretation: Why does the verse state: *Make the upright boards for the Tabernacle [lamishkan],* when it really should have said: "Make the upright boards that will form the Tabernacle?" [The wording gives the impression that the boards were ancillary to the structure, rather than a main component of the building itself.] Rabbi Hoshaya teaches: The term *lamishkan* should be understood as if it read *lamashkon* [meaning "as a pledge"]. For if the nation of Israel ever sinned so badly that they deserved to be destroyed, the nation would be able forfeit their pledge instead [and thereby save themselves through the Tabernacle's destruction]. Said Moshe to the Holy One, blessed be He: "But what will happen to Israel in an era when they have neither a Tabernacle nor a Temple to protect them that way?" God answered: "I will then take a single righteous individual from Israel who will serve as a pledge for the nation, and in order that I may forgive all of their sins." Another interpretation for this verse: Rabbi Avin taught the parable of a king who was very handsome. Said the monarch to one of his servants: "Fashion an image that is a perfect likeness of myself!" But the craftsman protested: "Sire, how can I possibly replicate your image precisely?" Answered the monarch: "You do the best you can with the materials you possess, and I will appear in My glory." Such did the Holy One, blessed be He, instruct Moshe: *Take care to make them* [the Tabernacle's accoutrements] *according to the design that is shown to you* (25:40). But Moshe protested: "Master of the Universe, am I a god who can fashion these objects exactly as You have made them?" Answered God: "You do your best to *make them according to the design,* using *sky-blue, purple, and scarlet wool* (25:4), as you try to imitate below what you have seen above." Thus when the verse states: *Make the upright boards for the Tabernacle,* it means: Just as they appear standing up in the heavens. (Teruma 35:2–6)

LEKAH TOV

עֲצֵי שִׁטִּים – *Acacia wood:* God could have picked any one of the varieties of cedar trees for the construction of the Tabernacle. However, He chose acacia wood [*atzei shittim*] to atone for the incident at Shittim [see Numbers 25, in which Israel engaged in idolatry in this place].

16 **Each board shall be ten cubits long and one and a half cubits**
17 **wide. Each board should have two matching tenons; all the**
18 **Tabernacle's boards should be made in this way. Make twenty**
19 **boards for the southern side of the Tabernacle, and forty sil-**
ver sockets under the twenty boards, two sockets under the

VERSE 18

LEKAH TOV

עֶשְׂרִים קֶרֶשׁ – *Twenty boards:* The Tabernacle comprised forty-eight boards altogether [twenty on the north side, twenty on the south side, and eight on the west side]. The Holy One, blessed be He, similarly commanded that similarly forty-eight cities of refuge be constructed [to shelter those guilty of manslaughter], to correspond to the number of boards in the structure. And there were seven types of coverings that lay on the Tabernacle: Finely spun linen, sky-blue wool, purple wool, scarlet wool, goats' hair, rams' hides, and fine leather. So did the Holy One, blessed be He, provide Israel with seven clouds of glory to protect them: one on each side of the camp, one above them, one below them, and a seventh to lead them through the wilderness.

VERSE 19

BARAITA DIMLEKHET HAMISHKAN

וְאַרְבָּעִים אַדְנֵי־כֶסֶף – *Forty silver sockets:* How were the Tabernacle boards erected? Twenty boards were put up to create the north wall, and twenty boards were used for the opposite south wall. This left eight boards for the western wall. The eastern wall of the structure contained no boards, but was defined by four posts that held a curtain in front of the Tabernacle, as the verse states: *Hang it on four gold-covered posts of acacia wood* (26:32). Hollow sockets were fashioned, and a groove was carved out of the boards' bottoms, leaving a quarter of wood on one side and a quarter of wood on the other side, with half of the bottom empty in the middle. Thus were created two pin-like tenons [on the boards' bottom edges] which were inserted into sockets. Two grooves were also carved out of the top of each board, but these were only each a fingerbreadth wide. A gold ring fit into neighboring grooves to prevent the boards from parting from each other, as the verse states: *Joined together at the top by a ring* (26:24). (1)

TALMUD YERUSHALMI

וְאַרְבָּעִים אַדְנֵי־כֶסֶף – *Forty silver sockets:* What construction actually took place in the formation of the Tabernacle? The craftsmen were required to insert the boards into the sockets. [The Talmud is discussing the basis for the labors that are forbidden on the Sabbath. A guiding principle regarding such labors is that they must effect some sort of permanent transformation. As such the Gemara asks:] But were the boards not placed into their sockets only on a temporary basis? Rabbi Yosei explained: Since the nation encamped and broke camp only upon God's orders, the people viewed any settlement as being permanent. However, Rabbi Yosei son of Rabbi Bun taught: Since the Holy One, blessed be He, had promised Israel that He planned to bring them to the promised land, each stop

כ תַּחַת־הַקֶּרֶשׁ הָאֶחָד לִשְׁתֵּי יְדֹתָיו: וּלְצֶלַע הַמִּשְׁכָּן הַשֵּׁנִית
כא לִפְאַת צָפוֹן עֶשְׂרִים קָרֶשׁ: וְאַרְבָּעִים אַדְנֵיהֶם כָּסֶף שְׁנֵי
אֲדָנִים תַּחַת הַקֶּרֶשׁ הָאֶחָד וּשְׁנֵי אֲדָנִים תַּחַת הַקֶּרֶשׁ
כב כג הָאֶחָד: וּלְיַרְכְּתֵי הַמִּשְׁכָּן יָמָּה תַּעֲשֶׂה שִׁשָּׁה קְרָשִׁים: וּשְׁנֵי
כד קְרָשִׁים תַּעֲשֶׂה לִמְקֻצְעֹת הַמִּשְׁכָּן בַּיַּרְכָתָיִם: וְיִהְיוּ תֹאֲמִם
מִלְּמַטָּה וְיַחְדָּו יִהְיוּ תַמִּים עַל־רֹאשׁוֹ אֶל־הַטַּבַּעַת הָאֶחָת
כה כֵּן יִהְיֶה לִשְׁנֵיהֶם לִשְׁנֵי הַמִּקְצֹעֹת יִהְיוּ: וְהָיוּ שְׁמֹנָה קְרָשִׁים
וְאַדְנֵיהֶם כֶּסֶף שִׁשָּׁה עָשָׂר אֲדָנִים שְׁנֵי אֲדָנִים תַּחַת הַקֶּרֶשׁ
כו הָאֶחָד וּשְׁנֵי אֲדָנִים תַּחַת הַקֶּרֶשׁ הָאֶחָד: וְעָשִׂיתָ בְרִיחִם
כז עֲצֵי שִׁטִּים חֲמִשָּׁה לְקַרְשֵׁי צֶלַע־הַמִּשְׁכָּן הָאֶחָד: וַחֲמִשָּׁה
בְרִיחִם לְקַרְשֵׁי צֶלַע־הַמִּשְׁכָּן הַשֵּׁנִית וַחֲמִשָּׁה בְרִיחִם
כח לְקַרְשֵׁי צֶלַע הַמִּשְׁכָּן לַיַּרְכָתַיִם יָמָּה: וְהַבְּרִיחַ הַתִּיכֹן בְּתוֹךְ
כט הַקְּרָשִׁים מַבְרִחַ מִן־הַקָּצֶה אֶל־הַקָּצֶה: וְאֶת־הַקְּרָשִׁים
תְּצַפֶּה זָהָב וְאֶת־טַבְּעֹתֵיהֶם תַּעֲשֶׂה זָהָב בָּתִּים לַבְּרִיחִם

TALMUD YERUSHALMI *(cont.)*

along the journey was considered temporary. This would imply that even non-permanent construction is tantamount to building. (Shabbat 7:2)

VERSE 26

LEKAH TOV

וְעָשִׂיתָ בְרִיחִם עֲצֵי שִׁטִּים – *Make crossbars, too, of acacia wood:* The crossbars that supported the walls fit into rings that were attached to the boards. Thus the crossbars ran through each of the Tabernacle's boards. Meanwhile, the middle crossbar that ran through the center of the boards from end to end was held in place miraculously. [According to this approach, there was a single middle crossbar that passed through all three walls, making ninety degree turns miraculously at the corners.]

VERSE 28

TARGUM YERUSHALMI

וְהַבְּרִיחַ הַתִּיכֹן – *The central crossbar:* [The definite article gives this impression that this item had already been fashioned.] The middle crossbar that ran through the center of the boards from one end to the other hand was fashioned from the tree that Avraham planted in Be'er Sheva [see Genesis 21:33]. When Israel walked through the Sea of Reeds, the angels chopped down the tree and cast into the water, where it floated on the surface. At that moment an angel spoke up and declared: "This is the very tree that Avraham planted in

20 first board for its two tenons, and two under the next. For the
second side of the Tabernacle, the northern side, there should
21 be twenty boards, along with their forty silver sockets, two un-
22 der the first board and two under each of the others. Make six
23 boards for the west side of the Tabernacle, and two additional
24 boards for the Tabernacle's rear corners. These should adjoin
each other at the bottom, and be joined together at the top by a
ring. So it should be for both sides; they shall form the two cor-
25 ners. So there should be eight boards and sixteen silver sockets,
26 two sockets under each board. Make crossbars, too, of acacia
27 wood, five for the boards of the first side of the Tabernacle, five
for the boards of the second side of the Tabernacle, and five for
28 the boards of the western side of the Tabernacle at the rear. The
central crossbar should go through the middle of the boards
29 from one end to the other. Overlay the boards with gold, and
make gold rings for the crossbars. The crossbars too should be

TARGUM YERUSHALMI *(cont.)*

Be'er Sheva after praying there and pronouncing the name of God!" The Israelites took hold of the tree and carved it into the middle crossbar, which was seventy cubits long. And the piece was wondrous, for when the people erected the Tabernacle, the rod wound like a snake all through the boards. [After passing through the northern boards, it miraculously turned the corner, ran through the western boards, and again bent to run back through the southern boards.] And when the Tabernacle was disassembled again, the middle crossbar emerged as straight as a single staff.

BERESHIT RABBA

וְהַבְּרִיחַ הַתִּיכֹן – *The central crossbar:* The Torah tells of the patriarch Yaakov: *And Yisrael took his journey with all that he had, and came to Be'er Sheva, and offered sacrifices to the God of his father Yitzḥak* (Genesis 46:1). Where had Yaakov gone in the meantime? Rav Naḥman taught: He went to chop down the trees that his grandfather Avraham had planted in Be'er Sheva [see Genesis 21:33]. Later, in describing the construction of the Tabernacle, the Torah states: *The central crossbar should go through the middle of the boards.* Rabbi Levi taught that the middle crossbar was thirty-two cubits in length. Where did the Israelites find such a long piece of wood? The trees must have been stored for this purpose since the time of Yaakov our patriarch. (Vayigash 94:4)

VERSE 29

BARAITA DIMLEKHET HAMISHKAN

בָּתִּים לַבְּרִיחִם – *For the crossbars:* How were the Tabernacle boards held upright? Forty sockets were fashioned for the north wall [each of the twenty boards had two tenons and hence required two sockets], forty sockets for the south wall, and sixteen sockets for the west wall. An additional four sockets were used in the east wall to reach a total of

ל וְצִפִּיתָ אֶת־הַבְּרִיחִם זָהָב׃ וַהֲקֵמֹתָ אֶת־הַמִּשְׁכָּן כְּמִשְׁפָּטוֹ
לא אֲשֶׁר הָרְאֵיתָ בָּהָר׃ וְעָשִׂיתָ פָרֹכֶת תְּכֵלֶת כ חמישי
וְאַרְגָּמָן וְתוֹלַעַת שָׁנִי וְשֵׁשׁ מָשְׁזָר מַעֲשֵׂה חֹשֵׁב יַעֲשֶׂה
לב אֹתָהּ כְּרֻבִים׃ וְנָתַתָּה אֹתָהּ עַל־אַרְבָּעָה עַמּוּדֵי שִׁטִּים
לג מְצֻפִּים זָהָב וָוֵיהֶם זָהָב עַל־אַרְבָּעָה אַדְנֵי־כָסֶף׃ וְנָתַתָּה
אֶת־הַפָּרֹכֶת תַּחַת הַקְּרָסִים וְהֵבֵאתָ שָׁמָּה מִבֵּית לַפָּרֹכֶת
אֵת אֲרוֹן הָעֵדוּת וְהִבְדִּילָה הַפָּרֹכֶת לָכֶם בֵּין הַקֹּדֶשׁ וּבֵין

BARAITA DIMLEKHET HAMISHKAN *(cont.)*

one hundred sockets, as the verse states: *A hundred talents for the hundred sockets* (38:27). Now each board was fitted with two gold rings, one situated near the top of the plank, and the other near the bottom, and crossbars were then inserted into these rings. The crossbars themselves were each thirty cubits long and hence equaled the combined length of a side's twenty boards [for each board was one and a half cubits wide]. However, the middle crossbars that ran through the centers of the northern and southern boards were only twelve cubits long and fit just eight boards on those sides, as the verse states, *The central crossbar should go through the middle of the boards* (26:28). Meanwhile, the crossbars on the western wall were only eight cubits long and supported six of that side's eight boards. The boards, the crossbars, the sockets, and the posts [mentioned in 26:32], were all covered in gold, as the verse dictates: *Overlay the boards with gold* (26:29).

VERSE 30

TALMUD YERUSHALMI

כְּמִשְׁפָּטוֹ – *According to the plan:* The boards that were selected for the north wall were always placed on that side, whereas those that were chosen for the south were always used there. (Shabbat 12:3)

PESIKTA RABBATI

כְּמִשְׁפָּטוֹ – *According to the plan:* When Moshe ascended to the heavens, the Holy One, blessed be He, opened up the seven heavens and showed him the celestial Temple, displaying before him the four colors to be used in the Tabernacle's construction. Hence the verse states: *So shall you set up the Tabernacle, according to the plan you were shown on the mountain.* For Moshe had protested: "Master of the Universe! I do not know what these colors are exactly." Responded God to him: "Look to your right." Moshe turned and there he saw a troop of angels wearing a color that resembled the sea. "This," He said, "is 'sky-blue.' Now look to your left." Moshe turned and there he saw people wearing red. "What do you see," He asked Moshe. Said Moshe: "I see men wearing the color red." "That is 'purple,'" God declared. Moshe looked behind him and saw a brigade wearing clothes that were neither red nor green. "That, Moshe," God said, "is what 'scarlet' is." Finally, Moshe looked in front of him and saw several brigades wearing white, and that was the finely spun linen. (20)

30 overlaid with gold. So shall you set up the Tabernacle, according
31 to the plan you were shown on the mountain. Make a HAMISHI
curtain of sky-blue, purple, and scarlet wool, and finely spun
32 linen with a design of cherubim worked into it. Hang it on four
gold-covered posts of acacia wood with gold hooks, set on
33 four sockets of silver. Hang the curtain under the clasps and
bring the Ark of the Testimony behind it, so that the curtain

VERSE 31

TALMUD YERUSHALMI

וְשֵׁשׁ מָשְׁזָר – *Finely spun linen:* Had the text used the word *ḥut* it would have meant a single thread, folded over once to create a double ply. The term *shazur* would suggest a combination of three, but *moshzar* [the term used in this verse] means six threads spun into one. And because there were four materials, there were altogether twenty-four strands.... Now one verse describes the Tabernacle's outer screen as being created "embroidered" (26:36), and that connotes a single design. However, our verse uses the term "worked into it" (26:31), implying that there were two images on the curtain. The interpretation of these instructions is debated by Rabbi Yehuda and Rabbi Neḥemya. One Sage argues that "embroidered" means that the same figure of a lion appeared on both faces of the screen, while "worked into it" indicated just a single figure of a lion on one side of the curtain. However, the other maintains that the terms' meanings should be reversed. (Shekalim 8:2)

TALMUD BAVLI

מַעֲשֵׂה חֹשֵׁב יַעֲשֶׂה אֹתָהּ כְּרֻבִים – *With a design of cherubim worked into it:* When the verse later mentions the Tabernacle's outer screen having been "embroidered" (26:36), it refers to figures that were embroidered over designs that had first been "worked into it." Such is the opinion of Rabbi Elazar. However, Rabbi Neḥemya argued that "worked into it" refers to needlework, which yields only one visible figure. However, "embroidery" [*maaseh ḥoshev*] is actually weaving work, from which results two different figures – one on either side of the cloth. (Yoma 72b)

VERSE 32

LEKAḤ TOV

וָוֵיהֶם זָהָב – *Gold hooks:* The hooks on top of the posts resembled reeds with bent tops, to accommodate the ropes. The ropes were used to tie down the curtain, which in turn was supported by the four posts held by four sockets.

VERSE 33

TALMUD BAVLI

וְהִבְדִּילָה הַפָּרֹכֶת לָכֶם – *So that the curtain separates:* Mishna: The High Priest would go through the Sanctuary [on Yom Kippur] until he reached the spot between the two curtains that separated the Sanctuary from the chamber of the Holy of Holies, with a space of one cubit between them. Rabbi Yosei argued: No, there was just a single

לד קֹדֶשׁ הַקֳּדָשִׁים: וְנָתַתָּ אֶת־הַכַּפֹּרֶת עַל אֲרוֹן הָעֵדֻת בְּקֹדֶשׁ
לה הַקֳּדָשִׁים: וְשַׂמְתָּ אֶת־הַשֻּׁלְחָן מִחוּץ לַפָּרֹכֶת וְאֶת־הַמְּנֹרָה
נֹכַח הַשֻּׁלְחָן עַל צֶלַע הַמִּשְׁכָּן תֵּימָנָה וְהַשֻּׁלְחָן תִּתֵּן עַל־

TALMUD BAVLI *(cont.)*

curtain hanging between those two spaces, as the verse states: *So that the curtain separates the holy place from the Holy of Holies.* Gemara: Rabbi Yosei's comment to the Rabbis seems correct; how would they respond? According to them, there was indeed but one curtain in the Tabernacle structure. However, in the Second Temple, there was no structure to take up the cubit's breadth of the partition wall that had existed in the First Temple. [In the First Temple there was a cubit-thick wall, called a *teraskin,* separating the Sanctuary from the Holy of Holies. Since the Sages were unsure of the status of that cubit, that is, to which of the two holy spaces it was considered to belong, two curtains were hung in the space of that cubit [to set off the ambiguous area]. (Yoma 51b) **וְהִבְדִּילָה הַפָּרֹכֶת לָכֶם** – *So that the curtain separates:* And why did the Sages not fashion a wall in the Second Temple [to separate between the Holy of Holies from the Sanctuary, as had been done in the First Temple]? A wall one cubit thick can hold up a wall that is thirty cubits high, but it cannot support a wall taller than that. And how do we know that the Second Temple was taller than the First Temple? For the prophet foretold: *The glory of this latter house shall be greater than that of the former, says the Lord of Hosts* (Haggai 2:9). Rav and Shmuel disagreed about that verse: According to one Sage, it promises that the Second Temple would be larger than the first, whereas the other held it means that the Second Temple would last longer than the first. Indeed, both interpretations were true. (Bava Batra 3a)

SHEMOT RABBA

וְהִבְדִּילָה הַפָּרֹכֶת לָכֶם – *So that the curtain separates:* Rabbi Berekhya opened his discourse by citing the verse: *Yours O Lord, is the greatness, and the power, and the glory, and the victory, and the majesty: for all that is in heaven and on earth is Yours* (I Chronicles 29:11). For we find that whatever the Holy One, blessed be He, created in the heavens, He fashioned a parallel creation on earth. For example, the Torah states, *Then God said, "Let an expanse stretch trough the water, let it separate water from water"* (Genesis 1:6). Corresponding to this heavenly partition, we find the instruction *So that the curtain separates the holy place from the Holy of Holies.* (Teruma 33:4)

VERSE 35

TALMUD YERUSHALMI

נֹכַח הַשֻּׁלְחָן עַל צֶלַע הַמִּשְׁכָּן תֵּימָנָה – *On the south side, opposite the table:* The presence of the table, the candelabrum, the altars, and the curtain is a prerequisite for the offering of the sacrifices. This is the opinion of Rabbi Meir. However, according to the Rabbis, only the basin and its base present such a requirement. But did not Rabbi Eliezer and Rabbi Yosei ben Ḥanina both state that the term "opposite" [*nokhaḥ,* also "present"] in reference to a certain item teaches that the presence of that item is necessary, whereas Rabbi Shmuel bar Naḥman

34 separates the holy place from the Holy of Holies. Put the cover
35 on the Ark of the Testimony in the Holy of Holies. The table
shall be placed on the north side of the Tabernacle outside the
curtain, and the candelabrum on the south side, opposite the

TALMUD YERUSHALMI *(cont.)*

said in the name of Rabbi Yonatan that even usage of the term "side" means that a feature is critical? Meanwhile, Rabbi Ila taught in the name of Rabbi Shmuel bar Naḥman that even the verb "to place" implies the critical nature of an item. [Since our verse contains all three terms under discussion, we would expect the table and candelabrum to be considered critical to the proper operation of the Tabernacle, in contradiction to the Rabbis' approach.] Rabbi Ḥanina explained: Indeed, any service that is performed inside the Sanctuary itself [such as lighting the lamps or burning incense] demands that all the listed features be in place. On the other hand, any service that is performed outside the Sanctuary [such as most sacrifices] is valid as long as the basin and its base are present. (Shekalim 4:2)

TALMUD BAVLI

וְשַׂמְתָּ אֶת־הַשֻּׁלְחָן מִחוּץ לַפָּרֹכֶת – *The table shall be placed outside the curtain:* The table was placed closest to the north wall [of the Sanctuary], and stood two and a half cubits from that wall. The candelabrum was positioned on the south side and stood two and a half cubits from that wall. The [golden incense] altar stood in the middle of the room, somewhat closer to the entrance. And why was the altar not situated on the same plane as the other two objects? Because God commanded: *And the candelabrum on the south side, opposite the table,* such that these two items were to be directly opposite each other [without the altar interposing]. (Yoma 33b)

וְאֶת־הַמְּנֹרָה נֹכַח הַשֻּׁלְחָן – *And the candelabrum opposite the table:* Mishna: How did they clear up the Temple courtyard for purification? They immersed the utensils which were in the Temple, and the priests were told: "Take care not to touch the table [and defile it]!" Gemara: A *tanna* taught an alternate version of the warning: "Take care not to touch the table nor the candelabrum." Now why does the mishna itself not mention the candelabrum? In connection with the table, the Torah employs the term "at all times" [*tamid,* in 25:30], whereas that word does not appear in conjunction with the candelabrum. [Hence the disqualification of table for even a short time would be a serious lapse]. If so, why does the other *tanna* mention the candelabrum as well? He bases his approach on the verse *And the candelabrum on the south side, opposite the table,* and argues that since the table and the candelabrum were juxtaposed in the text, the candelabrum too must be present uninterruptedly. (Ḥagiga 26a)

וְאֶת־הַמְּנֹרָה נֹכַח הַשֻּׁלְחָן – *And the candelabrum opposite the table:* Rabbi Yitzḥak taught: If one desires to become wise he should face the south [when praying], whereas if one wants to become rich he should face north. The way to remember this is that the table [symbolizing material blessing] stood in the north of the Sanctuary, whereas the candelabrum [representing wisdom] was situated in the south. Rabbi Yehoshua ben Levi, however taught: One should always face south, since wisdom can also lead to wealth, as the verse states: *Length of days is in her right hand; and in her left hand are riches and honor* (Proverbs 3:16). But did not Rabbi Yehoshua ben Levi teach that the Divine Presence rests in the

צֶלַע צָפוֹן׃ לו וְעָשִׂיתָ מָסָךְ לְפֶתַח הָאֹהֶל תְּכֵלֶת וְאַרְגָּמָן
וְתוֹלַעַת שָׁנִי וְשֵׁשׁ מָשְׁזָר מַעֲשֵׂה רֹקֵם׃ לז וְעָשִׂיתָ לַמָּסָךְ
חֲמִשָּׁה עַמּוּדֵי שִׁטִּים וְצִפִּיתָ אֹתָם זָהָב וָוֵיהֶם זָהָב וְיָצַקְתָּ
לָהֶם חֲמִשָּׁה אַדְנֵי נְחֹשֶׁת׃ כז א וְעָשִׂיתָ אֶת־הַמִּזְבֵּחַ ששי
עֲצֵי שִׁטִּים חָמֵשׁ אַמּוֹת אֹרֶךְ וְחָמֵשׁ אַמּוֹת רֹחַב רָבוּעַ יִהְיֶה

TALMUD BAVLI *(cont.)*

west? He meant that one should turn slightly to the south. Rabbi Ḥanina said to Rav Ashi: People like you, who live north of the land of Israel, should turn to the south. (Bava Batra 25b) **וְשַׂמְתָּ אֶת־הַשֻּׁלְחָן** – *The table shall be placed:* Our Sages taught: King Shlomo made ten tables [in addition to the one Moshe made for the Tabernacle], as the verse describes: *He made also ten tables, and placed them in the Temple, five on the right side, and five on the left* (II Chronicles 4:8). [Now what do the terms "right" and "left" connote in this verse?] If it means that he placed five tables to the right of the entrance on the north side of the Sanctuary, and five tables to the left of the entrance on the south side, that would seem to violate the command *The table shall be placed on the north side of the Tabernacle.* Rather, the verse means that while the table of Moshe was situated in the middle of the north section of the Sanctuary, five of Shlomo's tables were placed to its right and the other five to its left [all along the north wall of the Sanctuary.] (Menaḥot 98b)

VERSE 36

TARGUM YERUSHALMI

מַעֲשֵׂה רֹקֵם – *Embroidered:* Embroidered by needle.

CHAPTER 27, VERSE 1

PHILO

רָבוּעַ – *Square:* The altar has equal length and breadth because all the sacrificial victims that are offered by the heart of a pious mind ought to be equal, whether one offers a hundred bulls or brings merely roasted wheat. One should not presume that God is impressed by the sacrifices of the wealthy because they are wealthy; nor does He look down on the sacrifices of the impoverished because they are poor.

BARAITA DIMLEKHET HAMISHKAN

וְעָשִׂיתָ אֶת־הַמִּזְבֵּחַ – *Make the altar:* The outer altar was positioned in the middle of the courtyard with its ramp toward the south. The basin stood to the west of the altar [between the altar and the Sanctuary], and the slaughtering area was to the north [of the altar]. Meanwhile, the Israelites were restricted to the eastern area of the courtyard, as the verse states: *And they brought that which Moshe commanded before the Tent of Meeting: and all the congregation drew near and stood before the Lord* (Leviticus 9:5). The altar under discussion bore three names: The Burnt-Offering Altar, The Bronze Altar, and the Outer Altar. (11)

36 **table. Make a screen for the entrance to the Tent, embroidered**
with sky-blue, purple, and scarlet wool and finely spun linen.
37 **Make five posts of acacia wood for the screen and overlay them**
with gold; their hooks, also, shall be of gold. Cast for them, too,
27 1 **five sockets of bronze. Make the altar from acacia** SHISHI
wood. It should be square, five cubits long, five cubits wide,

TALMUD BAVLI

חָמֵשׁ אַמּוֹת אֹרֶךְ וְחָמֵשׁ אַמּוֹת רֹחַב – *Five cubits long, five cubits wide:* The verse should be understood as written, according to Rabbi Yosei. Rabbi Yehuda, however, points out that the verse states that *it should be square,* as does a verse in Ezekiel [43:16]. Now, in Yeḥezkel's vision, the prophet measured the distance in each direction from its center; so too here we should understand the verse as measuring the altar from its center. [Accordingly, the altar built for the Tabernacle was ten cubits by ten cubits.]… In describing the Tabernacle's altar, the Torah states: *It should be three cubits high.* According to Rabbi Yehuda, this statement should be understood as written. However, Rabbi Yosei maintains: The verse states here that the Tabernacle's altar *should be square,* while a separate verse similarly describes the incense altar (30:2). Hence, just as the height of the incense altar was twice its length, so too here, the height of the sacrificial altar was twice its length [i.e., ten cubits]. (Zevaḥim 59b)

וְעָשִׂיתָ אֶת־הַמִּזְבֵּחַ – *Make the altar:* The Sages taught: The horns [the protrusions at the top of each of the altar's corners described in the next verse], the ramp upon which the priests ascended the altar, the base of the altar, and the requirement that the altar must be exactly square – all these must be present for the altar to be fit for use. But the measurements of its length, width, and height are not indispensable. [That is, an altar with alternative dimensions will be valid.] How do we know this is so? Rav Huna taught: In reference to each of the crucial characteristics the verse employs the term "the altar" [*hamizbeaḥ*: Leviticus 4:18, 4:30, 27:1, and 6:7, where the word *lifnei* is an allusion to the ramp]. (Zevaḥim 62a)

רָבוּעַ יִהְיֶה הַמִּזְבֵּחַ – *It should be square:* Rav Yehuda taught: There were two small ramps protruding from the main ramp that led to the altar, on which the priests could turn to walk onto the base of the altar and onto the surrounding ledge of the altar. They were separated from the altar by a distance of a hairbreadth, because the verse states: *Sprinkle the blood round about upon the altar* [Leviticus 1:5; indicating that nothing can be attached anywhere on the entire perimeter of the altar]. However, Rabbi Abbahu cites a different source: *It should be square.* [If the ramps were connected to the altar, it would not be perfectly square.] (Zevaḥim 62b)

TANḤUMA

וְעָשִׂיתָ אֶת־הַמִּזְבֵּחַ עֲצֵי שִׁטִּים – *Make the altar from acacia wood:* Said the Holy One, blessed be He, to Moshe: Instruct Israel to construct an altar for sacrifices that will atone for their sins. For centuries ago I promised Avraham their ancestor that if his descendants should ever transgress My law, they would be cleansed by bringing offerings, as the verse states: *Take Me a heifer three years old, etc.* (Genesis 15:9). What does the word "altar" [*mizbeaḥ*] connote? Its four letters [*mem-zayin-bet-ḥet*] are an acronym for the words "forgiveness" [*meḥila*],

ב הַמִּזְבֵּחַ וְשָׁלֹשׁ אַמּוֹת קֹמָתוֹ: וְעָשִׂיתָ קַרְנֹתָיו עַל אַרְבַּע
ג פִּנֹּתָיו מִמֶּנּוּ תִּהְיֶיןָ קַרְנֹתָיו וְצִפִּיתָ אֹתוֹ נְחֹשֶׁת: וְעָשִׂיתָ
סִּירֹתָיו לְדַשְּׁנוֹ וְיָעָיו וּמִזְרְקֹתָיו וּמִזְלְגֹתָיו וּמַחְתֹּתָיו לְכָל־
ד כֵּלָיו תַּעֲשֶׂה נְחֹשֶׁת: וְעָשִׂיתָ לּוֹ מִכְבָּר מַעֲשֵׂה רֶשֶׁת נְחֹשֶׁת
וְעָשִׂיתָ עַל־הָרֶשֶׁת אַרְבַּע טַבְּעֹת נְחֹשֶׁת עַל אַרְבַּע קְצוֹתָיו:
ה וְנָתַתָּה אֹתָהּ תַּחַת כַּרְכֹּב הַמִּזְבֵּחַ מִלְּמָטָּה וְהָיְתָה הָרֶשֶׁת

TANḤUMA *(cont.)*

"merit" [*zekhut*], "blessing" [*berakha*] and "life" [*ḥayyim*]. The sacrifices burnt whole on the altar are called *ola* [meaning "ascend"] because when Israel offers the animal they are elevated, as King Shlomo wrote: *Who is this rising out of the wilderness like columns of smoke?* (Song of Songs 3:6). **עֲצֵי שִׁטִּים** – *Acacia wood:* The altar is made out of wood in honor of Avraham, about whose hospitality the verse states: *And he stood by them under the tree, and they ate* (Genesis 18:8). **עֲצֵי שִׁטִּים** – *Acacia wood:* Said God: The people of Israel performed an act of foolishness [*shetut*] and angered Me by making the golden calf, let the acacia wood [*shittim*] come and atone for their stupidity. Another interpretation: The word *shittim* is an acronym for the words "peace" [*shalom*], "goodness" [*tova*], "salvation" [*yeshua*], and "forgiveness" [*meḥila*]. **חָמֵשׁ אַמּוֹת אֹרֶךְ וְחָמֵשׁ אַמּוֹת רֹחַב** – *Five cubits long, five cubits wide:* The dimensions of the altar corresponded to the two tablets that contained the Ten Commandments: five on one tablet, and five on the other tablet. **וְשָׁלֹשׁ אַמּוֹת קֹמָתוֹ** – *And three cubits high:* The number of cubits corresponds to Israel's three redeemers, as the verse states: *For I brought you up out of the land of Egypt, and redeemed you out of the house of bondage; and I sent before you Moshe, Aharon, and Miriam* (Micha 6:4).

YALKUT SHIMONI

וְעָשִׂיתָ אֶת־הַמִּזְבֵּחַ – *Make the altar:* The word *mizbeaḥ* alludes to the following attributes of the altar: It removes [*meziaḥ*] sins, it sustains [*mezin*, since sacrifice calls down blessing from above], it endears [*meḥabbev*], and it atones [*mekhapper*]. But is not the action of removing sin the same as atoning? Instead say that the altar removes evil decrees and atones for sins. (Teruma 373)

VERSE 2

TALMUD BAVLI

קַרְנֹתָיו – *Horns for it:* [One Sukkot, when etrogim were pelted at a Sadducee priest who poured the water libation on his feet rather than on the altar – see Sukka 48b –] the horn of the altar was damaged as a result of the chaos. Thereupon they brought a fistful of salt and sealed the damaged section. They did this not in order to render the altar fit for the Temple service, but in deference to the altar, so that it would not be seen in its damaged state. (Zevaḥim 62a)

2 and three cubits high. Make horns for it on its four corners, the
horns being of one piece with it, and overlay it with bronze.
3 Make pots for removing its ashes, together with shovels, basins,
4 forks, and pans. Make all of these of bronze. Make a grate of
bronze mesh for it, and on the mesh make four bronze rings at
5 its four corners. The grate should be set below, under the ledge
of the altar, so that the mesh reaches the middle of the altar.

TANHUMA

וְצִפִּיתָ אֹתוֹ נְחֹשֶׁת – *And overlay it with bronze:* Rabbi Yehuda bar Shalum taught: Said Moshe to the Holy One, blessed be He: "Master of the Universe! You command me to construct an altar made out of acacia wood and to cover it in bronze. But You have also instructed that *the fire shall ever be burning upon the altar; it shall never go out* (Leviticus 6:6). Will not the fire burn right through the Ark's overlay and consume the structure?" The Holy One, blessed be He, responded to him: "Do the laws of physics that govern your world necessarily function in Mine? Consider the angels, who burn with a consuming flame, and yet inhabit My domain of snow and hail, as the verses state: *Have you entered the treasuries of the snow? Or have you seen the treasuries of the hail?* (Job 38:22), and *Who lays the beams of His chambers in the waters* (Psalms 104:3). Nevertheless the waters do extinguish their fires, nor does the fire boil off the water. See how dead matter enters My presence and emerges alive [see Numbers 17:16–26]; are you afraid that the wood comprising the altar will go up in flames? The altar itself exists only to serve Me. Furthermore, who has given fire the power to burn in the first place? You should have learned from your own experience, Moshe – when you walked between walls of fire, and passed through hosts of flames, should you not have been consumed? And when you came into My presence, as the verse states: *Moshe approached the thick darkness where God was* (20:18), you were not singed even slightly, even though I am all flame, as the verse states: *For the Lord your God is a consuming fire* (Deuteronomy 4:24). Why was that? Because you had ascended to heaven to honor Me. The same will be so with the sacrificial altar: Even though *the fire shall ever be burning upon the altar; it shall never go out,* the bronze that covers it will neither melt nor burn, and the wood that forms the structure will never be consumed." Why was the altar covered in bronze? To atone for Israel's "bronze forehead" [stubbornness], as the verse states: *Because I know that you are obstinate, and your neck is an iron sinew, and your forehead bronze* (Isaiah 48:4).

VERSE 5

TARGUM YERUSHALMI

וְנָתַתָּה אֹתָהּ תַּחַת כַּרְכֹּב הַמִּזְבֵּחַ – *The grate should be set below, under the ledge of the altar:* In that way, should a piece of sacrificial meat or a fiery coal tumble off the altar, it will fall onto the grate before reaching the ground. The priests can then pick it up from the grate and return it to the altar.

ו עַד חֲצִי הַמִּזְבֵּחַ: וְעָשִׂיתָ בַדִּים לַמִּזְבֵּחַ בַּדֵּי עֲצֵי שִׁטִּים
ז וְצִפִּיתָ אֹתָם נְחֹשֶׁת: וְהוּבָא אֶת־בַּדָּיו בַּטַּבָּעֹת וְהָיוּ הַבַּדִּים
ח עַל־שְׁתֵּי צַלְעֹת הַמִּזְבֵּחַ בִּשְׂאֵת אֹתוֹ: נְבוּב לֻחֹת תַּעֲשֶׂה
ט אֹתוֹ כַּאֲשֶׁר הֶרְאָה אֹתְךָ בָּהָר כֵּן יַעֲשׂוּ: וְעָשִׂיתָ שביעי
אֵת חֲצַר הַמִּשְׁכָּן לִפְאַת נֶגֶב־תֵּימָנָה קְלָעִים לֶחָצֵר שֵׁשׁ
י מָשְׁזָר מֵאָה בָאַמָּה אֹרֶךְ לַפֵּאָה הָאֶחָת: וְעַמֻּדָיו עֶשְׂרִים
וְאַדְנֵיהֶם עֶשְׂרִים נְחֹשֶׁת וָוֵי הָעַמֻּדִים וַחֲשֻׁקֵיהֶם כָּסֶף:
יא וְכֵן לִפְאַת צָפוֹן בָּאֹרֶךְ קְלָעִים מֵאָה אֹרֶךְ וְעַמֻּדָו עֶשְׂרִים
וְאַדְנֵיהֶם עֶשְׂרִים נְחֹשֶׁת וָוֵי הָעַמֻּדִים וַחֲשֻׁקֵיהֶם כָּסֶף:

TALMUD BAVLI

תַּחַת כַּרְכֹּב הַמִּזְבֵּחַ – *Under the ledge of the altar:* Our Sages taught: What was the *karkov* of the altar? It was the area between the altar's corners, and an additional walkway one cubit wide on top of the altar where the priests would walk. But does not the verse state: *He made a grate of bronze mesh beneath the ledge, extending downward to the middle of the altar* [38:4, suggesting that the *karkov* was on the side of the altar and not on top of it]? Rav Naḥman bar Yitzḥak said: There were actually two segments of the altar called *karkov*: One was a slight protrusion above the midway point of the altar for aesthetic purposes, and one was an indentation on top of the altar for the benefit of the priests, to ensure that they would not slip and fall off the top of the altar. (Zevaḥim 62a)

וְהָיְתָה הָרֶשֶׁת עַד חֲצִי הַמִּזְבֵּחַ – *So that the mesh reaches the middle of the altar:* A scarlet line was painted around the middle of the altar and surrounded it as a mark to separate the upper blood from the lower blood. [The blood of all sacrificial animals was cast against the corners of the altar. In most cases the blood was thrown at the lower half of the altar. However, in some cases the sacrifice's blood had to be splashed on the top part of the altar.] What is the source for this visual boundary? Rav Aḥa son of Rav Ketina taught: The verse which states: *So that the mesh reaches the middle of the altar,* shows that a marker was mandated to distinguish that point. (Zevaḥim 53a)

VERSE 8

MEKHILTA DERABBI YISHMAEL

נָבוּב לֻחֹת תַּעֲשֶׂה אֹתוֹ – *Make it hollow, with planks:* Rabbi Natan taught: The altar was constructed with empty space in its middle that was filled with earth whenever Israel made camp. Thus the verse states: *Make it hollow, with planks.* Isi ben Akiva emphasized that this altar that was filled with earth was covered in bronze, as the verse states [regarding King Shlomo's dedication ceremonies]: *The altar of bronze that was before the Lord was too little to receive the burnt offerings, and meal offerings, and the fat of the peace offerings* (I Kings 8:64). But was the altar in fact too small to service all of the sacrifices? Does not the verse state of the same altar: *A thousand burnt offerings did Shlomo offer upon that altar* (I Kings 3:4)?

6 And make staves of acacia wood for the altar, and overlay them
7 with bronze. Place the poles in the rings, so that the poles will
8 be on the two sides of the altar when it is carried. Make it hollow, with planks; make it as it was shown to you on the moun-
9 tain. Make the courtyard of the Tabernacle thus: on SHEVI'I
the south side there should be hangings a hundred cubits long
of finely spun linen, all the length of the courtyard on that side,
10 with twenty posts and their twenty bronze sockets. The hooks
11 and bands of the posts shall be of silver. Likewise on the north
side; the hangings shall be a hundred cubits long, with twenty
posts and their twenty corresponding bronze sockets, with

MEKHILTA DERABBI YISHMAEL *(cont.)*

When the verse states that the altar was "too little," that is a euphemistic way of saying that the altar had become unfit for use. (Massekhta Devaḥodesh 11)

LEKAḤ TOV

נְבוּב לֻחֹת תַּעֲשֶׂה אֹתוֹ – *Make it hollow, with planks:* The term *nevuv* connotes hollowness, as in the verse *But the empty [navuv] man shall become wise* (Job 11:12).

VERSE 9

BARAITA DIMLEKHET HAMISHKAN

וְעָשִׂיתָ אֵת חֲצַר הַמִּשְׁכָּן – *Make the courtyard of the Tabernacle:* How was the courtyard demarcated? Twenty bronze sockets were positioned along the northern side, and twenty sockets on the southern side, each holding a post. The posts in turn had rings affixed to their middles. Shafts were attached to ropes and to the posts, with the shafts having the length of six handbreadths and the width of three handbreadths. The rings were hung onto hooks, and around them was wound the hangings which resembled a ship's sails. Thus the curtain extended for two and a half cubits on either side of the post. The neighboring curtains were similarly spaced such that the posts stood a distance of five cubits from each other. The shafts that were tied to the posts with ropes were fastened to bronze pegs in the ground. (5)

VERSE 11

SHIR HASHIRIM RABBA

וְעַמֻּדָיו עֶשְׂרִים וְאַדְנֵיהֶם עֶשְׂרִים נְחֹשֶׁת – *With twenty posts and their twenty bronze sockets:* A later verse describes King Shlomo's palanquin, saying: *He made its pillars of silver, its back of gold, its seat of purple, the midst of it being inlaid lovingly, by the daughters of Jerusalem* (Song of Songs 3:10). The pillars of silver are reminiscent of the posts in the Tabernacle courtyard, about which the verse states: *With hooks and bands of silver* (27:11). Secondly, the back of gold is reminiscent of the boards that comprised the Tabernacle structure, about which the Torah states: *Overlay the boards with gold* (26:29). *Its seat of purple* is reminiscent of the dividing curtain, concerning which we are commanded: *Make a curtain of sky-blue and purple* (26:31). And as for the clause *The midst of it being inlaid lovingly,* Rabbi Yudan argues: That

יב וְרֹחַב הֶחָצֵר לִפְאַת־יָם קְלָעִים חֲמִשִּׁים אַמָּה עַמֻּדֵיהֶם
יג עֲשָׂרָה וְאַדְנֵיהֶם עֲשָׂרָה: וְרֹחַב הֶחָצֵר לִפְאַת קֵדְמָה
יד מִזְרָחָה חֲמִשִּׁים אַמָּה: וַחֲמֵשׁ עֶשְׂרֵה אַמָּה קְלָעִים לַכָּתֵף
טו עַמֻּדֵיהֶם שְׁלֹשָׁה וְאַדְנֵיהֶם שְׁלֹשָׁה: וְלַכָּתֵף הַשֵּׁנִית חֲמֵשׁ
טז עֶשְׂרֵה קְלָעִים עַמֻּדֵיהֶם שְׁלֹשָׁה וְאַדְנֵיהֶם שְׁלֹשָׁה: וּלְשַׁעַר
הֶחָצֵר מָסָךְ ׀ עֶשְׂרִים אַמָּה תְּכֵלֶת וְאַרְגָּמָן וְתוֹלַעַת שָׁנִי
וְשֵׁשׁ מָשְׁזָר מַעֲשֵׂה רֹקֵם עַמֻּדֵיהֶם אַרְבָּעָה וְאַדְנֵיהֶם
יז אַרְבָּעָה: כָּל־עַמּוּדֵי הֶחָצֵר סָבִיב מְחֻשָּׁקִים כֶּסֶף וָוֵיהֶם מפטיר
יח כֶּסֶף וְאַדְנֵיהֶם נְחֹשֶׁת: אֹרֶךְ הֶחָצֵר מֵאָה בָאַמָּה וְרֹחַב ׀
חֲמִשִּׁים בַּחֲמִשִּׁים וְקֹמָה חָמֵשׁ אַמּוֹת שֵׁשׁ מָשְׁזָר וְאַדְנֵיהֶם
נְחֹשֶׁת: לְכֹל כְּלֵי הַמִּשְׁכָּן בְּכֹל עֲבֹדָתוֹ וְכָל־יְתֵדֹתָיו וְכָל־
יְתֵדֹת הֶחָצֵר נְחֹשֶׁת:

SHIR HASHIRIM RABBA *(cont.)*

refers to the merit of the Torah and the merit of the righteous who occupy themselves with it. Rabbi Azarya said in the name of Rabbi Yehuda, who in turn was quoting Rabbi Simon: That phrase refers to the Divine Presence. (3:15)

VERSE 18

TALMUD BAVLI

אֹרֶךְ הֶחָצֵר מֵאָה בָאַמָּה – *The courtyard shall be a hundred cubits long:* Rabbi Yehuda taught: The area of two *beit se'a* exceeds that of a square seventy cubits and a fraction long by a very small margin, but the Sages did not indicate its exact dimensions. And what Is the area of two *beit se'a*? It is as large as the courtyard of the Tabernacle [which was fifty cubits by one hundred cubits]. From where is this derived? Rav Yehuda said: It is learned from the verse *The courtyard shall be a hundred cubits long, fifty cubits wide, and five cubits high.* To what does the plain meaning of the verse refer? Abaye taught: It means that [since the Tabernacle's tent was thirty cubits long and ten cubits wide, while the courtyard was a hundred cubits long and fifty cubits wide, Moshe was to] position the Tabernacle in the

12 hooks and bands of silver. The width of the hangings at the
western end of the courtyard shall be fifty cubits, and it should
13 have ten posts and their ten corresponding sockets. The width
of the courtyard at the front, facing east, shall be fifty cubits:
14 fifteen cubits of hangings with three posts and three sockets on
15 one side, and fifteen cubits of hangings with three posts and
16 three sockets on the other, and for the gate of the courtyard
there shall be an embroidered screen of twenty cubits of sky-
blue, purple, and scarlet wool and finely spun linen, with four
17 posts and four sockets. All the posts around the courtyard MAFTIR
should be banded with silver. Their hooks shall be of silver, and
18 their sockets of bronze. The courtyard shall be a hundred cubits long, fifty cubits wide, and five cubits high, with hangings
19 of finely spun linen and sockets of bronze. All the Tabernacle
utensils, for every use, as well as all its tent pegs and the tent
pegs of the courtyard, shall be of bronze.

TALMUD BAVLI *(cont.)*

middle of the courtyard, fifty cubits from the edge, so that there was a space of fifty cubits in front of it and a space of twenty cubits in every other direction, on each of the two sides and behind it. (Eruvin 23b)

LEKAḤ TOV

וְרֹחַב חֲמִשִּׁים בַּחֲמִשִּׁים – *Fifty cubits wide:* [Literally, "fifty by fifty."] What does the Torah mean by this? The length of the Tabernacle structure was thirty cubits, and it was placed twenty cubits from the back of the western fence of the courtyard. This meant that there was an open area of fifty cubits by fifty cubits in front of the Tabernacle, forming the courtyard up to the entrance to the compound. The space between the Tabernacle and the western fence measured twenty cubits, as did the space between the structure and the northern edge of the courtyard, and between the structure and the southern boundary. On the eastern border of the courtyard, the entrance spanned twenty cubits, and that was flanked on either side by fifteen cubits of hangings, for a total of fifty cubits across.

10TH CENTURY	RAV SE'ADYA GAON, 882, EGYPT – 942, IRAQ
11TH CENTURY	
	RASHI, 1040 – 1105, FRANCE
12TH CENTURY	RASHBAM, 1080 – 1160, FRANCE
	RABBI AVRAHAM IBN EZRA, 1089, SPAIN – 1164, ENGLAND
	RABBI YOSEF BEKHOR SHOR, 12TH CENTURY, FRANCE
13TH CENTURY	RABBI AVRAHAM BEN HARAMBAM, 1186 – 1237, EGYPT
	RAMBAN, 1194, SPAIN – 1270, ISRAEL
	RABBI ḤIZKIYA BEN MANOAḤ – *ḤIZKUNI*, 13TH CENTURY, FRANCE
14TH CENTURY	RABBEINU BAḤYA BEN ASHER, 1255 – 1340, SPAIN
	RALBAG, 1288 – 1344, PROVENCE
15TH CENTURY	
	RABBI YITZḤAK ABARBANEL, 1437, PORTUGAL – 1508, ITALY
16TH CENTURY	RABBI OVADYA SFORNO, 1475 – 1550, ITALY
	MAHARAL – *GUR ARYEH*, 1512 POLAND – 1609, BOHEMIA
17TH CENTURY	RABBI SHLOMO EFRAYIM LUNTSCHITZ – *KELI YAKAR*, 1550, POLAND – 1619, BOHEMIA

פרשת תרומה

PARASHAT TERUMA

THE **CLASSIC** COMMENTATORS

כה א ב וַיְדַבֵּר יְהוָה אֶל־מֹשֶׁה לֵּאמֹר: דַּבֵּר אֶל־בְּנֵי יִשְׂרָאֵל יח
וְיִקְחוּ־לִי תְּרוּמָה מֵאֵת כָּל־אִישׁ אֲשֶׁר יִדְּבֶנּוּ לִבּוֹ תִּקְחוּ

CHAPTER 25, VERSE 1

IBN EZRA

וַיְדַבֵּר יהוה – *The Lord spoke:* When Moshe ascended the mountain [at the end of the previous *parasha*], God transmitted to him the plans for the Tabernacle. The purpose of the project was to create a sanctuary for the glory of God's name, where He could dwell. It was there that God would communicate with Moshe so that the latter would not need to repeatedly climb the mountain.

וַיְדַבֵּר יהוה – *The Lord spoke:* Rav Se'adya Gaon makes the following point: "One might ask why God should abandon the purity of His celestial abode to settle His glory among filthy human beings. The explanation is that when the Divine Presence resides among the angels it is of a far greater intensity than the aura manifested when He dwells among Israel. This is because the angels reside on a much higher plane than do people." With this statement, Rav Se'adya has woken from the stupor he exhibits in his other writings where he claims that humans occupy a higher status than the celestial beings. Now the reason that the glory of God descended to Israel was to serve as a sign and a wonder, much like the divine cloud on Mount Sinai. Furthermore, the purpose of the Tabernacle was to provide a special location that would be designated for communication with God. The Tabernacle would be a site where wonders would occur and through which Israel's reputation would become known. An additional effect of God's presence within the community would be that the Israelites would be careful to avoid impurity, knowing that God was among them. They would similarly avoid sinning or taking false oaths during legal proceedings. Conversely, the people would feel comfortable turning to God in prayer, to ask Him to ease their personal suffering. The Tabernacle would also attract foreigners to seek God. (Short Commentary, 25:7)

RAMBAN

וַיְדַבֵּר יהוה – *The Lord spoke:* After God had spoken to Israel face to face in order to pronounce to them the Ten Commandments, Moshe was directed to command them in several principles that would serve as general guidelines of Torah law [listed in Parashat Mishpatim]. And now that Israel was to be a holy nation, they deserved to have a sanctuary in which the Divine Presence could dwell amongst them. God therefore first commanded the people to construct a Tabernacle to serve as a house dedicated to His name where His manifestation could dwell. Here God would continue to speak to Moshe and inform him what he was to relate to the people of Israel. The main function of the Tabernacle was to provide a place for the Divine Presence to rest, that being the Ark [see 25:22]. It is for this reason that the first items of the Tabernacle to be described are the Ark itself, as well as its cover, for these are the most important features of the whole enterprise. What emerged was that the glory of God that Israel enjoyed at Mount Sinai was a constant companion to the nation as they carried the Tabernacle through the wilderness. And when Moshe entered the Tent of Meeting God spoke to him just as He had on the mountaintop.

25 1 The Lord spoke to Moshe, saying, "Tell the Israelites to take an
2 offering for Me; take My offering from all whose heart moves

ḤIZKUNI

וַיְדַבֵּר יהוה – *The Lord spoke:* According to some scholars, God dictated the following passage to Moshe during the forty days mentioned above [in 24:18], when the prophet ascended the mountain to receive the two tablets and the rest of the Torah. It was at that point that the Holy One, blessed be He, commanded Moshe to construct a Tabernacle into which he would place the Ark of the Covenant to hold those tablets.

RABBEINU BAḤYA

וַיְדַבֵּר יהוה – *The Lord spoke:* The commandment to construct the Tabernacle was given on the day following Yom Kippur, after the sin of the golden calf [described later, in chapter 32]. For that transgression was committed on the seventeenth of Tamuz. Nevertheless, the text reports the later event first. For it is said of the Torah that *her ways are ways of pleasantness, and all her paths are peace* (Proverbs 3:17), and that is illustrated here, where the description of the Tabernacle which would serve for Israel's atonement is presented before the original sin is even mentioned. This demonstrates God's desire to give remedy for an ill before it strikes. As our Sages, of blessed memory, proclaim: The Holy One, blessed be He, creates the cure for Israel first, and then He strikes them (Megilla 13b). (25:6)

VERSE 2

RASHI

תִּקְחוּ אֶת־תְּרוּמָתִי – *Take My offering:* [The word "offering" appears three times in verses 2–3.] Our Sages teach that this text refers to three kinds of offerings. The first was the beka of silver donated by each man. These were fashioned into the Tabernacle's sockets as is detailed in Parashat Pekudei (38:26–27). The second offering was for the altar – also a beka from every man. The silver was deposited in chests and used to purchase animals for communal sacrifices. The third offering comprised donations that people volunteered for the construction of the Tabernacle [these had no prescribed amounts]. If you examine the thirteen materials listed in the following verses, you will find that all of them were required to fashion the Tabernacle and the priestly vestments.

IBN EZRA

וְיִקְחוּ־לִי תְּרוּמָה – *Take an offering for Me:* [Although everything belongs to God,] the words "for me" [*li*] is similar to the use of the word *elai* in the verse *Turn in to me* (Judges 4:18). In that story Sisera is being asked to turn aside from his path and to come toward Yael, who is beckoning him. Here too, the Israelites are being requested to take valuables from among their possessions and to set them aside for God.

ḤIZKUNI

תִּקְחוּ אֶת־תְּרוּמָתִי – *Take My offering:* Rashi explains that the people donated the thirteen types of materials listed here: gold, silver, bronze, sky-blue wool, purple wool, scarlet

CLASSIC COMMENTATORS

גּ אֶת־תְּרוּמָתִי: וְזֹאת֮ הַתְּרוּמָה֒ אֲשֶׁ֥ר תִּקְח֖וּ מֵאִתָּ֑ם זָהָ֥ב
ד וָכֶ֖סֶף וּנְחֹֽשֶׁת: וּתְכֵ֧לֶת וְאַרְגָּמָ֛ן וְתוֹלַ֥עַת שָׁנִ֖י וְשֵׁ֥שׁ וְעִזִּֽים:

——————————— ḤIZKUNI *(cont.)* ———————————

wool, linen, goats' hair, rams' hides, fine leather, acacia wood, oil, and fragrant incense. Actually, the incense was included in the oil since it had no real substance of its own. The tribal chiefs brought the precious stones mentioned in verse 7.

——————————— RABBEINU BAHYA ———————————

תִּקְחוּ אֶת־תְּרוּמָתִי – *Take My offering:* The Torah refers to these gifts as "My offering" because God is appreciative of generous donors and disdainful of the stingy. The phrasing also suggests that as soon as a person commits to offering goods for such a sacred endeavor, the valuables instantly belong to God, and if the Israelite reneges on his promise he will be punished. Furthermore the owner is responsible for the goods until he hands them over. These verses employ the word "offering" [*teruma*] three times to correspond to the three abstract types of gifts which were used to create the world: wisdom, understanding, and knowledge. As the verse states: *The* LORD *by wisdom founded the earth; by understanding He established the heavens. By His knowledge the depths were broken up, and the clouds drop down dew* (Proverbs 3:19–20). These verses allude to God's formation of the world because the construction of the Tabernacle corresponded to the acts of creation.

——————————— GUR ARYEH ———————————

תְּרוּמָה – *An offering:* According to Rashi, the term "offering" [*teruma*] connotes a setting-aside of donations from one's property. For God prohibited the Israelites from giving all of their possessions to the Tabernacle project, and hence what they offered had to be separated from the total of their wealth. Indeed, when our Sages discuss the limits of charity, they declare that a philanthropist may not yield more than twenty per cent of his estate [see Ketubbot 50a].

——————————— KELI YAKAR ———————————

תִּקְחוּ אֶת־תְּרוּמָתִי – *Take My offering:* [In these two verses, the Torah uses the word "offering" three times. The Midrash associates the first two donations with two half-shekel poll taxes and the third with voluntary offerings given by generous Israelites. Given this, the author asks:] Why are the first two instances of the word associated with God ["an offering for Me" and "My offering"], but not the third [simply "the offerings" in the next verse]? For whenever human beings express modesty and submission, the might of God resides among them. But when people make shows of pride, the Holy One, blessed be He, objects to any connection between them and Himself. Therefore, God was pleased to associate Himself with the first two types of donations, burdens which were shared equally among all the Israelites. With those gifts there was no opportunity for anyone to brag that he had given more money to the collections than his neighbor.

3 them to give. These are the offerings you shall receive from
4 them: gold, silver and bronze; sky-blue, purple, and scarlet

VERSE 3

IBN EZRA

זָהָב וָכֶסֶף וּנְחֹשֶׁת – *Gold, silver and bronze:* Rav Se'adya Gaon points that the only silver employed in the Tabernacle's construction was that which was collected during the counting of the people [in 30:11–14.] How then can silver be listed in this verse as one of the materials that was voluntarily offered? Rav Se'adya resolves the problem by suggesting that additional silver was collected to fashion a table, for he surmises that the Tabernacle must have required a table upon which to prepare, cut, and wash the sacrificial meat. [The Torah text does not mention such a piece of furniture.] However, in my opinion, such a conjecture of a silver table is unnecessary since an easier explanation is available. Although it lists sixteen different materials used to make the Tabernacle, and only fifteen were donated freely, the Torah did not bother to point out the one exception…. The text begins its list of required materials with the most valuable substance, gold, and ends its catalogue with similarly valuable items: *Rock crystal together with other precious stones* (25:7). And while only the tribal chiefs possessed these jewels, gold was widely owned by the people. Note that no iron was used in the building of the Tabernacle, a fact that is stated explicitly in the description of the construction of the Temple centuries afterward: *There was neither hammer nor axe nor any tool of iron heard in the house, while it was being built* (I Kings 6:7).

BEKHOR SHOR

וְזֹאת הַתְּרוּמָה – *These are the offerings:* Only materials that were suitable for the construction were to be brought by the Israelites. This was unlike later circumstances, when people were free to donate completed items, for example a cloak, which would then be sold and the money used to pay for sacrifices, or to make repairs in the Sanctuary. At this point, however, no such donations were accepted; for now the Tabernacle required raw materials.

RABBEINU BAḤYA

זָהָב – *Gold:* The Torah begins by mentioning gold as a principal type of donation. This hinted that Israel's sin of the golden calf [mentioned later, in chapter 32, but held by this author to have already occurred] had already been forgiven. It was for this reason that gold appears first on the list of required materials. (25:6)

ABARBANEL

וְזֹאת הַתְּרוּמָה – *These are the offerings:* Here the Torah lists fifteen different materials that the Israelites were encouraged to supply for the national project. Among these substances we find four types of minerals: gold, silver, and bronze mentioned at the start of the passage, and the precious stones appearing at its end. Similarly, the catalogue includes four items from the plant kingdom: linen, acacia wood, oil produced from olives, and incense, whose ingredients derive from various plants. Four materials represent the animal world: the wool dyed scarlet with a dye produced from a certain species of worm; the goats' hair; the rams' hides, and the fine leather. The Torah similarly mentions four different colors that were in demand for the Tabernacle's creation: sky-blue, purple, scarlet, and red.

ה וְעֹרֹ֨ת אֵילִ֧ם מְאָדָּמִ֛ים וְעֹרֹ֥ת תְּחָשִׁ֖ים וַעֲצֵ֥י שִׁטִּֽים׃ שֶׁ֖מֶן
ו לַמָּאֹ֑ר בְּשָׂמִים֙ לְשֶׁ֣מֶן הַמִּשְׁחָ֔ה וְלִקְטֹ֖רֶת הַסַּמִּֽים׃ אַבְנֵי־

VERSE 5

IBN EZRA

וְעֹרֹת תְּחָשִׁים – *And fine leather:* [The word *taḥash* might also denote a species of animal. According to Ibn Ezra,] this refers to a certain thick-skinned animal. In my opinion it was an ox, for sandals must be fashioned out of thick leather from that beast, and another verse states: *I shod you with taḥash skin* (Ezekiel 16:10). (Short Commentary) **וַעֲצֵי שִׁטִּים** – *Acacia wood:* [Regarding the availability of acacia wood in the wilderness,] some of our early scholars [see Rashi, citing the Midrash] have argued that the patriarch Yaakov planted these trees in Egypt after his descent to that land. Centuries later Moshe commanded Israel to chop down the timber and cart the wood with them upon leaving slavery. Evidence for this theory from the verse *Everyone who had acacia wood* [35:24, which seems to imply that people just happened to have acacia wood with them]. And yet, the language of that verse suggests that some Israelites had, on their own, taken wood with them upon their departure – why would they do that? What potential use would the people have envisioned for the acacia trees [to justify the effort of hauling them into the wilderness]? We should seek a different approach to the problem, and suggest that next to Mount Sinai grew a grove of acacia trees. When Israel arrived at that location, Moshe informed the people that they would be remaining there for some time, and so every man fashioned a booth for his family to live in. The tribal chiefs had even more impressive structures built for them, commensurate with their position. Thus was the entire forest of acacia trees felled to satisfy the needs of the large nation, all of whom required shelter. (Long Commentary) **וַעֲצֵי שִׁטִּים** – *Acacia wood:* Before being donated, the Israelites had been using the wood to erect tents for themselves, and these structures must have been exceptionally tall since we know that the boards required for the Tabernacle were ten cubits long [between five and six meters, or sixteen to twenty feet]. However, it is truly surprising that anybody would have possessed staves long enough to serve as the crossbars for the Tabernacle's boards. [Based on the measurements provided in 26:16–20, the crossbars would have had extended thirty cubits – up to eighteen meters, or sixty feet.] Nevertheless, some commentators explain that the crossbars were segmented [and were not crafted from a single lengthy piece of wood]. Some authorities identify the *shitta* [translated here as "acacia"] as a cedar tree, but this is inaccurate. (Short Commentary)

BEKHOR SHOR

וְעֹרֹת תְּחָשִׁים – *And fine leather:* This refers to very sumptuous leather that is used to craft beautiful shoes for noblemen and noblewomen, as in the verse *I shod you with taḥash skin* (Ezekiel 16:10). **וַעֲצֵי שִׁטִּים** – *Acacia wood:* There were forests in the wilderness where acacia trees [*shittim*] grew. Hence one verse reports that *Israel abode in Shittim* (Numbers 25:1), while a later verse states, *And Yehoshua the son of Nun sent out of Shittim two men to spy* (Joshua 2:1). The locale must have been named after the type of woodland that

5 wool; linen and goats' hair; rams' hides dyed red and fine leath-
6 er; acacia wood; oil for the lamps; spices for the anointing oil
7 and the fragrant incense; and rock crystal together with other

BEKHOR SHOR *(cont.)*

dominated the area. The prophet later quotes God predicting: *I will plant in the wilderness the cedar, the acacia, and the myrtle, and the oil tree;* (Isaiah 41:19). And it was from this area that the Israelites procured wood for the Tabernacle. Acacia wood is light, smooth, and attractive. The wood must have been extremely light, for the Tabernacle required forty-eight boards along with their sockets [to form the walls], and an additional five boards to hold the screen [that stood at the entrance], as well as another four boards to support the curtain [that separated the structure's two chambers]. There were also sixty pillars to hold the hangings surrounding the compound's courtyard, pieces which were also supported by sockets. And yet, the Merari family required just four wagons and eight oxen to transport all these boards, pillars, and the sockets to hold them, as specified in Parashat Naso (Numbers 7:8).

VERSE 6

IBN EZRA

שֶׁמֶן לַמָּאֹר – *Oil for the lamps:* The candelabrum burned at night.

BEKHOR SHOR

בְּשָׂמִים לְשֶׁמֶן הַמִּשְׁחָה – *Spices for the anointing oil:* The presence of this verse is quite surprising. The other four verses which catalogue materials list substances that were necessary for the actual construction of the Tabernacle. The items in this verse, however were meant to be used only for the services that were to take place in it. And yet we find that the Torah does not similarly demand that the people donate wheat to be baked for the showbread, nor lambs to be slaughtered for the sacrifices, nor wood to be burned on top of the altar. [What made the oil and spices, by contrast, worth mentioning here?] It seems that the three objects stated here were in fact required for the Tabernacle's construction. The anointing oil was used to consecrate the structure before its first use. Regarding the incense, we might describe the Tabernacle as a sort of palace, and just as it is customary to perfume the interior of such a structure before the royal family moves in, so was this home of the King of Kings suffused with the smell of incense before God's spirit entered the place. The oil for the lamps was required to similarly create the appropriate atmosphere for God's arrival. For it does not behoove a king to enter a house before his servants have illuminated the interior.

VERSE 7

IBN EZRA

אַבְנֵי־שֹׁהַם – *Rock crystal:* These stones were needed for the ephod [see 28:9]. **וְאַבְנֵי מִלֻּאִים** – *With other precious stones:* These gems were to be fastened to the breast piece. Yosef the Babylonian explains that these jewels were called *miluim* [literally, "fillings"] because the breast piece was folded in half with the stones placed in the middle. Other commentators suggest that they were so called because, unlike the ephod, the breast piece was covered [filled] with stones. The ephod was too large to be adorned

CLASSIC COMMENTATORS

ח שֹׁהַם וְאַבְנֵי מִלֻּאִים לָאֵפֹד וְלַחֹשֶׁן: וְעָשׂוּ לִי מִקְדָּשׁ וְשָׁכַנְתִּי
ט בְּתוֹכָם: כְּכֹל אֲשֶׁר אֲנִי מַרְאֶה אוֹתְךָ אֵת תַּבְנִית הַמִּשְׁכָּן

IBN EZRA *(cont.)*

completely with jewels, but sufficed with two rock crystals on its shoulder pieces. Finally, Rav Se'adya Gaon argues that the word intimates that the precious stones were to be arranged in rows on the breast piece.

RAMBAN

וְאַבְנֵי מִלֻּאִים – *With other precious stones:* [Literally, "filling stones."] The Torah refers to the jewels as "filling stones" because indentations were pressed into the gold settings, which the gems would fill. The rock crystals were designated for the ephod [see 28:9], while the other precious stones were to be arranged in the front of the breast piece. This is Rashi's explanation. However, it seems to me unlikely that the Torah would here refer to the stones as "filling stones" just because in the future the craftsman will be instructed to use them to fill holes that he fashioned. I believe instead that the stones were so called to teach that only specimens that had been mined whole [*male*, or "full"], just as they were created, could be used for the breast piece. The vestment was not to be adorned with jewels that had been chiseled from larger samples hewn out of a quarry. For it is well known that the powers inherent in precious jewels only endure when the rocks are in their original, smooth state, like those stones that are found on riverbeds. Thus when a subsequent verse states of these stones: *Each was engraved like a seal with the name of one of the twelve tribes* (39:14). This was not really the work of engravers at all. Rather, the only way Moshe was able to inscribe the stones with the names of the tribes was to employ the *shamir* [a miraculous worm which seared the names into the stones], as our Sages write in tractate Sota (48b).

VERSE 8

RAV SE'ADYA GAON

וְעָשׂוּ לִי מִקְדָּשׁ – *They shall make Me a Sanctuary:* When Israel constructs a sanctuary for Me out of all of these materials, I will bring My glory to dwell among them.

RABBEINU BAḤYA

וְעָשׂוּ לִי מִקְדָּשׁ – *They shall make Me a Sanctuary:* [The word *mikdash* usually refers to a Temple, a permanent structure.] The text here refers to the Tabernacle as a *mikdash* [literally, "sanctuary"] since the Divine Presence there would sanctify the space. Perhaps we can also say that the Sanctuary was called a *mikdash* because it mirrored the celestial Temple above.

RALBAG

וְעָשׂוּ לִי מִקְדָּשׁ – *They shall make Me a Sanctuary:* The Tabernacle is called a *mikdash* [a term usually reserved for a permanent Temple] because its designation as a place for the service of God makes it a holy [*kadosh*] space. By promising Israel that He would *dwell in their midst,* God meant that the construction of the Sanctuary would be the catalyst for God's

8 **precious stones for the ephod and breast piece. They shall make**
9 **Me a Sanctuary and I will dwell in their midst. Form the Taber-**
nacle and form all of its furnishings following the patterns that

RALBAG *(cont.)*

presence to descend to the site. It is fitting that the Tabernacle was built with materials supplied by the people. It is the masses whom God referred to in His request that *They shall make Me a Sanctuary.* And this makes perfect sense – the Tabernacle was a national project that would serve all of Israel. And so we find that contributions for the Tabernacle work were shared equally across the nation.

GUR ARYEH

וְעָשׂוּ לִי מִקְדָּשׁ – *They shall make Me a Sanctuary:* Rashi interprets this phrase as meaning: "They shall make a sacred structure in My Honor." What he implies by this is that Israel was not instructed to build a "sanctuary," but rather an ordinary structure that would only be sanctified after its completion [by God's presence]. For Israel was incapable of building anything inherently holy; they could only fashion a building worthy of becoming so.

VERSE 9

RASHBAM

כְּכֹל אֲשֶׁר אֲנִי מַרְאֶה אוֹתְךָ – *Following the patterns that I show you:* The Holy One, blessed be He, showed the plans of all the structures and the utensils to Moshe. We find a similar phenomenon in the book of Ezekiel regarding the construction of the Second Temple, when God revealed images of the future building to the prophet [in chapter 40]. There too God provided Yeḥezkel with pictures, while simultaneously explaining to him what He wanted done, as the text describes.

IBN EZRA

כְּכֹל אֲשֶׁר אֲנִי מַרְאֶה אוֹתְךָ – *Following the patterns that I show you:* Moshe saw the Tabernacle schematics with his own waking eyes. By contrast, the prophet Yeḥezkel received a parallel communication within a dream. **וְכֵן תַּעֲשׂוּ** – *Form:* [In the Hebrew this appears an independent clause concluding the verse: "And so you shall form," not specifying what is to be formed.] This phrase refers to the Tabernacle's accoutrements, because the command to fashion the actual structure already appears in the previous verse, *They shall make Me a Sanctuary.*

RABBI AVRAHAM BEN HARAMBAM

כְּכֹל אֲשֶׁר אֲנִי מַרְאֶה אוֹתְךָ – *Following the patterns that I show you:* Now one might ask why the Torah, when it reports Israel's fashioning of the Tabernacle, does not say that they did so "according to the images that the Lord had shown Moshe" [but rather: *As the Lord commanded Moshe* – 49:43]. There are two answers to this question, although one of them is more convincing than the other. The first, stronger explanation is that the Sages, of blessed memory, only received the verbal instructions for constructing the Sanctuary [and therefore the craftsmen themselves were not actually following visual schematics

CLASSIC COMMENTATORS

י וְאֵת תַּבְנִית כָּל־כֵּלָיו וְכֵן תַּעֲשׂוּ: וְעָשׂוּ אֲרוֹן
עֲצֵי שִׁטִּים אַמָּתַיִם וָחֵצִי אָרְכּוֹ וְאַמָּה וָחֵצִי רָחְבּוֹ וְאַמָּה
יא וָחֵצִי קֹמָתוֹ: וְצִפִּיתָ אֹתוֹ זָהָב טָהוֹר מִבַּיִת וּמִחוּץ תְּצַפֶּנּוּ

RABBI AVRAHAM BEN HARAMBAM *(cont.)*

when they worked]. Secondly, it is possible that although Moshe saw a rough image of what the Tabernacle should look like, the picture he saw did not show how the items would really look, but was rather just a vague outline.

RAMBAN

וְכֵן תַּעֲשׂוּ – *Form:* [In the Hebrew this phrase appears an independent clause concluding the verse: "And so you shall form," not specifying what is to be formed.] According to Rashi, this oblique clause hints that in future generations all new items fashioned for the Temple should be made according to the plans presented here. Nevertheless, it is unclear to me whether in his construction of the Temple, King Shlomo actually needed to design furniture that was identical to that used in the Tabernacle. For example, the bronze altar that Shlomo made was twenty cubits long by twenty cubits wide. [By contrast, the Tabernacle's altar was five cubits on each side; see 27:1.] Instead the phrase should be understood as merely strengthening and emphasizing the preceding instruction.

ABARBANEL

וְאֵת תַּבְנִית כָּל־כֵּלָיו – *All of its furnishings:* In his *Guide of the Perplexed* (3:45), Maimonides attempts to explain the symbolic meanings of each item of furniture introduced in this passage. He claims, for example, that the cherubim atop the Ark cover were intended to teach the existence of non-corporeal beings such as angels. The candelabrum was meant to provide honor and glory to the Tabernacle, since lights create an impressive atmosphere for a space. The incense was ostensibly supposed to counteract the foul smell resulting from the meat slaughtered for sacrifices. Still, Maimonides himself admits that he was unable to determine the significance of the table and the showbread that it held. The basin was clearly used to cleanse the priests, while the outer altar was where sacrifices were offered to God, affording the people a form of worship they were used to from their experiences with idolatry. And yet, I find these explanations for the Tabernacle's accoutrements to be weak.

SFORNO

וְכֵן תַּעֲשׂוּ – *Form:* Construct the Tabernacle so that I will dwell in your midst. It is there that I will communicate with you and receive the prayers and service of the people of Israel. This arrangement will differ from that which existed before the sin of the golden calf, when I said: *Wherever I cause My name to be invoked, I will come to you and I will bless you* (20:21).

GUR ARYEH

וְכֵן תַּעֲשׂוּ – *Form:* [The author responds to the Ramban's critique of Rashi; see above.] In fact, the difficulty raised by the Ramban regarding Shlomo's bronze altar poses no problem. Rashi's comment only referred to the movable furniture used in the Sanctuary,

10 I show you. Make an Ark of acacia wood, two and a
half cubits long, a cubit and a half wide, and a cubit and a half
11 high. Overlay it with pure gold, inside and out, and around it

GUR ARYEH *(cont.)*

whereas the altar stood outside and was fixed to the ground. Just as the structures of the Holy of Holies and the courtyard had different dimensions in the Temple than they had in the Tabernacle, so too did the altar.

VERSE 10

RAMBAN

וְעָשׂוּ אֲרוֹן עֲצֵי שִׁטִּים – *Make an Ark of acacia wood:* The command *ve'asu* [plural] here addresses the people of Israel. When the following verses use singular language to say: *Overlay it with pure gold* (25:11), and *Cast four gold rings for it* (25:12), they are directed at Moshe was the representative of all Israel. Perhaps the use of the plural here reflects God's will that the entire nation participate in the construction of the Ark, since it would serve as the most holy seat of the Divine Presence. Everybody who joined in the project would merit a share in the Torah [which was given to Moshe by a disembodied voice speaking from above the Ark]. Those who wished to participate did so by donating an item of gold to be used in making the Ark, or by assisting in some other manner.

RABBEINU BAḤYA

וְעָשׂוּ אֲרוֹן עֲצֵי שִׁטִּים – *Make an Ark of acacia wood:* The purpose of the Ark was straightforward: it was a receptacle in which to store the Tablets of the Law. And since the Torah is the most important of Israel's possessions, the Ark was the first item that God described to Moshe. The Hebrew term *"aron"* for the Ark derives from the word *or* [meaning "light"] since the Torah which it holds is referred to as light [in Proverbs 6:23]. The acacia wood [described as "upright" in 26:15] that was used for the Ark is an allusion to those who support the students of Torah.

ABARBANEL

וְעָשׂוּ אֲרוֹן עֲצֵי שִׁטִּים – *Make an Ark of acacia wood:* It seems to me that the Torah presents the Tabernacle's accoutrements in a sequence parallel to the list of materials that God requested for the project. Thus, Israel was first asked to donate *gold, silver and bronze* (25:3) and then *sky-blue, purple, and scarlet wool* (25:4). Logically, the text would then begin its description of the items to be made by explaining what was to be done with the gold. We therefore first read about the Ark, then the table, and then the candelabrum, all of which were fashioned out of gold. This explains why the Torah does not begin by laying out plans for the structure of the Tabernacle itself, but rather introduces the Ark first.

VERSE 11

RASHI

מִבַּיִת וּמִחוּץ תְּצַפֶּנּוּ – *Overlay it inside and out:* Betzalel [the craftsman, first mentioned by name in chapter 31] fashioned three boxes – two of gold and one of wood. Each

יב וְעָשִׂיתָ עָלָיו זֵר זָהָב סָבִיב: וְיָצַקְתָּ לּוֹ אַרְבַּע טַבְּעֹת זָהָב
וְנָתַתָּה עַל אַרְבַּע פַּעֲמֹתָיו וּשְׁתֵּי טַבָּעֹת עַל־צַלְעוֹ הָאֶחָת

RASHI *(cont.)*

box had four walls and a bottom, but was open on the top. The wooden chest fit into the larger gold one, while the smaller gold box slid into the wooden one. Meanwhile the top edges of the wood box were themselves covered in gold, such that the Ark as a whole was completely overlaid with gold inside and out. **זֵר זָהָב** – *A gold rim:* A sort of gold crown surrounded the entire Ark [protruding upward from the top edges of the chest]. This mean that the outer box extended to a slightly greater height than the inner box, such that this ornamental band rose just past the thickness of the Ark's cover. Thus when the Ark cover sat on the rim of the Ark, this gold decoration stretched a bit higher than its top. The gold rim symbolized the majesty of the Torah [since the Tablets of the Law were deposited inside the Ark].

BEKHOR SHOR

וְצִפִּיתָ אֹתוֹ זָהָב טָהוֹר – *Overlay it with pure gold:* It would have been appropriate for the Ark to be fashioned out of solid gold [instead of gilded wood], but that would have made it too heavy to carry. After all, the Levites were required to transport the Ark on their shoulders. We similarly find that God commanded that the altar be built *hollow, with planks* (27:8) so that it would not be too difficult to transport.

וְעָשִׂיתָ עָלָיו זֵר זָהָב סָבִיב – *And around it make a gold rim:* This rim was placed on top of the Ark's upper lip. For when the inner box of acacia wood was enveloped by one gold case, and then filled with another one, the upper surface of the wood box would be visible between the two. Hence God commanded that the inner golden box have a flat rim that folded outward, covering the top edge of the wooden box.

RABBEINU BAḤYA

וְצִפִּיתָ אֹתוֹ זָהָב טָהוֹר – *Overlay it with pure gold:* The gold reflects the anticipation that in the future God will extend a protective shelter over both the students of Torah and those who assist them [financially]. **מִבַּיִת וּמִחוּץ** – *Inside and out:* Our Sages employed this verse to teach that a person can only ever be considered a Torah scholar if his inner character matches his outer behavior. For a student of Torah is expected to be like the Ark, which was both lined and covered in gold. Our Sages taught further: Why are the words of Torah compared to glass, as the verse states, *Gold and glass cannot equal it* (Job 28:17)? We learn from here that just as glass is pure and clear, making its contents visible to all, so too should a Torah scholar be transparent. **עָלָיו** – *Around it:* [Literally, "on it."] When the Torah describes the rims of the table [in 25:24] and incense altar [in 30:3], it uses the word *lo* [literally, "for it"]. In our verse however, the Torah orders that the gold rim be fashioned "on it." The reason for this discrepancy is embedded in the symbolism of the three items. The table represents the crown of the Israelite monarchy [since the bread suggests material wealth], and the incense altar hints at the crown of the priesthood [since only the priests were permitted to burn incense in the Temple]. And of course, both the monarchy and the priesthood are transmitted dynastically; only direct descendants of King David may ascend to the

12 make a gold rim. Cast four gold rings for it and place them on
its four corners, two rings on one side and two on the other.

RABBEINU BAḤYA *(cont.)*

throne of Israel, and only those born into the family of Aharon can be priests. However, the Ark held the Torah, which is no one's by inheritance [but available to anyone with the will to master it]. This explains why the Torah instructs the gold rim of the Ark to be placed "on it" [the onus is on us to take it up] whereas the ornaments of the other two utensils are given "to them" outright.

RALBAG

וְצִפִּיתָ אֹתוֹ זָהָב טָהוֹר – *Overlay it with pure gold:* It is unlikely that the Torah is instructing that the Ark be gilded normally, since gold leaf does not adhere to wood as it would to other metals. The Torah therefore mandates the construction of three receptacles – a central chest made out of wood, a gold container to fit snugly inside, and an additional gold case to encompass the outside. This had the effect of covering the wood Ark in gold. Now the exact thickness of the gold boxes is unknown, but they certainly had to be thick enough to hold their shape. Still, it is unlikely that the thickness of either gold container would have been a whole handbreadth wide, as our Sages state [in Yoma 72], since this would have then used up all of the gold donated for the entire Tabernacle. This should be clear to anybody who has even the slightest understanding of engineering. Rather, the Sages' claim was made merely to emphasize that the gold chests had substantial thicknesses.

GUR ARYEH

מִבַּיִת וּמִחוּץ – *Inside and out:* Ibn Ezra poses the following question: Why not just make the Ark out of solid gold? The answer is profound: The Torah is referred to as *a tree of life to those who lay hold on her* (Proverbs 3:18), which is why the Ark had to be constructed out of wood. For just as a tree is planted forever, so are the words of Torah rooted in God's very being. Therefore, because God is eternal, the Torah too will last forever. And while gold is more valuable than wood, it is not a material of growth. Nevertheless, the wood was to be covered with gold to give the Ark a wondrous appearance.

VERSE 12

RASHI

פַּעֲמֹתָיו – *Its corners:* The Targum renders this as "corners" [*zaveyatei*]. The rings were situated at the upper corners of the Ark near its cover. They were fastened two on each of the Ark's long sides. Staves were inserted into the rings, with the length of the Ark separating them by a distance of two and a half cubits. This meant that two people carrying the Ark could walk comfortably between the poles. This is all explained in tractate Menaḥot (98b).

RASHBAM

וְיָצַקְתָּ לּוֹ – *Cast for it:* The four rings protruded from the body of the Ark. They were not made separately and attached. **עַל צַלְעוֹ הָאֶחָת** – *On one side:* The rings were to be placed on the narrow sides of the Ark, since the staves protruded toward the Sanctuary. That is, the

יג וּשְׁתֵּי טַבָּעֹת עַל־צַלְעוֹ הַשֵּׁנִית: וְעָשִׂיתָ בַדֵּי עֲצֵי שִׁטִּים
יד וְצִפִּיתָ אֹתָם זָהָב: וְהֵבֵאתָ אֶת־הַבַּדִּים בַּטַּבָּעֹת עַל צַלְעֹת
טו הָאָרֹן לָשֵׂאת אֶת־הָאָרֹן בָּהֶם: בְּטַבְּעֹת הָאָרֹן יִהְיוּ הַבַּדִּים

RASHBAM (cont.)

length of the Ark ran north to south, while the staves that held it stretched east to west. [The Tabernacle itself was oriented on an east-west axis.]

IBN EZRA

אַרְבַּע פַּעֲמֹתָיו – *Its four corners:* [The word *paamotav* is obscure.] I have searched all of Scripture and I have been unable to find the term *paam* used to denote corners [as the Targum interprets the word]. Rather, the word is always used to mean a foot, as in the verse *The steps [paamei] of the needy* (Isaiah 26:6) and many other instances. I am therefore forced to conclude that the Ark had feet, for it would certainly have been disgraceful to place this holy object directly on the ground. Furthermore, why does the verse need to say "And" two rings on one side? [The Hebrew contains the conjunctive letter *vav*.] One of the scholars of our times understands that although the staves were normally placed in the rings that were on the Ark's feet, they were removed from that position and inserted into separate upper rings when the Ark had to be transported. [Thus the "and" implies that there were really eight rings in total.] Still, I believe that once the staves were placed in the upper rings they were never removed from there, for the Torah demands: *The staves must stay in the rings of the Ark; they must not be removed* (25:15). And the four lower rings that were positioned on the Ark's feet were merely ornamental.

BEKHOR SHOR

וְיָצַקְתָּ לּוֹ אַרְבַּע טַבְּעֹת זָהָב – *Cast four gold rings for it:* According to the straightforward meaning of the text, since the second half of the verse literally means *And two rings on one side and two on the other,* there were altogether eight rings. The craftsman was first meant to cast four rings on to the sides of the Ark which were fixed there. Then four other, larger rings were joined to those, and the staves were permanently inserted into the latter. When the Ark was positioned inside the Holy of Holies, its attendants folded down the secondary rings, thereby lowering the staves so that they merely hung onto the Ark when it was at rest. For the staves were only raised to the height of the Ark when it was being transported.

RAMBAN

פַּעֲמֹתָיו – *Its corners:* I do not understand why Rashi felt compelled to state that the rings were situated at the upper corners of the Ark near its cover. For if that were really the case, the weight of the Ark would have been much more difficult to carry. Furthermore, it would certainly have been more respectful for the Ark to have been lifted up to rest high on the priests' shoulders when transporting it. In truth, I believe the rings were fastened to the lower corners of the Ark, which allowed it to be carried on high. Furthermore, I disagree with Ibn Ezra, who translates the term *paamotav* as "its feet," arguing that the Ark had legs. Rather, in our verse the word refers to the footsteps of the priests, who would be

13 Make staves of acacia wood and overlay them with gold; place
14 these staves in the rings on the sides of the Ark so that the Ark
15 may be carried. The staves must stay in the rings of the Ark;

RAMBAN *(cont.)*

carrying the Ark. By using this term the Torah makes two points: First, that the rings should be situated right at the bottom corners of the Ark where the base of the chest is located. Secondly, that the rings should be placed so that the length of the Ark interposes between them, so that the footsteps of the priests could be accommodated comfortably.

VERSE 13

IBN EZRA

בַּדֵּי עֲצֵי שִׁטִּים – *Staves of acacia wood:* The obscure term *baddim* also appears in the verse *So it became a vine, and brought forth branches [baddim], and sent out sprigs* (Ezekiel 17:7), referring to extensions on either side. The Torah does not indicate how long these staves were meant to be. (Short Commentary)

VERSE 14

RABBEINU BAḤYA

וְהֵבֵאתָ אֶת־הַבַּדִּים בַּטַּבָּעֹת – *Place these staves in the rings:* The staves used to transport the Ark symbolize the masses, who must support and strengthen Torah scholars. The phrase *So that the Ark may be carried* teaches that whoever provides for Torah learners allows them to ascend higher and higher.

VERSE 15

RASHI

לֹא יָסֻרוּ מִמֶּנּוּ – *They must not be removed:* Ever.

IBN EZRA

לֹא יָסֻרוּ מִמֶּנּוּ – *They must not be removed:* Except for when the Ark is in place, concealed behind the curtain, as I explain in comments to Numbers 4:6. (Short Commentary)

BEKHOR SHOR

לֹא יָסֻרוּ מִמֶּנּוּ – *They must not be removed:* Due to the sanctity of the Ark, God did not want the priests to be constantly handling it as they inserted and removed the staves from its rings. Rather, when the Ark was transported, the carriers merely took hold of the poles and moved it. And when they positioned the Ark in place, the put it down and walked away immediately out of reverence for the sacred object. Now, the Torah states that *the staves must stay in the rings of the Ark,* as a gesture of respect. Some commentators understand this phrase as indicating merely that when the poles are put in the rings they must fit tightly so that the Ark does not slide back and forth when carried. They hold that the poles could sometimes be taken out of the rings, as the verse states: *Aharon shall come, and his sons, and they shall…cover the Ark of the Testimony…and shall put in its poles* [Numbers 4:5–6, which suggests that the poles were inserted every time the Israelites broke camp]. Still, our Sages

טז לֹא יָסֻרוּ מִמֶּנּוּ: וְנָתַתָּ אֶל־הָאָרֹן אֵת הָעֵדֻת אֲשֶׁר אֶתֵּן
יז אֵלֶיךָ: וְעָשִׂיתָ כַפֹּרֶת זָהָב טָהוֹר אַמָּתַיִם וָחֵצִי אָרְכָּהּ וְאַמָּה שני

BEKHOR SHOR *(cont.)*

argue that the staves were never removed at all [see Makkot 21b]. They furthermore declare in tractate Yoma [72a] that anyone who takes the poles out of the Ark's rings is liable to be lashed. I therefore interpret the verses as explaining that the staves were taken out just once before being inserted on a permanent basis by the priests.

ḤIZKUNI

לֹא יָסֻרוּ מִמֶּנּוּ – *They must not be removed:* According to the straightforward meaning of the text, there was no reason for the staves to ever be removed from their rings. For the Ark sat in the Holy of Holies, where the poles were no bother to anyone. For the only person to ever enter that chamber was the High Priest, one day a year [as part of the Yom Kippur services]. However, the bronze altar stood in the courtyard, where there was much traffic of priests going to and fro. If its staves had been kept permanently fixed to it, it would have been difficult for people to maneuver in that space. Therefore, the altar's staves were only required to be in place when it was transported, as the verse states: *Place the poles in the rings, so that the poles will be on the two sides of the altar when it is carried* (27:7).

VERSE 16

RASHI

הָעֵדֻת – *The tablets of the Covenant:* [Literally, simply "the testimony."] This refers to the Torah, which is a testament that God commanded the people to observe the commandments recorded in it.

RASHBAM

הָעֵדֻת – *The tablets of the Covenant:* [Literally, simply "the testimony."] This refers to the two tablets which testified to the covenant between God and Israel. This is why the tablets are also referred to as the "Tablets of the Covenant."

IBN EZRA

הָעֵדֻת – *The tablets of the Covenant:* [Literally, simply "the testimony."] The two tablets were called a "testimony" because they served as a sort of marriage contract [between God and Israel]. Furthermore [the term here cannot refer to the entire Torah, for] Moshe had not yet written down the whole of the Torah. Also, the Torah scroll was later placed by the priests next to the Ark, not inside it [see Deuteronomy 31:26]. Additionally, a later verse affirms that *There was nothing in the ark save the two tablets of stone, which Moshe put there at Ḥorev* (I Kings 8:9). The following argument also proves that there was no Torah scroll inside the Ark [beside the tablets]: We know that Moshe placed the tablets in the Ark, which he then sealed with the Ark cover. Now since the glory of God rested on the cherubim – as the

16 **they must not be removed. Inside the Ark, place the tablets of**
17 **the Covenant that I will give you.** Make an Ark cover of pure SHENI
gold, two and a half cubits long and a cubit and a half wide.

———————————————— IBN EZRA *(cont.)* ————————————————

verse states: *You who are enthroned upon the cherubim* (Psalms 80:2) – how could Moshe have opened the Ark later to put the Torah there when it was complete? To do so he

would have had to have remove the cover with cherubim from the Ark [seeming to displace the Divine Presence].

———————————————— ḤIZKUNI ————————————————

וְנָתַתָּ אֶל־הָאָרֹן אֵת הָעֵדֻת – *Inside the Ark, place the tablets of the Covenant:* This explains the earlier directive to treat the Ark

reverentially, for the tablets of the Covenant were to be placed inside it.

VERSE 17

———————————————— RASHI ————————————————

כַּפֹּרֶת – *An Ark cover:* The *kapporet* was a cover placed on top of the Ark, which was itself only an open box. The cover was placed on top of it like a shelf. אַמָּתַיִם וָחֵצִי אָרְכָּהּ – *Two and a half cubits long:* Both the length and width of the Ark cover was equal to that of the Ark, which

it sealed. The lid rested on the tops of the Ark's four walls. And even though the Torah does not relate the thickness of the Ark cover, our Sages teach us that it was one handbreadth thick [see Sukka 5a].

———————————————— KELI YAKAR ————————————————

וְעָשִׂיתָ כַפֹּרֶת – *Make an Ark cover:* The Ark cover symbolized how that the Torah's secrets must be guarded and not revealed to the world at large. For what the Eternal has hidden must never be exposed, as the verse states: *A talebearer reveals secrets: but he that is of a faithful spirit conceals the matter* (Proverbs 11:13), while a subsequent verse states: *It is the glory of God to conceal a thing* (Proverbs 25:2). The two cherubim were crafted in the form of a type of angel of the same name, which resembled children. This symbolized the dictum that one must seek a teacher of Torah who resembles an angel of God and who is as free of sin like a one-year-old infant. Torah scholars should furthermore be well-regarded

both by God and their fellow human beings. To indicate this point, the wings of the cherubim were raised skyward, symbolizing loyalty to God, while they faced one another to signify concern for other people. This also taught that there can be no strife between people, only peace and friendship, when both parties love the Torah. When the verse states that *the cherubim…should face one another* (25:20), it means that their gaze should be constantly oriented inward toward the Torah that is in the Ark. These lessons are sometimes ignored by those who believe themselves to be wise men, but who are actually interested in their own personal aggrandizement rather than in promoting the honor due to the Torah.

יח וְחֶצְיִ רָחְבָּהּ: וְעָשִׂיתָ שְׁנַיִם כְּרֻבִים זָהָב מִקְשָׁה תַּעֲשֶׂה
יט אֹתָם מִשְּׁנֵי קְצָוֹת הַכַּפֹּרֶת: וַעֲשֵׂה כְּרוּב אֶחָד מִקָּצָה מִזֶּה
וּכְרוּב־אֶחָד מִקָּצָה מִזֶּה מִן־הַכַּפֹּרֶת תַּעֲשׂוּ אֶת־הַכְּרֻבִים
כ עַל־שְׁנֵי קְצוֹתָיו: וְהָיוּ הַכְּרֻבִים פֹּרְשֵׂי כְנָפַיִם לְמַעְלָה סֹכְכִים
בְּכַנְפֵיהֶם עַל־הַכַּפֹּרֶת וּפְנֵיהֶם אִישׁ אֶל־אָחִיו אֶל־הַכַּפֹּרֶת

VERSE 18

RAV SE'ADYA GAON

מִקְשָׁה – *Beaten:* The cherubim should be fashioned out of solid gold and should not be hollow.

RASHI

כְּרֻבִים – *Cherubim:* The figures had the faces of children. זָהָב מִקְשָׁה תַּעֲשֶׂה אֹתָם – *Make them of beaten gold:* Do not craft separate figures out of gold and then fasten them to the Ark cover, like welders, whose craft is called *souder* ["solder"] in Old French. Rather, begin with a large block of gold and hammer down its middle with a mallet so that material protrudes from its ends. Then fashion these projections into shapes to form the cherubim. מִקְשָׁה – *Beaten:* [The meaning of the Hebrew word is unclear. Rashi explains:] The Old French term for this is *battu* ["beaten"], as in the verse *And his knees smote [nakeshan] one against the other* (Daniel 5:6).

RASHBAM

כְּרֻבִים – *Cherubim:* The term *keruvim* denotes birds, as in the verse *You were a sublime, shielding cherub* (Ezekiel 28:14), which seems to describe a large bird with extended wings. Our Sages, however, claim that the term refers to a figure with the face of a child [see Sukka 5b].

IBN EZRA

מִקְשָׁה – *Beaten:* [Contrary to the translation in this edition,] the term *miksha* means "equal," as in the verse *And instead of evenly trimmed hair [maaseh miksheh], baldness* (Isaiah 3:24). The sense in our verse is that the two cherubim were positioned equidistant from the edge of the Ark cover.

RALBAG

מִקְשָׁה – *Beaten:* God instructed Moshe here to fashion the cover by striking the mass of gold with a mallet and punching out a cherub figure on either side of the lid. In this way the cherubim and the Ark cover would be formed out of a single block of metal.

VERSE 19

RASHI

מִן־הַכַּפֹּרֶת – *Of one piece with the cover:* The cherubim should be fashioned from the same piece of gold that the cover is made out of. This is what is meant by the clause *Make two cherubim of beaten gold* (25:18) – do not make each figure separately and then attach them to the cover.

18 Make two cherubim of beaten gold and place them at the
19 two ends of the cover: one cherub at one end and one at the
other; the cherubim shall be made of one piece with the cover.
20 These cherubim should have wings spread upward, sheltering
the cover. They should face one another, and look toward the

———————————————— RASHBAM ————————————————

מִקָּצָה מִזֶּה – *At one end:* The cherubim were
both fashioned in the middle of the Ark's
width, so that the Divine Presence [which

rested between the two] would be oriented
toward the Sanctuary [directly eastward, perpendicular to the orientation of the Ark].

VERSE 20

———————————————— RASHBAM ————————————————

וּפְנֵיהֶם אִישׁ אֶל־אָחִיו – *They should face one
another:* The two cherubim should be turned
toward the middle of the Ark cover, which is

also the sense of the phrase *And look toward
the cover.*

———————————————— IBN EZRA ————————————————

אֶל־הַכַּפֹּרֶת יִהְיוּ פְּנֵי הַכְּרֻבִים – *They should look
toward the cover:* The heads of the cherubim

should be bowed down toward the Ark cover.
(Short Commentary)

———————————— RABBI AVRAHAM BEN HARAMBAM ————————————

פֹּרְשֵׂי כְנָפַיִם לְמַעְלָה – *Wings spread upward:*
Note that angels have no physicality; they
are referred to as cherubim with human form
for two reasons. Firstly, when angels appear
to prophets within prophetic visions they
take on human visages. Secondly, the term
"cherub" alludes to the similarity that these
beings bear to people in their possession of
the power of speech. It is possible that the
raised wings allude to the angels' pursuit of
God's greatness and exaltedness. Furthermore, any person who is immersed in Torah
study and observance of the commandments

can be assured that angels will lift him up and
protect him, as the verse states: *For He shall
give His angels charge over you, to keep you in
all your ways. They shall bear you up in their
hands* (Psalms 91:11–12). It is possible that the
cherubim were said to cover the Ark cover
with their wings to symbolize their protection
of the community. The cherubim, when praising God and serving Him, move toward one
another, as the verse states: *And one cried to
another, and said, Holy, holy, holy, is the* LORD *of
Hosts* (Isaiah 6:3); this seems to be the sense of
the phrase here, *They should face one another.*

———————————————— ḤIZKUNI ————————————————

וּפְנֵיהֶם אִישׁ אֶל־אָחִיו – *They should face one
another:* This verse proves that the cherubim
were not created as images to be worshipped.
For if the command had been to fashion just a
single cherub, or if one of the two mandated
figures faced the worshipper while its partner

faced it, one could argue that the statues were
constructed to elicit reverence form the people. However, since the two cherubim were
made to face each other, and because they
both were turned inward to the Ark cover
where the Divine Presence rests, and toward

כא יִהְיוּ פְּנֵי הַכְּרֻבִים׃ וְנָתַתָּ אֶת־הַכַּפֹּרֶת עַל־הָאָרֹן מִלְמָעְלָה
כב וְאֶל־הָאָרֹן תִּתֵּן אֶת־הָעֵדֻת אֲשֶׁר אֶתֵּן אֵלֶיךָ׃ וְנוֹעַדְתִּי
לְךָ שָׁם וְדִבַּרְתִּי אִתְּךָ מֵעַל הַכַּפֹּרֶת מִבֵּין שְׁנֵי הַכְּרֻבִים

ḤIZKUNI *(cont.)*

the Ark which contains the Torah, it is clear that the sole function of the cherubim was aesthetic. Furthermore, the only human to ever see the cherubim was the High Priest, who entered the Holy of Holies on just one day a year [on Yom Kippur as part of the day's rituals]. The cherubim above the Ark were meant to represent God's attendants, as the verse states: *Seraphim stood above Him* (Isaiah 6:2).

SFORNO

וּפְנֵיהֶם אִישׁ אֶל־אָחִיו – *They should face one another:* The two statues of cherubim adorning the cover faced each other to demonstrate the transmission and reception of understanding which are only achieved by studying the Torah. Furthermore, the cherubim's wings reached upward, symbolizing the idea: *The way of life for the wise leads upward* (Proverbs 15:24).

VERSE 21

RASHI

וְאֶל־הָאָרֹן תִּתֵּן אֶת־הָעֵדֻת – *And inside the Ark place the tablets of the Covenant:* I do not know why the Torah repeats this command, for it has already been stated above: *Inside the Ark, place the tablets of the Covenant* (20:16). We might suggest that the above verse emphasizes that the tablets of the Covenant were to be placed inside the Ark while it stood uncovered, and that the Ark cover should be positioned on top only afterward. We find this stated explicitly when the Tabernacle was erected: *He took the covenant and put it in the Ark,* and then: *He inserted the carrying staves into the Ark and placed the cover on top of it* (40:20).

BEKHOR SHOR

וְאֶל־הָאָרֹן תִּתֵּן אֶת־הָעֵדֻת – *And inside the Ark place the tablets of the Covenant:* Here Moshe is commanded to put the tablets inside the Ark. The parallel language above [in verse 16] is merely explaining why the staves of the Ark must not be removed [out of respect for its precious cargo].

RAMBAN

וְאֶל־הָאָרֹן תִּתֵּן אֶת־הָעֵדֻת – *And inside the Ark place the tablets of the Covenant:* The Torah just mandated that the *cherubim should have wings spread upward* (25:20), but it has not explained what the purpose of these figures is, what they are doing in the Tabernacle, and why they should take the form that they do. Now, however, God tells Moshe what to do with the Ark cover along with its cherubim. For these components together all create a throne of glory for God, from which He would commune with Moshe, and where His Divine Presence would rest among Israel, as the verse states: *There, from above the cover, between*

21 cover. Place the cover on top of the Ark, and inside the Ark
22 place the tablets of the Covenant that I will give you. There,
from above the cover, between the two cherubim, above the

RAMBAN *(cont.)*

the two cherubim…I will meet with you and speak with you (25:22). God selected that spot, *above the Ark of the Testimony,* because the Ark represents the divine chariot witnessed in Yeḥezkel's vision: *This is the living creature that I saw under the God of Israel by the River Kevar; and I knew that they were cherubim. Each one had four faces, and each one four wings; and the likeness of the hands of a man was under their wings* (Ezekiel 10:20). And this is why God is referred to as the *Lord of Hosts, who sits upon the cherubim* (I Samuel 4:4) – the cherubim extended their wings to function as a steed transporting the glory of God. As the verse states, *Gold for the pattern of the chariot, that is the cherubim, that spread out their wings, and cover the Ark of the Covenant of the Lord* (I Chronicles 28:18).

VERSE 22

RASHI

וְדִבַּרְתִּי אִתְּךָ מֵעַל הַכַּפֹּרֶת – *From above the cover I will speak with you:* However, a later verse states: *And the Lord called to Moshe, and spoke to him out of the Tent of Meeting* (Leviticus 1:1), where the term "Tent of Meeting" refers to the area of the Tabernacle outside of the Holy of Holies. Although these verses seem to contradict each other, we can enlist a third verse to reconcile the difficulty: *And when Moshe had gone into the Tent of Meeting to speak with Him, then he heard the voice speaking to him from off the covering that was upon the Ark of Testimony, from between the two cherubim* (Numbers 7:89). When Moshe entered the Tabernacle structure, God's voice descended from heaven and emerged from between the two cherubim. Standing on the other side of the curtain, in the Tent of Meeting, Moshe was able to hear God's communication.

IBN EZRA

וְנוֹעַדְתִּי לְךָ שָׁם וְדִבַּרְתִּי אִתְּךָ – *There I will meet you and speak with you:* I do not understand how this verse allegedly [according to Rashi] contradicts the statement *And the Lord called to Moshe, and spoke to him out of the Tent of Meeting* (Leviticus 1:1). For the term "Tent of Meeting" can refer to any part of the Tabernacle [including the Holy of Holies].

BEKHOR SHOR

וְנוֹעַדְתִּי לְךָ שָׁם וְדִבַּרְתִּי אִתְּךָ – *There I will meet you and speak with you:* I will speak to you from between the cherubim, where the tablets are positioned. As for the later verse, *And the Lord called to Moshe, and spoke to him out of the Tent of Meeting* (Leviticus 1:1), that text means that the voice of God could be heard outside the Tabernacle structure when Moshe was there. But when he was inside, the voice was transmitted to him from above the Ark cover, as another verse states: *And when Moshe had gone into the Tent of Meeting to speak with Him, then he heard the voice speaking to him from off the covering that was upon the Ark of the Testimony, from between the two cherubim* (Numbers 7:89).

אֲשֶׁר עַל־אֲרֹן הָעֵדֻת אֵת כָּל־אֲשֶׁר אֲצַוֶּה אוֹתְךָ אֶל־בְּנֵי
יִשְׂרָאֵל׃
כג וְעָשִׂיתָ שֻׁלְחָן עֲצֵי שִׁטִּים אַמָּתַיִם אָרְכּוֹ וְאַמָּה רָחְבּוֹ וְאַמָּה
כד וָחֵצִי קֹמָתוֹ׃ וְצִפִּיתָ אֹתוֹ זָהָב טָהוֹר וְעָשִׂיתָ לּוֹ זֵר זָהָב
כה סָבִיב׃ וְעָשִׂיתָ לּוֹ מִסְגֶּרֶת טֹפַח סָבִיב וְעָשִׂיתָ זֵר־זָהָב

RALBAG

וְדִבַּרְתִּי אִתְּךָ מֵעַל הַכַּפֹּרֶת – *From above the cover I will speak with you:* It will thus be known to the nation that I issue your prophecies from that spot. This is only part of the significance of the forms of cherubim that were atop the Ark cover. But it is what Israel is capable of understanding.

וְנוֹעַדְתִּי לְךָ שָׁם – *There I will meet you:* It is at that location that you will see the divine cloud when I address you, and it will appear to you as if I am speaking to you from that place. The experience will be similar to the events at Mount Sinai when the glory of God descended to grace Moshe with prophecy.

SFORNO

וְנוֹעַדְתִּי לְךָ שָׁם וְדִבַּרְתִּי אִתְּךָ – *There I will meet you and speak with you:* Through the fashioning of the Ark cover with its attendant cherubim, the Divine Presence will be drawn to rest among Israel. Indeed, this presence will be found in any place where the sages of the generation dwell, people who are driven to understand and know God, as the verses state: *I will dwell in their midst…following the patterns that I show you* [25:8–9, implying that God will appear wherever there is teaching of Torah].

VERSE 23

BEKHOR SHOR

וְעָשִׂיתָ שֻׁלְחָן – *Make a table:* It is an honor for a king when his servants and priests share food off his table.

ABARBANEL

וְעָשִׂיתָ שֻׁלְחָן – *Make a table:* Because the Tabernacle was made to resemble the palace of a monarch, the inner sanctum known as the Holy of Holies was comparable to the inner chamber of a king's quarters. In such a room the ruler keeps his treasure chest and all his valuables, refusing to trust even his servants with the keys. And outside his most private and secure room, which nobody is allowed to enter, the king builds a throne room, which in the Tabernacle was paralleled by the Sanctuary. That is where the king spends his time, and hence it contains a table, a throne, and a light. Into that room are invited the king's servants and attendants, whose mission is to serve him. In God's House therefore, appears a table symbolizing His wealth, and a candelabrum which stands on the opposite wall. The incense altar represents God's royal seat, which is why incense is burned on it every morning and evening, just like a mortal king is served meals twice a day.

Ark of the Testimony, I will meet with you and speak with you,
and give you all My commands to the Israelites.
23 Make a table of acacia wood, two cubits long, a cubit wide, and
24 a cubit and a half high. Overlay it with pure gold and around it
25 make a gold rim. Make a frame a handbreadth wide all around,

VERSE 24

RASHI

זֵר זָהָב – *A gold rim:* This gold border symbolizes the crown of the Israelite monarchy, for the table as a whole represents earthly wealth and greatness. Thus do people say: "This food is fit for a king's table!"

BEKHOR SHOR

וְצִפִּיתָ אֹתוֹ זָהָב טָהוֹר – *Overlay it with pure gold:* Although the table would be covered in gold on the top and bottom, the wood would still be visible in between. Hence the verse instructs Moshe to *around it make a gold rim* to cover up the thickness of the table. The rim was to be fashioned like a border all around it.

RAMBAN

וְצִפִּיתָ אֹתוֹ זָהָב טָהוֹר – *Overlay it with pure gold:* Herein lies the secret of the Tabernacle's table. For since the close of creation, God has never created anything *ex nihilo*. Rather the world has always followed the natural laws built into it, as the verse states, *Then God saw all that He had made: and it was very good.* [Genesis 1:31; implying that nothing needed to be added later]. However, even when a thing already exists, God's blessing can still descend upon it and make it grow and flourish. This was so with the showbread that sat on the table – God's blessing infused these loaves, and from them plenitude extended to all of Israel. Hence our Sages claim: Every priest received just a morsel of food from the showbread, and yet was satisfied when he ate it (Yoma 39a).

VERSE 25

RASHI

מִסְגֶּרֶת – *A frame:* This should be understood as the Targum renders it: a "border" [*gedanefa*]. Now the Sages of Israel debate the position of this frame. According to some, the frame surrounded the table like a vertical ledge found on princes' tables. [That is, it stood upright, projecting above the tabletop like a fence.] Another approach claims that the frame ran beneath the tabletop and stretched from one leg to the next on all four sides. According to this second understanding, the tabletop sat on top of the frame. **וְעָשִׂיתָ זֵר־זָהָב לְמִסְגַּרְתּוֹ** – *And around the frame also make a gold rim:* This is the same rim as that mentioned above [in verse 24; the word "also" is absent from the Hebrew]. Our verse explains that this rim was attached to the frame.

BEKHOR SHOR

וְעָשִׂיתָ לּוֹ מִסְגֶּרֶת – *Make a frame:* A frame encircled the table to prevent the loaves of bread from falling off if the table was disturbed. The frame was one handbreadth

כו לְמִסְגַּרְתּוֹ סָבִיב: וְעָשִׂיתָ לּוֹ אַרְבַּע טַבְּעֹת זָהָב וְנָתַתָּ אֶת־
כז הַטַּבָּעֹת עַל אַרְבַּע הַפֵּאֹת אֲשֶׁר לְאַרְבַּע רַגְלָיו: לְעֻמַּת
הַמִּסְגֶּרֶת תִּהְיֶיןָ הַטַּבָּעֹת לְבָתִּים לְבַדִּים לָשֵׂאת אֶת־
כח הַשֻּׁלְחָן: וְעָשִׂיתָ אֶת־הַבַּדִּים עֲצֵי שִׁטִּים וְצִפִּיתָ אֹתָם זָהָב
כט וְנִשָּׂא־בָם אֶת־הַשֻּׁלְחָן: וְעָשִׂיתָ קְּעָרֹתָיו וְכַפֹּתָיו וּקְשׂוֹתָיו

BEKHOR SHOR *(cont.)*

wide and rested on the edge of the table. **וְעָשִׂיתָ זֵר־זָהָב לְמִסְגַּרְתּוֹ** – *And around the frame also make a gold rim:* Since the frame was fashioned out of wood, it needed a double border – on the inside and the outside – to conceal that material. Thus the whole Table was covered in gold.

KELI YAKAR

וְעָשִׂיתָ לּוֹ מִסְגֶּרֶת – *Make a frame:* The frame was meant to symbolize the Israelites' efforts to keep their passions at bay. A barrier serves to close oneself off and to set limits to one's behavior. **זֵר־זָהָב** – *A gold rim:* A person who shuts out and suppresses his cravings becomes his own master. Such people are truly free and rulers of their own destinies, in contrast to those who burst through their own boundaries and are therefore destined to be slaves to their desires. The Torah employs the word *zer* ["rim" here, but literally "crown" or "garland"] to teach that when we master our inclinations we assume a crown of power; but when we succumb to our wants, we become strangers [*zar*] and foreigners to our own character.

VERSE 27

RASHI

לְעֻמַּת הַמִּסְגֶּרֶת תִּהְיֶיןָ הַטַּבָּעֹת – *The rings should be attached next to the frame:* The rings were fixed in the legs opposite the ends of the frame.

ḤIZKUNI

לְעֻמַּת הַמִּסְגֶּרֶת תִּהְיֶיןָ הַטַּבָּעוֹת – *The rings should be attached next to the frame:* Fasten the rings on the underside of the table, near its frame, i.e., near to its edge. Do not place the rings in the middle of the table's surface.

VERSE 29

RASHI

וְעָשִׂיתָ קְּעָרֹתָיו וְכַפֹּתָיו – *You must also make its bowls, spoons:* [The meaning of all these terms is unclear. Rashi explains:] The *ke'arot* were pans formed in the shape of the loaves of bread they held. The showbread itself was shaped like an open box with two sides closed and two sides open. It had a bottom and was folded up on opposite sides to create two walls of bread. [That it, is looked like an elongated letter "U"]. The bread was therefore called *leḥem hapanim* [literally, "bread of faces"], since it had two faces on its sides, facing toward both sides of the Sanctuary. The long side of the loaves was oriented along the

26 and around the frame also make a gold rim. Make for it four
gold rings, and place the rings on the four corners where the
27 four legs are. The rings should be attached next to the frame
28 as holders for staves to carry the table. Make the staves of aca-
cia wood and overlay them with gold; by these the table shall
29 be carried. You must also make, out of pure gold, its bowls,

RASHI *(cont.)*

width of the table, while the walls of the bread stood upright opposite the edge of the table [and thereby faced the walls of the room]. A copy of this golden pan was made of iron. The bread was baked in the iron mold, but was removed from that when it was taken out of the oven and placed in the gold container. There it sat until the following day, the Sabbath, whereupon all the new loaves were placed on the table. Such a pan was called a *ke'ara*. **וְכַפֹּתָיו** – *Its spoons:* The *kappot* were utensils used to hold frankincense. There were two such containers to hold the two handfuls of frankincense, which were positioned on the two rows of bread, as the verse states: *And you shall put pure frankincense upon each row* (Leviticus 24:7). **וּקְשׂוֹתָיו** – *Its pitchers:* The *kesot* looked like halves of hollow canes that have been split along their length. Such forms were made out of gold, and three of them were arranged above each loaf of bread, to separate the loaves from one another. In this way air could circulate between the loaves and prevent mold from forming on them. In Arabic, anything hollow is called *kasweh*. **וּמְנַקִּיֹּתָיו** – *Its jars:* The Targum translates this word as *mekhilateih* [meaning "supports" for the tubes described above; see below]. These were fashioned like golden poles that stood on the ground and extended past the height of the table to the level of the loaves themselves. These poles had a series of six holes in them running up their lengths where the ends of the tubes were inserted between the loaves. This was so that the weight of the upper loaves would not overwhelm that of the lower loaves and cause them to break. The Targum's Aramaic term, *mekhilateih,* means "supports," as in the verse *I am weary of holding it in [hakhil]* (Jeremiah 6:11). Still, I do not know the connection of the Hebrew word *menakkiyyotav* to such a meaning. **אֲשֶׁר יֻסַּךְ בָּהֵן** – *For pouring libations:* [The word *yussakh* can also mean "be covered." Rashi follows this reading:] The clause means: By which the loaves of bread will be covered. This phrase refers to the tubes [*kesot*], for they sat like a roof [*sekhakh*] or a covering over the bread. Similarly, we read elsewhere: *The covering tubes [kesot hanasekh]* (Numbers 4:7). For both terms – *yussakh* and *nesekh* – are related to the words for roof and covering.

IBN EZRA

וְכַפֹּתָיו – *Its spoons:* These were small utensils shaped like spoons. A later verse uses the same word: *One spoon [kaf] of ten shekels of gold, full of incense* (Numbers 7:14). **וּקְשׂוֹתָיו** – *Its pitchers:* This word refers to cups, and it is regarding these that the verse later states: *For pouring libations.* Proof for this interpretation comes from a subsequent description which mentions *the libation pitchers [kesot hanasekh]* (Numbers 4:7). Some commentators argue that the phrase *With a writer's inkwell [keset, spelled with a letter samekh] by his side* (Ezekiel 9:2) contains a related term, since we sometimes find that the letter *sin* and the letter

ל וּמְנַקִּיֹּתָיו אֲשֶׁר יֻסַּךְ בָּהֵן זָהָב טָהוֹר תַּעֲשֶׂה אֹתָם׃ וְנָתַתָּ
עַל־הַשֻּׁלְחָן לֶחֶם פָּנִים לְפָנַי תָּמִיד׃
לא וְעָשִׂיתָ מְנֹרַת זָהָב טָהוֹר מִקְשָׁה תֵּיעָשֶׂה הַמְּנוֹרָה יְרֵכָהּ

BEKHOR SHOR *(cont.)*

samekh are interchangeable. For example, we find the phrase *Woe also to them when I depart [besuri] from them* [Hosea 9:12, where the word is spelled with a *sin* instead of the expected *samekh*]. There are many similar cases. (Short Commentary)

BEKHOR SHOR

קְעָרֹתָיו – *Its bowls:* These were bowls used to knead the dough for the loaves. **וְכַפֹּתָיו** – *Its spoons:* Frankincense was placed inside the spoons, and these in turn were put onto the array of bread. The incense was burned on a weekly basis as a token sacrifice from the bread. **וּקְשׂוֹתָיו** – *Its pitchers:* These were utensils into which water was placed to knead the dough, as the verse mentions *the jars for pouring out [kesot hanasekh]* (Numbers 4:7). For water was poured out from these vessels onto the flour before kneading it. The word *kesot* refers to containers, as the Talmud explains [see Sanhedrin 81b]. **וּמְנַקִּיֹּתָיו** – *Its jars:* [Contrary to the translation here, the author holds that] this refers to tools used to clean out [*lenakkot*] ashes from the oven and to scour the table before the loaves were placed there.

KELI YAKAR

וּמְנַקִּיֹּתָיו – *Its jars:* The description of the table ends with the Torah mentioning the jars, to teach that one should earn one's livelihood honestly, clear [*naki*] of all wrongdoing. Similarly, one should invite the poor to dine at his table in a respectful [*naki*] manner, not a deprecating way.

VERSE 30

RAV SE'ADYA GAON

לֶחֶם פָּנִים – *The showbread:* [Literally, "bread of faces."] The showbread was called thus because it had many faces [aspects, or dimensions].

RASHBAM

לֶחֶם פָּנִים – *The showbread:* The straightforward meaning of the term is that it is bread fit for a prince, wholesome bread, as the verse states: *And you shall take fine flour and bake twelve loaves* (Leviticus 24:5). Meanwhile an earlier verse states: *And he took and sent portions to them from before him [me'et panav]* [Genesis 43:34; the food that Yosef gave his brothers was naturally respectable due to his station].

ḤIZKUNI

לֶחֶם פָּנִים – *The showbread:* [Literally, "bread of faces."] The loaves were so called because they had multiple surfaces. Commenting on the Talmud [Menaḥot 71a] Rashi explains that the term *panim* is related to the word for walls – *defanot.* Alternatively, God referred to the showbread as *leḥem panim* as if to say that it should be perpetually in His presence [*lefanav*].

30 spoons, pitchers, and jars for pouring libations. On this table
the showbread must be placed before Me at all times.
31 Make a candelabrum of pure gold. Its base and shaft, cups,

VERSE 31

RASHBAM

וְעָשִׂיתָ מְנֹרַת זָהָב טָהוֹר – *Make a candelabrum of pure gold:* The light from the candelabrum would illuminate the table in the same room, as the verse states: *And the candelabrum [shall be placed] on the south side, opposite the table* (26:35). **מִקְשָׁה** – *Hammered:* Take a mallet to a single block of gold and hammer out the branches and the cups for the candelabrum. **יְרֵכָהּ** – *Its base:* This refers to the broad foot at the bottom of the candelabrum, which sat on the ground.

IBN EZRA

תֵּיעָשֶׂה – *Shall be:* I have examined copies of the Torah that have been checked by the scholars of Tiberias. Fifteen of these experts have sworn that they each reviewed the text three times, considering each word, every vowel, and all the instances of plene and deficient spellings. Through all of this I have discovered that the word *tei'aseh* in our verse is written with the letter *yod.* However, in Torah scrolls I have seen in Spain, France, and across the sea, the *yod* is absent. Early commentators have suggested that the extra letter *yod* alludes to the ten candelabra that Shlomo would later construct [for the first Temple; see I Kings 7:49; the numerical equivalent of the letter *yod* is ten]. Still, in general, it is unusual for this word to be written with a *yod.* The Midrash claims that the candelabrum made itself, since everyone who saw it was astonished at the item's complexity and wondered how human beings could have made it.

ḤIZKUNI

מִקְשָׁה – *Hammered:* According to Rashi, the word *miksha* alludes to the difficulty [*koshi*] Moshe had visualizing how the candelabrum should be fashioned. Moshe's trouble was that God did not specify how tall the object should be as He did when describing the other accoutrements of the Tabernacle. **גְּבִיעֶיהָ** – *Its cups:* The cups were a fixed feature that encircled the candelabrum's branches, and if the oil overflowed the lamps, it would drip down to the first cup. Should that cup become too full with oil, the excess would run down to the second, and so on to the third cup, and finally down to the cup situated on the candelabrum's base, into which all the extra oil flowed.

RABBEINU BAḤYA

וְעָשִׂיתָ מְנֹרַת זָהָב טָהוֹר – *Make a candelabrum of pure gold:* The straightforward understanding of this passage is that the candelabrum was placed in the Tabernacle and the Temple to impress upon observers the importance and grandeur of those structures, as the verse states: *You shall revere My Sanctuary* (Leviticus 19:30). It was for this reason that the candelabrum was positioned in the Sanctuary outside the curtain and not inside the Holy of Holies [where no one would see it]. Thus all people who came into the Sanctuary would see the candelabrum and be struck by its splendor. Another reason why the candelabrum was

לב וְקָנָהּ גְּבִיעֶיהָ כַּפְתֹּרֶיהָ וּפְרָחֶיהָ מִמֶּנָּה יִהְיוּ: וְשִׁשָּׁה קָנִים
יֹצְאִים מִצִּדֶּיהָ שְׁלֹשָׁה ׀ קְנֵי מְנֹרָה מִצִּדָּהּ הָאֶחָד וּשְׁלֹשָׁה
לג קְנֵי מְנֹרָה מִצִּדָּהּ הַשֵּׁנִי: שְׁלֹשָׁה גְבִעִים מְשֻׁקָּדִים בַּקָּנֶה
הָאֶחָד כַּפְתֹּר וָפֶרַח וּשְׁלֹשָׁה גְבִעִים מְשֻׁקָּדִים בַּקָּנֶה
הָאֶחָד כַּפְתֹּר וָפָרַח כֵּן לְשֵׁשֶׁת הַקָּנִים הַיֹּצְאִים מִן־הַמְּנֹרָה:
לד וּבַמְּנֹרָה אַרְבָּעָה גְבִעִים מְשֻׁקָּדִים כַּפְתֹּרֶיהָ וּפְרָחֶיהָ:
לה וְכַפְתֹּר תַּחַת שְׁנֵי הַקָּנִים מִמֶּנָּה וְכַפְתֹּר תַּחַת שְׁנֵי הַקָּנִים

RABBEINU BAḤYA *(cont.)*

placed on the outside of the curtain was to emphasize that God [whose presence rested on the inner side of the barrier] has no need for our physical illumination. In order to inspire all those who see it, the candelabrum was fashioned out of gold, the most superior of all metals. The candelabrum comprised seven branches because the number seven represents the cycle of the week. Now it is well known that the human soul finds pleasure in candlelight, because it reflects the light that is engraved upon the mind. This is why people are attracted to fire, even though a candle is physical whereas that of the soul is spiritual. And this is why King Shlomo compared a person's essence to fire, when he said: *The spirit of man is the candle of the Lord* (Proverbs 20:27). Homiletically however, the Midrash argues that the candelabrum contained seven lamps corresponding to the seven stars that circle the globe [that is, the sun, moon, and five clearly visible planets] and influence the lower realm of earth. The middle lamp of the candelabrum corresponded to the sun, which is ever present in our sky and stands as the middle star of these seven. We can also suggest that the candelabrum held seven arms to allude to the Torah, which is itself compared to light in the verse *For the commandment is a lamp; and Torah is light* (Proverbs 6:23), and Torah contains seven realms of wisdom. The six branches that emerged from the candelabrum's side corresponded to the six dimensions of the world [up, down, north, south, east, and west], which are all dependent upon the Torah that was given on the sixth of the month of Sivan. For the world can only endure if the Torah is observed, as the prophet declares: *This is what the Lord said: If not for my covenant day and night, I would not have established the laws of heaven and earth* (Jeremiah 33:25).

VERSE 33

RASHI

מְשֻׁקָּדִים – *Finely crafted:* The word *meshukkadim* should be understood as the Targum renders it – decorated in the way that gold and silver vessels are. In Old French this is called *nieller* ["filling in engraved designs with color"].

RASHBAM

שְׁלֹשָׁה גְבִעִים – *Three cups:* Hollow like cups, depressions made in the branch of the candelabrum. **מְשֻׁקָּדִים** – *Finely crafted:* Decorated with figures designed to look like

32 knobs, and flowers shall be hammered from a single piece. Six
branches shall extend from its sides, three on one side, three
33 on the other. On each branch there shall be three finely crafted
cups, each with a knob and a flower. All six branches extend-
34 ing from the candelabrum shall be like this. The shaft of the
candelabrum shall have four finely crafted cups, each with a
35 knob and a flower. For the six branches that extend from the

RASHBAM *(cont.)*

almonds [*shekedim*], raised on the surface of the cups. This feature is reminiscent of crafted silver made to resemble palms or apples.

כַּפְתֹּר וָפֶרַח – *A knob and a flower:* Knobs and flowers featured in the middle of every branch for decorative purposes.

IBN EZRA

מְשֻׁקָּדִים – *Finely crafted:* According to Rav Se'adya Gaon, the term *meshukkadim* suggests that the gold of the cups was shaped to look like almonds [*shekedim*]. Nevertheless, the word is in fact related to that appearing in the verse *Happy is the man who hearkens to me, attached [lishkod] daily at my gates, waiting at the posts of my doors* [Proverbs 8:34, meaning that the cups were attached to each other, or to the branches].

VERSE 35

RASHI

תַּחַת שְׁנֵי הַקָּנִים מִמֶּנָּה – *At the base of each pair of branches:* The branches that emerged from either side of the central shaft came out of knobs crafted in the middle branch. And these are the dimensions of the candelabrum as taught in Baraita Dimlekhet Hamishkan [a *baraita* appearing in Menaḥot 28b]: The height of the lamp was eighteen handbreadths, according to the following calculation: The feet that projected from the bottom of the base, together with the base itself, rose to three handbreadths, including the flower just above the base. This is the flower mentioned in the verse *And this was the work of the candlestick: it was of beaten gold, from its shaft, to its flower* (Numbers 8:4). Above that, the central shaft was smooth [unadorned] for two handbreadths, whereupon one handbreadth accounted for one cup out of the structure's four. Then appeared one knob and one flower out of the two that appeared on the main shaft of the candelabrum, as described in the verse *Each with a knob and a flower* (25:34). That verse teaches us that the middle branch held two knobs and two flowers aside from the three knobs at the points where the six branches emerged, which in turn are described by the phrase *A knob at the base of each pair of branches* (25:35). Now, above this ornamentation, were an additional two smooth handbreadths. This was followed by a handbreadth-long knob whence two branches emerged – one on either side. The branches were drawn out and rose to the height of the candelabrum. Above that point was another smooth handbreadth followed by an additional handbreadth with a knob, and two branches emerging from either side of it. Next there was a third smooth handbreadth before the third handbreadth-long knob. From that knob emerged the final two branches of the candelabrum to rise to the lamp's full height.

מִמֶּנָּה וְכַפְתֹּר תַּחַת־שְׁנֵי הַקָּנִים מִמֶּנָּה לְשֵׁשֶׁת הַקָּנִים
לו הַיֹּצְאִים מִן־הַמְּנֹרָה׃ כַּפְתֹּרֵיהֶם וּקְנֹתָם מִמֶּנָּה יִהְיוּ כֻּלָּהּ
לז מִקְשָׁה אַחַת זָהָב טָהוֹר׃ וְעָשִׂיתָ אֶת־נֵרֹתֶיהָ שִׁבְעָה
לח וְהֶעֱלָה אֶת־נֵרֹתֶיהָ וְהֵאִיר עַל־עֵבֶר פָּנֶיהָ׃ וּמַלְקָחֶיהָ
לט וּמַחְתֹּתֶיהָ זָהָב טָהוֹר׃ כִּכָּר זָהָב טָהוֹר יַעֲשֶׂה אֹתָהּ אֵת
מ כָּל־הַכֵּלִים הָאֵלֶּה׃ וּרְאֵה וַעֲשֵׂה בְּתַבְנִיתָם אֲשֶׁר־אַתָּה

RASHI *(cont.)*

Following that there were two smooth handbreadths. [At this point we have climbed fifteen handbreadths up the middle shaft]. This leaves three handbreadths which held three cups [out of the four on the central branch], and the second knob and flower set [of two on the central branch]. Altogether, the candelabrum held twenty-two cups: eighteen on the six outer branches – three on each branch – and an additional four on the central shaft. The number of knobs totaled eleven, with one on each of the six branches, three on the body of the middle shaft where the branches emerged, and an additional two knobs on the central shaft, as the verse states: *Finely-crafted knobs* (25:34). [Although the verse does not specify how many additional knobs should be crafted there, it uses a plural noun,] and the minimum plural is two. One of these appeared low on the central shaft near the base, with the other within the top three handbreadths of the structure with the three cups that were fashioned there. The total number of flowers on the candelabrum was nine. Each of the six branches had one flower, as the verse states: *On each branch there shall be... a flower* (25:33), and the central shaft had three flowers of its own, as the verse states: *Finely-crafted... flowers* (25:34). [Again the text does not give a number for how many flowers are to be fashioned on the central rod, but] the minimum plural is two, and we add to those two a third flower mentioned in Parashat Behaalotekha: *From its base to its flower* (Numbers 8:4). [Rashi concludes:] If you study the *baraita* cited above you will find all the components of the candelabrum according to their number and position.

VERSE 37

RASHBAM

וְהֵאִיר עַל־עֵבֶר פָּנֶיהָ – *So that they light the space in front of it:* The wicks of the lamps were to be lit such that they faced the front of the candelabrum, in the direction of the table which stood on the opposite wall.

RABBI AVRAHAM BEN HARAMBAM

וְהֶעֱלָה אֶת־נֵרֹתֶיהָ – *And mount them:* The verb "mount" here refers to lighting the lamps. The word derives from the root *alef-lamed-heh* ["to rise"] indicating that the flames ascend upward.

candelabrum, there must be a knob at the base of each pair of
36 branches. The knobs and their branches shall be of one piece
with it, the whole of it a single, hammered piece of pure gold.
37 Make its seven lamps and mount them so that they light the
38 39 space in front of it. Make its tongs and pans of pure gold. All
40 these items shall be made from a talent of pure gold. Take
care to make them according to that design that is shown to

HIZKUNI

וְעָשִׂיתָ אֶת־נֵרֹתֶיהָ – *Make its lamps:* This instruction indicates that the lamps used for the candelabrum were distinct objects which could be moved and removed from the branches where they sat. Proof for this assertion comes from a later verse, *Their knobs and branches were of one piece with it, so that the whole of it was a single piece of pure beaten gold* (37:22), omitting the lamps, which are mentioned later: *Its seven lamps and its tongs and pans were of pure gold* (37:23).

נֵרֹתֶיהָ שִׁבְעָה – *Its seven lamps:* The seven lamps correspond to the seven days of the week, as well as the seven celestial orbs: the sun, the moon, Mercury, Venus, Mars, Jupiter, and Saturn – stars that light up the world.

וְהֵאִיר עַל־עֵבֶר פָּנֶיהָ – *So that they light the space in front of it:* This command instructs that the seven lamps all be lit from the side where all the candelabrum's branches can be seen, i.e., from the front [rather than from the sides].

VERSE 40

RASHI

וּרְאֵה וַעֲשֵׂה – *Take care to make them:* [Literally, "see and make them."] God instructed Moshe to look at a diagram of the candelabrum that He showed him on the mountain. This tells us that Moshe had difficulty understanding how to construct this item, and only grasped its design once God Himself showed him a candelabrum of fire.

IBN EZRA

וּרְאֵה וַעֲשֵׂה – *Take care to make them:* [Literally, "see and make them."] It took great wisdom to fashion the candelabrum, and the craftsman had to be exceptionally clever to conceive of how to form all its features out of a single talent of gold.

RALBAG

אֲשֶׁר־אַתָּה מָרְאֶה – *That is shown to you:* According to this verse, Moshe was required to follow the plans that he was shown, although it was not critical that the candelabrum be made out of gold [see Menaḥot 28a], as long as the material was a beaten metal. Still, whatever substance was employed had to be free of slag, since the Torah emphasizes that when gold is used it should be pure [in verses 31 and 36]. Furthermore, should the candelabrum be fashioned out of a different metal, it is not necessary that it weigh a whole talent, because the weight mentioned by the Torah is not a crucial requirement. If another metal is already being substituted for the gold, the weight of material used can also vary.

כו א מָרְאֶה בָּהָר: וְאֶת־הַמִּשְׁכָּן תַּעֲשֶׂה עֶשֶׂר יט שלישי
יְרִיעֹת שֵׁשׁ מָשְׁזָר וּתְכֵלֶת וְאַרְגָּמָן וְתֹלַעַת שָׁנִי כְּרֻבִים

GUR ARYEH

וּרְאֵה וַעֲשֵׂה – *Take care to make them:* [Literally, "see and make them."] According to Rashi, God showed Moshe the appearance of all the Tabernacle's accoutrements. This was not because Moshe had difficulty conceptualizing the way they all looked; he only had trouble with the candelabrum. But having shown him that, God displayed the rest for him as well. For all the Tabernacle's furniture should be understood as a unified set, each one dependent on the others. Indeed, all the utensils must be present for any of them to be considered operative. Therefore, had God shown Moshe only the candelabrum, it would have been like explaining only part of a topic. It would have been inappropriate to demonstrate half of the schematics to Moshe. Hence our verse states: *Take care to make them according to that design,* indicating that God showed Moshe all the different accoutrements.

CHAPTER 26, VERSE 1

RAV SE'ADYA GAON

כְּרֻבִים – *Cherubim:* This refers to flat images of cherubim [as opposed to the sculptures on the Ark cover].

RASHI

כְּרֻבִים מַעֲשֵׂה חֹשֵׁב – *With a design of cherubim worked into them:* Images of cherubim were worked into the curtains as they were being woven. These were not embroidered through needlework [sewn on after the sheets were woven]; rather the cherubim were woven into the two sides of the curtain as they were being prepared. There were two different faces for the cherubim on either side of the sheet – on one side the figures' faces resembled lions; and on the other side the faces on the figures looked like eagles.

RASHBAM

וְאֶת־הַמִּשְׁכָּן – *As for the Tabernacle:* The first, innermost set of sheets was called the *mishkan.* [The sheets that covered the Tabernacle structure thereby serve as a synecdoche for the building.] These sheets deserved that title because the Ark stood directly beneath them, and the Ark was the spot where the Divine Presence rested.

IBN EZRA

כְּרֻבִים מַעֲשֵׂה חֹשֵׁב – *With a design of cherubim worked into them:* According to our Sages, there is a distinction between the crafts denoted by the terms *maaseh ḥoshev* and *maaseh rokem* [which appears in 26:36]. The first type of work involves creating figures with two faces [one on each side of the fabric], while the second art produces one image alone. This understanding is correct. Still, the straightforward meaning of the text is that *maaseh ḥoshev* suggests neither embroidery nor weaving, but rather a process familiar today for the crafting of silk clothing. For the image that one imagines producing on a material is the product of one's plan [*maḥashava*]. The artisan first draws the picture he has in mind on a board, and then he inserts the threads along that pattern.

26 1 you on the mountain. As for the Tabernacle itself, SHELISHI
make it with ten sheets of finely spun linen and sky-blue, purple, and scarlet wool, with a design of cherubim worked into

ḤIZKUNI

כְּרֻבִים מַעֲשֵׂה חֹשֵׁב – *With a design of cherubim worked into them:* The Torah here calls the craft of weaving *maaseh ḥoshev* because it demands substantial planning [*maḥashava*]. However, the phrase *maaseh rokem* [in 26:36] refers to mere needlework, which requires less intelligence.

RALBAG

שֵׁשׁ מָשְׁזָר – *Finely spun linen:* This refers to choice linen produced in Egypt, whose threads were folded six times. Now since the Tabernacle sheets were composed of *finely spun linen and sky-blue, purple, and scarlet wool,* it was appropriate for the other three materials to also comprise six strands. This ensured that the threads were all even and parallel. כְּרֻבִים מַעֲשֵׂה חֹשֵׁב – *With a design of cherubim worked into them:* Images of cherubim were woven into both sides of the fabric, for that is the implication of the phrase *maaseh ḥoshev*. The name of this craft may derive from the need of the weaver to keep track of the number [*ḥeshbon*] of fabric threads in the weave for the image to appear correctly.

ABARBANEL

וּתְכֵלֶת וְאַרְגָּמָן וְתֹלַעַת שָׁנִי – *Sky-blue, purple, and scarlet wool:* The linen was to be the warp, and these other three threads the weft to produce the design. Now according to our Sages [see Yoma 72a] each thread was itself six-ply consisting of a strand of gold, sky-blue, purple, scarlet, and finely spun linen. And yet it is difficult to accept this claim that all of the threads were identically composed, since if that were so, there could be no visible images of the cherubim woven into the fabric. Different colors would have to have been used disproportionately to present the pictures. And because of this sophisticated alternation of colors, the Torah refers to the effort as woven *maaseh ḥoshev,* a term meaning "the work of skillful craftsman." For the artisan had to delegate the threads in a way that would produce images on both sides of the sheet. This of course differs from mere needlework, where a picture is sewn onto material with a needle, in which case the design appears on just one side.

SFORNO

וְאֶת־הַמִּשְׁכָּן תַּעֲשֶׂה עֶשֶׂר יְרִיעֹת – *As for the Tabernacle itself, make it with ten sheets:* The sheets covering the Tabernacle were themselves called the *mishkan* since they defined the structure that contained a throne [the incense altar], a table, and a candelabrum to host the Divine Presence [*Shekhina*] of God. Fashioned into the sheets were images of cherubim similar to those mentioned in the verse *Seraphim stood above Him* (Isaiah 6:2), and *I saw the Lord sitting on His throne, and all the host of heaven standing by Him on His right hand and on His left.* (I Kings 22:19) These are the beings that the prophets saw in their visions.

KELI YAKAR

וְאֶת־הַמִּשְׁכָּן תַּעֲשֶׂה עֶשֶׂר יְרִיעֹת – *As for the Tabernacle itself, make it with ten sheets:* This verse should have started: "Make a Tabernacle," parallel to other such phrases in these chapters:

ב מַעֲשֵׂה חֹשֵׁב תַּעֲשֶׂה אֹתָם׃ אֹרֶךְ ׀ הַיְרִיעָה הָאַחַת שְׁמֹנֶה
וְעֶשְׂרִים בָּאַמָּה וְרֹחַב אַרְבַּע בָּאַמָּה הַיְרִיעָה הָאֶחָת מִדָּה
ג אַחַת לְכָל־הַיְרִיעֹת׃ חֲמֵשׁ הַיְרִיעֹת תִּהְיֶיןָ חֹבְרֹת אִשָּׁה
ד אֶל־אֲחֹתָהּ וְחָמֵשׁ יְרִיעֹת חֹבְרֹת אִשָּׁה אֶל־אֲחֹתָהּ׃ וְעָשִׂיתָ
לֻלְאֹת תְּכֵלֶת עַל שְׂפַת הַיְרִיעָה הָאֶחָת מִקָּצָה בַּחֹבָרֶת
וְכֵן תַּעֲשֶׂה בִּשְׂפַת הַיְרִיעָה הַקִּיצוֹנָה בַּמַּחְבֶּרֶת הַשֵּׁנִית׃
ה חֲמִשִּׁים לֻלָאֹת תַּעֲשֶׂה בַּיְרִיעָה הָאֶחָת וַחֲמִשִּׁים לֻלָאֹת
תַּעֲשֶׂה בִּקְצֵה הַיְרִיעָה אֲשֶׁר בַּמַּחְבֶּרֶת הַשֵּׁנִית מַקְבִּילֹת
ו הַלֻּלָאֹת אִשָּׁה אֶל־אֲחֹתָהּ׃ וְעָשִׂיתָ חֲמִשִּׁים קַרְסֵי זָהָב
וְחִבַּרְתָּ אֶת־הַיְרִיעֹת אִשָּׁה אֶל־אֲחֹתָהּ בַּקְּרָסִים וְהָיָה
ז הַמִּשְׁכָּן אֶחָד׃ וְעָשִׂיתָ יְרִיעֹת עִזִּים לְאֹהֶל עַל־הַמִּשְׁכָּן

KELI YAKAR *(cont.)*

Make a table (25:23) and *Make a candelabrum* (25:31). However, recognize that the *mishkan* is so called because God told Moshe, *I will dwell [veshakhanti] in their midst* (25:8). But it would inappropriate to directly associate the verb "to make" with regard to God's dwelling place, since only God can really create a space for Himself, as the verse states: *And I will set My dwelling among you* (Leviticus 26:11). This is why our verse starts by commanding Moshe to make sheets for the Tabernacle, rather than with an instruction to make the Tabernacle itself.

VERSE 3

RAV SE'ADYA GAON

חֹבְרֹת – *Sewn:* [Literally, "attached."] That the sheets were sewn together.

VERSE 4

RASHI

מִקָּצָה בַּחֹבָרֶת – *Of the end sheet in the first set:* The loops were fashioned on the border of the last [fifth] sheet of the set. Each set of five sheets that were joined together were referred to as a *ḥoveret* ["joining" or "set"]. **וְכֵן תַּעֲשֶׂה בִּשְׂפַת הַיְרִיעָה הַקִּיצוֹנָה בַּמַּחְבֶּרֶת הַשֵּׁנִית** – *And likewise on the upper edge of the outermost sheet* IN *the second set:* Another group of fifty loops was fashioned on the outer edge of the second *ḥoveret*. The term *kitzona* ["outermost"] is derived from *katzehi* ["edge"], that is, the loops were positioned at the end of the set of five sheets.

ḤIZKUNI

וְעָשִׂיתָ לֻלְאֹת תְּכֵלֶת – *Make loops of sky-blue wool:* God commanded Moshe to fashion the sheets into two sets to make it easier to transport them. He issued a similar instruction regarding the goats' hair sheets [in verses 7–11].

2 them. Each sheet shall be twenty-eight cubits long and four
3 cubits wide; all the sheets should be the same size. Five of the
4 sheets should be sewn together; the other five likewise. Make
loops of sky-blue wool on the upper edge of the end sheet in
the first set, and likewise on the upper edge of the outermost
5 sheet in the second set. Make fifty loops on each sheet on one
side and fifty on the upper edge of the corresponding sheets in
6 the other set, with the loops opposite one another. And make
fifty gold clasps. With the clasps, join the sheets together so
7 that the Tabernacle becomes one whole. Make sheets of goats'
hair as a tent over the Tabernacle; make eleven of these sheets.

VERSE 6

IBN EZRA

וְהָיָה הַמִּשְׁכָּן אֶחָד – *So that the Tabernacle becomes one:* The Torah refers to the entire Tabernacle, with all its components, as "one." Indeed every physical object can be considered a single entity even when it comprises many different parts. So too the glorious God who is One includes everything in Him. The same is true of humanity and the world itself.

RABBI AVRAHAM BEN HARAMBAM

בַּקְּרָסִים – *With the clasps:* The clasps resembled buttons which fit into the loops, attaching the two sets of sheets together. Each set of sheets comprised five sections, and these two large sets were brought together and fastened so that the loops on each set aligned with the ones opposite them. Clasps were fitted through the loops, one for every pair of loops. Thus was created one great sheet whose length matched that of the separate sheets, i.e., twenty-eight cubits, and whose width equaled the total of the individual sheets' widths, i.e., forty cubits. The Tabernacle's boards supported the coverings the way the walls of a house hold up its roof, as will be explained below. It is these coverings that united the Tabernacle into a single unit, which is why our passage begins with the statement *As for the Tabernacle itself, make it with ten sheets* (26:1) and ends with the summary *Join the sheets together so that the Tabernacle becomes one whole* (26:6).

VERSE 7

RABBI AVRAHAM BEN HARAMBAM

וְעָשִׂיתָ יְרִיעֹת עִזִּים – *Make sheets of goats' hair:* [Literally, "sheets of goats."] The verse refers to wool woven from goats' hair. There were two purposes to this second layer of sheets: The first was to increase the thickness of the roof, and the second was to protect the lower layer of more finely crafted sheets. Because this level was essentially protective, no great effort was expended in intricate weaving work. Rather, the material maintained its original black appearance.

ABARBANEL

וְעָשִׂיתָ יְרִיעֹת עִזִּים – *Make sheets of goats' hair:* This second level of goats' hair sheets was not artfully crafted. [Hence the term *maaseh ḥoshev,* used with regard to the inner

ח עַשְׁתֵּי־עֶשְׂרֵה יְרִיעֹת תַּעֲשֶׂה אֹתָם: אֹרֶךְ ׀ הַיְרִיעָה הָאַחַת
שְׁלֹשִׁים בָּאַמָּה וְרֹחַב אַרְבַּע בָּאַמָּה הַיְרִיעָה הָאֶחָת מִדָּה
ט אַחַת לְעַשְׁתֵּי עֶשְׂרֵה יְרִיעֹת: וְחִבַּרְתָּ אֶת־חֲמֵשׁ הַיְרִיעֹת
לְבָד וְאֶת־שֵׁשׁ הַיְרִיעֹת לְבָד וְכָפַלְתָּ אֶת־הַיְרִיעָה הַשִּׁשִּׁית
י אֶל־מוּל פְּנֵי הָאֹהֶל: וְעָשִׂיתָ חֲמִשִּׁים לֻלָאֹת עַל שְׂפַת
הַיְרִיעָה הָאֶחָת הַקִּיצֹנָה בַּחֹבָרֶת וַחֲמִשִּׁים לֻלָאֹת עַל שְׂפַת
יא הַיְרִיעָה הַחֹבֶרֶת הַשֵּׁנִית: וְעָשִׂיתָ קַרְסֵי נְחֹשֶׁת חֲמִשִּׁים
וְהֵבֵאתָ אֶת־הַקְּרָסִים בַּלֻּלָאֹת וְחִבַּרְתָּ אֶת־הָאֹהֶל וְהָיָה
יב אֶחָד: וְסֶרַח הָעֹדֵף בִּירִיעֹת הָאֹהֶל חֲצִי הַיְרִיעָה הָעֹדֶפֶת

ABARBANEL *(cont.)*

sheets in verse 1, does not appear here]. Nor were the figures of cherubim produced on it. For the main purpose of these sheets was to protect the layer that lay beneath them, which was intricately made and valuable. It is well known that an object made to protect something else is necessarily of inferior worth. This is what the Torah means when it states: *Make sheets of goats' hair as a tent over the Tabernacle*, that is, to shield the Tabernacle. Because of their secondary importance, the goats' hair sheets did not merit loops of sky-blue wool but of goats' hair, while the clasps that joined the sets were not of gold as they were for the sheets of linen and silk, but of inferior bronze.

SFORNO

לְאֹהֶל עַל־הַמִּשְׁכָּן – *As a tent over the Tabernacle:* For the Tabernacle itself [that is, the inner layer of coverings, also referred to as "Tabernacle"] was not meant to act as a shelter, but so that images of cherubim [woven into them] should surround the throne [the incense altar], the table, and the candelabrum.

VERSE 11

IBN EZRA

וְעָשִׂיתָ קַרְסֵי נְחֹשֶׁת חֲמִשִּׁים – *Make, also, fifty bronze clasps:* Since the inner layer of sheets was more valuable than the outer layer, which served to keep the rain out of the structure, the clasps for the exquisite lower sheets were fashioned out of gold, whereas those of the upper level were made out of less impressive bronze. Indeed, the Tabernacle's boards and rings [described later in the chapter] were also covered in gold, whereas I will later explain [in comments to Parashat Pekudei] why the sockets that held them were fashioned out of silver. The crossbars [that held the wall together] too were covered in gold, as were the pillars that held the curtain [separating the Tabernacle's two rooms]. But the sockets

8 Each sheet shall be thirty cubits long and four cubits wide, all
9 eleven sheets the same size. Join five of the sheets by themselves, and the other six by themselves. Fold the sixth sheet
10 over the front of the Tent. Make fifty loops on the edge of the
end sheet of one set, and fifty on the edge of the end sheet of the
11 other. Make, also, fifty bronze clasps. Put the clasps through the
loops, joining the tent together so that it becomes one whole.
12 As for the additional length of the tent sheets, the extra half

IBN EZRA (cont.)

that supported the hangings [surrounding the courtyard] were made out of bronze [as mandated in 27:18, because this external barrier was less important]. (Short Commentary)

VERSE 12

RASHI

וְסֶרַח הָעֹדֵף בִּירִיעֹת הָאֹהֶל – *As for the additional length of the tent sheets:* This refers to the extra material that exceeded the length of the lower layer of Tabernacle sheets. The term "curtains of the tent" refers to the upper layer of goats' hair sheets, called the "tent" in a later verse that states: *He made sheets of goats' hair for a tent over the Tabernacle* (36:14). The word "tent" connotes a roof, and it applies to these sheets because they formed a shelter and a covering over the lower layer of sheets. Now this second layer exceeded the length of the lower sheets on the west side by half a sheet-width [that is, by two cubits]. For one half of the additional, eleventh sheet overlapped the front of the Tabernacle [on the eastern side as mentioned in verse 9], and that left an excess of two cubits more than the lower layer, equal to half the width of a single sheet, which hung down in the west. תִּסְרַח עַל אֲחֹרֵי הַמִּשְׁכָּן – *Is to hang down at the rear of the Tabernacle:* This additional material covered up the two cubits of boards left exposed [by the shorter inner layer of sheets]. אֲחֹרֵי הַמִּשְׁכָּן – *At the rear of the Tabernacle:* The Torah calls the western side of the structure its back, because the opening to the Tabernacle stood in the east, and hence represented its front. The northern and southern walls were the Tabernacle's sides on the right and on the left.

RABBEINU BAHYA

וְסֶרַח הָעֹדֵף בִּירִיעֹת הָאֹהֶל – *As for the additional length of the tent sheets:* [There was one more of the outer sheets of goats' hair than there was of the inner sheets of wool and linen. The extra material was positioned as follows:] The Torah instructs that half of a sheet be folded down in front of the eastern side of the Tabernacle where the entrance to the building stood, as the verse states: *Fold the sixth sheet over the front of the Tent* (26:9). [Since each sheet was four cubits wide, this meant that two cubits of material hung over the edge of the structure's top.] Thus our Sages describe the Tabernacle as a bride who modestly covers her face with a veil. Meanwhile, half of a sheet extended the end of the cover on the western wall, as the verse states: *The extra half sheet is to hang down at the rear of the Tabernacle.* The western wall is referred to as the back of the Tabernacle, in contrast to the eastern wall which is called the front of the structure. (26:7)

יג תִּסְרַח עַל אֲחֹרֵי הַמִּשְׁכָּן׃ וְהָאַמָּה מִזֶּה וְהָאַמָּה מִזֶּה בָּעֹדֵף
בְּאֹרֶךְ יְרִיעֹת הָאֹהֶל יִהְיֶה סָרוּחַ עַל־צִדֵּי הַמִּשְׁכָּן מִזֶּה
יד וּמִזֶּה לְכַסֹּתוֹ׃ וְעָשִׂיתָ מִכְסֶה לָאֹהֶל עֹרֹת אֵילִם מְאָדָּמִים
וּמִכְסֵה עֹרֹת תְּחָשִׁים מִלְמָעְלָה׃
טו וְעָשִׂיתָ אֶת־הַקְּרָשִׁים לַמִּשְׁכָּן עֲצֵי שִׁטִּים עֹמְדִים׃ רביעי

VERSE 13

RASHI

וְהָאַמָּה מִזֶּה וְהָאַמָּה מִזֶּה – *The extra cubit at either end:* [The goats' hair sheets ran an extra cubit] down the north side and down the south side. בָּעֹדֵף בְּאֹרֶךְ יְרִיעֹת הָאֹהֶל – *At either end of each of the tent sheets:* The goats' hair sheets were each longer than those of the original layer by two cubits. [The sheets of this layer were thirty cubits long; the lower layer, twenty-eight cubits.] יִהְיֶה סָרוּחַ עַל־צִדֵּי הַמִּשְׁכָּן – *Should hang over the sides of the Tabernacle:* These hung down the northern and southern sides [completely covering the Tabernacle's walls] as I have explained above. The Torah thereby teaches us proper etiquette: One should always shelter and protect something precious.

RASHBAM

עַל־צִדֵּי הַמִּשְׁכָּן – *Over the sides of the Tabernacle:* The extra fabric of the goats' hair sheets covered up the cubit-high silver sockets [at the base of the boards], all the way down to the ground, since the height of the boards was ten cubits including the sockets. [The width of the goats' hair sheets was thirty cubits, and the Tabernacle was ten cubits wide. This interpretation assumes that the width of the walls themselves was negligible; see Shabbat 98b.]

BEKHOR SHOR

עַל צִדֵּי הַמִּשְׁכָּן – *Over the sides of the Tabernacle:* According to the most straightforward understanding of the verses, the Tabernacle's tent pegs were six cubits high, and the sheets were tied to the tops of these pegs spreading out like wings. [That is, the sheets descended to the ground diagonally. The author's perspective differs from the traditional view of the Tabernacle according to which the sheets hung straight down.] The exterior of the Tabernacle boards was covered with gold just like the inside surfaces were. And thus the gold of these walls was visible beneath the sheets which were held up.

VERSE 14

RASHI

מִכְסֶה לָאֹהֶל – *A covering for the tent:* The Torah now commands the fashioning of a cover for the goats' hair tent. Thus an additional covering was to be made, this one *from rams' hides dyed red*. On top of that would be another *covering of fine leather*. These curtains only covered the roof [and were not draped over the Tabernacle's walls], since they were only thirty cubits long and ten cubits wide. Such is the opinion of Rabbi Neḥemya [as expressed in Shabbat 28a], whereas Rabbi Yehuda maintains that our verse describes a single covering, half of which comprised *rams' hides dyed red* and half of which was *a covering of fine leather*.

13 sheet is to hang down at the rear of the Tabernacle. The extra
cubit at either end of each of the tent sheets should hang over
14 the sides of the Tabernacle to cover it on both sides. Make a
covering for the tent from rams' hides dyed red. Above it make
a covering of fine leather.
15 Make the upright boards for the Tabernacle of acacia wood. REVI'I

IBN EZRA

וְעָשִׂיתָ מִכְסֶה לָאֹהֶל – *Make a covering for the tent:* This was a covering over the goats' hair sheets to protect the lower coverings from rain.

ABARBANEL

וְעָשִׂיתָ מִכְסֶה לָאֹהֶל – *Make a covering for the tent:* After describing the sheets made out of goats' hair, which served as a shelter to protect the Tabernacle's valuable inner coverings, the text now mandates one additional layer of sheets. This was to be fashioned *from rams' hides dyed red* as well as *fine leather,* as a roof over the entire Tabernacle, including the sheets of goats' hair and the woven fabrics beneath it. This top canopy was intended to keep the rain and desert detritus out of the building. Thus there were three tents altogether: the first one composed of linen and silk, a second of goats' hair, and a final set made from rams' hides dyed red and fine leather, which was laid out above everything else. Now there are some commentators who believe that there were two covering layers: a rams' hide mantle which completely encompassed the goats' hair sheets, covering both the roof of the structure and its walls, and a covering of fine leather that only covered the top surface of the building – hence the phrase "above it" used with respect to the latter. I, however, take issue with this interpretation, since there was really only one protective layer of hides, not two. The Torah's later description of the Tabernacle's erection confirms this, as it states [in the singular]: *And placed the covering over the Tent, as the Lord had commanded him* (40:19).

VERSE 15

RASHI

וְעָשִׂיתָ אֶת־הַקְּרָשִׁים – *Make the boards:* It seems that the verse should have omitted the definite article and said merely "make upright boards." After all, such is the style used throughout this passage. [For example in verse 25:23, the Torah states: *Make a table,* not: "Make the table."] Why then does the text refer to the Tabernacle's boards as something already known? The Torah thereby teaches that the craftsmen were to fashion the walls out of wood that had already been designated for such usage. For our patriarch Yaakov planted trees in Egypt and on his deathbed instructed his sons to make sure to cut down the timber and transport it with them upon their departure from the country. Yaakov explained that the Holy One, blessed be He, would eventually command them to construct a Tabernacle in the wilderness out of acacia wood, and therefore it would behoove Israel to maintain a supply of that material for the project. This is what Shlomo Habavli [a tenth-century Italian Jewish liturgist] referred to in his poem [a *yotzer* for the morning of Passover] when he wrote: "He hurried to plant for the zealous, the cedar walls of our house

טז עֶשֶׂר אַמּוֹת אֹרֶךְ הַקָּרֶשׁ וְאַמָּה וַחֲצִי הָאַמָּה רֹחַב
יז הַקֶּרֶשׁ הָאֶחָד: שְׁתֵּי יָדוֹת לַקֶּרֶשׁ הָאֶחָד מְשֻׁלָּבֹת אִשָּׁה

RASHI (cont.)

[the Tabernacle]" – Israel eagerly prepared the materials for the structure long in advance. **עֲצֵי שִׁטִּים עֹמְדִים** – *Upright boards of acacia wood:* The Old French term for this position is *estantivs* ["upright"], meaning that the length of the boards must be arranged vertically to form the walls of the Tabernacle. Do not construct the walls by piling the boards on top of each other horizontally such that the widths of the boards comprise the structure's height.

IBN EZRA

וְעָשִׂיתָ אֶת־הַקְּרָשִׁים לַמִּשְׁכָּן – *Make the upright boards for the Tabernacle:* The term *mishkan* ["Tabernacle"] refers most specifically to the screens and the boards that defined the structure. **עֲצֵי שִׁטִּים עֹמְדִים** – *Upright boards of acacia wood:* The orientation of the wood in the boards was to be same as when it grew as trees, maintaining the height of the wood as the length of the boards [mentioned in the next verse]. The same is true when a person stands up [the direction of his growth is aligned vertically], as opposed to when he is lying down. Alternatively, the term might suggest that the wood should stand completely straight.

ḤIZKUNI

עֲצֵי שִׁטִּים עֹמְדִים – *Upright boards of acacia wood:* The Israelites were not to take acacia trees that had been felled long before, since their wood was likely rotten. Rather, this instruction demands that wood be harvested from standing trees that were still attached to the ground and growing in their natural position. The Torah further teaches us that is best to construct buildings from non-fruit-bearing trees.

VERSE 17

RASHI

שְׁתֵּי יָדוֹת לַקֶּרֶשׁ הָאֶחָד – *Each board should have two matching tenons:* The carpenter cut a groove down the middle of the bottom of each board to a height of a cubit, leaving a quarter [of the total width] intact on one side and a quarter intact on the other side. These two pins formed the tenons that our verse introduces. The groove between the tenons occupied half the width of the board, and it was situated precisely in the middle. The two tenons on each board were inserted into two hollow sockets, each one cubit long. Forty sockets [on each wall] were thus positioned one next to the other. Now the tenons themselves were chiseled on three sides before being inserted into their sockets, to a width equal to that of the sockets so that the board would cover the entire upper surface of the socket. For if shoulders were not carved around the tenons, the outside widths of the sockets of neighboring boards would create a space between adjoining planks. This is the meaning of the phrase *These should adjoin each other at the bottom* (26:24) – the thickness of each tenon should be pared down so that the boards could be positioned right next to each other. **מְשֻׁלָּבֹת** – *Matching:* The tenons were fashioned to look like rungs [*shelivot*] on a ladder,

16 **Each board shall be ten cubits long and one and a half cubits**
17 **wide. Each board should have two matching tenons; all the**

RASHI *(cont.)*

which have space in between them. Furthermore, the ends of the tenons were beveled to facilitate their insertion into the hollows of the socket, like a rung fits into a hole on the side of a ladder. **אִשָּׁה אֶל־אֲחֹתָהּ** – *Matching:* The two tenons on the end of each board were mirror images of each other, such that the shoulders around them were of identical dimensions. In other words, the stock removed from around one tenon could not be so great that that tenon would be situated closer to the middle of the board, while the other had less material carved away, thereby positioning it closer to the edge of the board. Rather, the shoulders should be of equal size across the handbreadth of the board, and the tenons would stand parallel to each other. The Targum renders the term *yadot* ["tenons"] as *tzirin* ["hinges"] since they resemble door hinges that fit into sockets in the doorframe.

RAMBAN

מְשֻׁלָּבֹת אִשָּׁה אֶל־אֲחֹתָהּ – *Matching:* [Alternatively, "flush with one another."] According to Rashi, the word *meshullavot* ["flush"] teaches that the ends of the tenons should be beveled so that they fit easily into the sockets. On the other hand, the phrase *isha el aḥotah* ["with one another"] reflects the requirement that the boards stand immediately adjacent one next to the other. But if this were so, the phrase should have been masculine – *ish el aḥiv* – considering that the Hebrew word *kerashim* ["boards"] is masculine. Still, Rashi might have meant that the *shelivot* [the rungs, or tenons, a feminine word] should align with each other, and that the shoulders created around the tenons should be exactly identical so that the boards would touch when erected next to each other. The ends of the tenons were thus not pared diagonally, since the interiors of the sockets were angled perfectly straight. Rather, the tenons were only cut on their sides to allow the boards to fit together. However, in the Baraita Dimlekhet Hamishkan I have found the following description: "Two pegs emerged from the boards, and these were inserted into corresponding holes, as the verse uses the word *meshullavot* – for the pegs resembled the rungs [*shelivot*] of a ladder." This seems to imply that our verse is commanding Moshe to fashion dowels on the sides of the boards that fit into holes on their neighboring boards. And here, the phrase in question is certainly referring to the to the rungs [or pegs, *shelivot*] themselves, a term which is feminine.

ABARBANEL

מְשֻׁלָּבֹת אִשָּׁה אֶל־אֲחֹתָהּ – *Matching:* This clause refers to tenons on neighboring boards [rather than the two tenons on each individual board], and states that these two pins should share a socket that holds the two boards together. What emerges is that each board had two sockets beneath it. [That is, every board had two tenons, but these were not inserted into the same socket. Rather, one tenon fit into a mortise that it shared with a tenon from the board to its right, and the other tenon fit into a mortise that it shared with a tenon from the board to its left.] Each socket sat beneath half of one board and half of another. The term for

יח אֶל־אֲחֹתָהּ כֵּן תַּעֲשֶׂה לְכֹל קַרְשֵׁי הַמִּשְׁכָּן: וְעָשִׂיתָ אֶת־
הַקְּרָשִׁים לַמִּשְׁכָּן עֶשְׂרִים קֶרֶשׁ לִפְאַת נֶגְבָּה תֵימָנָה:
יט וְאַרְבָּעִים אַדְנֵי־כֶסֶף תַּעֲשֶׂה תַּחַת עֶשְׂרִים הַקָּרֶשׁ שְׁנֵי
אֲדָנִים תַּחַת־הַקֶּרֶשׁ הָאֶחָד לִשְׁתֵּי יְדֹתָיו וּשְׁנֵי אֲדָנִים
כ תַּחַת־הַקֶּרֶשׁ הָאֶחָד לִשְׁתֵּי יְדֹתָיו: וּלְצֶלַע הַמִּשְׁכָּן הַשֵּׁנִית
כא לִפְאַת צָפוֹן עֶשְׂרִים קָרֶשׁ: וְאַרְבָּעִים אַדְנֵיהֶם כָּסֶף שְׁנֵי
אֲדָנִים תַּחַת הַקֶּרֶשׁ הָאֶחָד וּשְׁנֵי אֲדָנִים תַּחַת הַקֶּרֶשׁ
כב כג הָאֶחָד: וּלְיַרְכְּתֵי הַמִּשְׁכָּן יָמָּה תַּעֲשֶׂה שִׁשָּׁה קְרָשִׁים: וּשְׁנֵי
כד קְרָשִׁים תַּעֲשֶׂה לִמְקֻצְעֹת הַמִּשְׁכָּן בַּיַּרְכָתָיִם: וְיִהְיוּ תֹאֲמִם
מִלְּמַטָּה וְיַחְדָּו יִהְיוּ תַמִּים עַל־רֹאשׁוֹ אֶל־הַטַּבַּעַת הָאֶחָת

ABARBANEL *(cont.)*

these sockets is *eden*, which means "ear" in Arabic or Aramaic, since the letter *dalet* replaces the Hebrew letter *zayin*. [The Hebrew word for ear is *ozen*.] They were so called because they resembled that organ.

VERSE 18

RAMBAN

לִפְאַת נֶגְבָּה תֵימָנָה – *For the southern side:* [The Ramban discusses the Torah's terminology for directions.] The Torah uses the phrase *kedma mizraḥa* to refer to the east [in 27:13] because it always refers to the east as *kedem* [literally, "forward"], as in the verse *And you shall measure from outside the city on the east side [kedma] two thousand cubits* (Numbers 35:5). Scripture calls the west *aḥor* ["backward"], as in the verse *Behold, I go east, but He is not there; and west [aḥor], but I cannot perceive Him* (Job 23:8). Similarly, the text refers to the Mediterranean as *the Westward [haaḥaron] Sea* (Deuteronomy 34:2), since it lies to the west of the land of Israel. Both *kedem* and *aḥor* are colloquial terms, in which the language expresses the perspective of a person facing the light of the rising sun.... Now the Torah refers to the south as *negev* because the sun makes that direction arid [*nagguv*].... The west can also be called "seaward" [*yama* as in verse 22 of our chapter] since the Torah takes the perspective of people living in the land of Israel, of which the Mediterranean Sea forms the western border. The north, however, is merely called by its name – *tzafon* [as in verse 20], an appellation that derives from its "hidden" [*tzafun*] nature, since the sun is not visible there. The term *darom*, used to denote south in, for example, the verse *The wind goes toward the south [darom]* (Ecclesiastes 1:6), is really a contraction of two words – *dar rum* [meaning "lives in the height"] – since the sun attains its greatest height in that direction. The south is also called *yamin* ["right"] and the north *semol* ["left"], based on the orientation of a person facing east as I have mentioned.

18 Tabernacle's boards should be made in this way. Make twenty
19 boards for the southern side of the Tabernacle, and forty silver
sockets under the twenty boards, two sockets under the first
20 board for its two tenons, and two under the next. For the second
side of the Tabernacle, the northern side, there should be twen-
21 ty boards, along with their forty silver sockets, two under the
22 first board and two under each of the others. Make six boards
23 for the west side of the Tabernacle, and two additional boards
24 for the Tabernacle's rear corners. These should adjoin each
other at the bottom, and be joined together at the top by a ring.
So it should be for both sides; they shall form the two corners.

VERSE 22

RASHBAM

תַּעֲשֶׂה שִׁשָּׁה קְרָשִׁים – *Make six boards:* The total width of the six boards running north to south along the western wall was nine cubits [since each of the six boards was one and a half cubits wide]. This means that half a cubit was left exposed in the northwest corner and half a cubit was similarly not filled in in the southwest corner. [The interior of the Tabernacle building was ten cubits, with the back wall of the Holy of Holies covering just nine of those ten required cubits. This meant that on either side of the six boards there remained half a cubit that had to be accounted for. This explains] the need for *two additional boards for the Tabernacle's rear corners* (26:23). These boards too were cut to a width of one and a half cubits – one was positioned at the end of the northern wall to comprise the final half cubit of that side, while the other was placed at the end of the southern wall to make up the final half cubit in that direction. Meanwhile the extra cubit on each of the two corner boards was covered by the width of the north wall on one side and of the south wall on the opposite one. [Running perpendicular to the west wall were the north and south boards, which were all one cubit thick.] Thus the north and south walls covered the protruding cubit on either side of the western wall, and the interior space of the Tabernacle remained ten cubits wide. On the outside of the building the corners were therefore perfect right angles.

VERSE 24

RASHI

אֶל־הַטַּבַּעַת הָאֶחָת – *By a ring:* Two slits were cut across the width of the boards on either side [near the edge of the board]. The width of these slits was equal to the thickness of the rings that would be placed in them. A ring [like a bracket] was thus placed through the slits of two neighboring boards, holding them together. I do not know whether these rings were placed on the boards permanently or whether they were movable. Meanwhile the corner boards had a ring that encompassed both the thickness of the southern or northern wall board and the top of the adjacent corner board on the western side, thus joining the perpendicular walls.

כה כֵּן יִהְיֶה לִשְׁנֵיהֶם לִשְׁנֵי הַמִּקְצֹעֹת יִהְיוּ: וְהָיוּ שְׁמֹנָה קְרָשִׁים
וְאַדְנֵיהֶם כֶּסֶף שִׁשָּׁה עָשָׂר אֲדָנִים שְׁנֵי אֲדָנִים תַּחַת הַקֶּרֶשׁ
כו הָאֶחָד וּשְׁנֵי אֲדָנִים תַּחַת הַקֶּרֶשׁ הָאֶחָד: וְעָשִׂיתָ בְרִיחִם
כז עֲצֵי שִׁטִּים חֲמִשָּׁה לְקַרְשֵׁי צֶלַע־הַמִּשְׁכָּן הָאֶחָד: וַחֲמִשָּׁה
בְרִיחִם לְקַרְשֵׁי צֶלַע־הַמִּשְׁכָּן הַשֵּׁנִית וַחֲמִשָּׁה בְרִיחִם

RALBAG

וְיִהְיוּ תֹאֲמִם מִלְּמַטָּה – *These should adjoin each other at the bottom:* What this means is that the two corner boards should be both aligned with the western wall boards and attached to the adjoining north and south walls. The corner pieces were to be held in place at their tops with rings just like all the boards along the two long walls. These attachments would have the additional effect of ensuring that the heights of all the boards aligned. The rings on the corner boards were positioned along their thickness and lined up with the rings that were oriented along the widths of the northern and southern boards. What emerged is that when the crossbars [described in verses 26–29] were inserted through the rings on the long sides they culminated on the rings of the western wall thereby strengthening the structure. The rings were fixed permanently into the boards so that the building would take shape when the crossbars were placed through them.

VERSE 26

RASHI

בְרִיחִם – *Crossbars:* The five crossbars mentioned in this verse were actually only three, for both the top bar and the bottom bar on each side of the structure were composed of two separate pieces. The first piece [of the upper and lower horizontal crossbars] stretched the length of half the wall it was supporting, while a second piece held together the second half of the wall. In other words, one piece was inserted in the ring from one side of the structure until it reached the halfway mark of the wall, while a second piece was inserted from the other direction meeting its partner in the middle. Thus the upper crossbar and the lower crossbar were really two sections each, for a total of four pieces. However, the middle crossbar was a single long piece that stretched the whole length of the wall it was supporting. It passed clear through from one end of the wall to the other, as the verse states: *The central crossbar should go through the middle of the boards from one end to the other* (26:28). The upper and lower crossbars were held in place by a series of rings, two of which were fastened to each of the boards [one near the top for the upper crossbar, and a lower ring near the base for the bottom crossbar]. The ten cubits of the boards' height were thereby divided into four equal sections. The space from the upper ring to the top of the board was the first, and the space between the lower ring to the bottom was the last. Each of these spaces took up one quarter of the board's length. The space between those two rings was further divided into two additional sections [by the middle crossbar]. Following this arrangement, all of the rings were evenly placed in straight rows next to each other. The middle crossbar, however, had no rings, because the boards were bored through the middle of the boards

25 So there should be eight boards and sixteen silver sockets, two
26 sockets under each board. Make crossbars, too, of acacia wood,
27 five for the boards of the first side of the Tabernacle, five for the
boards of the second side of the Tabernacle, and five for the

RASHI *(cont.)*

themselves. The holes were perfectly aligned, allowing that crossbar to pass directly from one board to the next. This is what the verse means when it states: *The central crossbar should go through the middle of the boards* (26:28). Now the lengths of the four upper and lower crossbars, which were oriented along the north and south walls of the Tabernacle, were each fifteen cubits long [half the total length of the structure], whereas the length of the middle crossbar stretched the full thirty cubits, as the verse states: *From one end to the other,* i.e., from the east wall to the west wall. With regard to the five crossbars that supported the west wall, the upper and the lower crossbars were each six cubits long [so that the two upper crossbars together and the two lower crossbars together covered the twelve-cubit width of the Tabernacle], while the middle crossbar [running through the wall's center] ran the full length of twelve cubits that comprised the total of the eight boards on this side. This description follows Baraita Dimlekhet Hamishkan.

ḤIZKUNI

וְעָשִׂיתָ בְרִיחִם – *Make crossbars:* According to Rashi, the ten-cubit height of the boards was divided to host the crossbars. The same pattern was followed for the placement of the crossbars of the Tabernacle boards as is employed today for stitching together Torah scrolls with animal sinew, and the same spacing is followed for the establishment of cities of refuge in the land of Israel. [When sewing the separate parchment sheets of a Torah scroll together, the sinew thread is not sewn either right to the top or bottom to prevent the tearing of the scroll, but some distance from the two edges, and again in the middle. Regarding the cities, six towns were set up in the land of Israel to harbor manslaughterers – three on the west side of the Jordan River and three on the east side. The northern cities were not placed directly at the northern border of the country, nor were the southern cities situated at the furthest southern point of the land, but some distance from the ends of the country.]

VERSE 27

RASHBAM

וַחֲמִשָּׁה בְרִיחִם לְקַרְשֵׁי צֶלַע־הַמִּשְׁכָּן – *Five crossbars for the side of the Tabernacle:* Each board was fitted with five rings, one beneath the other on a vertical line, to hold the supportive crossbars. In addition to these pieces there was a middle pole that ran through the centers of the planks. Holes were bored through the widths of the boards to accommodate this middle crossbar. Thus the Tabernacle walls were held together by sockets at the bottoms of the boards, external crossbars, and one internal crossbar, with the latter providing the greatest amount of strength to the building. Now according to the straightforward meaning of the text, there were three internal crossbars running the length of the three walls – one inside the north wall, one in the south side, and the third through the western wall. Thanks to holes in the corner pieces, the north and south crossbars connected those walls to the

כח לְקַרְשֵׁי צֶלַע הַמִּשְׁכָּן לַיַּרְכָתַיִם יָמָּה: וְהַבְּרִיחַ הַתִּיכֹן בְּתוֹךְ
כט הַקְּרָשִׁים מַבְרִחַ מִן־הַקָּצֶה אֶל־הַקָּצֶה: וְאֶת־הַקְּרָשִׁים
תְּצַפֶּה זָהָב וְאֶת־טַבְּעֹתֵיהֶם תַּעֲשֶׂה זָהָב בָּתִּים לַבְּרִיחִם
ל וְצִפִּיתָ אֶת־הַבְּרִיחִם זָהָב: וַהֲקֵמֹתָ אֶת־הַמִּשְׁכָּן כְּמִשְׁפָּטוֹ
לא אֲשֶׁר הָרְאֵיתָ בָּהָר: וְעָשִׂיתָ פָרֹכֶת תְּכֵלֶת כ חמישי

RASHBAM *(cont.)*

western side, linking all three walls together. However, according to our Sages [see Shabbat 98b], there was one central crossbar that, when inserted, miraculously made a right-angle turn when it reached each corner [and thus was able to hold together all three walls].

VERSE 29

RASHI

בָּתִּים לַבְּרִיחִם – *Rings for the crossbars:* The rings that you fasten to the boards will serve as holders for the crossbars after you insert them. **וְצִפִּיתָ אֶת־הַבְּרִיחִם זָהָב** – *The crossbars too should be overlaid with gold:* The poles that comprised the crossbars were not themselves actually overlaid with gold; they had no covering at all. Rather, the rings held gold tubes that served as sheaths for the crossbars like hollow reeds. These pieces extended on either side of the ring such that they spanned the width of the boards from the ring [in the middle of each board] to either edge. The crossbars entered the opening of one holder and extended from it to the opening of the next sheath at the next ring. Thus the crossbars truly were wrapped in gold when they were fastened to the boards. Note that the crossbars supported the walls from the outside of the Tabernacle, such that they projected on the exterior side of the walls and were not visible on the inside, just as the rings and tubes were also not apparent from the structure's interior. The insides of the walls were completely smooth [with nothing protruding from them].

SFORNO

וְאֶת־טַבְּעֹתֵיהֶם תַּעֲשֶׂה זָהָב – *And make gold rings:* [Literally, "and make their rings of gold." But no such rings have been introduced yet. Sforno explains:] Unless otherwise stated, we expect crossbars to be supported by rings. Hence the text makes special note of the exceptional arrangement for the central crossbar, which ran through the middle of the boards and was not held in place by rings, as the verse states: *The central crossbar should go through the middle of the boards* (26:28).

VERSE 30

RAV SE'ADYA GAON

כְּמִשְׁפָּטוֹ – *According to the plan:* Moshe would follow the schematics he was shown by God.

RASHI

וַהֲקֵמֹתָ אֶת־הַמִּשְׁכָּן – *So shall you set up the Tabernacle:* Set up the Tabernacle after all the components have been produced. **הָרְאֵיתָ בָּהָר** – *You were shown on the*

28 boards of the western side of the Tabernacle at the rear. The
central crossbar should go through the middle of the boards
29 from one end to the other. Overlay the boards with gold, and
make gold rings for the crossbars. The crossbars too should be
30 overlaid with gold. So shall you set up the Tabernacle, according
31 to the plan you were shown on the mountain. Make a HAMISHI

RASHI (cont.)

mountain: As you will be shown prior to assembling the Tabernacle, for I will demonstrate to you the sequence of setting up the structure. [A more fitting translation according to Rashi would be "you will have been shown."]

IBN EZRA

וַהֲקֵמֹתָ אֶת־הַמִּשְׁכָּן – *So shall you set up the Tabernacle:* [Moshe would not set up the structure all by himself, but rather] instruct wise men in how to do so. Alternatively, Moshe was given the order to begin the activity of assembling the Tabernacle, while others were encouraged to join him. For many hands were required to aid in putting the structure together.

RABBI AVRAHAM BEN HARAMBAM

כְּמִשְׁפָּטוֹ – *According to the plan:* This term derives from the word *mishpat* [meaning "law"]. For Moshe was legally bound to follow the plans he was shown prophetically.

GUR ARYEH

וַהֲקֵמֹתָ אֶת־הַמִּשְׁכָּן – *So shall you set up the Tabernacle:* According to Rashi, this command means that Moshe was to set up the Tabernacle "only after it was finished." [This is the literal sense of Rashi's first comment on this verse; the translation in this edition has been emended to give Rashi's sense, which the author will now explain:] What the exegete is trying to say is that the instruction to set up the Tabernacle is not meant to follow directly on the heels of the directive to manufacture the structure's boards [which immediately precedes it]. In other words, it does not mean: "Erect the Tabernacle right after you finish fashioning the boards." The Torah could not possibly intend such a thing, since after the planks were prepared there were still other components of the Tabernacle that had to be made. For example, after discussing the planks for the boards, the Torah introduces the curtain [in verse 31], the outer altar [in chapter 27], and the golden incense altar [in chapter 30]. Hence why would the Torah instruct Moshe to set up the Tabernacle with merely the boards? This then is why Rashi explains that the command in this verse must only take effect after all the parts of the enterprise have been finished.

VERSE 31

RASHBAM

פָּרֹכֶת – *A curtain:* This curtain was to serve as a barrier separating one chamber of the Tabernacle from the other. מַעֲשֵׂה חֹשֵׁב – *Worked into it:* [Literally, "the work of a

וְאַרְגָּמָן וְתוֹלַעַת שָׁנִי וְשֵׁשׁ מָשְׁזָר מַעֲשֵׂה חֹשֵׁב יַעֲשֶׂה
לב אֹתָהּ כְּרֻבִים׃ וְנָתַתָּה אֹתָהּ עַל־אַרְבָּעָה עַמּוּדֵי שִׁטִּים
לג מְצֻפִּים זָהָב וָוֵיהֶם זָהָב עַל־אַרְבָּעָה אַדְנֵי־כָסֶף׃ וְנָתַתָּה
אֶת־הַפָּרֹכֶת תַּחַת הַקְּרָסִים וְהֵבֵאתָ שָׁמָּה מִבֵּית לַפָּרֹכֶת
אֵת אֲרוֹן הָעֵדוּת וְהִבְדִּילָה הַפָּרֹכֶת לָכֶם בֵּין הַקֹּדֶשׁ וּבֵין

RASHBAM *(cont.)*

designer."] The Torah here commands that a craftsman be employed to fashion the curtain. The term *maaseh ḥoshev* connotes the artful weaving of figures into the fabric. This differs from the alternative term *maaseh rokem* [appearing in verse 36], which describes a design embroidered onto the surface of material with a needle.

IBN EZRA

וְעָשִׂיתָ פָרֹכֶת – *Make a curtain:* King Shlomo similarly fashioned a curtain for the entrance to the Holy of Holies in the Temple, covering an opening in a wall built there – a structure that was perhaps made of wood. The length of that building stood at sixty cubits, with Rashi arguing that the Sanctuary [the outer room in the Temple building] measured forty cubits, and the Holy of Holies twenty cubits. The posts that held the curtain in the Tabernacle were inserted into *sockets of silver* (26:32), to honor the Ark [which stood inside]. Now the Holy of Holies in the Temple was twice as long, twice as wide, and twice as high as the same space in the Tabernacle.

KELI YAKAR

וְעָשִׂיתָ פָרֹכֶת תְּכֵלֶת – *Make a curtain of sky-blue:* There were three differences between the curtain [described here], which separated the Holy of Holies chamber from the Sanctuary room, and the screen that closed the Tabernacle building off from the courtyard outside [outlined in verses 36–37]. Firstly, the curtain was woven with images of cherubim – *maaseh ḥoshev* – while the screen was decorated through embroidery – *maaseh rokem*. Secondly, the curtain was held up by four posts, and the screen by five pillars. And thirdly, the curtain's pillars stood in silver sockets, whereas those of the screen were supported by bronze sockets. These variances can be explained by the fact that the High Priest was only permitted to enter the Holy of Holies on Yom Kippur. On that day, the people of Israel are compared to the ministering angels, also known as cherubim, because their physicality is suppressed [through fasting], leaving the nation defined solely by their intellectual side – called *maaseh ḥoshev* [literally, "the product of a thinker"]. This is why the curtain leading into the Holy of Holies was woven with this art to produce designs of angels. Similarly, the silver sockets of the curtain's posts symbolize the day's character of forgiveness, since silver-white is the color of atonement, as we hope that our sins will be washed clean like snow. Furthermore, on Yom Kippur, the High Priest conducted the service wearing four white garments, as described in Parashat Aḥarei Mot [Leviticus 16:4, which explains why the curtain was held up by four pillars]. However, the screen that stood at the entrance to

curtain of sky-blue, purple, and scarlet wool, and finely spun
32 **linen with a design of cherubim worked into it. Hang it on four**
gold-covered posts of acacia wood with gold hooks, set on
33 **four sockets of silver. Hang the curtain under the clasps and**
bring the Ark of the Testimony behind it, so that the curtain

KELI YAKAR *(cont.)*

the Tabernacle separated the Sanctuary from the altar, an object that atoned for sins and transgressions committed through our five senses, which are represented by the five pillars that supported the screen. And since the catalyst for all human disobedience was the original serpent [*naḥash*], the screen's pillars stood within sockets of bronze [*neḥoshet*]. Finally, the images on the screen were produced with embroidery [*maaseh rokem*] as a symbol of the creation of mankind, as the verse states: *I was made in secret, and curiously wrought [rukkamti] in the lowest parts of the earth* (Psalms 139:15).

VERSE 32

RASHBAM

וָוֵיהֶם זָהָב – *Gold hooks:* Hooks like forks were attached to the posts, which in turn held the top hem of the curtain in place.

ḤIZKUNI

עַל־אַרְבָּעָה עַמּוּדֵי שִׁטִּים – *On four posts of acacia wood:* These four posts stood within the interior of the Holy of Holies, across its width. They presented no real obstruction to movement within the building, since the inner room was only used one day a year, during the Yom Kippur services. On the other hand, there were five posts situated at the entrance to the Sanctuary [as mandated by verse 26:37]. One of those was placed near the south wall of the Tabernacle, one near the north wall, and the remaining three were situated in the middle of the entrance space leading into the building. Since the priests entered and left the structure at that spot, having more than three posts there would have impeded easy movement in and out. Some commentators explain that the interior curtain was supported by just four posts because these were erected between the two sides of the Tabernacle, making it possible to stretch a rod to hold the curtain by affixing its two ends to the north and south walls. But the screen positioned in front of the entrance to the structure hung under the open sky, and its rod could not be attached to the walls on either side. Thus five posts were required to support the screen. However, this approach seems illogical to me, since it was the posts that held up the screen [and not the walls] – note that Rashi writes that the ends of hooks were bent so that a rod could rest on them. Rather, the first understanding I have offered is correct.

VERSE 33

RASHBAM

וְנָתַתָּה אֶת־הַפָּרֹכֶת תַּחַת הַקְּרָסִים – *Hang the curtain under the clasps:* This refers to the gold clasps [that joined the two sets of five sheets together; see 26:6] twenty cubits from the Tabernacle's entrance. For the building had a total length of thirty cubits, and the row of

לד קֹדֶשׁ הַקֳּדָשִׁים: וְנָתַתָּ אֶת־הַכַּפֹּרֶת עַל אֲרוֹן הָעֵדֻת בְּקֹדֶשׁ
לה הַקֳּדָשִׁים: וְשַׂמְתָּ אֶת־הַשֻּׁלְחָן מִחוּץ לַפָּרֹכֶת וְאֶת־הַמְּנֹרָה
נֹכַח הַשֻּׁלְחָן עַל צֶלַע הַמִּשְׁכָּן תֵּימָנָה וְהַשֻּׁלְחָן תִּתֵּן עַל־
לו צֶלַע צָפוֹן: וְעָשִׂיתָ מָסָךְ לְפֶתַח הָאֹהֶל תְּכֵלֶת וְאַרְגָּמָן

RASHBAM *(cont.)*

clasps was located in the middle of the forty-cubit-long covering of ten sheets. [The first set of ten sheets, twenty cubits long, began at the east side of the building and ended ten cubits from the rear. The second stretched from there ten cubits to the Tabernacle's back edge and hung down ten cubits over the wall.] The curtain was thus twenty cubits from the eastern entrance to the Sanctuary. The additional ten cubits that separated the curtain from the back, or western, wall of the structure comprised the length of the Holy of Holies.

RAMBAN

וְהֵבֵאתָ שָׁמָּה מִבֵּית לַפָּרֹכֶת אֵת אֲרוֹן הָעֵדוּת – *And bring the Ark of the Testimony behind it:* God did not command Moshe to fulfill the commands of this verse in the sequence they were issued. That is, he did not have to first *hang the curtain under the clasps,* and only then *bring the Ark of the Testimony behind it.* For this passage does not actually represent instructions for the erection of the Tabernacle, but merely provides designs for the components that had to be fashioned for it. Similarly, when the verse states: *Put the cover on the Ark of the Testimony in the Holy of Holies* (26:34), that does not mean that the Ark's cover was to be put into place only after the Ark was placed inside that chamber. Here, the purpose of our verse was to explain to Moshe that the curtain should be hung directly beneath the row of clasps, with the Ark on the inside of the partition, *so that the curtain separates the holy place from the Holy of Holies.* Thus we are informed that the Ark cover with its cherubim was situated within the Holy of Holies, which in turn is located behind the curtain. However, when the Torah later commands that the Tabernacle be assembled, it first instructs: *Put [the tablets] in it the Ark of the Testimony,* and only then: *Screen the Ark with the curtain* (40:3). Subsequent verses report that this sequence was indeed followed, as the text first states: *He took the covenant and put it in the Ark. He inserted the carrying staves into the Ark and placed the cover on top of it. He brought the Ark into the Tabernacle* (40:20–21), followed by: *And hung the cloth curtain, screening off the Ark of the Testimony, as the Lord had commanded him* (40:21).

RABBEINU BAḤYA

וְהִבְדִּילָה הַפָּרֹכֶת – *So that the curtain separates:* Behind the curtain stood the Ark of the Covenant, the Ark cover, and the cherubim that adorned it. This sat upon the Foundation Stone [in the Temple built later] at the west end of the Holy of Holies. Sitting in front of the Ark were the jar of manna [mentioned in 16:33], the jar of anointing oil, Aharon's staff complete with its almonds and blossoms [as described in Numbers 17:21–26], and the High Priest's garments. On the other side of the curtain [in the Sanctuary room] stood the table, the candelabrum, and the incense altar. The table was positioned near the northern wall, and the candelabrum near the southern wall, with the altar situated between them but placed somewhat closer to the hall's entrance.

34 separates the holy place from the Holy of Holies. Put the cover
35 on the Ark of the Testimony in the Holy of Holies. The table
shall be placed on the north side of the Tabernacle outside the
curtain, and the candelabrum on the south side, opposite the
36 table. Make a screen for the entrance to the Tent, embroidered
with sky-blue, purple, and scarlet wool and finely spun linen.

ABARBANEL

וְהִבְדִּילָה הַפָּרֹכֶת לָכֶם – *So that the curtain separates:* What this description implies is that should any person look into the Sanctuary, he would not be able to view the Ark cover or the cherubim that emerged from its top. As for the word *lakhem* ["for you," plural, untranslated in this edition], it refers only to Israelites and the priests [who were prohibited from entering the Holy of Holies], but not to Moshe, who was able to enter the inner sanctum at any time to commune with God face to face.

VERSE 35

RASHI

וְשַׂמְתָּ אֶת־הַשֻּׁלְחָן – *The table shall be placed:* The table [described in chapter 25] sat on the north side of the Tabernacle room, two and a half cubits from the northern wall. The candelabrum opposite it stood two and a half cubits from the southern wall. The golden incense altar was situated in the space between the table and the candelabrum, but it was positioned closer to the east opening [than the other furniture]. But all three items stood past the halfway mark of the chamber. How was that? There were twenty cubits from the opening of the Tabernacle to the curtain separating the first room from the Holy of Holies, and the altar, the table, and the candelabrum were all placed in the western half of that space.

ḤIZKUNI

וְאֶת־הַמְּנֹרָה נֹכַח הַשֻּׁלְחָן – *And the candelabrum opposite the table:* The candelabrum was so placed in order to illuminate the table. As a later verse states: *When you light the lamps, the seven lamps shall give light opposite the body of the candelabrum* (Numbers 8:2), meaning that the seven lamps are intended to cast light toward the table standing on the opposite wall. **עַל צֶלַע הַמִּשְׁכָּן תֵּימָנָה** – *On the south side:* The light should always be in the south, corresponding to the sun which travels toward that direction. [In the northern hemisphere, the sun is always in the southern half of the sky.]

VERSE 36

IBN EZRA

מַעֲשֵׂה רֹקֵם – *Embroidered:* The term *maaseh rokem* connotes needlework that is inferior to *maasei ḥoshev* [the term used above to describe the curtain]. The posts from which the screen hung were covered in gold, as were the hooks attached to them, out of respect for God. However, the sockets that held these pillars were fashioned out of bronze [rather than silver], because this screen was in the middle. [That is, it was in an intermediate position between the curtain, which concealed the Holy of Holies, and the outer screen at the entrance to the Tabernacle's courtyard. The two outer screens were considered less holy than the one that concealed the inner sanctum, and as such they were made of more mundane materials.]

לז וְתוֹלַעַת שָׁנִי וְשֵׁשׁ מָשְׁזָר מַעֲשֵׂה רֹקֵם: וְעָשִׂיתָ לַמָּסָךְ
חֲמִשָּׁה עַמּוּדֵי שִׁטִּים וְצִפִּיתָ אֹתָם זָהָב וָוֵיהֶם זָהָב וְיָצַקְתָּ
כז א לָהֶם חֲמִשָּׁה אַדְנֵי נְחֹשֶׁת: וְעָשִׂיתָ אֶת־הַמִּזְבֵּחַ ששי
עֲצֵי שִׁטִּים חָמֵשׁ אַמּוֹת אֹרֶךְ וְחָמֵשׁ אַמּוֹת רֹחַב רָבוּעַ יִהְיֶה
ב הַמִּזְבֵּחַ וְשָׁלֹשׁ אַמּוֹת קֹמָתוֹ: וְעָשִׂיתָ קַרְנֹתָיו עַל אַרְבַּע

RABBI AVRAHAM BEN HARAMBAM

וְעָשִׂיתָ מָסָךְ – *Make a screen:* This was meant to be a divider similar to the curtain, but fashioned differently. Because of this, the Torah refers to them by distinct names, labeling the first a "curtain" [*parokhet*], and the second a screen [*masakh*]. The latter word is related to the term *sukka,* and both are built from the root *samekh-kaf-kaf,* meaning "covering." Thus a later verse states: *He brought the Ark into the Tabernacle, and hung the cloth curtain [parokhet hamasakh], screening off [vayasekh] the Ark of the Testimony, as the Lord had commanded him* (40:21). **מַעֲשֵׂה רֹקֵם** – *Embroidered:* The difference between *maaseh rokem* and *maasei ḥoshev* [the term used with regard to the curtain], is that the latter produces identical pictures on both sides of the fabric, whereas the former is only capable of creating an image on one side of the material.

CHAPTER 27, VERSE 1

RAV SE'ADYA GAON

וְעָשִׂיתָ אֶת־הַמִּזְבֵּחַ – *Make the altar:* The Torah now introduces the altar upon which sacrifices would be offered.

RABBI AVRAHAM BEN HARAMBAM

וְעָשִׂיתָ אֶת־הַמִּזְבֵּחַ – *Make the altar:* According to the basic description of the altar provided by the text, it comprised planks nailed together to form a square box. Its corners were pronounced as they are on a chest. The dimensions of the object measured five cubits long by five cubits wide. According to our Sages, of blessed memory [see Zevaḥim 59b], the height of the altar was ten cubits. And as for the figure of three cubits mentioned in our verse, that number refers only to the height of the wood pile [the top section of the altar where the wood for the fire was placed].

RALBAG

רָבוּעַ יִהְיֶה הַמִּזְבֵּחַ – *It should be square:* By including this detail, it seems that the Torah does not insist that the altar be exactly five cubits long by five cubits wide, since if it did, the words "it should be square" would be redundant. However, the Torah does insist that the altar be square and three cubits tall – corresponding to the height of a human being. Still, since we find that the altar fashioned by Shlomo was ten cubits high, we must conclude that [since Moshe's altar must have been ten cubits tall as well] the three cubits mentioned in our verse cannot refer to the entire height of the object. Rather the number three relates to the height from the top of the ledge [*karkov,* on the side of the altar]

37 Make five posts of acacia wood for the screen and overlay them
with gold; their hooks, also, shall be of gold. Cast for them, too,
27 1 five sockets of bronze. Make the altar from acacia SHISHI
wood. It should be square, five cubits long, five cubits wide,
2 and three cubits high. Make horns for it on its four corners, the
horns being of one piece with it, and overlay it with bronze.

RALBAG *(cont.)*

to the wood pile [on the altar's top surface]. Now the *karkov* is the same as the *sovev* [a parallel term mentioned in the Talmud], and it was situated at the midpoint of the structure. This is made clear in the subsequent verse *The grate should be set below, under the ledge of the altar, so that the mesh reaches the middle of the altar* (27:5). Beneath it was the base of the altar mentioned in Parashat Vayikra [Leviticus 4:7]. Now that we have established that the altar's height was greater than three cubits, we must nevertheless concede that since the verse does state: *And three cubits high,* should an altar be made even to that minimum height, it would be acceptable as fit for sacrifice.

ABARBANEL

וְעָשִׂיתָ אֶת־הַמִּזְבֵּחַ – *Make the altar:* The Torah here commands that *the* altar be made, employing the definite article. This hints at how the entire nation of Israel had been waiting for God to command the construction of the altar upon which the sacrifices would be offered. This was the item that would make Israel like all the other ancient nations who worshipped their deities through offerings and sacrifices. So too did Adam, Noaḥ, Avraham, Yitzḥak, and Yaakov, bring animal oblations to God. Note that Israel had already been commanded at Mount Sinai: *Make for Me an altar of earth and on that sacrifice your burnt offerings and peace offerings, your sheep and your cattle* (20:21), and the Torah reports that Moshe, upon establishing the Torah covenant, built an altar at the foot of the mountain [see 24:4–8]. Hence, when God states here: *Make the altar,* it means that the altar that the nation would employ to offer sacrifices to God should be constructed in the courtyard of the Tabernacle, in front of the entrance to the Sanctuary.... The verse instructs that the altar should be made *from acacia wood,* referring to just the walls of the structure. The walls, but not the top, were constructed out of planks of wood, and the interior was filled with earth. Hence the earlier text calls it *an altar of earth* (20:21). Had the entire structure been composed of solid wood, it would have quickly burned to the ground, since the Torah states: *The fire shall ever be burning upon the altar; it shall never go out* (Leviticus 6:6). The altar is called a *mizbeaḥ* in Hebrew because that was where the priests would sacrifice – *yizbeḥu* – the animals and cast their blood. Still, the incense altar is also referred to as a *mizbeaḥ* [even though it did not host any animal sacrifices] because its design resembled that of the larger altar.

VERSE 2

ABARBANEL

וְעָשִׂיתָ קַרְנֹתָיו עַל אַרְבַּע פִּנֹּתָיו – *Make horns for it on its four corners:* The protrusions on the corners of the altar are called "horns" because they rise at the sides like an animal's

ג פִּנֹּתָיו מִמֶּנּוּ תִּהְיֶיןָ קַרְנֹתָיו וְצִפִּיתָ אֹתוֹ נְחֹשֶׁת: וְעָשִׂיתָ
סִּירֹתָיו לְדַשְּׁנוֹ וְיָעָיו וּמִזְרְקֹתָיו וּמִזְלְגֹתָיו וּמַחְתֹּתָיו לְכׇל־
ד כֵּלָיו תַּעֲשֶׂה נְחֹשֶׁת: וְעָשִׂיתָ לּוֹ מִכְבָּר מַעֲשֵׂה רֶשֶׁת נְחֹשֶׁת
וְעָשִׂיתָ עַל־הָרֶשֶׁת אַרְבַּע טַבְּעֹת נְחֹשֶׁת עַל אַרְבַּע קְצוֹתָיו:

ABARBANEL *(cont.)*

horns. These fixtures were hollow, and this allowed blood to be poured through them down to the ground to the base of the altar. From there, the blood descended to the depths of the earth and was never seen at all. **מִמֶּנּוּ תִּהְיֶיןָ קַרְנֹתָיו** – *The horns being of one piece with it:* This clause means that the horns should extend directly in a straight line out from the wooden altar. They should not veer inward or stick outward. Rather, they should be aligned with the walls of the main body of the structure. **וְצִפִּיתָ אֹתוֹ נְחֹשֶׁת** – *And overlay it with bronze:* Although the altar was covered in bronze, it was done so equally everywhere. For the bronze was only applied from the midpoint upward, as I will explain [in comments on verse 5].

KELI YAKAR

וְעָשִׂיתָ קַרְנֹתָיו – *Make horns for it:* The function of the horns is to atone for sinners, who are compared to horned rams attempting to gore heaven in rebellion. Thus the verses state: *I said to the arrogant, Deal not arrogantly! and to the wicked, Lift not the horn. Lift not your horn on high: speak not with an insolent neck* (Psalms 75:5–6). **וְצִפִּיתָ אֹתוֹ נְחֹשֶׁת** – *And overlay it with bronze:* According to Rashi, the bronze alludes to the insolence of a sinner, as the verse states: *Because I know that you are obstinate, and your neck is an iron sinew, and your forehead bronze* (Isaiah 48:4). This supports what we have written above, since all horns emerge from an animal's forehead.

VERSE 3

RASHI

לְדַשְּׁנוֹ – *For removing its ashes:* The ashes from the top of the altar were swept into these pots. Thus Onkelos translates the phrase as "to remove the ashes into them." [The word *ledashen,* which literally seems to mean "to ash," thus actually means "to remove ash."] For there are certain words in the Hebrew language that can express opposite meanings, denoting both construction and destruction. For example, we read in one verse: *You did cause it to take deep root [vatashresh]* (Psalms 80:10), and similarly, *I have seen the foolish taking root [mashrish]* (Job 5:3). But the same term appears with the opposite meaning in the verse, *would root out [tesharesh] all my increase* (Job 31:12). In our verse as well, the term *ledasheno* actually means "to clear away the ashes." **וּמִזְרְקֹתָיו** – *Basins:* These utensils would be used to collect the blood from the sacrificial animals. **וּמִזְלְגֹתָיו** – *Forks:* These were fashioned like hooks which were stuck into the flesh of the sacrifice to turn the meat over on top of the wood coals. This action would expedite the burning of the sacrifice. **וּמַחְתֹּתָיו** – *Pans:* These were receptacles used to carry coals from the outer altar to the inner altar where they were employed to burn the incense. The objects were referred to as *maḥtot* because of the raking [*ḥatiyya*] done with them.

3 Make pots for removing its ashes, together with shovels, basins,
4 forks, and pans. Make all of these of bronze. Make a grate of
bronze mesh for it, and on the mesh make four bronze rings

IBN EZRA

לְדַשְּׁנוֹ – *For removing its ashes:* The pots were used to remove the ashes from the altar. Now the word *ledashen* can have three possible interpretations. The first is as mentioned. The second means "to fatten," as in the verse: *The light of the eyes rejoices the heart: and a good report makes the bones fat [tedashen]* (Proverbs 15:30). The third sense appears in the verse *May He remember all your offerings and accept with favor [yedasheneh] your burnt offering* (Psalms 20:4). The latter verse appeals to God to accept our burnt offerings, such that the fire engulfs the entire sacrifice, leaving only the fat. [It is thus related to the second definition offered here.] וְיָעָיו – *Shovels:* The term here is related to that used in the verse *And the hail shall sweep away [veyaa] the refuge of lies* (Isaiah 28:17). וּמִזְלְגֹתָיו – *Forks:* Forks were needed to handle the flesh on the altar, as when the text recounts: *The priest's lad came, while the meat was cooking, with a fork having three teeth in his hand; and he struck it into the pan, or kettle, or cauldron, or pot* (I Samuel 2:13–14). וּמַחְתֹּתָיו – *Pans:* These utensils were prepared for the purpose of transporting hot coals. Although the text does not specify how many of these pans were to be fashioned, I imagine that there were two of them, which is the minimum plural possible. (Short Commentary)

RABBI AVRAHAM BEN HARAMBAM

וְיָעָיו – *Shovels:* These were used to sweep up the ashes from the altar into the pots prepared for that purpose. The shovels were likely similar to the bronze pans used by chemists. וּמִזְרְקֹתָיו – *Basins:* The priests were to use these tools to collect the blood from the sacrificial animals and cast it against the altar. The basins were fashioned such that they were wide on top but narrow at their bases, like the design of a watering can. וּמִזְלְגֹתָיו – *Forks:* The forks were like spits that were used to turn over the sacrifice's limbs once they were on the altar. לְכָל־כֵּלָיו תַּעֲשֶׂה נְחֹשֶׁת – *Make all of these of bronze:* [Literally, "make for all its utensils of bronze."] According to the grammarians, the letter *lamed* ["for"] prefixed to the word *lekhol* is unnecessary. However, my grandfather argued that indeed the letter is required. For he claimed that had the verse omitted it, we might have supposed that there were other utensils used to service the altar in addition to the ones listed here. Hence, when the verse includes the preposition "for," we are meant to understand that the following phrase, "all its utensils," refers only to those mentioned in the verse.

VERSE 4

RASHI

מִכְבַּר – *A grate:* The term *mikhbar* here is related to the Hebrew word for a sieve – *kevara* – called *cruvel* in Old French. This item was fashioned as sort of a garment for the altar, and it was perforated with holes like a net. The wording of the verse is inverted, and what it really means is: "Make a bronze grate shaped like a mesh," rather than "Make a grate shaped like a bronze mesh."

ה וְנָתַתָּה אֹתָהּ תַּחַת כַּרְכֹּב הַמִּזְבֵּחַ מִלְּמָטָּה וְהָיְתָה הָרֶשֶׁת

RABBI AVRAHAM BEN HARAMBAM

מִכְבָּר – *A grate:* The mesh appears to have surrounded the altar on all four of its walls, situated midway up the structure. According to Rav Se'adya Gaon, the sides of the altar were themselves not completely covered with wooden walls, but were open, defined only by pillars at the corners that were topped by the horns. The surrounding mesh covered the top part of the altar's sides, while the bottom half of the walls were completely open and hollow. This approach, however, seems to be contradicted by the subsequent verse, which states: *Make it hollow, with planks* (27:8). It is more likely that the four walls of the altar were made of planks that completely enclosed an empty interior space. These boards were covered in bronze, and atop them sat the mesh, which was there for ornamental purposes. **וְעָשִׂיתָ עַל־הָרֶשֶׁת אַרְבַּע טַבְּעֹת** – *And on the mesh make four rings:* There is no way of knowing whether the rings were placed at the top of the mesh, in its middle, or on the mesh's lower edge. **עַל אַרְבַּע קְצוֹתָיו** – *At its four corners:* The rings were fastened to the edges of the altar near the corners. [That is, they emerged parallel to the walls, not at a forty-five-degree angle.]

ABARBANEL

מִכְבָּר – *A grate:* The command here is to fashion a bronze mesh perforated with holes. This should be affixed to the four sides of the altar, rising from the midpoint of the structure up to the edge of its surrounding ledge. The mesh featured four rings made of bronze on its four corners, which were the four corners of the altar.

GUR ARYEH

מִכְבָּר – *A grate:* According to Rashi, this verse is inverted, and what it means is: "Make a bronze grate shaped like a mesh." For God cannot be commanding Moshe to make a grate designed as a bronze mesh, because nets are not made out of bronze, but out of ropes.

KELI YAKAR

מִכְבָּר – *A grate:* The bronze mesh on the altar was meant to evoke the net that the evil inclination spreads to trap its prey. To counter this, the mesh on the altar is intended to rescue us from the snares of our passions. We find that miracles abounded on the altar. For example, it was never consumed by the fire that burned on top of it day and night. Nor did the altar's bronze melt from the heat of that flame. Similarly, the altar was protected from water, and its fire was never extinguished from rain falling onto its wood pile. No wind ever overcame the pillar of smoke that rose straight up from the altar. Meanwhile, the altar itself was constructed as a hollow shell and filled with earth. A later altar [that was built in the Temple in Jerusalem] was composed of rocks that had not been hewn by sword. And all these features allude to human beings, who are saved from the ravages of the four elements [in punishment of their sins] by bringing sacrifices to the altar.

5 **at its four corners. The grate should be set below, under the ledge of the altar, so that the mesh reaches the middle of the**

VERSE 5

RASHI

כַּרְכֹּב הַמִּזְבֵּחַ – *The ledge of the altar:* The *karkov* mentioned in this verse is also known [in the Talmud] as the *sovev* [literally, "that which encircles"], for anything that surrounds something else is called a *karkov*. [The *sovev* described here was merely ornamental. However on the altar in the Temple of Jerusalem there was a second] *sovev* upon which the priests walked, which did not feature in the brass altar [employed in the Tabernacle]. That additional *sovev* was located on the top of the altar and ran between the structure's corners. The *karkov* that was attached to the Tabernacle's altar's walls was put there for decorative purposes, and the grate was fastened below it. The bottom of the grate sat at the midpoint of the altar [five cubits from the ground], and it served to identify the exact middle of the altar's height and thereby separate between the blood [of certain sacrifices] that had to be applied to the altar's upper half and that [of others] which had to be sprinkled on the lower half. Later, the Temple's altar would sport a red painted line running around its midpoint as a replacement for the grate on this altar. A ramp led up to the top of the altar, and even though it is not described in the current passage, the Torah alludes to that structure when it introduces the altar of earth, stating: *Do not ascend to My altar with steps* (20:23). Indeed, the "altar of earth" (20:21) mentioned in that passage is the same as the bronze altar being discussed here. The Torah initially refers to this altar as being made of earth because its hollow was filled with soil whenever Israel made camp. The ramp stood on the south side of the altar, but it was separated from the altar itself by a hair's breadth of empty space. The bottom of the ramp ended one cubit away from the hangings surrounding the southern side of the courtyard. Such is the description of the ramp according to the opinion that the altar reached a height of ten cubits. However, based on the alternative approach which argues that verse 1 should be understood as written and that the altar was in fact three cubits high, the ramp was only ten cubits long [and thus ended some distance from the wall of the courtyard].

RABBI AVRAHAM BEN HARAMBAM

תַּחַת כַּרְכֹּב הַמִּזְבֵּחַ – *Under the ledge of the altar:* The word *karkov* is obscure. Rav Se'adya Gaon writes that it denotes the "surface" of the altar. This means that the altar had a protruding surface that the priests could walk on. This is what the Mishna refers to as a *ziz* [meaning "projection"]. עַד חֲצִי הַמִּזְבֵּחַ – *Reaches the middle of the altar:* My grandfather had a tradition from Rabbi Yitzḥak Ibn Ghayyat that the bronze mesh was actually positioned within the hollow space of the altar. The ashes from the top would fall through the mesh's holes and descend to the ground. This theory is based on God's commandment *that the mesh reaches the middle of the altar.* Now according to the assumption that the height of the altar that Moshe fashioned for the Tabernacle was ten cubits, we can account as follows: The base of the structure constituted one cubit, the ledge was three cubits, and the mesh was one cubit as well, for a total of five cubits. This brings us to the midpoint of the altar, which seems to be the sense of the verse, *so that the mesh reaches the middle of the altar.* [The

ו עַד חֲצִי הַמִּזְבֵּחַ׃ וְעָשִׂיתָ בַדִּים לַמִּזְבֵּחַ בַּדֵּי עֲצֵי שִׁטִּים
ז וְצִפִּיתָ אֹתָם נְחֹשֶׁת׃ וְהוּבָא אֶת־בַּדָּיו בַּטַּבָּעֹת וְהָיוּ הַבַּדִּים
ח עַל־שְׁתֵּי צַלְעֹת הַמִּזְבֵּחַ בִּשְׂאֵת אֹתוֹ׃ נְבוּב לֻחֹת תַּעֲשֶׂה

RABBI AVRAHAM BEN HARAMBAM *(cont.)*

author holds that this measurement is from the bottom.] It is possible that the mesh divided the altar's height into two parts from within the structure. The mesh would therefore be a square perforated plate through which the ashes would fall to the ground. Such an arrangement would work even if the height of the altar was less than ten cubits, that is if we take the figure of three cubits literally [in verse 27:1]. If this understanding is correct, the mesh did not have a thickness of one cubit [as it would if we viewed is as a screen affixed to the sides of the altar], which would be excessive, but had a negligible thickness [being spread out horizontally].

ABARBANEL

תַּחַת כַּרְכֹּב הַמִּזְבֵּחַ – *Under the ledge of the altar:* The verse instructs that the mesh be affixed to the walls of the altar such that it extend from the ledge, which was the altar's upper rim, down to the midpoint of the altar. Now the mesh must have been twenty cubits in length so that it could be wrapped around the altar [whose sides were each five cubits long], and a cubit and a half in width. For the total height of the altar was three cubits, and the mesh occupied one half of the utensil's height. The commentators claim that the mesh had an ornamental purpose only, but it seems to me that this feature served a practical function as well. For if the bronze that covered the altar was solid all the way around the structure, it would have made the thing extremely heavy to transport. However, because the mesh used much less bronze, it reduced the weight of the altar, thereby making it easier to carry, even though the mesh only covered half of the object's height. Furthermore, the soil that filled the altar [when it was at rest] weighed a great deal, and it pressed downward inside the utensil. Had there been another mesh around the bottom of the altar the tremendous pressure would have caused the perforated structure to break. This is why the mesh only covered the upper half of the altar, whereas from the midpoint of the utensil, the covering was solid bronze which could bear the weight of the earth inside. Meanwhile, the function of the ledge was to prevent fire from slipping off the top of the altar and damaging its walls.

SFORNO

כַּרְכֹּב הַמִּזְבֵּחַ – *The ledge of the altar:* It is usual for all wooden vessels to have a rim, as our Sages state [in Ḥullin 25a]: "The following are considered unfinished wood utensils: Whatever still needs to be polished and hollowed out [*ulkharkev*]."

VERSE 6

RABBEINU BAḤYA

וְעָשִׂיתָ בַדִּים לַמִּזְבֵּחַ בַּדֵּי עֲצֵי שִׁטִּים – *And make staves of acacia wood for the altar:* [In the Hebrew, the word "staves" appears twice. Rabbeinu Baḥya explains:] The reason that the Torah uses wordy language to describe the staves is to allude to their miraculous

6 altar. And make staves of acacia wood for the altar, and over-
7 lay them with bronze. Place the poles in the rings, so that the
poles will be on the two sides of the altar when it is carried.
8 Make it hollow, with planks; make it as it was shown to you on

RABBEINU BAHYA *(cont.)*

length, as stated in the verse: *The poles extended* [I Kings 8:8; the Sages understand that the staves could miraculously change their length.] And our Sages teach: Said the Holy One, blessed be He: The staves' lives are destined to extend 487 years after the children of Israel leave Egypt, as the verse states: *The poles extended.* [Construction of the First Temple began 480 years after the exodus. The building was completed seven years later.]

VERSE 8

RASHBAM

נָבוּב – *Hollow:* The term *nevuv* means "hollow," as in the verse *But the empty [navuv] man shall become wise* (Job 11:12). When traveling through the wilderness, the Israelites would fill the inner space of the altar with earth whenever they made camp. Then it would be ready to receive sacrifices.

IBN EZRA

כֵּן יַעֲשׂוּ – *Make it:* [The altar is the final item of furniture described in this *parasha.*] The Torah does not mention the washing basin here [it is first mentioned in 30:17–21], because it was not fashioned from materials donated by the entire nation of Israel. Rather, the bronze used to make the laver was supplied by the women alone [see 38:8]. It was for this reason that the priests' basin is listed together with the spices, which were also not given by the whole nation, but just the by tribal princes [see 30:22–26].

HIZKUNI

נְבוּב לֻחֹת תַּעֲשֶׂה אֹתוֹ – *Make it hollow, with planks:* Making the altar hollow meant that it would be easy to transport. The altar was to be placed within the grate [that is, the grate was affixed on the altar's exterior], whose edge reached to the midpoint of the altar. Whenever Israel reached a new camp site, they filled the altar's hollow space with soil; it is that soil upon which the sacrifices were offered. And when the time arrived for the nation to move on, they would lift up the altar by the staves fixed to the edge of the utensil's grate. This would cause the earth inside the structure to fall through the holes, since the grate was perforated like a mesh. When they reached the next destination, Israel would once again fill in the altar with fresh earth.

RABBEINU BAHYA

נְבוּב לֻחֹת תַּעֲשֶׂה אֹתוֹ – *Make it hollow, with planks:* The hollow space inside the altar was filled with soil. Each time Israel arrived at a new camp site they would collect soil for the altar and offer their sacrifices on that earth. This explains the earlier verse, *Make for Me an altar of earth and on that sacrifice etc.* (20:21). Now there was a great miracle performed on the altar's behalf: Although fire burned on the altar's surface day and night, the wood that comprised its structure was not consumed, nor did the bronze that coated it melt. Centuries later, the

ט אֹתוֹ כַּאֲשֶׁר הֶרְאָה אֹתְךָ בָּהָר כֵּן יַעֲשׂוּ׃ שביעי וְעָשִׂיתָ
אֵת חֲצַר הַמִּשְׁכָּן לִפְאַת נֶגֶב־תֵּימָנָה קְלָעִים לֶחָצֵר שֵׁשׁ
י מָשְׁזָר מֵאָה בָאַמָּה אֹרֶךְ לַפֵּאָה הָאֶחָת׃ וְעַמֻּדָיו עֶשְׂרִים
וְאַדְנֵיהֶם עֶשְׂרִים נְחֹשֶׁת וָוֵי הָעַמֻּדִים וַחֲשֻׁקֵיהֶם כָּסֶף׃
יא וְכֵן לִפְאַת צָפוֹן בָּאֹרֶךְ קְלָעִים מֵאָה אֹרֶךְ וְעַמֻּדָו עֶשְׂרִים

RABBEINU BAḤYA *(cont.)*

altar in the Temple enjoyed its own wonder, which was that rain never extinguished the fire that rose from the altar there. The altar in the Temple stood exposed to the elements in that compound's courtyard, as it had in the Tabernacle's courtyard. In the Midrash Tanḥuma (Teruma 11), our Sages report an assurance that God offered Moshe, who feared that the fire would engulf the wooden altar. "Said the Holy One, blessed be He, to him: Moshe, what are you afraid of? Who is it that commands fire to consume? So too regarding the bronze altar – even though I have commanded that *the fire shall ever be burning upon the altar; it shall never go out* (Leviticus 6:6), the bronze will not soften, nor will the acacia wood burn up. And lest you argue that the bronze did not dissolve because it was too thick, note that Rabbi Neḥemya taught that the bronze sheathing the altar was no thicker than a dinar coin. Rabbi Pinḥas bar Ḥama taught: The altar that Moshe constructed was more beloved than the one that King Shlomo built, although the latter altar was larger, as the verse states: *A thousand burnt offerings did Shlomo offer upon that altar* (I Kings 3:4).

RALBAG

נְבוּב לֻחֹת תַּעֲשֶׂה אֹתוֹ – *Make it hollow, with planks:* The altar was constructed out of planks of acacia wood and was hollow like a box. The reason for this design is that the altar was intended to be portable. However, once the nation of Israel reached the promised land and settled there permanently, they constructed a solid altar of stone that was not hollow. This fulfilled the commandment given later, *You shall build the altar of the Lord your God of whole stones* (Deuteronomy 27:6).

VERSE 9

RASHI

קְלָעִים – *Hangings:* These curtains were fashioned like the sails of a ship, but perforated with holes [to permit the wind to flow through]. They were plaited not woven, as the Targum's translation of the word *kela'im* – *seradin* ["network"] – suggests. Onkelos similarly renders the term *mikhbar* ["grate," in verse 4] as *serada,* because that piece was perforated like a sieve. **לַפֵּאָה הָאֶחָת** – *On that side:* Each side of the Tabernacle is referred to as a *pe'a* [which can also mean a "corner" or "fringe"].

RASHBAM

קְלָעִים – *Hangings:* According to Menaḥem ben Saruq, the term *kela'im* refers to curtains. But he offers a second definition to accommodate the verses *The two doors also were of*

9 the mountain. Make the courtyard of the Tabernacle SHEVI'I
thus: on the south side there should be hangings a hundred cubits long of finely spun linen, all the length of the courtyard on
10 that side, with twenty posts and their twenty bronze sockets.
11 The hooks and bands of the posts shall be of silver. Likewise

RASHBAM *(cont.)*

olive wood; and he carved [vekala] upon them carvings of cherubim and palm trees and open flowers (I Kings 6:32), and *The cedar of the house within was carved [miklaat] with colocynths and open flowers* (I Kings 6:18). But it seems to me that these hangings that surrounded the Tabernacle's courtyard were also decorated with images and figures [such that the word has the same sense in both contexts].

VERSE 10

RASHI

וַחֲשֻׁקֵיהֶם – *And bands:* The courtyard posts were filleted with bands of silver. But I do not know whether these pieces covered the entire surface of the posts, or whether they were wrapped around the posts' tops or middles. However, I do know that the term *ḥishuk* connotes a girdle, for we find the word employed in the story of the concubine from Giva, as the verse states, *and there were with him two donkeys saddled [ḥavushim]* (Judges 19:10), and the Targum renders *ḥavushim* as *ḥashikim.*

RALBAG

וְעַמֻּדָיו עֶשְׂרִים – *With twenty posts:* The posts holding the hangings were to be spaced five cubits apart all around the courtyard. These pillars were supported by bronze sockets and bore silver hooks at their tops to which the hangings were attached. Additionally, silver threads were affixed to the posts, which were in turn tied to the hangings to prevent them from moving to and fro with the wind. In my estimation there were more of these threads than there were posts, such that the hangings were tied tightly to the pillars.

SFORNO

וְעַמֻּדָיו עֶשְׂרִים – *With twenty posts:* Measures of five cubits surrounded the courtyard, where each unit comprised the width of a post and the distance to the next pillar. However, the twenty pillars on the north side and the twenty pillars on the south side did not stand exactly parallel to one another. Rather, the first post on each side was offset a full unit of space [that is, five cubits] from its respective corner, and so too on the eastern and western sides. [Accordingly, the last post of each side stood exactly at the corner, such that one post stood at each corner to define the corners of the courtyard.] וַחֲשֻׁקֵיהֶם כָּסֶף – *The bands shall be of silver:* These were circular pieces of silver that encompassed the pillars for ornamentation.

VERSE 11

IBN EZRA

וַחֲשֻׁקֵיהֶם – *And bands:* The term *ḥashuk* denotes a thing that is attached [*davuk*]. Note how the phrase *And his soul was drawn [vatidbak] to Dina the daughter of Yaakov* (Genesis

וְאַדְנֵיהֶם עֶשְׂרִים נְחֹשֶׁת וָוֵי הָעַמֻּדִים וַחֲשֻׁקֵיהֶם כָּסֶף׃
יב וְרֹחַב הֶחָצֵר לִפְאַת־יָם קְלָעִים חֲמִשִּׁים אַמָּה עַמֻּדֵיהֶם
יג עֲשָׂרָה וְאַדְנֵיהֶם עֲשָׂרָה׃ וְרֹחַב הֶחָצֵר לִפְאַת קֵדְמָה
יד מִזְרָחָה חֲמִשִּׁים אַמָּה׃ וַחֲמֵשׁ עֶשְׂרֵה אַמָּה קְלָעִים לַכָּתֵף
טו עַמֻּדֵיהֶם שְׁלֹשָׁה וְאַדְנֵיהֶם שְׁלֹשָׁה׃ וְלַכָּתֵף הַשֵּׁנִית חֲמֵשׁ
טז עֶשְׂרֵה קְלָעִים עַמֻּדֵיהֶם שְׁלֹשָׁה וְאַדְנֵיהֶם שְׁלֹשָׁה׃ וּלְשַׁעַר
הֶחָצֵר מָסָךְ ׀ עֶשְׂרִים אַמָּה תְּכֵלֶת וְאַרְגָּמָן וְתוֹלַעַת שָׁנִי
וְשֵׁשׁ מָשְׁזָר מַעֲשֵׂה רֹקֵם עַמֻּדֵיהֶם אַרְבָּעָה וְאַדְנֵיהֶם
יז אַרְבָּעָה׃ כָּל־עַמּוּדֵי הֶחָצֵר סָבִיב מְחֻשָּׁקִים כֶּסֶף וָוֵיהֶם מפטיר

IBN EZRA *(cont.)*

34:3), is synonymous with the phrase in the subsequent verse, *The soul of my son Shekhem longs [ḥasheka] for your daughter* (Genesis 34:8).

VERSE 12

IBN EZRA

חֲמִשִּׁים אַמָּה – *Fifty cubits:* The width of the courtyard was thus half of the compound's length. According to the commentaries, the entrance of the Tabernacle building was situated fifty cubits from the eastern edge of the courtyard. And since the courtyard was fifty cubits wide, this explains the sense of the verse *The courtyard shall be a hundred cubits long, fifty* [literally, "fifty by fifty"] *cubits wide* [26:18, where "fifty by fifty" gives the area of the open space in front of the Tabernacle tent]. In my opinion, however, the verse merely means that the courtyard was rectangular, such that it was fifty cubits wide on both sides.

VERSE 14

RASHBAM

וַחֲמֵשׁ עֶשְׂרֵה אַמָּה קְלָעִים לַכָּתֵף – *Fifteen cubits of hangings on one side:* The eastern side of the Tabernacle courtyard, which contained the entrance to the compound, had a total width of fifty cubits. Of those, fifteen were covered by curtains on either side of the opening, while a screen twenty cubits long stood in front of the site's access point. Thus were the fifty cubits completely covered. [The twenty cubit screen was removed somewhat to the east of the hangings on either side of it. People wishing to enter the courtyard would walk around this screen and then behind it to gain entry to the area.]

VERSE 16

ḤIZKUNI

עַמֻּדֵיהֶם אַרְבָּעָה – *With four posts:* Actually, only three posts stood at the entrance gate to the Tabernacle courtyard, while a total of eleven pillars were employed across the fifty cubit

on the north side; the hangings shall be a hundred cubits long,
with twenty posts and their twenty corresponding bronze
12 sockets, with hooks and bands of silver. The width of the hangings at the western end of the courtyard shall be fifty cubits,
and it should have ten posts and their ten corresponding sock-
13 ets. The width of the courtyard at the front, facing east, shall
14 be fifty cubits: fifteen cubits of hangings with three posts and
15 three sockets on one side, and fifteen cubits of hangings with
16 three posts and three sockets on the other, and for the gate of
the courtyard there shall be an embroidered screen of twenty
cubits of sky-blue, purple, and scarlet wool and finely spun
17 linen, with four posts and four sockets. All the posts around MAFTIR
the courtyard should be banded with silver. Their hooks shall

ḤIZKUNI *(cont.)*

width of the holy site. One of those eleven was situated either in the southeast corner or the northeast corner, whichever you choose, and that leaves ten posts and ten spaces to cover that fifty cubit distance, with every gap of five empty cubits followed by a post. Three of those space-post units [with a total of four posts counting the corner post] comprised the northern half of the eastern edge of the courtyard, and another three the southern half. The remaining four five-cubit spaces accounted for the twenty-cubit long screen that stood in front of the courtyard's entrance. Thus all the courtyard hangings were arranged. Examine it and you will understand.

VERSE 17

RASHI

כָּל־עַמּוּדֵי הֶחָצֵר סָבִיב – *All the posts around the courtyard:* [This would seem to have already been conveyed in verses 10–11. Rashi explains:] Earlier, the text only specified that the posts on the northern and southern sides should be equipped with silver hooks and bands and bronze sockets. But the Torah has not yet stated that the posts standing on the eastern and western sides should similarly be fashioned. Our verse now clarifies that indeed all the courtyard posts were outfitted identically.

BEKHOR SHOR

וָוֵיהֶם כָּסֶף – *Their hooks shall be of silver:* The verse refers to fork-like fixtures resembling the Hebrew letter *vav*, but inverted. These hooks were affixed to the pillars and the curtains were hung from them using loops.

ḤIZKUNI

מְחֻשָּׁקִים כֶּסֶף – *Banded with silver:* Since these posts were not completely covered in metal like the Tabernacle's other boards were, the silver bands had to be strongly affixed to the posts to prevent the adornments from cracking in the desert heat.

יח כֶּסֶף וְאַדְנֵיהֶם נְחֹשֶׁת׃ אֹרֶךְ הֶחָצֵר מֵאָה בָּאַמָּה וְרֹחַב ׀
חֲמִשִּׁים בַּחֲמִשִּׁים וְקֹמָה חָמֵשׁ אַמּוֹת שֵׁשׁ מָשְׁזָר וְאַדְנֵיהֶם
יט נְחֹשֶׁת׃ לְכֹל כְּלֵי הַמִּשְׁכָּן בְּכֹל עֲבֹדָתוֹ וְכָל־יְתֵדֹתָיו וְכָל־
יִתְדֹת הֶחָצֵר נְחֹשֶׁת׃

VERSE 18

RASHBAM

וְרֹחַב חֲמִשִּׁים בַּחֲמִשִּׁים – *Fifty cubits wide:* [Literally, "fifty by fifty cubits wide."] How is this to be understood? The courtyard was one hundred cubits long from west to east, which we know because the north wall comprised one hundred cubits of hangings [as verse 27:11 commands]. The south side was the same length [as stated in verse 27:9]. Meanwhile, the distance between the north and the south walls of the courtyard was fifty cubits [as attested to by verses 27:12 and 27:13]. Now the Tabernacle building itself stood thirty cubits long by ten cubits wide, and its entrance was set back fifty cubits from the entrance to the courtyard. This meant that the available area in front of the Tabernacle was a square region fifty cubits wide by fifty cubits long. Furthermore, there were twenty cubits of open space between the other three of the Tabernacle's walls [the north, south, and west sides] and the boundaries of the courtyard. Since the length of the structure was thirty cubits, that left twenty cubits out of the total length of one hundred that was unused space behind the western wall of the building. And taking into account the ten-cubit width of the Tabernacle, there were twenty cubits between its north wall and the north side of the courtyard, and another twenty cubits between its south wall and the south side of the courtyard.

ḤIZKUNI

וְרֹחַב חֲמִשִּׁים בַּחֲמִשִּׁים – *Fifty cubits wide:* The dimensions of the [eastern half of the courtyard] were not exactly fifty cubits by fifty cubits, for while there were fifty cubits between the north and south sides of the compound, there were only forty-nine cubits between the eastern entrance to the site and the Tabernacle building. How so? Consider that the total length of the courtyard stood at one hundred cubits, while its width was fifty cubits. Now the length of the Tabernacle structure, including the width of the boards comprising its western wall and the width of the sockets on the eastern wall, was thirty-two cubits. [The interior space of the building was thirty cubits long, and the boards and sockets were each one cubit thick. Using similar calculations, we find that the total] width of the Tabernacle was twelve cubits including the thickness of the [southern and northern] boards. The length of the Tabernacle was positioned down the length of the courtyard and in the middle of its width, starting forty-nine cubits from the hanging at the courtyard's entrance. This means that the area in front [to the east] of the structure was actually forty-nine cubits long by fifty cubits wide. The open area in the west [behind the Tabernacle] was fifty cubits wide [from the north to the south walls], with nineteen cubits between the wall and the building. [Thus the one-hundred-cubit length of the courtyard first yielded forty-nine cubits of empty space, then thirty-two cubits for the building, and lastly nineteen cubits of additional empty space.] Similarly, the unused areas on the far north and the far south of

18 be of silver, and their sockets of bronze. The courtyard shall be
a hundred cubits long, fifty cubits wide, and five cubits high,
19 with hangings of finely spun linen and sockets of bronze. All
the Tabernacle utensils, for every use, as well as all its tent pegs
and the tent pegs of the courtyard, shall be of bronze.

ḤIZKUNI *(cont.)*

the courtyard measured one hundred cubits long [in a straight line from the western to the eastern walls] by nineteen cubits wide [between the Tabernacle's north side and the north wall, and between its south side and the south wall]. **וְקֹמָה חָמֵשׁ אַמּוֹת** – *And five cubits high:* According to the straightforward understanding of this verse, the fence surrounding the courtyard rose five cubits high with hangings of finely spun linen, aside from the sockets of bronze. What emerges is that together with the one-cubit height of the sockets, the curtains stood six cubits tall. However, according to the Talmud (Zevaḥim 59b), the height of the hangings was equal to their length of fifteen cubits [given in 27:14]. How then are we to understand the clause *And five cubits high*? That figure represents the difference between the top of the altar [which stood a total of ten cubits high] and the top of the hangings. This follows Rabbi Yosei, who believes that the altar was twice as high as it was wide [i.e., ten cubits, since the width of the altar, stated in 27:1, was five cubits].

VERSE 19

RAV SE'ADYA GAON

לְכֹל כְּלֵי הַמִּשְׁכָּן – *All the Tabernacle utensils:* This refers to all the utensils required for service in the Tabernacle.

RASHI

לְכֹל כְּלֵי הַמִּשְׁכָּן – *All the Tabernacle utensils:* This clause refers to the tools that were needed to assemble and disassemble the Tabernacle. For example, the mallets that were used to strike the pegs and posts were also fashioned out of bronze. **יִתְדֹת** – *Tent pegs:* These were bronze pins whose purpose was to secure the sheets covering the Tabernacle and the hangings surrounding the courtyard. Ropes tied to the hems of those materials were wound around the bottom of these dowels to prevent the wind from lifting them up. Now I do not know whether the pegs were pounded into the ground, or whether these fixtures were merely tied to the sheets and the hangings and left loose, with their sheer weight preventing the bottom edges from flapping around in the wind. However, it seems to me that the name of this tool proves that the pegs were in fact driven into the desert floor. For the name *yated* suggests that usage, and a biblical text supports me: *Your eyes shall see Jerusalem a quiet habitation, a tent that shall not be taken down; its pegs [yetedotav] shall not be removed for ever* [Isaiah 33:20, implying that such pegs fasten the tent firmly to the ground].

RABBI AVRAHAM BEN HARAMBAM

לְכֹל כְּלֵי הַמִּשְׁכָּן – *All the Tabernacle utensils:* [Literally, "for all etc."] My grandfather interpreted the prefixed letter *lamed* [meaning "for"] as suggesting that the courtyard [mentioned in the previous verse] would be used "for" all the Tabernacle utensils. Thus the *lamed*

RABBI AVRAHAM BEN HARAMBAM *(cont.)*

is not superfluous, as other commentators have suggested, but is instead necessary. **וְכָל־יְתֵדֹתָיו** – *All its tent pegs:* According to the above understanding, these words represent a new clause, referring back to the Tabernacle itself. [The verse would hence be better translated: "…for all the Tabernacle utensils, for every use. Its tent pegs as well, and the tent pegs of the courtyard, shall be of bronze."]

ḤIZKUNI

וְכָל־יְתֵדֹתָיו – *All its tent pegs:* When it came time to assemble the Tabernacle, the Israelites tied ropes that were attached to the hems of the courtyard hangings to tent pegs, all along the south and north sides of the compound. These ropes were pulled taut, and the pegs were set firmly into the ground, causing the hangings to stiffen. The curtains were thus prevented from falling into the courtyard due to their weight and cluttering the space of the holy site.

RALBAG

לְכֹל כְּלֵי הַמִּשְׁכָּן בְּכֹל עֲבֹדָתוֹ – *All the Tabernacle utensils, for every use:* This clause refers to all the tools that would be needed to assemble the Tabernacle and to take it apart. For example, hammers would be required to knock the crossbars into their rings on the boards, whereas punches would be used to remove them. Mallets would similarly extract the pillars from their sockets and pound the pegs into the ground so the courtyard hangings could be tied to them. And all these tools used to erect the Tabernacle were made out of bronze. Even though gold was used extensively in fashioning the Tabernacle furniture, it was nevertheless appropriate to select a slightly inferior metal for the more ancillary tools.

ABARBANEL

לְכֹל כְּלֵי הַמִּשְׁכָּן בְּכֹל עֲבֹדָתוֹ – *All the Tabernacle utensils, for every use:* Do not imagine that these descriptions about the construction of the Tabernacle, the fashioning of its accoutrements, the sequence of its assembly, disassembly and transport, the sacred vestments of the priests, or ultimately the system of sacrifices itself, have no significance to us today during these centuries of exile. Do not suggest that the listing of the tribal chiefs, the donations they made to the Tabernacle, or any of the events of those generations of antiquity have no relevance to us, or that it is not worth our while to study the Torah passages that describe them. Neither should you allow such an attitude to pervade your study of those commandments that are dependent on the land of Israel, or treat with disinterest the laws of purity and impurity or the rules governing proper priestly behavior in the Temple. We must still study this material in our age because the presence of these ideas and phenomena in the Torah retain one purpose: the study of the word of our God. And whoever engages in the understanding of these concepts perfects his soul by enriching it with knowledge and perception. When Jews learn about the Tabernacle, its utensils, and all the allusions those structures convey, that scholarship affects and improves the pupil as much as the actual construction of the holy objects would. When one considers the issue from that perspective, one will conclude that in fact the sacrificial service was never actually suspended [in the absence of the Temple], nor did the laws of impurity and purity become void, even though these rules can no longer be properly realized. The inquiry into these matters still occurs and must not be neglected.

18TH CENTURY

RABBI ḤAYYIM IBN ATTAR – *OR HAḤAYYIM*, 1696, MOROCCO – 1743, ISRAEL

RABBI ISAAC SAMUEL REGGIO, 1784 – 1855, ITALY

19TH CENTURY

RABBI YAAKOV TZVI MECKLENBURG – *HAKETAV VEHAKABBALA*, 1785 – 1865, GERMANY

SHADAL, 1800 – 1865, ITALY

RABBI SAMSON RAPHAEL HIRSCH, 1808 – 1888, GERMANY

MALBIM, 1809 – 1879, UKRAINE

RABBI NAFTALI TZVI YEHUDA BERLIN – *HAAMEK DAVAR*, 1816, BELARUS – 1893, POLAND

RABBI YOSEF ḤAYYIM OF BAGHDAD – *BEN ISH ḤAI*, 1835 – 1909, IRAQ

20TH CENTURY

RABBI MEIR SIMḤA OF DVINSK – *MESHEKH ḤOKHMA*, 1843, LITHUANIA – 1926, LATVIA

RABBI ABRAHAM ISAAC KOOK, 1865–1935, LATVIA/ISRAEL

RABBI AHARON KOTLER – *MISHNAT RABBI AHARON*, 1891, BELARUS – 1962, USA

RABBI JOSEPH B. SOLOVEITCHIK, 1903, LITHUANIA – 1993, USA

RABBI MENACHEM MENDEL SCHNEERSON – THE LUBAVITCHER REBBE, 1902, UKRAINE – 1994, USA

NEHAMA LEIBOWITZ, 1905, LATVIA – 1997, ISRAEL

פרשת תרומה
PARASHAT TERUMA

CONFRONTING
MODERNITY

כה א ב וַיְדַבֵּר יְהוָה אֶל־מֹשֶׁה לֵּאמֹר: דַּבֵּר אֶל־בְּנֵי יִשְׂרָאֵל וְיִקְחוּ־ יח
לִי תְּרוּמָה מֵאֵת כָּל־אִישׁ אֲשֶׁר יִדְּבֶנּוּ לִבּוֹ תִּקְחוּ אֶת־

CHAPTER 25, VERSE 1

SHADAL

וַיְדַבֵּר יהוה אֶל־מֹשֶׁה – *The* Lord *spoke to Moshe:* After Israel had accepted God's laws and statutes and acknowledged that He was King over Israel, the next step was to construct a Temple in His honor, to suggest that God dwelled in their midst. Such a religious center would provide a strong incentive to preserve the nation's unity and would ensure that the people maintained the Torah's code of behavior. And even though the decree that would keep Israel in the wilderness for forty years had not yet been passed, God did not want the nation to wait until they had conquered and divided the land of Israel before building Him a Sanctuary. God wished Israel to establish the Sanctuary even before they had chosen a location in the promised land to serve as the permanent heart of their state. He thus commanded that Israel construct a portable Tabernacle which they could erect and use anywhere, even after they had entered the land, based on their needs at the time. The Tabernacle that the nation built in the desert served Israel for 480 years, until Shlomo built the First Temple.

THE LUBAVITCHER REBBE

וַיְדַבֵּר יהוה אֶל־מֹשֶׁה – *The* Lord *spoke to Moshe:* After the sin of the golden calf, Moshe had to ascend to Mount Sinai again, intercede with God on the people's behalf and reinstate the relationship that had been forged at the revelation and that had been abrogated by the sin [of the golden calf]. There were two aspects to the relationship: the rational, contractual aspect; and the essential, covenantal aspect. God indicated His restoration of the contractual side of the relationship by replacing the broken tablets and the commandments inscribed on them. He indicated His restoration of the covenantal side of the relationship by allowing the people to build the Tabernacle, so His presence could indeed dwell among them. The Torah therefore gives the details of the Tabernacle and its operation here, deferring the account of the sin of the golden calf and the subsequent reconciliation until later on, in order to first complete its description of both aspects of the bond between God and the people that was established at Mount Sinai.

VERSE 2

OR HAḤAYYIM

מֵאֵת כָּל־אִישׁ אֲשֶׁר יִדְּבֶנּוּ לִבּוֹ – *From all whose heart moves them to give:* According to the Sages, the Tabernacle was meant to atone for Israel's sin with the golden calf [see chapter 32]. The Sages report a conversation between Moshe and God. Said Moshe: "Is it possible for Israel to construct a Tabernacle for you?" [That is, will they be able to afford it?] Said God: "Even the most destitute person can build a sanctuary for Me." And lo, when the manna descended to earth it was accompanied by jewels and pearls [which the Israelites collected and used to pay for the project]. Our Sages also tell us that when the Israelites gathered the wealth that washed up on the shores of the Sea of Reeds following the drowning of

25 1 2 The LORD spoke to Moshe, saying, "Tell the Israelites to take an offering for Me; take My offering from all whose heart moves

OR HAḤAYYIM (cont.)

the Egyptian cavalry, even the least industrious of the people assembled a stash of silver, gold, and precious stones requiring forty donkeys to transport. Finally, the Sages tell us that the haul that Israel combed from the beaches was greater than the possessions they took off the Egyptians' hands before departing from their land. Thus it is clear whence the Israelites had sufficient wealth to build the Tabernacle.

RABBI ISAAC SAMUEL REGGIO

אֲשֶׁר יִדְּבֶנּוּ לִבּוֹ – *Whose heart moves them to give:* Generosity is a great virtue, for generous people give not for their own sake but to benefit others. Sometimes one will donate some of his own wealth to address another's deprivation, while other times we might dedicate time and effort to those who need assistance. And occasionally, a person might even endanger his own life to come to the aid of someone less fortunate. All those who are truly altruistic are prepared to give of themselves with no expectation of reward at all. In our case, God informed Moshe that the donations He was requesting were not obligatory but voluntary, such that the people would be encouraged to offer only the amounts and the goods that they felt a desire to supply.

SHADAL

וְיִקְחוּ־לִי תְּרוּמָה – *Take an offering for Me:* [Why does the Torah use the word "take" rather than "give"?] This was a command for the nation to appoint officers who would collect ["take"] the people's donations, as the verse continues to state: *Take My offering from all whose heart moves them to give.*

HAKETAV VEHAKABBALA

וְיִקְחוּ־לִי תְּרוּמָה – *Take an offering for Me:* When the recipient of a gift is an important person, the status of the donor is raised as a result of his gift. This is why our verse employs the verb "take" and not "give." [That is, since the Israelites will be donating valuables to God, they will "take" some benefit in prestige.] We find similar language when Avraham addresses his guests [the three angels], saying: *I will take a morsel of bread* (Genesis 18:5), rather than "I will give." For in this case, the donor considered himself a recipient [of honor when his gift was received].

HAAMEK DAVAR

וְיִקְחוּ־לִי תְּרוּמָה – *Take an offering for Me:* The significance of the statement *Take an offering for Me,* is that Moshe should appoint officers and collectors to "take" the appropriate amounts from each Israelite. Thus we understand Rashi's interpretation of the term "for me" [*li*] as meaning "in My name." For when the treasurers seized materials for the Sanctuary, the items became consecrated property even above the owners' objections. [Only God possesses such power of eminent domain.] The verse proceeds to state: *Take My offering from all whose heart moves them to give* [which suggests that donations were not compulsory]. But this means only that should some people be willing to donate their wealth without being forced to, those riches should be accepted as well. For the

ג תְּרוּמָתִי: וְזֹאת הַתְּרוּמָה אֲשֶׁר תִּקְחוּ מֵאִתָּם זָהָב וָכֶסֶף

——————— HAAMEK DAVAR *(cont.)* ———————

collection of the materials mentioned here was unlike that of the silver gathered for the sockets, about which the Torah states: *The rich*

shall not give more, and the poor shall not give less, than this half shekel (30:15).

——————— SEFAT EMET ———————

וְיִקְחוּ־לִי תְּרוּמָה – *Take an offering for Me:* The language of the text is difficult; why does the verse employ the verb "take" when it would have more reasonable to use the word "give"? The Torah recognizes the inherent absurdity of the situation – how can a person of flesh and blood give something to God [who owns everything]? Indeed, all we have to give the Almighty is our own goodwill and the devotion of our souls. That is what the verse alludes to. For with regard to all of the Torah's commandments and the good deeds that people are called upon to do, the essence of the performance depends on the doer's intention. It

is that willingness to serve that elevates one's behavior toward God, may He be blessed. And all the while, we must recognize how truly distant we remain from the One who has issued those instructions to us. Thus must a person be prepared to dedicate his life and spend all of his resources in order to achieve that purpose of observance. This then is the sense of the command *Tell the Israelites to take an offering for Me.* For everything depends on and begins with the will of the human being; and God subsequently supports that eagerness by assisting His servants in fulfilling His decrees.

——————— RABBI JOSEPH B. SOLOVEITCHIK ———————

אֲשֶׁר יִדְּבֶנּוּ לִבּוֹ – *Whose heart moves them to give:* Yonatan ben Uziel [the Targum Yerushalmi] clarifies this phrase to mean: "Do not use force or methods of coercion for this collection." Although everyone, whether poor or rich, must give the half-shekel [see 30:13], the contribution to the Tabernacle was voluntary. The collection of money for the Tabernacle is different from the collection of charity. Maimonides in the *Guide of the Perplexed* (3:53) explains that charity is an act of justice (as the word *tzedaka* implies), not mercy or grace. The Torah allows the taking of charity by force [see e.g., Bava Batra 8b]. Why did the Torah eliminate the construction of the Tabernacle from that class of activity which does not require consent on the part of the giver? Man is basically a homeless being. No matter how large and opulent his home, he

is exposed. He is subject to the vicissitudes of life, subject to nature – which at best is indifferent to man, at worst is hostile – and subject to an inscrutable future. There is only one home where man gains security: God is called *Me'ona* ["an abode," in Deuteronomy 33:27]. The only home where man can find security is in the Almighty. God told Moshe not to collect the money for the Tabernacle by using force, because the Tabernacle was to be built only if the nation felt the need to build a home for God on their own. For God to descend from infinity into an earthly dwelling built by man is, as it were, a sacrificial act on His part. This act of self-contraction was a sacrifice He was willing to make, but only if the people themselves wanted a Tabernacle and were willing to contribute to build it.

₃ them to give. These are the offerings you shall receive from

VERSE 3

OR HAHAYYIM

וְזֹאת הַתְּרוּמָה אֲשֶׁר תִּקְחוּ – *These are the of-ferings you shall receive:* [The opening to this verse seems superfluous. Since the previous sentence declared that Israel should make do-nations, our verse could have begun straight-away to list the required materials. The author explains:] Perhaps by stating: *These are the of-ferings,* the verse emphasizes that the people should not donate only one or three of these kinds of substances; rather, all the items on the list must be procured. Israel would not fulfill its obligation unless the people supplied all the necessary metals and textiles. Now this

certainly does not imply that each individual Israelite was obligated to supply gold, silver, bronze, sky-blue wool, and so on. Rather, the point is that the sum of the donations col-lected from the nation had to include all the elements mentioned here. Alternatively, the verse might be suggesting that all donations toward the national project should be ac-cepted even if one brings the least expensive of the thirteen substances. No person's gift should be disparaged, if it consists only of linen or hides.

MALBIM

וְזֹאת הַתְּרוּמָה אֲשֶׁר תִּקְחוּ – *These are the offer-ings you shall receive:* This command indicates that only the fifteen specific materials required for the Tabernacle's construction were to be accepted by the Israelite donors. The treasur-ers who receive the gifts could not accept goods that were of no immediate use for the building, and which had to be sold or traded

to procure the necessary substances. Now since the Tabernacle, as our Sages tell us, was a microcosm of the entire world, which was created with the letters *yod* and *heh* [the let-ters of God's name that have numerical values of ten and five], Israel was asked to provide a total of fifteen substances to make it.

HAAMEK DAVAR

וְזֹאת הַתְּרוּמָה אֲשֶׁר תִּקְחוּ – *These are the of-ferings you shall receive:* Starting with this sentence and through verse 7, the text seems to be wholly unnecessary, since the materials required for the construction of the Tabernacle are made clear by the Torah's instructions later. [For example, since verse 10 commands that an Ark be made of acacia wood, and verse 11 explains that it should be sheathed in gold, it is clear that those two materials had to be col-lected.] Rather, the text teaches the way the Holy One, blessed be He, commanded that the people's possessions were to be evaluated

and demanded. [This follows the author's ap-proach that the donations were obligatory rather than voluntary.] That is, the treasurers were not merely to take a tax from each per-son which would then be used to purchase the items on the list. Instead, the assessors were to determine the nature of every Israel-ite's possessions, and whether they held the necessary substances. He who did not own the required items was exempt from donating anything, even though he might have had an abundance of other riches.

ה וּנְחֹשֶׁת: וּתְכֵלֶת וְאַרְגָּמָן וְתוֹלַעַת שָׁנִי וְשֵׁשׁ וְעִזִּים: וְעֹרֹת

ו אֵילִם מְאָדָּמִים וְעֹרֹת תְּחָשִׁים וַעֲצֵי שִׁטִּים: שֶׁמֶן לַמָּאֹר

ז בְּשָׂמִים לְשֶׁמֶן הַמִּשְׁחָה וְלִקְטֹרֶת הַסַּמִּים: אַבְנֵי־שֹׁהַם

──────── RABBI JOSEPH B. SOLOVEITCHIK ────────

זָהָב וָכֶסֶף וּנְחֹשֶׁת – *Gold, silver and bronze:* The slaves in Egypt had no property rights – slaves are not compensated. The Israelite would pass an Egyptian woman and see her beautiful clothing, while all the Israelites had were rags. Suddenly they were liberated and given so many gifts: clothing, utensils of gold and silver. Suddenly the people acquired great wealth. When one undergoes privation, it is natural to want to be compensated for the years of poverty and destitution when the period of privation ends. But then God makes an announcement: We are ready to accept contributions for the Temple. The people's willingness to give up these hard-earned possessions that they received from the Egyptians is precisely what hallowed and sanctified the Sanctuary.

VERSE 5

──────── RABBI ABRAHAM ISAAC KOOK ────────

וְעֹרֹת תְּחָשִׁים – *Fine leather:* [According to the Sages, the *taḥash* was the name of an animal.] As a practical matter, we think of purity as "good" and impurity as "bad." Still, these terms are only relative, for we know that all of God's creations are ultimately good, and there is really no such thing as ultimate evil without some ancillary benefit as a result. Nevertheless, all of morality and religion is founded on a person's duty to distinguish between good and evil. For although we might know in the abstract that everything bad in the world serves some good purpose, that knowledge is not meant to influence our idea of moral behavior, which must be based on our emotional and visceral abhorrence of evil and appreciations of good. As such only pure objects are considered suitable as means of religious observance. And even if we might theorize that impure things are created to serve some higher purpose, they are still not fit for use in the service of God and accomplishment of mitzvot. Only the hides of kosher animals are appropriate for such tasks. This explains the great pains our Sages took to establish that the animal known as a *taḥash* in Moshe's time was kosher. (*Ein Aya* 2:77)

VERSE 6

──────── HAKETAV VEHAKABBALA ────────

שֶׁמֶן לַמָּאֹר – *Oil for the lamps:* The materials that the Torah has listed so far have all been preceded by the conjunctive letter *vav* [literally, "*and* silver, *and* bronze, *and* rams' hides, etc."]. But now we reach verse 6 and the conjunction is absent, the Torah stating merely, "oil for the lamps" [with no "and"]. The reason for this is that all those materials that appear with the letter *vav* were brought by the rich and the poor alike, donated to the national project by the heads of families and the elders as one. However, those which are apparently listed

4 them: gold, silver and bronze; sky-blue, purple, and scarlet wool;
5 linen and goats' hair; rams' hides dyed red and fine leather; aca-
6 cia wood; oil for the lamps; spices for the anointing oil and the
7 fragrant incense; and rock crystal together with other precious

HAKETAV VEHAKABBALA *(cont.)*

separately were not supplied by the community but by the tribal chiefs alone, as is attested in Parashat Vayakhel: *The leaders brought rock crystal stones and other precious stones for setting in the ephod and the breast piece* (35:27).

בְּשָׂמִים לְשֶׁמֶן הַמִּשְׁחָה וְלִקְטֹרֶת הַסַּמִּים – *Spices for the anointing oil and the fragrant incense:* Some commentators understand the term *sammim* [appearing at the end of the verse] as referring to curatives such as frankincense and galbanum, which are medicinal. On the other hand, the word *besamim* [earlier in the verse], connotes edible spices that provide food with a flavorful scent. According to this approach, *sammim* are distinct from *besamim.* [That is, this phrase lists two separate items: "spices for the anointing oil" and "fragrant incense."] However, the Ramban believed that the more important scented or perfumed substances are referred to simply as *besamim* – choice spices which are well known – and that *sammim* denotes the larger category of the former.

HAAMEK DAVAR

שֶׁמֶן לַמָּאֹר – *Oil for the lamps:* The verse requests oil for the lamps yet neglects to mention that it would also be needed for the anointing oil [see 30:22–33]. This is because a hin [the volume of oil required for the anointing] was readily available from any Israelite, and constituted a common food item. Thus this was not a material which people had to be coerced into donating [see commentary on verse 2]. On the other hand, oil for the lamps was produced in a different manner and was therefore an expensive good that individuals did not have on hand. This explains why the text here demands that Israel supply *oil for the lamps; spices for the anointing oil and the fragrant incense* during the construction of the Tabernacle, while wheat flour for the meal offerings and animals for the daily burnt offerings [both of which were plentiful] were not sought at this point.

VERSE 7

HAKETAV VEHAKABBALA

אַבְנֵי־שֹׁהַם – *Rock crystal:* [The term *shoham* is obscure.] Onkelos translates this term into Aramaic as "*burla* stones," where *burla* is a Greek word for "passing a thread through the eye of a needle." For there exist two types of precious stones. The first lack holes and can only be fastened to fabric by being placed into settings. Such jewels are referred to as "*miluim* stones" [also mentioned in this verse; literally, "filling stones"], because, as Rashi explains, the stones were meant to fill these cavities. On the other hand, there are some attractive minerals which are porous. Golden threads can be threaded through their small holes like tiny pins to affix the stone to the concavity where the jewel is to sit. Regarding these two types of rocks, the verse requests "*shoham* stones" – stones that are to be pierced, and "*miluim* stones" – those which are to be set into sockets.

ח וְאַבְנֵי שֹׁהַם וְאַבְנֵי מִלֻּאִים לָאֵפֹד וְלַחֹשֶׁן: וְעָשׂוּ לִי מִקְדָּשׁ וְשָׁכַנְתִּי

VERSE 8

OR HAHAYYIM

וְעָשׂוּ לִי מִקְדָּשׁ – *They shall make Me a Sanctuary:* We must clarify why this verse refers to the holy site as a "Sanctuary" [*mikdash*], whereas in the very next sentence the Torah calls the structure a "Tabernacle" [*mishkan*]. It seems to me that the initial instruction *They shall make Me a Sanctuary,* is a general obligation incumbent upon all generations, starting with the Israelites in the wilderness, and continuing with those who would subsequently enter the land of Israel. Thus the verse represents a positive commandment for all times [to erect and sustain a Tabernacle or a Temple]. As such, Israel really should be responsible to erect such a structure even when they find themselves in exile from their land. However, we find that once the Temple was built in Jerusalem, God forbade the construction of any other such structures.

RABBI SAMSON RAPHAEL HIRSCH

וְעָשׂוּ לִי מִקְדָּשׁ – *They shall make Me a Sanctuary:* The Torah thus informs us that when Israel *shall make Me a Sanctuary,* God *will dwell in their midst*. Therefore, the term "Sanctuary" [*mikdash*] connotes nothing less than a general expression for what it takes to guarantee that the Divine Presence dwells among Israel. The current verse thereby expresses two concepts which are symbolized by the construction of the Tabernacle and its accoutrements. These two principles are: "Sanctuary" [*mikdash*] and "Tabernacle" [*mishkan*]. *Mikdash* [which derives from the root meaning "holy"] connotes the responsibility that Israel must fulfill in their relationship toward God, whereas *mishkan* [deriving from the verb "to dwell"] reflects the promises that God undertakes to deliver when we complete our side of the bargain. Furthermore, *mikdash* signifies the sanctification and elevation of every dimension of our private and communal lives as we devote our existences to obeying God's laws. Conversely, the term *mishkan* suggests the expectation we hold that God will endow our nation with the revelation and actuality of His essence within our borders, granting us divine protection, blessing, and prosperity.

HAAMEK DAVAR

וְעָשׂוּ לִי מִקְדָּשׁ – *They shall make Me a Sanctuary:* All the details incorporated into the Tabernacle correspond to the particulars of the world at large, which God Himself fashioned and in which He dwells. This is why the Almighty commanded Moshe to create the Tabernacle and its utensils in such a way as to resemble the universe as a whole, as I will presently explain. And once the Tabernacle was constructed as a microcosmos, it would be possible for the Divine Presence to dwell there.

MISHNAT RABBI AHARON

וְעָשׂוּ לִי מִקְדָּשׁ – *They shall make Me a Sanctuary:* The main function of this project was to provide a site where human beings could get as close as physically possible to God, through the appearance of the Divine Presence on earth. Furthermore, all of the miracles that were performed in the Temple, and the oracle of the Urim and Tumim, which provided

8 stones for the ephod and breast piece. They shall make Me a

MISHNAT RABBI AHARON *(cont.)*

a prophetic guide toward appropriate conduct, were manifestations of this proximity that God granted the nation in the Sanctuary. In addition, the Temple served as a conduit through which the people could transmit their prayers and requests to God and have them heard and fulfilled. Of course, the ultimate goal of the relationship between God and the nation of Israel was for the latter to appreciate and adopt the Torah and its laws. For the manifestation of God's providence in the Tabernacle and the palpable sanctity of the place induced the character of the people to become more amenable to a pious way of life. (Shemot Rabba 33:1)

RABBI JOSEPH B. SOLOVEITCHIK

וְשָׁכַנְתִּי בְּתוֹכָם – *And I will dwell in their midst:* According to Rabbi Ḥayyim of Volozhin, there is no truer Temple than the personality of the individual. The Divine Presence resides within us. Conversely, sin involves the removal of God's presence from within the individual. Because sin is equated to the destruction of the Temple, in a very real sense a sinner does to himself what the tyrants Nevuzaradan and Titus did to the two Temples.

THE LUBAVITCHER REBBE

וְעָשׂוּ לִי מִקְדָּשׁ – *They shall make Me a Sanctuary:* The idea of making a physical "dwelling" for the Creator seems absurd. First of all, how can the Creator of heaven and earth – spiritually and physically – "dwell" in a physical structure? Second, why is such a "dwelling" needed in the first place? Isn't God everywhere? What does it mean that God "resides" in a certain place? Of course, God is indeed everywhere, but unfortunately He is hidden; His presence is not revealed and we don't feel Him. This is so because the world at present is by and large simply not able to express the fact that it and everything in it is divinity. If we would liken the world to a radio receiver, we would say that the divine "wavelength" is for the most part out of its range of reception. It cannot presently be "tuned in" to God. There are exceptions, of course. People feel the presence of God – to some extent – in many places: in the unspoiled panoramas of nature; in acts of kindness, of love or of mercy; when studying His Torah; in the presence of holy individuals; in places of worship or study that have been hallowed by years of heartfelt prayer or diligent study of the holy books. But these experiences are the exception rather than the rule. Moreover, they are subjective. God's presence in them is so dilute that it can be clouded by our own subjective yearnings and predispositions. We are often unsure of or even mistaken about the implications they hold for us. We thus live our lives intermittently uplifted by moments of transcendence, but the goal of making this world God's home in the fullest sense of the word eludes us. These experiences in and of themselves are neither intense, nor profound, nor objective enough to enable us to permanently transform the fabric of our lives. The experience of God in the Tabernacle (and later, in the Temple), however, was altogether different. The Tabernacle was a place where the presence of God on earth was a fact, a reality that could not be denied, and the message this presence held for our lives was clear. To be sure, the Tabernacle did

ט בְּתוֹכָם: כְּכֹל אֲשֶׁר אֲנִי מַרְאֶה אוֹתְךָ אֵת תַּבְנִית הַמִּשְׁכָּן
י וְאֵת תַּבְנִית כָּל־כֵּלָיו וְכֵן תַּעֲשׂוּ: וְעָשׂוּ אֲרוֹן
עֲצֵי שִׁטִּים אַמָּתַיִם וָחֵצִי אָרְכּוֹ וְאַמָּה וָחֵצִי רָחְבּוֹ וְאַמָּה

THE LUBAVITCHER REBBE *(cont.)*

not take away a person's free will: he could choose not to internalize the experience of divinity available to him there. But whoever so desired could, through the Tabernacle, feel God's presence in his life on an ongoing basis.

NEHAMA LEIBOWITZ

וְשָׁכַנְתִּי בְּתוֹכָם – *And I will dwell in their midst:* The Holy One who is the heart of Israel summons the people once more to draw near unto Him, knocking at the door, as it were, and expressing a wish to dwell amidst them. This is the message of the verse *They shall make Me a Sanctuary and I will dwell in their midst.* The *Tzeida Laderekh* [an early-seventeenth-century commentary on Rashi] notes that what God is seeking here is not entering into the Sanctuary but into their hearts. The use of the plural pronoun "in their midst" [referring to the people] instead of the singular "in it" [in reference to the Tabernacle] is meant to teach us that: "The Divine Presence does not rest in the Sanctuary on account of the Sanctuary, but on account of Israel, for they constitute the Temple of God."

VERSE 9

RABBI SAMSON RAPHAEL HIRSCH

וְכֵן תַּעֲשׂוּ – *Form:* [In the Hebrew, this appears as a separate concluding phrase, introduced by a conjunctive *vav*, literally, "and so shall you do." Rabbi Hirsch explains:] This final clause is not a continuation of the sentence that immediately precedes it, but a new commandment altogether. The sense of the concluding phrase is: "And so shall you perform in subsequent generations" – for just as the Tabernacle was only constructed through the command and direction of Moshe, similarly, in the future any issues regarding the Temple [such as expansions or renovations of the site] may only be undertaken under the auspices of the Sanhedrin, which comprises the official representatives of the nation [see Sanhedrin 16b].

HAAMEK DAVAR

כְּכֹל אֲשֶׁר אֲנִי מַרְאֶה אוֹתְךָ – *Following the patterns that I show you:* This implies that all those who are involved in building the structure must consistently consult the blueprint provided by God, i.e., the physical and spiritual universe. It was only when Betzalel fully understood all this and directed his subordinates in their sacred work that it was possible for the Divine Presence to descend to the Tabernacle. Similarly, when the First Temple was built, the text [in I Kings 7:14] reports that Ḥiram [the chief artisan of that project] was imbued with wisdom, understanding, and skill, which indicates that he too was possessed with divine inspiration for his task. However, when the Second Temple was erected centuries later, the contractors of that structure lacked the comparable insight of the nature of the cosmos. Hence, even though all the Temple's utensils were made appropriately, the second iteration of Jerusalem's Sanctuary was not graced with God's Divine Presence.

9 Sanctuary and I will dwell in their midst. Form the Tabernacle and form all of its furnishings following the patterns that I
10 show you. Make an Ark of acacia wood, two and a
half cubits long, a cubit and a half wide, and a cubit and a half

VERSE 10

OR HAHAYYIM

וְעָשׂוּ אֲרוֹן – *Make an Ark:* [In the Hebrew, this appears to be addressed in the third person plural: "They shall make."] There must be a reason why God altered His terminology when commanding the construction of the Ark in contrast to the language used for the other utensils' instructions, for example: *Make* [literally, "you shall make"] *a table of acacia wood* (25:23). Furthermore, the subsequent details related to the Ark itself are also described in the second person singular [despite the initial command being given in the third person plural]. Perhaps the anomaly in our phrase hints that Torah law can only be maintained when the entire population of Israel is devoted to its observance. For there does not exist within the nation any single individual who is capable of fulfilling all of the Torah's many laws [symbolized by the Ark, which housed the tablets of the Covenant]. For example, a priest is exempt from donating the twenty-four gifts that other Israelites are obligated to provide for that caste, nor may he redeem his own firstborn son [as non-priestly fathers must]. On the other hand, common Israelites are not permitted to fulfill the positive commandments of offering sacrifices [duties restricted to the priests] and are therefore barred from the numerous laws which attend to that system of services. Hence it is only the community at large which can ensure that the full range of the Torah laws are fulfilled, and it is to reflect that fact that the initial verb describing the Ark appears in the plural form.

RABBI SAMSON RAPHAEL HIRSCH

וְעָשׂוּ אֲרוֹן – *Make an Ark:* Now that the Torah has embarked on a description of the Tabernacle, it begins listing the Sanctuary's most important accoutrements. In other words, the Tabernacle was constructed to house these items of furniture; the vessels were not themselves fashioned just to fill up the Tabernacle structure. This category includes the Ark, the table, the candelabrum, and the altar. These objects are the true Sanctuary, and it is they that realize the sanctity of Israel's physical lives, the people's dedication to God, and their elevation toward Him. The structure of the Tabernacle, on the other hand, reflects the result of that human devotion – the fulfillment of God's promise to dwell in the midst of the nation, responding to Israel's efforts to build Him a Sanctuary.

MALBIM

וְעָשׂוּ אֲרוֹן עֲצֵי שִׁטִּים – *Make an Ark of acacia wood:* The instructions for the Ark's construction appear first in the text, before all the other vessels of the Tabernacle [in contrast to the actual order of construction recounted in Parashat Vayakhel, which began with the structure of the building]. This is because all of these commandments were issued during the forty days that Moshe spent receiving the Tablets of the Law. For the initial plan was for the leader to deliver this record of the Ten Commandments to Israel, and to thereupon immediately begin the project of building the Tabernacle. Hence the Ark had to be made first, for it was

יא וָחֵצִי קֹמָתוֹ׃ וְצִפִּיתָ אֹתוֹ זָהָב טָהוֹר מִבַּיִת וּמִחוּץ תְּצַפֶּנּוּ
יב וְעָשִׂיתָ עָלָיו זֵר זָהָב סָבִיב׃ וְיָצַקְתָּ לּוֹ אַרְבַּע טַבְּעֹת זָהָב
וְנָתַתָּה עַל אַרְבַּע פַּעֲמֹתָיו וּשְׁתֵּי טַבָּעֹת עַל־צַלְעוֹ הָאֶחָת
יג וּשְׁתֵּי טַבָּעֹת עַל־צַלְעוֹ הַשֵּׁנִית׃ וְעָשִׂיתָ בַדֵּי עֲצֵי שִׁטִּים
יד וְצִפִּיתָ אֹתָם זָהָב׃ וְהֵבֵאתָ אֶת־הַבַּדִּים בַּטַּבָּעֹת עַל צַלְעֹת

MALBIM *(cont.)*

to serve as a receptacle for those tablets. However, after Israel sinned by worshipping the golden calf [and the tablets were broken], God ordered Moshe to *make for yourself an Ark of wood* (Deuteronomy 10:1) in which to place the fragments of the first set of tablets. And then there was no pressing need for a proper Ark to be built. This was true even though God had forgiven Israel for their sin and Moshe was permitted to begin work on the Tabernacle. For the new set of tablets were also inserted in the temporary [wooden] ark next to the shards of the first tablets until the Tabernacle was erected. This is why when it came time to actually construct the Tabernacle, Betzalel began with the structure before starting on the furniture.

VERSE 11

RABBI SAMSON RAPHAEL HIRSCH

וְעָשִׂיתָ עָלָיו זֵר זָהָב סָבִיב – *And around it make a gold rim:* This gold rim surrounded the Ark at its upper border. It extended from the top of the Ark's outer gold covering and rose above the horizontal plane of the Ark cover. The term *zer* derives from a root connoting otherness and distance from others due to a strange and unique character. It seems that the purpose of this *zer* was thus to embody the quality of holiness inherent in the Tabernacle's vessels that made them off-limits to touch by human hands. This is also the sense of the term *nezer* – a crown [which signals that its wearer is set above and apart from his subjects]. In the case of the Ark, the *zer* did not represent a distinct piece, but was rather fashioned by extending the border of the external container. This feature symbolized the hope that if only Israel maintains its stability, shielding both its private and communal lives from the world of impurity, then it will be able to protect itself from all external threats, as God assures us: *And all people of the earth shall see that you are called by the name of the Lord; and they shall be afraid of you* (Deuteronomy 28:10).

VERSE 12

HAKETAV VEHAKABBALA

וְיָצַקְתָּ לּוֹ אַרְבַּע טַבְּעֹת זָהָב – *Cast four gold rings for it:* Note that with regard to all the items which are to have rings, other than the Ark, the Torah employs the verb "make" [*asiyya*] to command their creation [see 25:26, 27:4, and 30:4]. However, it is not difficult to explain why our verse's directive uses the alternative verb "cast." For the Ark was a large object comprising three nested containers [the main box of wood and its inner and outer gold covers], made even heavier by the tablets that sat within it. Furthermore, it was topped by an Ark cover of solid gold one handbreadth thick that also had two golden cherubim emerging

11 **high. Overlay it with pure gold, inside and out, and around it**
12 **make a gold rim. Cast four gold rings for it and place them on**
its four corners, two rings on one side and two on the other.
13 14 **Make staves of acacia wood and overlay them with gold; place**
these staves in the rings on the sides of the Ark so that the Ark

HAKETAV VEHAKABBALA *(cont.)*

from it to a height of ten handbreadths. All of this combined to make the Ark an extremely heavy object, meaning that the rings that held the staves to transport the utensil had to be exceptionally strong. This then is why it was insufficient to "make" these rings – they had to be "cast." For forged gold becomes strong and durable as its parts meld together. Notice that even though Betzalel was not required to "cast" the rings for the table or for the altar, he did so anyway [see 37:13 and 38:5]. Betzalel put in the extra effort so as to ensure the vessels' quality and perform his duties in a superlative way.

HAAMEK DAVAR

וְיָצַקְתָּ לּוֹ אַרְבַּע טַבְּעֹת זָהָב – *Cast four gold rings for it:* This sentence emphasizes that when the rings are cast they should be fashioned with the intention of being affixed to the Ark specifically. The craftsman should not merely construct several sets of rings for the Tabernacle's vessels [including the table and the altar, and then select some for the Ark].

VERSE 13

RABBI SAMSON RAPHAEL HIRSCH

וְעָשִׂיתָ בַדֵּי עֲצֵי שִׁטִּים – *Make staves of acacia wood:* The Ark's staves symbolize Israel's duty and destiny: to carry the Ark and its contents [the Torah], even beyond their accustomed locations in the hour of need. Now the commandment demanding that the staves never be removed from the Ark's rings establishes for all generations the concept that the Torah and its messages are not rooted to a specific location where the Tabernacle or the Temple stand. The perpetual presence of the staves testifies that observance of the Law is not restricted to any particular place. This stands in stark contrast to the other Tabernacle vessels, especially the table and the candelabrum, which were not outfitted with permanent staves. What those objects symbolize – the fullness of the nation's material lifestyle [represented by the bread of the table] and the complete development of its spiritual dimension [suggested by the light of the lamps] – were both dependent on the presence of Israel in its land. But the Torah's commandments are applicable and required always and everywhere.

VERSE 14

HAAMEK DAVAR

וְהֵבֵאתָ אֶת־הַבַּדִּים בַּטַּבָּעֹת – *Place these staves in the rings:* This task fell to the craftsman Betzalel as part of the process of making the Ark. We similarly find such a task as part of the construction of the large altar: *Place the poles in the rings, so that the poles will be on the two sides of the altar when it is carried* (27:7). These two instructions differ from those received regarding the table and the inner altar. In those cases, the Torah only commands that the poles be fashioned, and does not emphasize that the staves must be placed in their

טו הָאָרֹן לָשֵׂאת אֶת־הָאָרֹן בָּהֶם: בְּטַבְּעֹת הָאָרֹן יִהְיוּ הַבַּדִּים
טז לֹא יָסֻרוּ מִמֶּנּוּ: וְנָתַתָּ אֶל־הָאָרֹן אֵת הָעֵדֻת אֲשֶׁר אֶתֵּן

HAAMEK DAVAR *(cont.)*

rings. Now it seems that the purpose of this is to teach that the ideas symbolized by the Ark and the outer altar [the Torah and the sacrificial system] are carried with the Jewish people throughout the generations, to wherever exile takes them. Of course, it is well known that prayer has taken the place of the Temple services. Note however, that when it comes to the Ark, the Torah uses active language: *Place these staves in the rings,* meaning that the craftsman who creates the Ark is the one who must do this. However, the verse discussing the outer altar uses passive language: *Place the poles [vehuva et badav* – literally, "the poles should be placed"] *in the rings* (27:7), signaling that anyone working on the project was permitted to insert those staves. The difference is because Betzalel, who crafted the Ark, himself was learned in the Torah. He was thus the person who carried the Ark of the Torah and its study. However, Betzalel was not equally associated with the sacrificial service, represented by the altar, than anyone else.

VERSE 15

MESHEKH ḤOKHMA

בְּטַבְּעֹת הָאָרֹן יִהְיוּ הַבַּדִּים – *The staves must stay in the rings:* Based on this verse, our Sages declare that whoever removes the staves from the Ark is liable to punishment. By contrast, with regard to the altar, the Torah states: *Place the poles in the rings, so that the poles will be on the two sides of the altar when it is carried* (27:7), and regarding the table we read: *Make the staves of acacia wood.…by these the table shall be carried* [25:28; the verses imply that these staves were only inserted when they were carried]. However, the arrangement with the Ark was different – the staves were meant to remain in their places forever. Now according to the Midrash, the Ark represents expertise in Torah, a title which can be claimed by any person. And it is clear that a Torah scholar requires financial support from wealthy patrons – such as Thaddeus of Rome [discussed in Pesaḥim 53b] – so that he can pursue his studies. This is what the staves signify – they are always present to hold up the Ark, symbolizing the aid that the community must extend to their sages. For a Torah scholar is himself a testament to God and His laws, and it is therefore incumbent on the masses to sustain their teachers at all times – *they must not be removed.* This is why the staves must be permanent fixtures on the sides of the Ark.

NEHAMA LEIBOWITZ

לֹא יָסֻרוּ מִמֶּנּוּ – *They must not be removed:* The prohibition against the removal of the poles from the Ark is puzzling. No such prohibition applies to the poles of the table or those of the two altars. This prohibition, which is included in all of the enumerations of the 613 divine precepts, seems purely a technical matter. What is its point? Admittedly, it would seem sufficient that the Torah has so commanded. We are not to probe the reasons. But though we must never make the reason the be-all and end-all of the precept, we may certainly study it from all angles and look for reasons, but not *the* reason, which can be no other than the

15 may be carried. The staves must stay in the rings of the Ark;
16 they must not be removed. Inside the Ark, place the tablets of

NEHAMA LEIBOWITZ *(cont.)*

fact that God ordained it. In the conviction that every precept possessed its own inner reason, our Sages and commentators, ancient and modern, suggested various reasons for them. Some, like the *Sefer Haḥinukh*, were satisfied with attributing a purely technical role to the prohibition: "We are bidden not to remove its poles, since we might be called upon to go forth with the Ark in haste, and in the hurry of the moment forget to examine whether the poles are properly secured, and, God forbid, the Ark might slip from our hold".... [However] the *Keli Yakar* regards the permanent attachment of the poles to the Ark as symbolic of the unbreakable links between Israel and the Torah.

VERSE 16

HAKETAV VEHAKABBALA

וְנָתַתָּ אֶל־הָאָרֹן אֵת הָעֵדֻת – *Inside the Ark, place the tablets of the Covenant:* [The Hebrew word *el* literally means "to" not "inside."] According to Rashi, the verse should be understood as an instruction to place the tablets inside the Ark. Now according to our Sages, the commands to construct the Tabernacle appearing here in Parashat Teruma were issued before the sin of the golden calf. Based on that understanding, we can suggest why the Torah does not use the more natural language "inside the Ark [with a prefix letter *bet*]. For God knew that the first set of tablets which are mentioned in the current verse, would in fact not be placed inside the Ark at all, because they would be smashed into pieces. Only the fragments of those first tablets were positioned inside the Ark, beneath the second set of tablets, as the Talmud describes [see Bava Batra 14b]. And since the presence of the first tablets was of secondary importance, the verse employs the preposition *el* ["to"] here, which suggests that although the pieces technically were placed inside the Ark, they were incidental to the main contents of the container, as if they were kept outside and nearby.

RABBI SAMSON RAPHAEL HIRSCH

הָעֵדֻת – *The tablets of the Covenant:* The Torah has been entrusted to the Jewish people, who are expected to maintain it and carry it with them forever. For the Torah possesses the purity and stability of gold, while constantly expanding and developing like the wood of a tree. The tablets of the Covenant represented the Torah itself, since they testified for all generations that God revealed His Torah to the nation at Mount Sinai. By delivering this proof of revelation to Israel, God anticipated that in the future, some would deny the divine authorship of the Torah and blaspheme its contents as inconsequential. In order to combat such claims, God provided His people with this *edut* [literally, "testimony"]. For evidence is only required to prove a point before skeptics.

HAAMEK DAVAR

הָעֵדֻת – *The tablets of the Covenant:* [Literally, "the testimony."] The term *edut* derives from the root meaning "witness," as Rashi explains, and is related to the word *ye'ud* [meaning "designation"]. For the tablets connect the Holy One, blessed be He, to Israel, so to speak.

יז אֵלֶיךָ׃ וְעָשִׂיתָ כַפֹּרֶת זָהָב טָהוֹר אַמָּתַיִם וָחֵצִי אָרְכָּהּ וְאַמָּה שני
יח וָחֵצִי רָחְבָּהּ׃ וְעָשִׂיתָ שְׁנַיִם כְּרֻבִים זָהָב מִקְשָׁה תַּעֲשֶׂה
יט אֹתָם מִשְּׁנֵי קְצוֹת הַכַּפֹּרֶת׃ וַעֲשֵׂה כְּרוּב אֶחָד מִקָּצָה מִזֶּה
וּכְרוּב־אֶחָד מִקָּצָה מִזֶּה מִן־הַכַּפֹּרֶת תַּעֲשׂוּ אֶת־הַכְּרֻבִים
כ עַל־שְׁנֵי קְצוֹתָיו׃ וְהָיוּ הַכְּרֻבִים פֹּרְשֵׂי כְנָפַיִם לְמַעְלָה סֹכְכִים
בְּכַנְפֵיהֶם עַל־הַכַּפֹּרֶת וּפְנֵיהֶם אִישׁ אֶל־אָחִיו אֶל־הַכַּפֹּרֶת
כא יִהְיוּ פְּנֵי הַכְּרֻבִים׃ וְנָתַתָּ אֶת־הַכַּפֹּרֶת עַל־הָאָרֹן מִלְמָעְלָה
כב וְאֶל־הָאָרֹן תִּתֵּן אֶת־הָעֵדֻת אֲשֶׁר אֶתֵּן אֵלֶיךָ׃ וְנוֹעַדְתִּי
לְךָ שָׁם וְדִבַּרְתִּי אִתְּךָ מֵעַל הַכַּפֹּרֶת מִבֵּין שְׁנֵי הַכְּרֻבִים

VERSE 17

RABBI ISAAC SAMUEL REGGIO

וְעָשִׂיתָ כַפֹּרֶת – *Make an Ark cover:* The term *kapporet* connotes a lid for the Ark, which was open at the top. The Ark cover was positioned like a plate or a shelf across the length of the Ark, and since it covered [*kipper al*] the utensil, it was called a *kapporet*.

VERSE 18

RABBI ISAAC SAMUEL REGGIO

מִקְשָׁה – *Beaten:* What the Torah means by this instruction is that the cherubim must not be fashioned separately and then attached to the Ark cover. Rather, they must be pounded out of the same block of gold that the surface is made from. Taking a mallet to center of the gold mass, the craftsman was to form the images on the ends of the cover.

RABBI SAMSON RAPHAEL HIRSCH

וְעָשִׂיתָ שְׁנַיִם כְּרֻבִים – *Make two cherubim:* In the Bible, the cherub is an entity that serves two functions: On the one hand, these angels are protectors and guardians; on the other, they are said to carry the Divine Presence above them. We thus read, for example: *He placed the cherubim and the flaming, whirling sword to guard the way to the Tree of life* (Genesis 3:24), demonstrating the role of these beings as watchers. With regard to their role as bearers of the glory of God we read: *And He rode upon a cherub, and did fly: He soared on the wings of the wind* (Psalms 18:11), and we find God described as *enthroned upon the cherubim* (Psalms 80:2).

VERSE 20

HAAMEK DAVAR

סֹכְכִים בְּכַנְפֵיהֶם עַל־הַכַּפֹּרֶת – *Sheltering the cover:* The cherubim's outspread wings were meant to guard the Torah [kept in the Ark] lest it be forgotten. The joint preservation of the Torah by God and Israel was mirrored by the stature of the two cherubim. **וּפְנֵיהֶם אִישׁ אֶל־אָחִיו** – *They should face one another:* The cherubim were to face each other

17 the Covenant that I will give you. Make an Ark cover of pure SHENI
gold, two and a half cubits long and a cubit and a half wide.
18 Make two cherubim of beaten gold and place them at the
19 two ends of the cover: one cherub at one end and one at the
other; the cherubim shall be made of one piece with the cover.
20 These cherubim should have wings spread upward, sheltering
the cover. They should face one another, and look toward the
21 cover. Place the cover on top of the Ark, and inside the Ark
22 place the tablets of the Covenant that I will give you. There,
from above the cover, between the two cherubim, above the

HAAMEK DAVAR *(cont.)*

in a display of devoted love, similar to the way a groom gazes at his bride, thrilling at the sight of her. **אֶל־הַכַּפֹּרֶת יִהְיוּ פְּנֵי הַכְּרֻבִים** – *They should look toward the cover:* The image of the two cherubim looking at the Ark's cover reminds us that together Israel and God are focused on the Torah inside. In this sense, God, Israel, and Torah are united as one.

VERSE 21

SHADAL

וְאֶל־הָאָרֹן תִּתֵּן אֶת־הָעֵדֻת – *And inside the Ark place the tablets:* This statement emphasizes to Moshe that it is the tablets inside the Ark that make it holy. It is because of the tablets within the Ark, not the cover or its cherubim without, that made the vessel a conduit for God's communication to humanity. This is why our verse introduces God's promise that *there, from above the cover...I will meet with you and speak with you* (25:22).

MESHEKH ḤOKHMA

וְאֶל־הָאָרֹן תִּתֵּן אֶת־הָעֵדֻת – *And inside the Ark place the tablets:* When the Second Temple was constructed, all of the Tabernacle's utensils [which had been lost with the destruction of the First Temple] were recreated except for the Ark. This was because the tablets of the Covenant had earlier been hidden away [see Yoma 22b], and the central function of the Ark was to house those items. For whenever the Torah repeats an instruction regarding sacred items, that indicates that their presence is indispensable. [The command to place the tablets inside the Ark appears twice, in verses 16 and 21.] Because of this repetition, we can conclude that the box only truly counts as the Ark once the tablets are put inside it. And since Israel was no longer in possession of the tablets when they built the Second Temple, no Ark was crafted. On the other hand, the Ramban informs us that when the tablets are extant, an Ark must be made to hold them, such that if the Ark is broken, a new one must be fashioned.

VERSE 22

RABBI SAMSON RAPHAEL HIRSCH

וְנוֹעַדְתִּי לְךָ שָׁם – *There I will meet with you:* The verb *venoadti* derives from the root *yod-ayin-dalet* [meaning "designation"] which is similar to *yod-ḥet-dalet* [meaning "unite"].

אֲשֶׁר עַל־אֲרוֹן הָעֵדֻת אֵת כָּל־אֲשֶׁר אֲצַוֶּה אוֹתְךָ אֶל־בְּנֵי
יִשְׂרָאֵל׃
כג וְעָשִׂיתָ שֻׁלְחָן עֲצֵי שִׁטִּים אַמָּתַיִם אָרְכּוֹ וְאַמָּה רָחְבּוֹ וְאַמָּה
כד וָחֵצִי קֹמָתוֹ׃ וְצִפִּיתָ אֹתוֹ זָהָב טָהוֹר וְעָשִׂיתָ לּוֹ זֵר זָהָב
כה סָבִיב׃ וְעָשִׂיתָ לּוֹ מִסְגֶּרֶת טֹפַח סָבִיב וְעָשִׂיתָ זֵר־זָהָב
כו לְמִסְגַּרְתּוֹ סָבִיב׃ וְעָשִׂיתָ לּוֹ אַרְבַּע טַבְּעֹת זָהָב וְנָתַתָּ אֶת־

RABBI SAMSON RAPHAEL HIRSCH *(cont.)*

Hence, centered at the Ark cover, God would designate a time and a place to commune with Moshe. Still, God did not intend to speak with Moshe out of any personal friendship that He shared with the man, but rather based on the covenant God had forged with the people of Israel that had brought them close to Him. The Divine Presence rested among Israel because the people agreed to abide by God's Torah. That is why God offers to speak to Moshe *from above the cover, between the two cherubim.* For His willingness to communicate with Moshe was always dependent on the nation remaining in God's good graces [symbolized by the cherubim's stance facing one another].

RABBI JOSEPH B. SOLOVEITCHIK

וְדִבַּרְתִּי אִתְּךָ מֵעַל הַכַּפֹּרֶת – *Above the cover I will speak with you:* Rashi notes an inconsistency regarding where precisely Moshe heard God's voice. This verse suggests that Moshe heard the voice from atop the Ark in the Holy of Holies. The opening chapter of Leviticus (1:1), however, indicates that God spoke with Moshe in the Tent of Meeting outside the Holy of Holies. To resolve the apparent contradiction, Rashi cites yet a third verse: *He would hear the Voice speaking to him from above the cover over the Ark of the Covenant* (Numbers 7:89). God's voice emanated from the Holy of Holies, but Moshe heard it as soon as he entered the Tabernacle. If Moshe had been required to enter the Holy of Holies to speak with God, he would have had to separate himself from the rest of the nation, since the Holy of Holies was off limits to the rest of the people. Moshe's greatness was entirely dependent on his connection to the people, in accordance with what God later said to Moshe in the wake of the golden calf incident (see Rashi on 32:7): "Go descend from your position of greatness – I bestowed greatness upon you only for the sake of Israel."

VERSE 23

RABBI SAMSON RAPHAEL HIRSCH

וְעָשִׂיתָ שֻׁלְחָן עֲצֵי שִׁטִּים – *Make a table of acacia wood:* The Tabernacle's table was meant to hold the showbread and the frankincense. It hardly needs to be said that the bread represents sustenance. Meanwhile, it is similarly obvious that odors invoke emotions – good or ill – and that some sort of stimulation is intended by the spice present here. To support this interpretation, it is enough to quote a single verse: *They said to them, "May the* L*ORD* *look on you and judge, because you have made us repellent* [literally, "you have made our

Ark of the Testimony, I will meet with you and speak with you,
and give you all My commands to the Israelites.
23 Make a table of acacia wood, two cubits long, a cubit wide, and
24 a cubit and a half high. Overlay it with pure gold and around it
25 make a gold rim. Make a frame a handbreadth wide all around,
26 and around the frame also make a gold rim. Make for it four
gold rings, and place the rings on the four corners where the

RABBI SAMSON RAPHAEL HIRSCH *(cont.)*

smell rancid"] *in the eyes of Pharaoh"* (5:21). For a pleasant odor awakens feelings of comfort and satisfaction in an experience. Now the relationship between the frankincense [placed in bowls on the table], and the incense [see 30:34–38] was the contrast between natural and synthetic materials. The scent of the "pure" frankincense [see Leviticus 24:7] evoked a purity and contentment that is at once simple and natural. Thus the table bore nourishment for the nation while offering emotions of comfort and familiarity. And together these two facets of national life create an atmosphere of prosperity, meaning that this item was the source of material blessing. Therefore the table had to be constructed primarily out of acacia wood, since trees grow as the ultimate example of renewal and development. A plant, like the nation, is bound only by the limitations that it places on itself when striving to flower and flourish. Still, the table was sheathed in gold, the symbol of strength and stability. Yet the gold was subordinate to the principle meaning of the table.

VERSE 25

SHADAL

וְעָשִׂיתָ לּוֹ מִסְגֶּרֶת – *Make a frame:* The frame was fashioned on the top of the table to bound it off and thereby prevent its contents from falling to the floor. Had the frame been situated below to provide structural support [an approach taken by Rashi], it seems to me that this feature would not have been called a "frame," since it would not have been enclosing anything. My student, Yitzḥak Pardo, adds that even though the frame was placed at the top of the structure, it nevertheless contributed to the reinforcement of the table. For it is likely that the table's top did not merely rest upon the tops of the legs; rather, they were inserted into its thickness and that of the frame.

VERSE 26

HAAMEK DAVAR

עַל אַרְבַּע הַפֵּאֹת אֲשֶׁר לְאַרְבַּע רַגְלָיו – *On the four corners where the four legs are:* [The term *pe'a*, translated here as "corner," is unclear.] The primary sense of the term *pe'ot* is explained by Rashi on tractate Eruvin (11b) as a plait of vines trained from one post to another. In the current usage as well, the Torah refers to a stretcher that connects one leg of a table to another. The table had four of these – one along each side. And do not wonder that the Torah nowhere explicitly commands the construction of this feature. For similarly, we find that the text mentions a ring on the corner boards of the Tabernacle walls [see 26:24], without having previously commanded that such an item be crafted. The resolution of this

כז הַטַּבָּעֹת עַל אַרְבַּע הַפֵּאֹת אֲשֶׁר לְאַרְבַּע רַגְלָיו: לְעֻמַּת
הַמִּסְגֶּרֶת תִּהְיֶיןָ הַטַּבָּעֹת לְבָתִּים לְבַדִּים לָשֵׂאת אֶת־
כח הַשֻּׁלְחָן: וְעָשִׂיתָ אֶת־הַבַּדִּים עֲצֵי שִׁטִּים וְצִפִּיתָ אֹתָם זָהָב
כט וְנִשָּׂא־בָם אֶת־הַשֻּׁלְחָן: וְעָשִׂיתָ קְּעָרֹתָיו וְכַפֹּתָיו וּקְשׂוֹתָיו

HAAMEK DAVAR *(cont.)*

difficulty is simple: The Torah only mentions structural details that correspond to some element of the heavens and the earth. [According to the author, the Tabernacle is a representation of God's creation of the world.] However, the rings on the corner boards and the stretchers on the table [served no symbolic purpose but] were used solely to assist the structural integrity of their respective parts. Now according to my interpretation, the rings that were affixed to the table were not situated on its corners. Rather, one ring was placed in the center of each of the four stretchers. Each ring hosted its own pole, and thus eight people altogether were required to carry the object. Due to this arrangement, the staves could only be inserted into the rings when the table was to be carried. For because each pole was inserted into a single ring, it would not have remained steady if left unattended, but would rather have tilted and slid out. Only when the two ends of each pole rested on the shoulders of its bearers would the stave stay straight.

VERSE 28

RABBI SAMSON RAPHAEL HIRSCH

וְעָשִׂיתָ אֶת־הַבַּדִּים עֲצֵי שִׁטִּים – *Make the staves of acacia wood:* The staves for the table were constructed for the sole practical purpose of facilitating its transport. Hence they were inserted into the table's rings only when the object was to be moved. Note that the previous verse first states: *The rings should be attached…as holders for staves to carry the table,* and then repeats: *By these the table shall be carried.* The repetition emphasizes that these poles bore no symbolic meaning [and were there merely for transport].

VERSE 29

HAKETAV VEHAKABBALA

אֲשֶׁר יֻסַּךְ בָּהֵן – *For pouring libations:* [The meaning of the word *yussakh* is ambiguous.] According to Rashi, the verse refers to tubes which sat like a roof or covering [*sekhakh*]. However, this cannot be right, since these three narrow rods, which stretched across a space that was twelve handbreadths long and six handbreadths wide, could hardly be said to be covering the loaves. Rather, the word should be seen as connoting separation and protection, as in the verse *Screen [vesakkota] the Ark with the curtain* [40:3; here the screen shielded the Ark but did not cover it from above]. Now the tubes and supports mentioned in our verse functioned together to create a space between the loaves, thereby preventing them from attracting mold and from crumbling. Air was thus able to circulate around the bread, keeping it fresh. The supports were like hollow reeds that were laid

27 four legs are. The rings should be attached next to the frame as
28 holders for staves to carry the table. Make the staves of acacia
wood and overlay them with gold; by these the table shall be
29 carried. You must also make, out of pure gold, its bowls, spoons,

HAKETAV VEHAKABBALA *(cont.)*

horizontally between the loaves, with their ends inserted into rods that stood upright on the sides of the table. This separation kept the loaves of bread from sitting directly on each other, which would have caused them to break. The "spoons" that served as receptacles for the frankincense also separated the two columns of loaves, such that a scent wafted between them in a space two handbreadths across. Meanwhile, the "bowls" were molds made to hold the loaves after they had been baked. The outer walls of these utensils were yet a further protection against the possibility that the bread might become spoiled, as the Mishna states (Menaḥot 11:1): When the loaves were removed from the oven they were placed straightaway into molds lest they become damaged and crumble. Thus the phrase in question actually modifies all four of the fixtures listed in this verse – the bowls, the spoons, the tubes, and the supports all combined to separate the loaves from each other and to protect the bread from mold and damage.

RABBI SAMSON RAPHAEL HIRSCH

קְעָרֹתָיו וְכַפֹּתָיו וּקְשׂוֹתָיו וּמְנַקִּיֹּתָיו – *Its bowls, spoons, pitchers and jars:* The term "bowls" [*ke'arotav*] refers to the molds that the loaves were put into upon their removal from the oven to maintain the their shape until they were placed on the table. The showbread, which symbolized Jewish prosperity, was baked in specially designed metal forms, and hence the shape of the bread had subsequently to be preserved. For this purpose gold molds were fashioned to hold the bread until they were stacked on the table. Rabbi Ḥanina [see Menaḥot 94b] provides a convincing argument that the mold resembled an open box, that is, a flat bottom with both ends folded upward. Because identical forms were employed, each loaf took up the same amount of space (or very nearly so) as the one above and below it. This conformity symbolizes the necessity of every individual to sacrifice his own interests for that of his fellow, in unselfish altruism. For a sense of community is absolutely necessary for the prosperity and wellbeing of the whole. Thus must every person acquire as much capital for others as he does for himself and provide for his neighbor's table as much food (or nearly as much) as he does for his own family. This sense of comradery is so prevalent in everything having to do with the showbread, that we must see the institution of citizenship as critical to achieving material wellbeing on a national level.... Now, frankincense was placed in cups throughout the table, and these were burned as incense before God. This spice signified an atmosphere of comfort, satisfaction and contentment which transformed the bread, symbolizing mere sustenance, into prosperity. Having the frankincense in the bowls, ready to be offered to God, suggests His approval of man's behavior. In other words, humanity can never be happy with its own achievements unless its actions have found favor in the eyes of God.

ל וּמְנַקִּיֹּתָיו אֲשֶׁר יֻסַּךְ בָּהֵן זָהָב טָהוֹר תַּעֲשֶׂה אֹתָם׃ וְנָתַתָּ
עַל־הַשֻּׁלְחָן לֶחֶם פָּנִים לְפָנַי תָּמִיד׃
לא וְעָשִׂיתָ מְנֹרַת זָהָב טָהוֹר מִקְשָׁה תֵּיעָשֶׂה הַמְּנוֹרָה יְרֵכָהּ
לב וְקָנָהּ גְּבִיעֶיהָ כַּפְתֹּרֶיהָ וּפְרָחֶיהָ מִמֶּנָּה יִהְיוּ׃ וְשִׁשָּׁה קָנִים
יֹצְאִים מִצִּדֶּיהָ שְׁלֹשָׁה ׀ קְנֵי מְנֹרָה מִצִּדָּהּ הָאֶחָד וּשְׁלֹשָׁה
לג קְנֵי מְנֹרָה מִצִּדָּהּ הַשֵּׁנִי׃ שְׁלֹשָׁה גְבִעִים מְשֻׁקָּדִים בַּקָּנֶה
הָאֶחָד כַּפְתֹּר וָפֶרַח וּשְׁלֹשָׁה גְבִעִים מְשֻׁקָּדִים בַּקָּנֶה
הָאֶחָד כַּפְתֹּר וָפָרַח כֵּן לְשֵׁשֶׁת הַקָּנִים הַיֹּצְאִים מִן־הַמְּנֹרָה׃

VERSE 30

RABBI ISAAC SAMUEL REGGIO

לֶחֶם פָּנִים – *Showbread:* [Literally, "bread of faces"]: It seems that the showbread was called this because it had multiple faces, i.e., all sides of the breads were prominent and visible. It is also possible that the showbread resembled a human face in that it was a single unit with features that were mostly doubled, like two eyes, two ears, and two nostrils. So too were the loaves of bread stacked on the table in symmetrical columns, while altogether representing just one offering.

VERSE 31

HAAMEK DAVAR

וְעָשִׂיתָ מְנֹרַת זָהָב טָהוֹר – *Make a candelabrum of pure gold:* The very nature of this utensil was pure. The light that shone from the candelabrum would only ever be bright and strong if the generation of Israel at the time was free of sin. This explains why the lamps of the candelabrum were extinguished during the period of the Second Temple [see Yoma 39b] when the people of that time chose to disobey the law. Furthermore, the symbolism of the candelabrum was that it illuminated the world of Torah scholarship, which could only shine by virtue of truth. Hence the fires of the candelabrum went out when Israel quarreled unnecessarily and divided the Torah into factions.

BEN ISH ḤAI

וְעָשִׂיתָ מְנֹרַת זָהָב טָהוֹר – *Make a candelabrum of pure gold:* It seems to me that the candelabrum symbolizes the *Amida* prayer, as I will explain below. The utensil's pure gold suggests how one's petitions to God should be eloquent and without error. **מִקְשָׁה תֵּיעָשֶׂה הַמְּנוֹרָה** – *Shall be hammered from a single piece:* Just as the candelabrum must be fashioned from a single block of gold, so too one's prayer to God must comprise one uninterrupted speech. We can see in the various parts of the candelabrum parallels to the structure of the *Amida* service. The base of the utensil represents the petitions lodged at the end of the prayer. [This refers to the paragraph beginning *Elohai netzor*.] The shaft

30 pitchers, and jars for pouring libations. On this table the showbread must be placed before Me at all times.
31 Make a candelabrum of pure gold. Its base and shaft, cups,
knobs, and flowers shall be hammered from a single piece.
32 Six branches shall extend from its sides, three on one side,
33 three on the other. On each branch there shall be three finely
crafted cups, each with a knob and a flower. All six branches

BEN ISH ḤAI *(cont.)*

of the candelabrum and the branches emerging from the central pillar symbolize the various blessings that comprise the service. In the course of the prayer, the individual must transition smoothly from one paragraph to the next, just as the candelabrum's branches are seamlessly attached to one another. The verse continues to describe the object by stating: *Its cups, knobs and flowers shall be hammered from a single piece.* The cups that adorned the candelabrum are parallel to the letters and the words that comprise the *Amida*'s blessings. The knobs on the candelabrum's shaft and branches are an allusion to the thoughts that the exercise of prayer demands. When standing before God a Jew must focus his thoughts on the meaning of the words being recited; the supplicant is warned not to allow his thoughts to wander, even to ruminations on the Torah or contemplation of commandments. Rather, one's mind must be devoted to it – the prayers – just like the knobs are fused to the body of the candelabrum. Finally, the flowers symbolize the additions that a person is permitted or encouraged to add within the separate blessings. As long as the petitioner's private insertions match the theme of whatever blessing he is reading, the content of the request can still be described as *from a single piece.* (First Year)

NEHAMA LEIBOWITZ

וְעָשִׂיתָ מְנֹרַת זָהָב טָהוֹר – *Make a candelabrum of pure gold:* How do we distinguish between legitimate and futile allegorical explanation? Should we rest content with stating the general purpose of the Tabernacle, regarding all its various appurtenances as belonging to the category of those details of the precept which the divine wisdom demanded should be parts of His work which have no specific significance? Or perhaps each appurtenance is itself a general precept serving a certain aim, the details (i.e., materials, measurements, components etc.) only possessing no significance? Let us see how these two approaches find expression in their respective explications of the candelabrum. The Rambam is brief: "The candelabrum was placed in front of the curtain to enhance the glory and splendor of the house. For an abode illuminated by a continual light concealed by a curtain makes a deep psychological impact." [Abarbanel, on the other hand, offers an] allegorical explanation of the candelabrum's components: "The candelabrum symbolizes man, who is like a lamp, ready to give light with the help of the Lord through Torah and good works. It is therefore eighteen handbreadths high, the height of a medium-sized man. Though formed of gross matter, he should make himself pure and free of dross and sin like pure gold…"

לד וּבַמְּנֹרָה אַרְבָּעָה גְבִעִים מְשֻׁקָּדִים כַּפְתֹּרֶיהָ וּפְרָחֶיהָ׃
לה וְכַפְתֹּר תַּחַת שְׁנֵי הַקָּנִים מִמֶּנָּה וְכַפְתֹּר תַּחַת שְׁנֵי הַקָּנִים
מִמֶּנָּה וְכַפְתֹּר תַּחַת־שְׁנֵי הַקָּנִים מִמֶּנָּה לְשֵׁשֶׁת הַקָּנִים
לו הַיֹּצְאִים מִן־הַמְּנֹרָה׃ כַּפְתֹּרֵיהֶם וּקְנֹתָם מִמֶּנָּה יִהְיוּ כֻּלָּהּ
לז מִקְשָׁה אַחַת זָהָב טָהוֹר׃ וְעָשִׂיתָ אֶת־נֵרֹתֶיהָ שִׁבְעָה

VERSE 34

RABBI ISAAC SAMUEL REGGIO

מְשֻׁקָּדִים – *Finely crafted:* Based on the cantillation marks that we have before us [which serve to aid in parsing the verse], we must conclude that this term modifies the following words, *A knob and a flower.* Nevertheless, our Sages, of blessed memory, have included our verse on their list of five instances where the Torah's language is ambiguous [see Yoma 52b; indeed, in this edition's translation, the term "finely crafted" modifies the cups, not the knobs and flowers]. It seems the Sages found it difficult to see the term *meshukkadim* as related to the knobs and flowers, since in all the other verses dealing with construction of the Tabernacle [such as those immediately preceding], we find the adjective associated solely with the cups and never with those other two features.

HAAMEK DAVAR

מְשֻׁקָּדִים – *Finely crafted:* There is a well-known talmudic discussion [see Yoma 52a] on how exactly to parse the subsequent verse, *The shaft of the candelabrum shall have four finely crafted cups, each with a knob and a flower* (25:34). Does the term "finely crafted" [*meshukkadim*] modify the cups or the knobs? Commenting on the matter, Tosafot ask why this case is even listed in that passage, which lists several other uncertain verses, considering that the other examples raised there, although unclear, tend to lean toward one interpretation over the other. On the other hand, in our case, there seems to be no way at all to determine what exactly the verse means. Now according to Onkelos, the term *meshukkadim*, means "finely crafted." But it seems to me that this only squares with the interpretation that sees the word as modifying the knobs. However, if one argues that the term describes the cups, as it must in our current verse [since it clearly does so in the preceding verses], then the term more likely implies a design that looks like an almond [*shaked*]. Thus the cups were narrow at their bottoms and wide at their tops. However, unlike almonds, which are rounded and closed at the top, the cups were open.

VERSE 36

OR HAḤAYYIM

מִמֶּנָּה יִהְיוּ – *Shall be of one piece with it:* By including the phrase *Shall be of one piece with it,* the Torah emphasizes that only those features of the candelabrum which are fashioned

34 extending from the candelabrum shall be like this. The shaft of
the candelabrum shall have four finely crafted cups, each with
35 a knob and a flower. For the six branches that extend from the
candelabrum, there must be a knob at the base of each pair of
36 branches. The knobs and their branches shall be of one piece
with it, the whole of it a single, hammered piece of pure gold.
37 Make its seven lamps and mount them so that they light the

OR HAḤAYYIM *(cont.)*

out of the single gold block are indispensable to the utensil's operation. [That is, any omission of these details renders the whole invalid, unlike, for example, the lamps, which were fashioned separately and inserted into the top of the candelabrum.] On the other hand, perhaps the lamps too were necessary, since they functioned as the extension of the candelabrum's seven branches. Thus if a lamp is missing, it is as if the branch itself has been neglected and the whole candelabrum is worthless.

VERSE 37

RABBI SAMSON RAPHAEL HIRSCH

וְעָשִׂיתָ אֶת־נֵרֹתֶיהָ שִׁבְעָה – *Make its seven lamps:* The meaning of the candelabrum and its lamps is self-evident, for it radiates light, and light symbolizes knowledge. The candelabrum therefore represents the spirit of understanding, especially since the lamp stood near the Ark of the Covenant which held the Torah. Furthermore, the candelabrum was positioned opposite the table, which signified physical prosperity, and together, the two utensils encapsulate the entire character of the Israelite nation – a community founded on God's Torah, devoted to its commandments, can hope for both material wellbeing and spiritual development.... Nevertheless, there are plenty of instances in the Bible where candles and light are employed metaphorically to suggest the source of life's success, perfection and growth, advancement, happiness, contentment, and joy. Thus the verses state: *Oh that I were as in months past, as in the days when God preserved me; when His candle shone upon my head, and when by His light I walked through darkness* (Job 29:2–3); and *How often is the candle of the wicked put out? and when does their calamity come upon them?* (Job 21:17); and *There will I make the horn of David to shoot up: I have set up a lamp for My anointed* (Psalms 132:17). If we were to summarize all that we know about the Bible's usage of the light throughout numerous verses, we must concede that the appearance of light as a metaphor for wisdom is but one limited way in which luminosity appears poetically in the Scripture. For the other approach to understanding light is as movement – motion together with knowledge provide us with the full understanding of what light represents. By "movement" I do not mean a mechanical change of location, but alteration on an organic level suggesting change and progress, transformation necessary for any sort of spiritual development. Light illuminates and brightens life, which makes light the perfect metaphor for intellectual advancement, and hence for the joy of life. For happiness is nothing but the thrill of life's flourishing.

לח וְהֶעֱלָה֙ אֶת־נֵרֹתֶ֔יהָ וְהֵאִ֖יר עַל־עֵ֣בֶר פָּנֶ֑יהָ: וּמַלְקָחֶ֥יהָ
לט וּמַחְתֹּתֶ֖יהָ זָהָ֥ב טָה֑וֹר: כִּכָּ֛ר זָהָ֥ב טָה֖וֹר יַעֲשֶׂ֣ה אֹתָ֑הּ אֵ֥ת
מ כָּל־הַכֵּלִ֖ים הָאֵֽלֶּה: וּרְאֵ֖ה וַעֲשֵׂ֑ה בְּתַבְנִיתָ֔ם אֲשֶׁר־אַתָּ֥ה

כו א מָרְאֶ֥ה בָּהָֽר: וְאֶת־הַמִּשְׁכָּ֣ן תַּעֲשֶׂ֣ה עֶ֣שֶׂר יְ *שלישי*

VERSE 38

MALBIM

זָהָב טָהוֹר – *Pure gold:* In verse 36, the Torah states that *the knobs and their branches shall be of one piece with it*, meaning that all of the details listed in this passage – the cups, the knobs, and the flowers – must be crafted into the candelabrum when the utensil is made out of pure gold. However, should the candelabrum be fashioned out of some other kind of metal, all of these adornments are not required – such a utensil would be valid even if it lacked the cups, knobs, and flowers. However, even a non-gold candelabrum must contain branches, since otherwise it is just a candlestick. Now our verse which states: *Make its tongs and pans of pure gold,* distinguishes these utensils from the candelabrum and its built-in features, since the tongs and pans were not molded out of the same single mass

of gold used to create the main object. We can infer that in the event that the candelabrum is not made out of gold, the tongs and pans still must be. We must therefore conclude that the subsequent verse, which reads: *All of these items shall be made from a talent of pure gold* (25:39), refers only to the amount of material required when the candelabrum is made of gold. However, if silver, for example, is being used for the candelabrum, it need not be pounded out of a talent of that metal. This too is specified in Parashat Behaalotekha, where the verse states: *And this was the work of the candelabrum: it was of beaten gold* (Numbers 8:4), meaning only gold had to be beaten when used. Other metals need not be so treated if they were to be used for the candelabrum.

VERSE 40

HAAMEK DAVAR

אֲשֶׁר־אַתָּה מָרְאֶה – *That is shown to you:* This verse uses the verb *raa* [meaning "to see"] twice. For God showed Moshe the image of the candelabrum, demonstrating to him what the cups, knobs, and flowers [mentioned in 25:31] that would adorn the utensil should look like. But when He declared that Moshe should *take care* [literally, "see"] *to make them*

thus, God was instructing Moshe to look at the world of creation around him and to find the elements in nature that corresponded to the candelabrum and its details. When he set out to fashion the object, Moshe was to have this goal in mind. It was with this that Moshe had special difficulty, and this is why God had to illustrate the candelabrum and its plans to him.

SEFAT EMET

אֲשֶׁר־אַתָּה מָרְאֶה – *That is shown to you:* Rashi writes that Moshe had difficulty imagining what the candelabrum was meant to

look like, and so God showed him an image of the object. He continues to say that even with that illustration, Moshe still struggled

38 39 space in front of it. Make its tongs and pans of pure gold. All
40 these items shall be made from a talent of pure gold. Take care
to make them according to that design that is shown to you on
26 1 the mountain. As for the Tabernacle itself, make it SHELISHI
with ten sheets of finely spun linen and sky-blue, purple, and

SEFAT EMET *(cont.)*

with the assignment until the God told him: "Cast the talent of gold into the fire and the candelabrum will become formed all on its own." But if such a method for fashioning the candelabrum was available, why then did God bother to show Moshe the object's design first? After all, the Creator must have known that Moshe would be unable to make the candelabrum without assistance. Hence we must conclude that in fact the candelabrum was not entirely created on its own – since if it were, what would be left for the Israelites to fashion? Surely it was the people who were the main builders and craftsmen of the Tabernacle. Rather, once God showed Moshe what He meant for the candelabrum to look like, and Moshe finally understood the piece's design through the demonstration, he was fully prepared to set to work crafting the piece. Still, Moshe found that he was unable to actually execute the artisanship necessary until he completely focused on his intent to complete the task. This is what is meant by the candelabrum being formed on its own. [That is, only when the craftsman was totally fixated on the candelabrum, with the latter becoming paramount in his thoughts could the object be made. This is what the midrash cited by Rashi means metaphorically by arguing that the candelabrum created itself.] When the verse states" *Take care to make them,* the sense of the clause is that only through careful consideration and intense investigation into the Torah, with untiring efforts and a willingness to properly obey the commandments, comes the guarantee of divine assistance, as the verse states: *I will cry to God most high; to God who performs all things for me* (Psalms 57:3). Based on this, we can explain God's direction to Moshe to "cast it into the fire" as referring to the Torah itself, which is often compared to fire. When one throws oneself utterly into the pursuit of Torah, one attains success.

CHAPTER 26, VERSE 1

OR HAḤAYYIM

תַּעֲשֶׂה עֶשֶׂר יְרִיעֹת – *Make it with ten sheets:* The ten sheets that formed the cover of the Tabernacle were an allusion to the ten statements that God employed in His creation of the world. This emphasizes that the construction of the Tabernacle symbolized the formation of the cosmos. And when Israel fulfilled the command to craft these ten sheets, they accrued merit as if they had actually built the universe itself.

RABBI ISAAC SAMUEL REGGIO

וְאֶת־הַמִּשְׁכָּן – *As for the Tabernacle itself:* The term "Tabernacle" [*mishkan*] refers specifically to the combination of the first layer of covering sheets together with the interior of the structure up to the five pillars standing at the building's entrance. This space with its roof is so called because that is where the glory of God resided [*shakhan*].

יְרִיעֹת שֵׁשׁ מָשְׁזָר וּתְכֵלֶת וְאַרְגָּמָן וְתֹלַעַת שָׁנִי כְּרֻבִים
ב מַעֲשֵׂה חֹשֵׁב תַּעֲשֶׂה אֹתָם׃ אֹרֶךְ ׀ הַיְרִיעָה הָאַחַת שְׁמֹנֶה
וְעֶשְׂרִים בָּאַמָּה וְרֹחַב אַרְבַּע בָּאַמָּה הַיְרִיעָה הָאֶחָת מִדָּה
ג אַחַת לְכָל־הַיְרִיעֹת׃ חֲמֵשׁ הַיְרִיעֹת תִּהְיֶיןָ חֹבְרֹת אִשָּׁה
ד אֶל־אֲחֹתָהּ וְחָמֵשׁ יְרִיעֹת חֹבְרֹת אִשָּׁה אֶל־אֲחֹתָהּ׃ וְעָשִׂיתָ
לֻלְאֹת תְּכֵלֶת עַל שְׂפַת הַיְרִיעָה הָאֶחָת מִקָּצָה בַּחֹבָרֶת
וְכֵן תַּעֲשֶׂה בִּשְׂפַת הַיְרִיעָה הַקִּיצוֹנָה בַּמַּחְבֶּרֶת הַשֵּׁנִית׃

SHADAL

שֵׁשׁ מָשְׁזָר וּתְכֵלֶת וְאַרְגָּמָן וְתֹלַעַת שָׁנִי – *Finely spun linen and sky-blue, purple, and scarlet wool:* According to the straightforward meaning of the text, each kind of thread was employed separately by the craftsmen, depending on the color needed to fashion the design. This enabled the artisans to create patterns with different shades. However, in the opinion of our Sages, composite threads were spun out of strands from the four materials listed here.

RABBI SAMSON RAPHAEL HIRSCH

מַעֲשֵׂה חֹשֵׁב – *Worked into them:* The Talmud (Yoma 72b) compares the work referred to as *maaseh rokem* [appearing in verse 36] to *maaseh ḥoshev* [mentioned here], and explains that the former is mere needlework that creates a face or figure on one side of the fabric. *Maaseh ḥoshev,* on the other hand, requires the design to be part of the weave itself, such that two images are formed – one on either side of the material. When needlework is employed for embroidery, a picture is formed on top of the material, and only one image emerges.

MALBIM

וְאֶת־הַמִּשְׁכָּן – *As for the Tabernacle itself:* Altogether the Tabernacle roof comprised three layers of covering. The first, lowest level was called "the Tabernacle" [*mishkan*] because the Divine Presence [*shekhina*] rested directly beneath them. The second layer was composed of goats'-hair sheets; it is referred to as the "tent over the Tabernacle" [in verse 7]. Lastly, the top covering of rams' hides dyed red and fine leather that rested on top of the goats'-hair layer was called "the covering for the tent" [in verse 14]. Thus a subsequent verse refers to all three layers together when it mentions *the Tabernacle, its tent, and its covering* (35:11).

HAAMEK DAVAR

שֵׁשׁ מָשְׁזָר וּתְכֵלֶת וְאַרְגָּמָן וְתֹלַעַת שָׁנִי – *Finely spun linen and sky-blue, purple, and scarlet wool:* When later describing the same materials in the context of the Tabernacle's curtain and screen, the text presents an alternative sequence: *Sky-blue, purple, and scarlet wool, and finely spun linen* (26:31, 27:16). Those verses clearly mention the most valuable substances first. Here, the main component of the covering sheets was linen, whereas the principal threads of the other items was the sky-blue wool. It is well known that the color sky blue

scarlet wool, with a design of cherubim worked into them.
2 Each sheet shall be twenty-eight cubits long and four cu-
3 bits wide; all the sheets should be the same size. Five of the
4 sheets should be sewn together; the other five likewise. Make
loops of sky-blue wool on the upper edge of the end sheet in
the first set, and likewise on the upper edge of the outermost

HAAMEK DAVAR *(cont.)*

represents royalty, exaltedness, and sanctity. **כְּרֻבִים מַעֲשֵׂה חֹשֵׁב תַּעֲשֶׂה אֹתָם** – *With a design of cherubim worked into them:* When describing the Tabernacle's curtain, the text uses the same words, but ordered differently. [The Hebrew word for cherubim in 26:31 appears at the end of the phrase; here it is situated at the beginning.] This distinction indicates a difference in the way the two materials were created. For when the craftsmen set out to fashion the Tabernacle covers, they did not need to plan a whole image for each individual fabric, since the pictures were formed only by sewing the individual sheets together. However, with regard to the curtain [which comprised a single piece of material], it was necessary to map out at the start precisely how the picture would be crafted to ensure that the image was not all squeezed into the center of the curtain. This is why, when describing the sheets, the text begins with the term *keruvim*, [the word is deemphasized since the images were a less integral part of the work], whereas with regard to the curtain the Torah switches the sequence.

VERSE 3

HAAMEK DAVAR

אִשָּׁה אֶל־אֲחֹתָהּ – *Together:* The text here emphasizes that neighboring sheets had to be perfectly aligned because the images of the cherubim were fashioned in parts and were made visible when the separate sheets were brought together.

VERSE 4

RABBI SAMSON RAPHAEL HIRSCH

לֻלָאֹת – *Loops:* The root *lamed-vav-lamed* connotes integration, which is why the same term is used to describe a winding staircase [which gives the impression of a mixing movement]. By extension, *layil* means night, for that is the time when people are mixed up and disoriented.

HAAMEK DAVAR

הַקִּיצֹנָה – *Outermost:* This clause describes the end of the set of sheets sitting above the less holy, outer space of the Sanctuary, i.e., the end of that space that bordered on the Holy of Holies. Hence the text uses the term *kitzona* here [in contrast to the synonymous word *katza* used earlier in the verse] to evoke the word *katzin* [meaning "captain"] with its implication of importance. For this edge was the most significant point of the outer set, being privileged to attach to the sheets above the Holy of Holies.

ה חֲמִשִּׁים לֻלָאֹת תַּעֲשֶׂה בַּיְרִיעָה הָאֶחָת וַחֲמִשִּׁים לֻלָאֹת
תַּעֲשֶׂה בִּקְצֵה הַיְרִיעָה אֲשֶׁר בַּמַּחְבֶּרֶת הַשֵּׁנִית מַקְבִּילֹת
ו הַלֻּלָאֹת אִשָּׁה אֶל־אֲחֹתָהּ: וְעָשִׂיתָ חֲמִשִּׁים קַרְסֵי זָהָב
וְחִבַּרְתָּ אֶת־הַיְרִיעֹת אִשָּׁה אֶל־אֲחֹתָהּ בַּקְּרָסִים וְהָיָה
ז הַמִּשְׁכָּן אֶחָד: וְעָשִׂיתָ יְרִיעֹת עִזִּים לְאֹהֶל עַל־הַמִּשְׁכָּן
ח עַשְׁתֵּי־עֶשְׂרֵה יְרִיעֹת תַּעֲשֶׂה אֹתָם: אֹרֶךְ ׀ הַיְרִיעָה הָאַחַת
שְׁלֹשִׁים בָּאַמָּה וְרֹחַב אַרְבַּע בָּאַמָּה הַיְרִיעָה הָאֶחָת מִדָּה
ט אַחַת לְעַשְׁתֵּי עֶשְׂרֵה יְרִיעֹת: וְחִבַּרְתָּ אֶת־חֲמֵשׁ הַיְרִיעֹת
לְבָד וְאֶת־שֵׁשׁ הַיְרִיעֹת לְבָד וְכָפַלְתָּ אֶת־הַיְרִיעָה הַשִּׁשִּׁית
י אֶל־מוּל פְּנֵי הָאֹהֶל: וְעָשִׂיתָ חֲמִשִּׁים לֻלָאֹת עַל שְׂפַת
הַיְרִיעָה הָאֶחָת הַקִּיצֹנָה בַּחֹבָרֶת וַחֲמִשִּׁים לֻלָאֹת עַל שְׂפַת

VERSE 5

RABBI SAMSON RAPHAEL HIRSCH

מַקְבִּילֹת הַלֻּלָאֹת – *With the loops opposite:* The root *kof-bet-lamed* also appears in the verse *And Shalum the son of Yavesh conspired against him and smote him before [kovol] the people* (II Kings 15:10). There, the word means "before" or "opposite." The root itself connotes accepting something willingly from another; and so the causative form *hikbil* refers to making oneself ready to receive someone, to look directly at him. Because the loops were attached to their counterparts, they received one another by the hooks that bound them.

VERSE 6

RABBI SAMSON RAPHAEL HIRSCH

קַרְסֵי – *Clasps:* The term *kerasim* derives from the root *kof-resh-samekh*, meaning "bend over." Thus we find the verses *Bel bows down, Nevo stoops [kores]…. They stoop [karesu], they bow down together* (Isaiah 46:1–2). Indeed this root is related to *gimmel-resh-samekh* [which means "grind"] since *keres* likely suggests that something that is being pushed down forcefully to its breaking point. Thus *kerasim* were hooks that were bent and therefore suited to holding the loops that were threaded through them.

SEFAT EMET

וְחִבַּרְתָּ אֶת־הַיְרִיעֹת אִשָּׁה אֶל־אֲחֹתָהּ – *Join the sheets together:* Midrash Tanḥuma [Teruma 25:2] tells a parable of two merchants, one of whom sells silk and the other peppers. These men exchange their goods with each other, since the item that one has, the other lacks. We find a similar situation with Torah scholars: one might be an expert in Zera'im [the order of the Mishna dealing largely with agricultural laws], while another has mastered the order Mo'ed [which discusses the Sabbath and festivals]. If they share their knowledge with each other, they will find that each possesses two full orders of Mishna. The point is that every Jew

5 sheet in the second set. Make fifty loops on each sheet on one
side and fifty on the upper edge of the corresponding sheets in
6 the other set, with the loops opposite one another. And make
fifty gold clasps. With the clasps, join the sheets together so
7 that the Tabernacle becomes one whole. Make sheets of goats'
hair as a tent over the Tabernacle; make eleven of these sheets.
8 Each sheet shall be thirty cubits long and four cubits wide, all
9 eleven sheets the same size. Join five of the sheets by themselves, and the other six by themselves. Fold the sixth sheet
10 over the front of the Tent. Make fifty loops on the edge of the
end sheet of one set, and fifty on the edge of the end sheet of the

SEFAT EMET *(cont.)*

manages to learn one specific area of the Torah, and the Torah thereby serves to connect Israel's individual souls together, as the verse states, *The Torah of the Lord is perfect, restoring the soul* (Psalms 19:8). Such is the power of the Torah that it unites all the nation's disparate characters, as the verse states: *Moshe commanded us a Torah, the inheritance of the congregation of Yaakov* (Deuteronomy 33:4). We each benefit from the knowledge of others. Similar to this is the collection of materials for construction of the Tabernacle, which was undertaken as a request for voluntary donations. The Tabernacle project was a mechanism that brought all the Israelites together. And that in turn enabled the Divine Presence to dwell amongst the nation. For unity of speech and thought are critical for the spiritual health of Israel. And we find that in the time of the Tabernacle and the Temple, the people acted as one to build those structures, while representing a unified effort in their speech – that is, their study of the Torah – and in their contemplation of the Divine. This is how a single nation is forged.

MESHEKH ḤOKHMA

וְהָיָה הַמִּשְׁכָּן אֶחָד – *So that the Tabernacle becomes one whole:* It is likely that the two sets of loops were never disengaged from the clasps [that is, the two sets of sheets were never separated], even when the nation broke camp and journeyed elsewhere. A similar arrangement governed the upper layer of sheets that sat above these coverings.

VERSE 7

HAAMEK DAVAR

וְעָשִׂיתָ יְרִיעֹת עִזִּים – *Make sheets of goats' hair:* [Literally, simply "sheets of goats."] Rabbi Shlomo Ibn Parḥun [a Spanish grammarian of the 12th century] writes that the term *izzim* ["goats"] in this verse connotes a type of well-known wool, and that the final two letters of the word do not even indicate the plural form of the word *ez* ["goat"]. Rather, according to him, *izzim* is simply the name of the material. Nevertheless, the Talmud in tractate Shabbat (99a) comments on the verse *All the women whose hearts inspired them used their skill to spin the goats' hair [ha'izzim* – literally, "spin the goats"] (35:26) claims that the women washed the wool and spun it while it was still on the animals. This indicates that the term *izzim* refers to goats' hair, as Rashi writes.

יא הַיְרִיעָה הַחֹבֶרֶת הַשֵּׁנִית: וְעָשִׂיתָ קַרְסֵי נְחֹשֶׁת חֲמִשִּׁים
וְהֵבֵאתָ אֶת־הַקְּרָסִים בַּלֻּלָאֹת וְחִבַּרְתָּ אֶת־הָאֹהֶל וְהָיָה
יב אֶחָד: וְסֶרַח הָעֹדֵף בִּירִיעֹת הָאֹהֶל חֲצִי הַיְרִיעָה הָעֹדֶפֶת
יג תִּסְרַח עַל אֲחֹרֵי הַמִּשְׁכָּן: וְהָאַמָּה מִזֶּה וְהָאַמָּה מִזֶּה בָּעֹדֵף
בְּאֹרֶךְ יְרִיעֹת הָאֹהֶל יִהְיֶה סָרוּחַ עַל־צִדֵּי הַמִּשְׁכָּן מִזֶּה
יד וּמִזֶּה לְכַסֹּתוֹ: וְעָשִׂיתָ מִכְסֶה לָאֹהֶל עֹרֹת אֵילִם מְאָדָּמִים
וּמִכְסֵה עֹרֹת תְּחָשִׁים מִלְמָעְלָה:

VERSE 12

RABBI ISAAC SAMUEL REGGIO

תִּסְרַח עַל אֲחֹרֵי הַמִּשְׁכָּן – *Is to hang down at the rear of the Tabernacle:* One cubit [of the additional two cubits of the goats' hair sheets] covered the cubit of the exposed silver sockets at the base of the western wall, while the last cubit dragged on the ground behind the structure. Thus our Sages, of blessed memory, write [see Shabbat 98b]: To what may the Tabernacle be compared? To a woman strolling through the market place with her skirts trailing after her. אֲחֹרֵי הַמִּשְׁכָּן – *At the rear of the Tabernacle:* This western side of the Tabernacle is called the rear, while the eastern side with the entrance was the front of the structure. Meanwhile, the south and north walls of the building were its right and left sides, respectively.

VERSE 13

RABBI ISAAC SAMUEL REGGIO

עַל־צִדֵּי הַמִּשְׁכָּן – *Over the sides of the Tabernacle:* This verse refers to how the coverings should hang down the north and south walls of the structure…. The additional material across the width of the Tabernacle descended equally on the two walls – those who assemble the structure were not to drape all of the extra covering on one side.

VERSE 14

HAAMEK DAVAR

וּמִכְסֵה עֹרֹת תְּחָשִׁים מִלְמָעְלָה – *Above it make a covering of fine leather:* [Scholars debate whether this verse instructs the fashioning of two additional coverings, as the translation here indicates, or just one layer comprising two kinds of materials.] According to the opinion arguing that there was just one top layer, the term "above it" [does not mean "above the first layer," but rather] refers to the Holy of Holies chamber, which was higher in holiness than the outer area of the Sanctuary. [That is, the layer was fashioned by stitching together two kinds of hides. One third of the covering, which was made up of the fine leather, sat above the Holy of Holies at the western, or "higher" end of the building. The remaining two thirds of the covering was crafted out of rams' hides and sat above the outer Sanctuary room.] Now in his comments to tractate Shabbat (28a), Rashi argues that the term "above" [*milma'la*] refers to both components of the layer, that is to the entire covering [which sat

11 other. Make, also, fifty bronze clasps. Put the clasps through the
loops, joining the tent together so that it becomes one whole.
12 As for the additional length of the tent sheets, the extra half
13 sheet is to hang down at the rear of the Tabernacle. The extra
cubit at either end of each of the tent sheets should hang over
14 the sides of the Tabernacle to cover it on both sides. Make a
covering for the tent from rams' hides dyed red. Above it make
a covering of fine leather.

HAAMEK DAVAR *(cont.)*

above the layer of goats'-hair sheets]. But it is difficult to reconcile that interpretation with later verses (40:19 and Numbers 4:25), which use the composite phrase *alav milma'la* [redundantly meaning "over above it"]. Why do those texts use both words? [If Rashi were correct, it would be sufficient to say just once that the third layer was to be laid atop the second layer.] Rather, my understanding is more accurate: The word *alav* refers to the entire covering [which sheltered the tent], and the term *milma'la* refers specifically to the fine leather portion of it, which sat above the Holy of Holies.

MESHEKH ḤOKHMA

וְעָשִׂיתָ מִכְסֶה לָאֹהֶל – *Make a covering for the tent:* Rabbi Yehuda and Rabbi Neḥemya disagree as to whether this verse commands the fashioning of one covering or two. Now it seems that the same number of barriers one had to cross to access the Holy of Holies at the ground level would have paralleled the number of coverings above that chamber. [The curtain at the entrance to the Holy of Holies paralleled the innermost layer of wool and linen sheets, and both are thus discounted in the following discussion.] The Tabernacle comprised a Sanctuary, outside of which was a courtyard, which means that these were two barriers [two gateways] that one had to traverse before reaching the Holy of Holies. Still, we find that *tanna'im* debate whether the sanctity of the outer Sanctuary room and that of the *ulam* [an outer entrance hall that existed in the Temple of Jerusalem but was not a distinct area in the Tabernacle] were of the same degree. At the start of tractate Eruvin (2a) the Talmud declares Rabbi Yehuda's belief that the sanctity of the Sanctuary was greater than that of the entrance. Therefore according to Rabbi Yehuda, there were actually three barriers [with one invisible in the Tabernacle but distinct in the Temple]. This means that according to Rabbi Yehuda, parallel to these three boundaries, the Torah demands three coverings above the Tabernacle [that is, in addition to the linen and wool sheets]: First lay the goats' hair tent covering, second was a layer of rams' hides dyed red, and above that a covering of fine leather. [This is why Rabbi Yehuda believes that our verse refers to two separate coverings.]

THE LUBAVITCHER REBBE

עֹרֹת תְּחָשִׁים – *Fine leather:* The *taḥash* skins are to be placed highest, because they are the most beautiful of all the skins, and because their beauty is intrinsic to the hide rather than added to it by dying.

טו טז וְעָשִׂיתָ אֶת־הַקְּרָשִׁים לַמִּשְׁכָּן עֲצֵי שִׁטִּים עֹמְדִים׃ עֶשֶׂר רביעי
אַמּוֹת אֹרֶךְ הַקָּרֶשׁ וְאַמָּה וַחֲצִי הָאַמָּה רֹחַב הַקֶּרֶשׁ הָאֶחָד׃
יז שְׁתֵּי יָדוֹת לַקֶּרֶשׁ הָאֶחָד מְשֻׁלָּבֹת אִשָּׁה אֶל־אֲחֹתָהּ כֵּן

VERSE 15

OR HAḤAYYIM

עֲצֵי שִׁטִּים עֹמְדִים – *Upright boards of acacia wood:* The adjective "upright" emphasizes that when the Tabernacle boards are erected they should be positioned in the same orientation that they grew in. Meanwhile, the term *kerashim* ["boards"] is an allusion to the word *kesharim* ["attachments"] to indicate that it is through these boards that all levels of higher and lower holiness were to be connected and united.

RABBI SAMSON RAPHAEL HIRSCH

עֲצֵי שִׁטִּים עֹמְדִים – *Upright boards of acacia wood:* The Talmud [see Yoma 72a] interprets the term "upright" as instructing that the boards should be oriented as they grew when they were trees. This means that the planks should be positioned with the side toward the roots below, and the side of the branches above. Thus the character of the tree was preserved even after it had been sawn into a board. Alternatively, the Talmud suggests that the word "upright" means that the wood supported its metallic sheathing. Even though gold was used to adorn the boards, that covering was considered subordinate to the wood, whose character defined the nature of the boards. This was similarly so with the table [which was also constructed out of wood and covered in gold].

MALBIM

לַמִּשְׁכָּן – *For the Tabernacle:* Note that the term "Tabernacle" properly refers to the first layer of coverings, as the Talmud states in tractate Shabbat (28a). Boards were necessary to support these sheets. Hence the text uses the definite article to refer to the boards [as if they have already been introduced. For once we have encountered the "Tabernacle" sheets it goes without saying that they would need boards to support them].

MESHEKH ḤOKHMA

עֹמְדִים – *Upright:* Israel was required to set up the boards in the same orientation that they had grown as trees. But this demand only applied to the beams, which were repeatedly taken apart and transported when the nation traveled. However, the Ark, the table, and the altar [which were also constructed of wood] were never disassembled, and hence there was no need to ensure that their wood was positioned in the way it grew.

RABBI JOSEPH B. SOLOVEITCHIK

עֹמְדִים – *Upright:* This verse is utilized to teach the rule that the planks for the Tabernacle must be cut from the acacia tree parallel to the direction of the tree's original growth and laid so the lower part of the board corresponds to the lower part of the original acacia tree.

15 Make the upright boards for the Tabernacle of acacia wood. REVI'I
16 Each board shall be ten cubits long and one and a half cubits
17 wide. Each board should have two matching tenons; all the

RABBI JOSEPH B. SOLOVEITCHIK *(cont.)*

If the board were to be turned upside down, with the upper part of the tree corresponding to the lower part of the board, it would be invalid. Deriving from this rule regarding acacia planks, the Talmud [see Sukka 45b] generalizes that all commandments which are based on plant life, such as the lulav, hadasim, and aravot, must be held in their original growth orientation. This generalization of the Talmud suggests that such orientation is not merely a condition for properly observing the commandment, but that in its lack the object itself is invalid. An acacia plank erected in the wrong direction is not considered an acacia plank at all, and a lulav that is held upside down is not considered a lulav. Although the canopy that covers a sukka also derives from plant life, it does not require growth-orientation because it can be derived from any number of sources. Only when a specific species is stipulated for fulfillment of a commandment does the object become invalid through improper orientation.

THE LUBAVITCHER REBBE

שִׁטִּים – *Acacia:* The Hebrew word for acacia [*shitta*] means "bending." The acacia tree is called the "bending" tree because it tends to bend to the side as it grows, rather than growing straight up. "Foolishness" [*shetut*] is another form of this word, since foolishness is an act of "bending" from the path dictated by logic. Foolishness can be either holy or unholy. Unholy foolishness is the illogical thinking that leads us to go against God's will. Holy "foolishness" is our willingness to go beyond the strict requirements of the Torah in fulfilling our Divine mission or in refining ourselves. Allegorically, then, placing the "bending" acacia planks vertically means using our power to be "foolish" for holy purposes. We can thereby turn this often negative character trait into a positive force in our lives, enabling us to reach levels of dedication to God and union with Him that we would not be able to reach otherwise.

VERSE 17

RABBI ISAAC SAMUEL REGGIO

מְשֻׁלָּבֹת – *Matching:* In rabbinic terminology, the rungs of a ladder are referred to as *shelivot* [see e.g., Makkot 7b]. This is because the steps of a ladder are inserted [*meshullavot*] into the sides of that object. Thus in our verse the text employs the same term to refer to the tenons that are to be fitted into the sockets, where the form of the word suggests that these pegs will be inserted into those mortises once the Tabernacle is assembled.... Meanwhile the phrase *isha el aḥotah* [literally, "to each other"] connotes that the tenons on the bottom of each board must align with one another, and that the grooves carved on either side of these fixtures should be of equal size.

יח תַּעֲשֶׂה לְכֹל קַרְשֵׁי הַמִּשְׁכָּן: וְעָשִׂיתָ אֶת־הַקְּרָשִׁים לַמִּשְׁכָּן
יט עֶשְׂרִים קֶרֶשׁ לִפְאַת נֶגְבָּה תֵימָנָה: וְאַרְבָּעִים אַדְנֵי־כֶסֶף
תַּעֲשֶׂה תַּחַת עֶשְׂרִים הַקָּרֶשׁ שְׁנֵי אֲדָנִים תַּחַת־הַקֶּרֶשׁ
הָאֶחָד לִשְׁתֵּי יְדֹתָיו וּשְׁנֵי אֲדָנִים תַּחַת־הַקֶּרֶשׁ הָאֶחָד לִשְׁתֵּי
כ יְדֹתָיו: וּלְצֶלַע הַמִּשְׁכָּן הַשֵּׁנִית לִפְאַת צָפוֹן עֶשְׂרִים קָרֶשׁ:
כא וְאַרְבָּעִים אַדְנֵיהֶם כָּסֶף שְׁנֵי אֲדָנִים תַּחַת הַקֶּרֶשׁ הָאֶחָד
כב וּשְׁנֵי אֲדָנִים תַּחַת הַקֶּרֶשׁ הָאֶחָד: וּלְיַרְכְּתֵי הַמִּשְׁכָּן יָמָּה
כג תַּעֲשֶׂה שִׁשָּׁה קְרָשִׁים: וּשְׁנֵי קְרָשִׁים תַּעֲשֶׂה לִמְקֻצְעֹת
כד הַמִּשְׁכָּן בַּיַּרְכָתָיִם: וְיִהְיוּ תֹאֲמִם מִלְּמַטָּה וְיַחְדָּו יִהְיוּ תַמִּים
עַל־רֹאשׁוֹ אֶל־הַטַּבַּעַת הָאֶחָת כֵּן יִהְיֶה לִשְׁנֵיהֶם לִשְׁנֵי

SHADAL

מַשְׁלָבֹת – *Matching:* According to the second definition for *shalav* in the *Arukh* dictionary, the term *sheliva* refers to spigots on a pot from which water pours. From this we can surmise that the word *meshullavot* connotes a protrusion. Similarly, in Rabbinic Hebrew, *shelivot* are the rungs of a ladder, which stick out from the vertical stiles and upon which the climber steps. Thus Rashi argues that the word *meshullavot* connotes a resemblance to rungs.

VERSE 18

SHADAL

לִפְאַת נֶגְבָּה תֵימָנָה – *For the southern side:* [The words *negba* and *teimana* both mean "southern."] It seems that the second word serves to elucidate the first, since the word *teimana* is more common. Similarly, in the phrase *kedma mizraḥa* ["eastern," twice], the word *mizraḥ* is fairly well known, but the term *kedma* is more obscure. Now the word *teiman* derives from *yamin,* meaning "right," whereas the word *semol* ["left"] is used to denote north. This is because when a person faces east ["forward," the literal meaning of *kedma*], south is to the right and left is to the north.

RABBI SAMSON RAPHAEL HIRSCH

לִפְאַת נֶגְבָּה תֵימָנָה – *For the southern side:* Both *negba* and *teimana* are names for south. The term *negev* is related to the word *nekev* ["hole"] presumably because the sun's rays in the south strike one's head in a piercing way. Meanwhile, the term *teiman* derives from the word *yamin,* meaning "right." This is because when a person faces the sun as it rises in the east, the south reaches out to his right. Perhaps the text includes this second term for south to emphasize that the front of the Tabernacle was in the east, and hence the south was to the right.

18 **Tabernacle's boards should be made in this way. Make twenty**
19 **boards for the southern side of the Tabernacle, and forty silver**
sockets under the twenty boards, two sockets under the first
20 **board for its two tenons, and two under the next. For the second**
side of the Tabernacle, the northern side, there should be twen-
21 **ty boards, along with their forty silver sockets, two under the**
22 **first board and two under each of the others. Make six boards**
23 **for the west side of the Tabernacle, and two additional boards**
24 **for the Tabernacle's rear corners. These should adjoin each**
other at the bottom, and be joined together at the top by a ring.
So it should be for both sides; they shall form the two corners.

VERSE 24

RABBI SAMSON RAPHAEL HIRSCH

אֶל־הַטַּבַּעַת – *By a ring:* It is unclear whether rings were used only to connect each wall's end boards to the corner posts, or whether this system was also employed to join the boards all along those two walls.

MALBIM

תֹאֲמִם מִלְּמַטָּה – *Adjoin each other at the bottom:* The shoulders that are carved out around the tenons at the bottom of the boards should equal the width of the sockets, such that the sockets will not create a space between the boards [as they would if they were wider than the boards above]. Because the term *toamim* usually refers to twins – two babies sharing a single womb, it is borrowed here to refer to two sockets that are affixed to a single board The sockets resemble identical siblings performing the same task. [According to this author, the tenons of neighboring boards were inserted into a single socket, a method that held the beams together. This meant that the tenons of each board were placed into two different sockets.]

HAAMEK DAVAR

לִשְׁנֵי הַמִּקְצֹעֹת יִהְיוּ – *They shall form the two corners:* The term "they shall form" [*yihyu*] in this clause is unnecessary. [The verse would read smoother as: "...for both sides for the two corners."] Furthermore, the presence of the same word in the verse that describes the actual construction [36:29; the word is not reflected in this edition's translation] seems superfluous as well. We must therefore explain that the form of the word teaches that the two rings that joined the corner boards to the south and to the north walls could be placed in either position whenever the Tabernacle was assembled. [That is, there was not one ring that had to always be placed in the southwest corner, while the other was designated for the northwest corner – either fixture could be put in either corner. Thus the word *yihyu* suggests: In the future the rings can be placed where you will.] This allowance stood in contrast to the Tabernacle boards, which were assigned specifically to one side or the other [see Yerushalmi Horayot 3:5]. The reason for this flexibility regarding the rings is

כה הַמִּקְצֹעֹת יִהְיוּ: וְהָיוּ שְׁמֹנָה קְרָשִׁים וְאַדְנֵיהֶם כֶּסֶף שִׁשָּׁה
עָשָׂר אֲדָנִים שְׁנֵי אֲדָנִים תַּחַת הַקֶּרֶשׁ הָאֶחָד וּשְׁנֵי אֲדָנִים
כו תַּחַת הַקֶּרֶשׁ הָאֶחָד: וְעָשִׂיתָ בְרִיחִם עֲצֵי שִׁטִּים חֲמִשָּׁה
כז לְקַרְשֵׁי צֶלַע־הַמִּשְׁכָּן הָאֶחָד: וַחֲמִשָּׁה בְרִיחִם לְקַרְשֵׁי
צֶלַע־הַמִּשְׁכָּן הַשֵּׁנִית וַחֲמִשָּׁה בְרִיחִם לְקַרְשֵׁי צֶלַע
כח הַמִּשְׁכָּן לַיַּרְכָתַיִם יָמָּה: וְהַבְּרִיחַ הַתִּיכֹן בְּתוֹךְ הַקְּרָשִׁים
כט מַבְרִחַ מִן־הַקָּצֶה אֶל־הַקָּצֶה: וְאֶת־הַקְּרָשִׁים תְּצַפֶּה
זָהָב וְאֶת־טַבְּעֹתֵיהֶם תַּעֲשֶׂה זָהָב בָּתִּים לַבְּרִיחִם וְצִפִּיתָ

HAAMEK DAVAR *(cont.)*

connected to what I have already explained, that these fixtures were employed merely for the support of the structure, and were not instituted as a feature corresponding to some element in the natural world. Hence they lacked such laws governing their usage. We learn from this distinction that objects that are used in a synagogue do not need to be treated like the boards [i.e., they can be reversed or turned upside down if they fill their function just as well that way].

VERSE 26

RABBI ISAAC SAMUEL REGGIO

חֲמִשָּׁה לְקַרְשֵׁי צֶלַע־הַמִּשְׁכָּן הָאֶחָד – *Five for the boards of the first side:* Although the text demands that five crossbars be employed to support the boards across the long sides of the Tabernacle, these poles really strengthened the walls at just three points. For the top and the bottom bars were composed of two sections, each one running just half of the wall. For example, one half of the top crossbar was inserted in a ring situated at the far western side of the south wall, while a pole of equal length was placed into a ring affixed to the far eastern side of the same wall. These bars slid through rings fastened in every board on the wall until the two halves met in the middle. There were therefore two crossbars at the top of the wall and two at its bottom for a total of four poles per wall. The fifth crossbar was called the center support because it was positioned in the middle of the walls. Now this single bar stretched the full length of the walls and was fed through holes that had been bored through the widths of the boards.

VERSE 28

RABBI SAMSON RAPHAEL HIRSCH

וְהַבְּרִיחַ הַתִּיכֹן – *The central crossbar:* [The verse could be more literally understood to mean: "The middle crossbar should go through the inside of the boards, etc."] The term *tikhon* generally refers to the "middle" of something rather than the "inside" of it, as in the phrase *The beginning of the middle watch* (Judges 7:19). This is why, having established

25 So there should be eight boards and sixteen silver sockets, two
26 sockets under each board. Make crossbars, too, of acacia wood,
27 five for the boards of the first side of the Tabernacle, five for the
boards of the second side of the Tabernacle, and five for the
28 boards of the western side of the Tabernacle at the rear. The
central crossbar should go through the middle of the boards
29 from one end to the other. Overlay the boards with gold, and
make gold rings for the crossbars. The crossbars too should be

RABBI SAMSON RAPHAEL HIRSCH *(cont.)*

that this is the "middle" crossbar [i.e., situated between the upper and lower crossbars], the verse must add that it passed through the "inside" of the boards. [These are two different pieces of information.] In addition to this central bar, there were four other crossbars on each wall of the Tabernacle, which were held in place by gold rings on the outside of the boards and were themselves covered in gold. On the other hand, the central crossbar was not visible from outside the boards because it passed through a series of holes that were bored through the boards' widths for this purpose. There was another distinction between the middle crossbar and the others in that it was composed of a single piece of wood, whereas the upper and lower supports were each a set of two bars that met in the middle of the Tabernacle's length. Thus only the middle crossbar stretched from one end of the structure to the other, down the full lengths of the walls. Furthermore, according to the Talmud [see Shabbat 98b], a single pole sufficed for all three walls [the north, west, and south sides of the building, excluding the eastern wall, which framed the entrance], because it miraculously was able to make right angle turns at the two corners without snapping. Thus was fulfilled the verse *So that the Tabernacle becomes one whole* (26:6).

HAAMEK DAVAR

מַבְרִחַ מִן־הַקָּצֶה אֶל־הַקָּצֶה – *From one end to the other:* According to the straightforward meaning of the text, the central crossbar stretched from one end of a wall to the other end, and hence this piece measured thirty cubits [on the north and south walls]. This is why the Talmud [see Shabbat 98b] states that the crossbars stayed intact miraculously – despite their great length, these thin pieces of wood did not break. However, Rashi and Tosafot [commenting on the Talmud] explain otherwise. [They explain that the miracle of the crossbar was that a single pole ran miraculously through all three walls of the building.]

VERSE 29

RABBI ISAAC SAMUEL REGGIO

וְאֶת־הַקְּרָשִׁים תְּצַפֶּה זָהָב – *Overlay the boards with gold:* The boards were covered in gold at the spots where they held the crossbars. How was this done? Each board was fitted with a [horizontally-oriented] gold cylinder that was one and a half cubits long [the width of the board itself]. These pipes ran through holes in the width of the boards, where the crossbars were to be located. [Thus the gold insulated the crossbars from direct contact with the wood of the boards.]

ל אֶת־הַבְּרִיחִם זָהָב׃ וַהֲקֵמֹתָ אֶת־הַמִּשְׁכָּן כְּמִשְׁפָּטוֹ אֲשֶׁר
לא הָרְאֵיתָ בָּהָר׃ וְעָשִׂיתָ פָרֹכֶת תְּכֵלֶת וְאַרְגָּמָן כ חמישי
וְתוֹלַעַת שָׁנִי וְשֵׁשׁ מָשְׁזָר מַעֲשֵׂה חֹשֵׁב יַעֲשֶׂה אֹתָהּ כְּרֻבִים׃
לב וְנָתַתָּה אֹתָהּ עַל־אַרְבָּעָה עַמּוּדֵי שִׁטִּים מְצֻפִּים זָהָב וָוֵיהֶם
לג זָהָב עַל־אַרְבָּעָה אַדְנֵי־כָסֶף׃ וְנָתַתָּה אֶת־הַפָּרֹכֶת תַּחַת
הַקְּרָסִים וְהֵבֵאתָ שָׁמָּה מִבֵּית לַפָּרֹכֶת אֵת אֲרוֹן הָעֵדוּת

VERSE 30

OR HAHAYYIM

וַהֲקֵמֹתָ אֶת־הַמִּשְׁכָּן – *So shall you set up the Tabernacle:* According to Rabbi Avraham Ibn Ezra, Moshe was not meant to set up the Tabernacle himself; rather, this instruction meant that he should enlist capable and skilled workers to do so on his behalf. That commentator has taken the same general approach to the entire passage of the Tabernacle designs, explaining that although God speaks to Moshe in the second person throughout His communications on this matter, He did not intend for Moshe himself to personally construct the building and all of its accoutrements. And just as Moshe needed to employ craftsman to manufacture the various parts of the Tabernacle, so too here other people would be given the job of actually erecting the structure. But this understanding is incorrect. Actually, every direction that Moshe received directly from God was meant for him and nobody else. The exception to this rule would be in instances where God explicitly directed that others should be involved. In those cases we would argue that God nevertheless spoke to Moshe in the second person since he would be the one directing the labor being performed by those other people. For when Moshe served as the foreman he was credited as if he had performed the work himself. Therefore the building of the Tabernacle was attributed to Moshe even though later verses specify the involvement of Betzalel (31:2–3), Oholiav (38:23), and other Israelites (31:6). So while Moshe was never supposed to execute all of God's instructions himself, still, when it came to assembling the Tabernacle, we find no verse where God mentions anyone else helping to erect the structure. We must therefore accept the text as presented, meaning that Moshe alone was charged with this responsibility. And indeed we see that Moshe did in fact put up the Tabernacle building, as the verse states: *Moshe set up the Tabernacle, placed its sockets, erected its frames, inserted its bars, and put up its posts* (40:18). Moshe did it himself with no assistance from anyone else.

VERSE 31

HAKETAV VEHAKABBALA

וְעָשִׂיתָ פָרֹכֶת – *Make a curtain:* The term *parokhet* connotes a barrier, which the Sages call a *pargod*. Rashi argues that this is a divider that separates a king from his subjects, so that the line between the domain of the monarch and that of the people is clearly delineated. Now in both the Tabernacle and the Temple the partition was intended to bound off the glory of God and to clearly divide the area of the Holy of Holies, where the Divine Presence

30 overlaid with gold. So shall you set up the Tabernacle, according
31 to the plan you were shown on the mountain. Make a HAMISHI
curtain of sky-blue, purple, and scarlet wool, and finely spun
32 linen with a design of cherubim worked into it. Hang it on four
gold-covered posts of acacia wood with gold hooks, set on
33 four sockets of silver. Hang the curtain under the clasps and

HAKETAV VEHAKABBALA *(cont.)*

resides, from the adjoining space of the Sanctuary, as the verse states: *So that the curtain separates the holy place from the Holy of Holies* (26:33). The term *parokhet* is only ever used to refer to the partition in the Tabernacle and the Temple. But it is incorrect to understand that the *parokhet* must always be a hanging curtain; this barrier can also be constructed as a wall. Indeed, in the First Temple, it was not a curtain but an actual wall, one cubit thick, that was built to separate the two chambers.

RABBI SAMSON RAPHAEL HIRSCH

וְעָשִׂיתָ פָרֹכֶת – *Make a curtain:* The term *parokhet* denotes a barrier, that is, a veil that separates and divides one space into different areas. These parts nevertheless remain connected in the way that the limbs of a human body are distinct but joined together. The purpose of the curtain was to separate, as verse 33 makes clear. Elsewhere the Torah calls this feature a "cover" [*masakh*] (39:34), while in a later verse Moshe is also told: *Screen the Ark with the curtain* (40:3), Thus we see that the *parokhet,* whose job was primarily to separate the two chambers, also served as a cover to protect the Ark. It therefore stands to reason that the curtain did not merely hang vertically from the ceiling of the Tabernacle to the floor, acting as a mere screen. Rather, at the top of the room it turned inward horizontally to act as a sort of inner roof and cover above the tablets of the Covenant.

MALBIM

וְעָשִׂיתָ פָרֹכֶת – *Make a curtain:* It seems to me that this curtain was not a permanent fixture in the Sanctuary. For in the First Temple it was replaced with a wall. As for what I wrote in *Hatorah Vehamitzva* (Leviticus 222), that a curtain did in fact hang in the Temple, I was referring there to the screen which hung in front of the entrance to the structure. That object did not possess the design of the *parokhet* curtain that divided the Sanctuary on the inside. Now the builders of the Second Temple introduced two curtains to separate the space. For they were unsure whether the thickness of the wall of the First Temple counted as part of the Holy of Holies or the Sanctuary [and therefore placed a curtain on either side of where the wall would have been]. Since there nobody knew which of the two curtains was the real one, neither one could be woven with figures of cherubim.

VERSE 33

OR HAHAYYIM

וְנָתַתָּה אֶת־הַפָּרֹכֶת תַּחַת הַקְּרָסִים – *Hang the curtain under the clasps:* These verses give the impression that Moshe was meant to first hang the curtain between the two rooms and

וְהִבְדִּילָה הַפָּרֹכֶת לָכֶם בֵּין הַקֹּדֶשׁ וּבֵין קֹדֶשׁ הַקֳּדָשִׁים׃
לד וְנָתַתָּ אֶת־הַכַּפֹּרֶת עַל אֲרוֹן הָעֵדֻת בְּקֹדֶשׁ הַקֳּדָשִׁים׃
לה וְשַׂמְתָּ אֶת־הַשֻּׁלְחָן מִחוּץ לַפָּרֹכֶת וְאֶת־הַמְּנֹרָה נֹכַח
הַשֻּׁלְחָן עַל צֶלַע הַמִּשְׁכָּן תֵּימָנָה וְהַשֻּׁלְחָן תִּתֵּן עַל־צֶלַע
לו צָפוֹן׃ וְעָשִׂיתָ מָסָךְ לְפֶתַח הָאֹהֶל תְּכֵלֶת וְאַרְגָּמָן וְתוֹלַעַת
לז שָׁנִי וְשֵׁשׁ מָשְׁזָר מַעֲשֵׂה רֹקֵם׃ וְעָשִׂיתָ לַמָּסָךְ חֲמִשָּׁה עַמּוּדֵי
שִׁטִּים וְצִפִּיתָ אֹתָם זָהָב וָוֵיהֶם זָהָב וְיָצַקְתָּ לָהֶם חֲמִשָּׁה

OR HAḤAYYIM *(cont.)*

only then to position the Ark inside the Holy of Holies. On the other hand, in Parashat Pekudei, God instructs Moshe: *Put in it the Ark of the Testimony, and screen the Ark with the curtain* (40:3), which suggests that the two actions should be performed in the opposite order. In practice, we find that Moshe first placed the Ark inside its designated chamber and only then hung the curtain in front of it [see 40:21]. Apparently, the reason our verse describes the placement of the curtain out of order is because it has just been discussing the creation of that component of the Tabernacle. The only reason the Ark is even mentioned in this verse is to clarify the purpose of the curtain – its job was to separate the holiness of the Sanctuary from the more sacred Holy of Holies, where the Ark was housed. Thus the current verse is not meant to convey the order in which the Tabernacle's various components were installed – that will be explored in its proper place.

RABBI SAMSON RAPHAEL HIRSCH

וְנָתַתָּה אֶת־הַפָּרֹכֶת תַּחַת הַקְּרָסִים – *Hang the curtain under the clasps:* Note that the text first orders that the curtain be hung in front of the Holy of Holies, and then that the cover of the Ark be put into position [in the next verse]. Thus the text emphasizes the importance of the division that the curtain contributes toward our entire understanding of the Ark cover's symbolism. When the Tabernacle was actually assembled, the Ark with its cover was first brought into the structure, and only then was the curtain hung before it to separate the room from the rest of the Sanctuary [see 40:21].

HAAMEK DAVAR

וְנָתַתָּה אֶת־הַפָּרֹכֶת – *Hang the curtain:* [Literally, "place the curtain."] The sense of the verb "place" [*venatatta*] in this clause is really to "hang." The text waits to explains the curtain's purpose until after describing how the Ark is to be brought into the chamber. That will create a state wherein *the curtain separates the holy place from the Holy of Holies* by hanging between the two rooms.

RABBI JOSEPH B. SOLOVEITCHIK

וְהִבְדִּילָה הַפָּרֹכֶת – *So that the curtain separates:* From the time I was young, I learned to restrain my feelings and not to demonstrate what was happening in my emotional world.

bring the Ark of the Testimony behind it, so that the curtain
34 separates the holy place from the Holy of Holies. Put the cover
35 on the Ark of the Testimony in the Holy of Holies. The table
shall be placed on the north side of the Tabernacle outside the
curtain, and the candelabrum on the south side, opposite the
36 table. Make a screen for the entrance to the Tent, embroidered
with sky-blue, purple, and scarlet wool and finely spun linen.
37 Make five posts of acacia wood for the screen and overlay them
with gold; their hooks, also, shall be of gold. Cast for them, too,

RABBI JOSEPH B. SOLOVEITCHIK *(cont.)*

My father would say that the holier and more intimate the feeling, the more it should be concealed. There is a hidden curtain that separates between one's interior and the exterior: *So that the curtain separates the holy place from the Holy of Holies.* What location is more sanctified than the inner sanctum one's emotional life? If all is going well and one's heart overflows with happiness, he should reveal the deep interior of his soul to God, but he should not reveal it to others lest a stranger profane his Holy of Holies. If, on the other hand, someone is in dire straits, mired in a cloud of pain and suffering, finding himself abandoned and alone, he should reveal his thoughts before the Creator; he should cry to Him and supplicate behind the curtain. A stranger should not approach the Holy of Holies lest in his apathy he profanes the sanctity of the mute pain that burdens the sufferer. *No one shall be in the Tent of Meeting from the time Aharon enters to make atonement in the Sanctuary until he comes out* (Leviticus 16:17). The High Priest's rendezvous with his Creator is in solitude.

VERSE 35

MALBIM

וְשַׂמְתָּ אֶת־הַשֻּׁלְחָן – *The table shall be placed:* There are two commandments contained in this instruction. Firstly, the verse teaches that the table was to be placed in the Sanctuary before the candelabrum was brought in, as is in fact reported in Parashat Pekudei (40:22–25). Secondly, this sentence informs us that the candelabrum was to be positioned along the south wall and the table opposite it against the north wall of the building. This is because the north side wakes first, as the verse requests: *Awake, O north wind; and come, you south; blow upon my garden* (Song of Songs 4:16), while an earlier verse states, *His left hand is under my head, and his right hand embraces me* [Song of Songs 2:6; the left side corresponds to the north and the right is south].

VERSE 37

HAAMEK DAVAR

וְעָשִׂיתָ לַמָּסָךְ חֲמִשָּׁה עַמּוּדֵי שִׁטִּים – *Make five posts of acacia wood for the screen:* The prepositional *lamed* that starts the word *lamasakh* means "for" the screen [implying that they must be made with the specific intention of being used for the screen], since anything that is not constructed for the express purpose of the Sanctuary is invalid for use there. But if this is so, the following difficulty emerges: Why, regarding the posts for the curtain described

כז א אַדְנֵי נְחֹשֶׁת׃ וְעָשִׂיתָ אֶת־הַמִּזְבֵּחַ עֲצֵי שִׁטִּים ששי
חָמֵשׁ אַמּוֹת אֹרֶךְ וְחָמֵשׁ אַמּוֹת רֹחַב רָבוּעַ יִהְיֶה הַמִּזְבֵּחַ

HAAMEK DAVAR *(cont.)*

previously, does the text not similarly specify that the posts are to be "for" the curtain? Instead, it simply instructs: *Hang it on four gold-covered posts* (26:32). But those pillars too must have been fashioned specifically to hold the curtain. Nevertheless, the Torah did not need to specify this fact with regard to those inner pillars because the requirement of special intent is mandated with regard to *all* components of the Tabernacle by the verse *They shall make Me a Sanctuary* [25:8; i.e., everything must be specially made "for Me" and cannot be repurposed from other projects]. But this only begs the question: Why in our verse does the Torah feel the need to specify that these posts in particular must be made "for" the screen? This answer is that this added phrase teaches that some extra step was required to create the posts for the screen, something not needed for the similar structures which supported the curtain. Thus it was forbidden for the Tabernacle builders to merely make nine posts to serve the curtain, which was holier, and of those nine to repurpose five to suspend the screen at the eastern entrance of the tent. Without the special detail present on the screen's pillars, it would have in fact been possible to do so. This will be made clear in Parashat Vayakhel, which states that these pillars possessed an additional sheathing that the curtain's posts lacked. [As the later verse states: *He overlaid their [the five posts] tops and bands with gold, but their five sockets were of bronze* – 36:38.]

CHAPTER 27, VERSE 1

OR HAHAYYIM

וְעָשִׂיתָ אֶת־הַמִּזְבֵּחַ – *Make the altar:* Note that the verse uses the definite article when introducing the alter, where it could have merely said: Make an altar. It is possible that the altar had already been tacitly introduced in the general statement at the start of these chapters, *Form the Tabernacle and form all of its furnishings following the patterns that I show you* (25:9). It was at that point that God showed Moshe a picture of the altar. And hence the sense of God's command here is: Make the altar whose image I previously illustrated.

HAKETAV VEHAKABBALA

רָבוּעַ יִהְיֶה – *It should be square:* These words appear to be superfluous. Once the verse states that the altar is to be *five cubits long and five cubits wide*, it is obvious that the item was square! Why then is this detail included in the altar's description? It teaches us that actually, the exact dimensions given here are not absolutely necessary. Even a much smaller altar measuring one cubit by one cubit would be valid as long as it was square. Furthermore, when the text mandates that the structure should be "three cubits high," that represents a minimum height for the altar, but it need not be built to precisely that specification. At the very least, the altar must rise to a height of three cubits, which is the size of an average person. Based on this it seems that we should not understand the term "three cubits high" literally, since in fact the Tabernacle altar was ten cubits tall. Rather, the term "high" [*komato*] implies merely that the altar should stand upright, perpendicular to the ground.

27 1 five sockets of bronze. Make the altar from acacia SHISHI
wood. It should be square, five cubits long, five cubits wide,

RABBI SAMSON RAPHAEL HIRSCH

רָבוּעַ יִהְיֶה – *It should be square:* The squareness of the altar is a necessary requirement for its construction. [That is, any other shape would invalidate the structure.] Now it is well known that most forms produced by the natural world are round or curved. It is only human beings who exercise their free will and act with forethought, willingly limiting their behavior. Only they fashion their creations with straight lines and measured angles. Hence, while the circle belongs to the world of submission, to a state devoid of freedom, to impurity, a square by contrast symbolizes our recognition that we possesses the liberty to extend our mastery over the physical world and devote ourselves to the pursuit of purity. From this general perspective it becomes readily apparent why the square, and systems of straight lines and right angles constitute the fundamental architectural principles for the Tabernacle. For the entire project was meant to stand in opposition to the cult of nature worship prevalent in those days.

HAAMEK DAVAR

וְעָשִׂיתָ אֶת־הַמִּזְבֵּחַ – *Make the altar:* Why does the verse not simply command: Make an altar? [What is the significance of the definite article?] The answer is that God introduced the altar earlier when He commanded: *Make for Me an altar of earth* (20:21). At this point the text returns to describe exactly what kind of altar God intended Israel to fashion. This fact explains why the current passage does not bother to mention that [although the altar should be hollow, as instructed in verse 8] it was to be filled with earth. For that particular was already decreed back in Parashat Yitro.

RABBI JOSEPH B. SOLOVEITCHIK

וְעָשִׂיתָ אֶת־הַמִּזְבֵּחַ – *Make the altar:* Maimonides apparently maintains that were we not obligated to offer sacrifices in the Tabernacle, there would be no commandment to build it at all. We can infer his opinion from the wording at the outset of *Hilkhot Beit Habekhira:* "It is a positive commandment to build a house for God which is set for offering sacrifices." Along similar lines, he writes in *Sefer Hamitzvot* (20): "We are commanded to build a chosen house for sacrifice, within it is the offering and the continual burning of the fire." When Maimonides uses the term "a house for God," he means a house in which sacrifices are offered. He does not use this idiom in the more literal sense, that is, as a place where the Divine Presence resides, in the way that Ibn Ezra and Ramban use it. Maimonides rejects the entire concept of *tzimtzum* [literally, "limiting" or "withdrawing"], negating the possibility that God could reside in a building. In his opinion, the purpose of the Sanctuary was only for the offering of sacrifices within it. The words *They shall make Me a Sanctuary and I will dwell in their midst* (25:8) are fulfilled only through sacrifices [*korbanot*], which is derived from the word "closeness" [*hitkarevut*] because man becomes exceedingly close to God, enraptured by the sacrificial service.

וְשָׁלֹשׁ אַמּוֹת קֹמָתוֹ: וְעָשִׂיתָ קַרְנֹתָיו עַל אַרְבַּע פִּנֹּתָיו מִמֶּנּוּ ב
תִּהְיֶיןָ קַרְנֹתָיו וְצִפִּיתָ אֹתוֹ נְחֹשֶׁת: וְעָשִׂיתָ סִּירֹתָיו לְדַשְּׁנוֹ ג
וְיָעָיו וּמִזְרְקֹתָיו וּמִזְלְגֹתָיו וּמַחְתֹּתָיו לְכָל־כֵּלָיו תַּעֲשֶׂה
נְחֹשֶׁת: וְעָשִׂיתָ לּוֹ מִכְבָּר מַעֲשֵׂה רֶשֶׁת נְחֹשֶׁת וְעָשִׂיתָ ד

VERSE 2

HAKETAV VEHAKABBALA

וְעָשִׂיתָ קַרְנֹתָיו – *Make horns for it:* The Hebrew language borrows the word "horn" [*keren*] to refer to any feature that protrudes from the top of an object as an animal's horns do. Thus the verse states: *My beloved had a vineyard on the top [keren] of a rich hill* (Isaiah 5:1). The term is similarly employed in association with anything outstanding or prominent, as in the verses *There will I make the horn of David to shoot up* (Psalms 132:17), and *In My name shall his horn be exalted* (Psalms 89:25). Now the horns introduced here sat on the top of the altar and covered one square cubit of each corner of that surface. Thus these were "horns" in two senses, for the protuberances stuck out of the top of the altar, and they were also situated on its corners.

HAAMEK DAVAR

וְעָשִׂיתָ קַרְנֹתָיו – *Make horns for it:* [Literally, "make its horns."] This language is inaccurate, since it implies that the horns are already familiar to the reader. Instead of saying: *Make its horns*, as if the Torah had already commanded that such be fashioned, the verse should have said: "Make horns for the altar." We find a similar difficulty below when the text states: *The grate should be set below, under the ledge of the altar* (27:5), where no mention has yet been made of a ledge. Furthermore, it is surprising that the text omits the dimensions of the altar's base, given that the base of the altar is necessary for offering libations [see Zevaḥim 62a]. Nevertheless, all of these questions can be resolved by recourse to the later verse *Make it [the altar] as it was shown to you on the mountain* (27:8). We do not find such language associated with most of the other Tabernacle furniture, although the text does make a similar general statement about the Tabernacle as a whole [in 25:9] and the candelabrum specifically [in 25:40]. Now I have explained elsewhere that Moshe did not actually see images of the Tabernacle and its vessels, but the "forms" of the items that God wished him to fashion, by which I mean elements in the natural world that served as models for the various components of the Tabernacle. However, with regard to the altar, when the verse states: *Make it as it was shown to you on the mountain* (27:8), it indicates that Moshe was shown an actual picture of the altar itself. [Hence Moshe knew what God was referring to when He mentioned the altar's horns, and he did not need to be told specifically about the altar's base.]… Now in Rashi's commentary to the verse *Overlay it with pure gold on its top* [30:3, referring to the golden incense altar], the exegete explains that although the incense altar had a roof [that is, a top surface], the sacrificial altar lacked one. Rather, the altar was filled in with earth each time the Israelites settled in a new camp. Thus, in Rashi's opinion, the altar comprised just four walls sheathed in bronze, but was open on top as well as on the bottom. That is how he understands the phrase "make it hollow" (27:8). But that is quite a surprising interpretation in my opinion, since it implies that whenever the

2 and three cubits high. Make horns for it on its four corners, the
horns being of one piece with it, and overlay it with bronze.
3 Make pots for removing its ashes, together with shovels, basins,
4 forks, and pans. Make all of these of bronze. Make a grate of

HAAMEK DAVAR *(cont.)*

nation traveled the fire had to be removed from the top of the altar. That is, since the altar could be transported only after the earth sitting inside had had been removed, and the fire sat upon that soil, according to Rashi, the altar could not be moved with its fire intact. However, the Talmud in tractate Zevaḥim (61b) states that a fire burned continuously atop the altar from the time of Israel's sojourn in the wilderness until King Shlomo built the First Temple. I believe that, contrary to Rashi's understanding, the walls of the altar were not in fact covered with bronze – only the top surface of the utensil was. The bottom of the structure was open, allowing earth to be inserted when the people encamped, and easily left behind when the altar was picked up and carried away. However, the fire was ever present atop the altar, even during Israel's journeys.

THE LUBAVITCHER REBBE

וְצִפִּיתָ אֹתוֹ נְחֹשֶׁת – *Overlay it with bronze:* Although most of the other furnishings of the Tabernacle are to be overlaid with gold, you must overlay this altar with bronze, because the word for bronze [*neḥoshet*] is similar to the word for stubbornness [*naḥush*], and the sacrifices offered up on this altar atone for inadvertent sins, which a person generally commits out of his stubborn deference to the animal side of his personality.

VERSE 3

HAAMEK DAVAR

לְכָל־כֵּלָיו תַּעֲשֶׂה נְחֹשֶׁת – *Make all of these of bronze:* [Literally, "make bronze for all of these tools."] Should the verse not have more logically read: "Make all of these tools out of bronze"? In fact, the language of the verse indicates that it was not critical that the listed tools all be fashioned out of bronze, in contrast to the body of the altar itself, whose acacia wood could not have been covered in silver or in gold. For in future generations, the Temple certainly employed basins crafted out of silver and gold. Indeed, we find that the tribal chiefs presented silver basins which they dedicated for use at the Tabernacle's altar in the desert [see Numbers 7]. For sometimes copper is worked directly after being mined from the ground, whereas at other times it is annealed to form a material more amenable for construction. [Bronze is an alloy of copper and tin.] Thus when the verse states: "Make bronze for all of these tools," it means literally that the craftsmen should fashion the type of metal appropriate for the specific tool being made for the altar.

VERSE 4

SHADAL

וְעָשִׂיתָ עַל־הָרֶשֶׁת אַרְבַּע טַבְּעֹת נְחֹשֶׁת – *On the mesh make four bronze rings:* The four rings were to hold two staves, which in turn would be used to transport the altar, as mentioned below [see 38:5–7]. The rings were situated just above the grate, but they were not

עַל־הָרֶשֶׁת אַרְבַּע טַבְּעֹת נְחֹשֶׁת עַל אַרְבַּע קְצוֹתָיו׃
ה וְנָתַתָּה אֹתָהּ תַּחַת כַּרְכֹּב הַמִּזְבֵּחַ מִלְּמָטָּה וְהָיְתָה הָרֶשֶׁת
ו עַד חֲצִי הַמִּזְבֵּחַ׃ וְעָשִׂיתָ בַדִּים לַמִּזְבֵּחַ בַּדֵּי עֲצֵי שִׁטִּים

SHADAL *(cont.)*

attached to it, being affixed instead to the altar itself. Furthermore, the grate itself was not welded to the altar and could be removed. We know this because the text later reports: *They brought the Tabernacle to Moshe…the bronze altar with its bronze mesh, its staves and all its utensils* (39:33–39). And that passage mentions not a single fixture that was attached to, or was a permanent feature of, the item to which it belonged. For example the Torah does not state that the craftsman brought to Moshe for his inspection the loops that connected the sets of sheets [described in 26:5], the frame surrounding the table [demanded in 25:25], or its gold rim [required by 25:24]; and the text neglects to count the cups, knobs, and flowers [that adorned the candelabrum – see 25:31] as items distinct from the candelabrum itself. [Thus we can infer that, because the grate is stated separately from the altar, it was always considered a distinct piece from the main body of the item.]

MALBIM

וְעָשִׂיתָ לּוֹ מִכְבַּר מַעֲשֵׂה רֶשֶׁת נְחֹשֶׁת – *Make a grate of bronze mesh for it:* The term *mikhbar* derives from the same root that gives us *kevara* [meaning "sieve"], a term found in the verse *I will sift the house of Israel among all nations, as grain is sifted in a sieve* (Amos 9:9). In the current context, the word refers to a decorative mesh that was fashioned around the altar. Now logically, this verse should have appeared earlier [before verse 3, which discusses the tools associated with the functioning of the altar] since the grate was apparently a fixture on the altar itself. After that the text could have gone on to state: *Make pots for removing its ashes etc.* We find a more appropriate sequence in the Torah's presentation of the table, where the entire object is described before the text continues with its *bowls, spoons, pitchers and jars* (25:29). We are therefore justified in concluding that the grate did actually not form part of the body of the altar. Rather, this item was built as a separate ornament, which was then wrapped around the altar. Thus Rashi is careful to state: "The grate was fashioned as a sort of garment for the altar." Note that the altar in the Temple had no grate, but was instead marked around the middle of its height with a line of red paint. That border delineated the upper part of the altar, where the blood of particular sacrifices was sprinkled, separating it from the bottom half of the structure where the blood of other kinds of offerings was splashed. It seems to me that the purpose of the grate was to allow a place for the attachment of the rings. For since the altar had to be perfectly square and smooth all around, there was really no place for the rings to protrude. Hence Moshe was instructed to affix the rings to the grate that encompassed the altar. And because the grate was a distinct item of its own, even though it fit tightly around the altar such that it did not slide down its walls, we can still characterize the altar itself as a perfect square. This explains why the grate was perforated – that design meant that it would not appear to be a true part of the altar, since the latter could be seen through the holes of the grate. But all this was

bronze mesh for it, and on the mesh make four bronze rings at
5 its four corners. The grate should be set below, under the ledge
of the altar, so that the mesh reaches the middle of the altar.
6 And make staves of acacia wood for the altar, and overlay them

MALBIM *(cont.)*

only required in the wilderness when rings were needed to transport the altar. The altar in the Temple was never moved, and hence did not require a grate.

VERSE 5

HAKETAV VEHAKABBALA

תַּחַת כַּרְכֹּב הַמִּזְבֵּחַ – *Under the ledge of the altar:* The altar was not one smooth surface all the way up from the ground to its top. After six cubits, counting from the bottom, a ledge surrounded the object. This was a protrusion that adorned the altar and encompassed it. Beneath the ledge, also running all around the altar, was an additional feature called a grate. Affixed to this mesh were four bronze rings, into which were inserted the staves used to transport the altar. Now the Targum of Yonatan ben Uziel [Targum Yerushalmi] explains that the function of the projecting ledge was to catch anything that might tumble off the altar's surface. Thus he writes: "The grate was situated halfway up the altar, such that if any piece of sacrificial flesh or a flaming coal fell off, it would be caught by the grill and would not reach the ground. Should that happen, the priests would pick up the fallen item and replace it on top of the altar." Thus it becomes clear that the ledge and the grate that held the rings and the staves both protruded from the surface of the altar, giving it a stepped appearance beneath the top level of the wood pile itself. However, from that point upward – a span of three cubits – the altar was a straight vertical plane on all four sides. This then is the meaning of the requirement that the altar be "three cubits high" [27:1, although it was actually much higher].

HAAMEK DAVAR

תַּחַת כַּרְכֹּב הַמִּזְבֵּחַ – *Under the ledge of the altar:* The ledge mentioned in this verse is synonymous with the *sovev* mentioned by Onkelos. This was an indispensable feature of the altar [i.e., in its absence the altar was rendered invalid]. We must conclude that Moshe was shown an image of the altar from above, so that he was able to see the ledge. For this would explain why the text does not explicitly command that Moshe construct a ledge, for that detail was included in the general instruction: *Make it [the altar] as it was shown to you on the mountain* (27:8). [That is, since Moshe witnessed the ledge when God demonstrated to him how the altar should look, there was no need to issue a specific command regarding this detail.]

VERSE 6

HAAMEK DAVAR

וְעָשִׂיתָ בַדִּים לַמִּזְבֵּחַ בַּדֵּי עֲצֵי שִׁטִּים – *And make staves of acacia wood for the altar:* [Literally, "and make staves for the altar, staves of acacia wood."] This verse is rather wordy and could

ז וְצִפִּיתָ אֹתָם נְחֹשֶׁת: וְהוּבָא אֶת־בַּדָּיו בַּטַּבָּעֹת וְהָיוּ הַבַּדִּים
ח עַל־שְׁתֵּי צַלְעֹת הַמִּזְבֵּחַ בִּשְׂאֵת אֹתוֹ: נְבוּב לֻחֹת תַּעֲשֶׂה
ט אֹתוֹ כַּאֲשֶׁר הֶרְאָה אֹתְךָ בָּהָר כֵּן יַעֲשׂוּ: וְעָשִׂיתָ שביעי
אֵת חֲצַר הַמִּשְׁכָּן לִפְאַת נֶגֶב־תֵּימָנָה קְלָעִים לֶחָצֵר שֵׁשׁ

HAAMEK DAVAR *(cont.)*

have read more simply: And make staves of acacia wood for the altar. Now the staves fashioned for the Ark and the bronze altar differed from those made for the other utensils. Betzalel was required to insert the poles of the main altar and those of the Ark so that they remained perpetually in their rings. This contrasted with the staves of the table and the inner altar, which were put into place only when those items had to be transported. This feature symbolized the power of the Torah that inhered in the Ark, and the importance of the sacrificial service represented by the altar. These aspects of Jewish life are two constants that accompany the nation forever and wherever they find themselves. [The fixed staves symbolize these areas' mobile character. The sacrifices have been replaced by the institution of prayer, as the author discusses below]. On the other hand, the dimension of the Israelite monarchy [reflected in the materialism of the table] and the significance of the High Priesthood [attached to the incense altar] are areas of Jewish life which only become relevant when the nation resides in the land of Israel. Nevertheless, the strength of the Torah does differ from the system of sacrifices, in that as the Torah is carried through Jewish history, it travels in the same manner that it was conveyed through the wilderness and into the land of Israel. This remains so even though there are occasional alterations in the modes through which the Torah is studied, something that is contingent on varying lifestyles and conditions. Still, the efforts to interpret the Torah and derive its lessons do not change. In our times, however, prayer substitutes for sacrifice, and the two forms of religious expression are inherently different. This is what our verse alludes to when it uses the word "staves" twice.

VERSE 7

HAAMEK DAVAR

וְהוּבָא אֶת־בַּדָּיו בַּטַּבָּעֹת – *Place the poles in the rings:* It has already been explained that the staves were inserted upon the completion of the Tabernacle as the structure was about to be assembled. But these poles needed to be *on the two sides of the altar* only when the nation began their first journey. When the finished altar was first presented to the leader, the staves only needed to be symbolically inserted in the rings, as a sign that the altar would really be carried throughout the generations. Afterward, the staves would really have to be on the two sides of the alter only *when it is carried*. And once the altar came to rest at the nation's new location, its staves were removed. For it is only regarding the poles of the Ark that the Torah commands: *The staves must stay in the rings of the Ark; they must not be removed* (25:15).

עַל־שְׁתֵּי צַלְעֹת הַמִּזְבֵּחַ – *On the two sides of the altar:* The arrangement of the staves on the altar differed from that of the table, which was

7 with bronze. Place the poles in the rings, so that the poles will
8 be on the two sides of the altar when it is carried. Make it hollow, with planks; make it as it was shown to you on the moun-
9 tain. Make the courtyard of the Tabernacle thus: on SHEVI'I
the south side there should be hangings a hundred cubits long
of finely spun linen, all the length of the courtyard on that side,

HAAMEK DAVAR *(cont.)*

carried by four poles – each side of the table held a ring into which was inserted a different pole. The inner gold altar was constructed in an identical manner. However, the sacrificial altar had two rings on each of two sides, and each pair of rings served a single pole.

VERSE 8

HAAMEK DAVAR

נְבוּב לֻחֹת תַּעֲשֶׂה אֹתוֹ – *Make it hollow:* This verse explains that the altar is not to be filled permanently with earth that is sealed inside the structure with boards. Rather, the planks framed a hollow vessel which was emptied of all of its earth each time the nation broke camp. When Israel arrived at its new campsite, the altar was again filled up with soil. The reason for this design was to realize God's command to construct an altar that was attached to the ground, as the Talmud explains [see Zevaḥim 58a]. This idea is supported by the Mekhilta on Parashat Yitro, which states: "Rabbi Yishmael taught: When the verse states: *Make for Me an altar of earth* (20:21), it means that the altar should not be erected on a platform or raised to sit on pillars." Because the altar was hollow [with an open bottom] the earth contained within its walls was in direct contact with the ground wherever the structure stood.

VERSE 9

HAKETAV VEHAKABBALA

קְלָעִים – *Hangings:* According to Rashi, the hangings were so called because they resembled the sails [*kela'im*] of a ship, only they were perforated with holes [to permit the wind to flow through]. Rashbam, on the other hand, writes that the Tabernacle hangings were constructed with braided [*miklaot*] designs. In fact, both approaches convey the intention of the verse. Firstly, the hangings were meant to be suspended like curtains. Indeed the Aramaic word for a hanging is *kela*, as we find in the verse: *They could not spread the sail* (Isaiah 33:23) translated as *lemifras kela*, referring to the sails of a ship. But the term *kela* also teaches us how these curtains were fashioned – they should be constructed out of braided ropes [*keli'a*].

RABBI SAMSON RAPHAEL HIRSCH

וְעָשִׂיתָ אֵת חֲצַר הַמִּשְׁכָּן – *Make the courtyard of the Tabernacle:* The usual understanding of the word *ḥatzer* is an open space surrounding some structure to which it is attached. Thus the areas and rooms in front of the main Temple building, where sacred activities were undertaken, are in fact referred to as *azarot*, since those places served as outdoor annexes that facilitated [*azar*] the overall compound. Now the courtyard encompassed the Tabernacle

י מָשְׁזָר מֵאָה בָאַמָּה אֹרֶךְ לַפֵּאָה הָאֶחָת: וְעַמֻּדָיו עֶשְׂרִים
וְאַדְנֵיהֶם עֶשְׂרִים נְחֹשֶׁת וָוֵי הָעַמֻּדִים וַחֲשֻׁקֵיהֶם כָּסֶף:
יא וְכֵן לִפְאַת צָפוֹן בָּאֹרֶךְ קְלָעִים מֵאָה אֹרֶךְ וְעַמֻּדָו עֶשְׂרִים
וְאַדְנֵיהֶם עֶשְׂרִים נְחֹשֶׁת וָוֵי הָעַמֻּדִים וַחֲשֻׁקֵיהֶם כָּסֶף:
יב וְרֹחַב הֶחָצֵר לִפְאַת־יָם קְלָעִים חֲמִשִּׁים אַמָּה עַמֻּדֵיהֶם
יג עֲשָׂרָה וְאַדְנֵיהֶם עֲשָׂרָה: וְרֹחַב הֶחָצֵר לִפְאַת קֵדְמָה
יד מִזְרָחָה חֲמִשִּׁים אַמָּה: וַחֲמֵשׁ עֶשְׂרֵה אַמָּה קְלָעִים לַכָּתֵף
טו עַמֻּדֵיהֶם שְׁלֹשָׁה וְאַדְנֵיהֶם שְׁלֹשָׁה: וְלַכָּתֵף הַשֵּׁנִית חֲמֵשׁ

RABBI SAMSON RAPHAEL HIRSCH *(cont.)*

building on all four sides, but its most important space comprised the area in front of the tent. The measurements of this specific zone are given below as fifty cubits square [in 27:18].

קְלָעִים – *Hangings:* The hangings introduced in this verse ran all around the borders of the compound. It is possible that the term *kela* derives from a root that connotes shooting [at a target] or throwing something from a distance. For the hangings suspended around the Sanctuary were light and kept some way apart from the items and service inside the area. This stood in contrast to the coverings above the Tabernacle building, which were not only thick, but also closely adjacent to the structure they protected. Our Sages use the word *ikla* to denote a happenstance encounter between individuals, and this relates to the literal sense of the term: to be cast into a place with no prior intention of arriving there. This understanding seems also to reflect an alternative meaning of *keli'a* ["braiding"] which involves threads that are thrown at, i.e., woven over, each other. Thus it is also possible that the word *kela'im* suggests thin coverings such as curtains made of materials interwoven as in a braid.

MALBIM

קְלָעִים לֶחָצֵר – *Hangings for the courtyard:* Rashi believes that these hangings were perforated, whereas Radak argues that the hangings were so called because they seemed to be carved, as in the phrase "carvings of bulbs" [*miklaat peka'im* – I Kings 6:18].

THE LUBAVITCHER REBBE

קְלָעִים לֶחָצֵר – *Hangings for the courtyard:* These hangings were made of linen because flax, from which linen is made, differs from other plants in that only a single stalk grows from each seed. One of the words for linen in biblical Hebrew [*bad*] reflects this attribute, since it also means "alone." Since the Jews are distinguished from the other nations by virtue of their absolute monotheism, it is appropriate that the curtain separating the Tabernacle from the surrounding world be made of this material.

10 with twenty posts and their twenty bronze sockets. The hooks
11 and bands of the posts shall be of silver. Likewise on the north
side; the hangings shall be a hundred cubits long, with twenty
posts and their twenty corresponding bronze sockets, with
12 hooks and bands of silver. The width of the hangings at the
western end of the courtyard shall be fifty cubits, and it should
13 have ten posts and their ten corresponding sockets. The width
of the courtyard at the front, facing east, shall be fifty cubits:
14 fifteen cubits of hangings with three posts and three sockets on
15 one side, and fifteen cubits of hangings with three posts and

VERSE 10

RABBI ISAAC SAMUEL REGGIO

וָוֵי הָעַמֻּדִים – *The hooks of the posts:* This term refers to the hooks by which the hangings were attached. These were perhaps ornately designed as capitals atop the pillars. **וַחֲשֻׁקֵיהֶם** – *Bands:* The root *ḥet-shin-kof* usually refers to something attached or joined, as when a person loves somebody and cleaves to them, his soul intertwined with theirs. Thus the verse states: *And his soul cleaved to Dina the daughter of Yaakov, and he loved the girl* (Genesis 34:3), a statement followed by the verse: *The soul of my son Shekhem longs [ḥasheka] for your daughter* (Genesis 34:8). Hence we can explain that the hooks were firmly attached to the posts with silver bands which encompassed the pillars.... And since these hooks were burdened with the heavy weight of the hangings, and were pulled by the pegs stuck into the ground to which they were tied, their contact point on the pillars had to be reinforced to prevent them from being yanked out. This was achieved by welding them to silver fillets that held them in place.

RABBI SAMSON RAPHAEL HIRSCH

וַחֲשֻׁקֵיהֶם – *Bands:* In verse 17 we read that *All the posts around the courtyard should be banded [meḥushakim] with silver.* These strips of silver were not mere accessories, negligible features of the pillars. Rather, the fillets represented an essential attribute of these posts, since the root *ḥet-shin-kof* connotes a strong adherence to something. It is employed to describe a tight grip on a person or object, here indicating that the bands were firmly embedded into the posts they circled.

VERSE 13

RABBI ISAAC SAMUEL REGGIO

חֲמִשִּׁים אַמָּה – *Fifty cubits:* The fifty-cubit eastern edge of the compound was not covered entirely with the hangings, because that side held the entrance to the Sanctuary. Rather, there were fifteen cubits of material on either side of the opening, leaving a space of twenty cubits for the entrance. Hence the subsequent verse states: *And for the gate of the courtyard there shall be an embroidered screen of twenty cubits* (27:16); this screen fit the open area precisely.

טז עֶשְׂרֵה קְלָעִים עַמֻּדֵיהֶם שְׁלֹשָׁה וְאַדְנֵיהֶם שְׁלֹשָׁה: וּלְשַׁעַר
הֶחָצֵר מָסָךְ ׀ עֶשְׂרִים אַמָּה תְּכֵלֶת וְאַרְגָּמָן וְתוֹלַעַת שָׁנִי
וְשֵׁשׁ מָשְׁזָר מַעֲשֵׂה רֹקֵם עַמֻּדֵיהֶם אַרְבָּעָה וְאַדְנֵיהֶם
יז אַרְבָּעָה: כָּל־עַמּוּדֵי הֶחָצֵר סָבִיב מְחֻשָּׁקִים כֶּסֶף וָוֵיהֶם מפטיר
יח כָּסֶף וְאַדְנֵיהֶם נְחֹשֶׁת: אֹרֶךְ הֶחָצֵר מֵאָה בָאַמָּה וְרֹחַב ׀
חֲמִשִּׁים בַּחֲמִשִּׁים וְקֹמָה חָמֵשׁ אַמּוֹת שֵׁשׁ מָשְׁזָר וְאַדְנֵיהֶם
יט נְחֹשֶׁת: לְכֹל כְּלֵי הַמִּשְׁכָּן בְּכֹל עֲבֹדָתוֹ וְכָל־יְתֵדֹתָיו וְכָל־
יִתְדֹת הֶחָצֵר נְחֹשֶׁת:

VERSE 16

HAAMEK DAVAR

תְּכֵלֶת וְאַרְגָּמָן – *Sky-blue, purple:* The design of this screen was like that on the fabric that hung in front of the entrance to the Tabernacle building itself [mentioned in 26:36], and it also resembled the curtain suspended in front of the Holy of Holies [described in 26:31]. It was not at all similar to the other hangings that surrounded the courtyard [comprising the walls] which all in turn differed considerably from the roof coverings of the structure. The distinction between this embroidered screen at the compound's entrance and the hangings that stood nearby teaches us the following point: When one prepares to enter a holy area, he must sanctify himself even before he has reached the inner area of the Sanctuary and still stands outside the precincts of the Tabernacle. True, before crossing the threshold of the holy space, one is permitted to act in a thoroughly secular manner. But as he approaches the place where the Divine Presence rests, he must focus his thoughts and begin to conduct himself appropriately. Thus the screen that was situated in front of the courtyard was composed of sky-blue wool to recall the throne of glory [known to be the same color – see 24:10]. And this symbolism was significant even though, after moving into the courtyard, one still remained outside the Tabernacle structure itself. The screen of the tent served as a sign for those who sought further entrance to that area, to compose and consecrate themselves.

VERSE 17

RABBI SAMSON RAPHAEL HIRSCH

מְחֻשָּׁקִים כֶּסֶף – *Banded with silver:* Imagine what the courtyard in front of the Tabernacle must have looked like! The space was surrounded by white sheets fashioned from threads of linen twisted six times. The hangings themselves were suspended with silver hooks on pillars that were filleted with silver bands, and which were held in place by bronze sockets. All of this stood in concert with the symbolism of the Tabernacle compound these hangings encompassed, and the altar that stood within it, while it was the altar itself which lent the whole courtyard its significance. The area surrounding the altar, like the altar itself announced to all who visited it: "Behold! You are standing at the entrance to

16 three sockets on the other, and for the gate of the courtyard
there shall be an embroidered screen of twenty cubits of sky-
blue, purple, and scarlet wool and finely spun linen, with four
17 posts and four sockets. All the posts around the courtyard MAFTIR
should be banded with silver. Their hooks shall be of silver, and
18 their sockets of bronze. The courtyard shall be a hundred cubits long, fifty cubits wide, and five cubits high, with hangings
19 of finely spun linen and sockets of bronze. All the Tabernacle
utensils, for every use, as well as all its tent pegs and the tent
pegs of the courtyard, shall be of bronze.

RABBI SAMSON RAPHAEL HIRSCH *(cont.)*

a place dedicated to purification." The starkest impression a visitor must have received was the glaring whiteness emanating from the Tabernacle environment. The white linen shimmering in the desert heat symbolized purification, especially the taming of those areas of human nature closest to animal instinct, such as sexual desire and physical indulgences. For mastery over those inclinations represents the first task of the religious personality, since their influence over the individual is purely negative. When a person seeks a closeness with God he must distance himself from the profane, and must minimize association with whatever damages the purity of the soul. Since it is those elements that prevent an individual from fulfilling his sacred destiny, all spiritual progress is dependent upon reaching a level of distance from them. All this lies within the realm of the possible; we are not expected to ignore our human nature or to thoroughly suppress our needs or inclinations. After all, it is our Creator who calls upon us to rise and meet our potential; God would not demand anything that was beyond our abilities, or command us to perform at a level outside of our powers. On the contrary, God made us for the express purpose of purifying our souls. We alone among His creations are able to express the image of God that we have been granted. The foundational character of human beings is the freedom they possesses to act in a moral fashion, and the first expression of that nature is purity.

HAAMEK DAVAR

וְאַדְנֵיהֶם נְחֹשֶׁת – *And their sockets of bronze:* Surely it is unnecessary for both verses 17 and 18 to state that the sockets holding the courtyard posts should be constructed out of bronze. It seems that the repetition here is to stress that the sockets must be made out of bronze and cannot be fashioned out of iron. These sockets are called *adanim,* a name that derives from the word for foundation – *eden.* Furthermore, the phrase *All the Tabernacle utensils…shall be of bronze* (27:19) teaches that even the tools used to assemble the Tabernacle and to take it apart also had be made of bronze and not iron, just like those used to build the Temple.

VERSE 19

RABBI ISAAC SAMUEL REGGIO

וְכָל־יְתֵדֹתָיו – *All its tent pegs:* This term refers to the bronze stakes used to tie down the courtyard hangings. These pegs were pounded into the ground to prevent the curtains

RABBI ISAAC SAMUEL REGGIO *(cont.)*

from billowing up in the wind. It seems likely that the pegs were situated at the midpoint between the hangings' posts, since that is where the material would have been most susceptible to movement.

RABBI JOSEPH B. SOLOVEITCHIK

לְכֹל כְּלֵי הַמִּשְׁכָּן – *All the Tabernacle utensils:* How must a religious couple furnish their home? The Tabernacle that the children of Israel made in the desert as a house for God can serve as an example. In Parashat Teruma, God commands to make the vessels of the Tabernacle: the Ark, the table, and the candelabrum. God also commanded to make the incense altar, but this item is not mentioned until Parashat Tetzaveh (30:1–10). In Parashat Vayakhel (chapter 37), all four vessels are mentioned together at the time they were made. However, the fact that the incense altar is not mentioned in Parashat Teruma suggest that the character of this vessel is different from the other three (see Ibn Ezra on 25:22). It appears that the purpose of the building of the Tabernacle was not merely to offer sacrifices. For this purpose a simple altar would be sufficient; the beautiful building and the vessels within this building would be unnecessary. The main purpose behind the building of the Tabernacle was to create a house for God. Ibn Ezra explains that only the three vessels mentioned in Parashat Teruma (the Ark, the table, and the candelabrum) were necessary to create such a house. Even without the incense altar, the Sanctuary would have fulfilled the function of a house. Precisely how to furnish a guest can be derived from the incident of the Shunamite woman who told her husband: *Let us make him a small enclosed upper chamber and provide him with a bed, table, chair, and lamp there, so that whenever he comes to us, he can turn in there* (II Kings 4:10). If, according to Ibn Ezra, the Tabernacle can transform into a house, the private house of the Jew can transform into a Tabernacle. We welcome God into our homes through establishing what the Shunamite woman mentioned: the bed, the table, the chair, and the lamp. Homiletically, the bed represents family purity, the table represents keeping kosher as well as the commandment of welcoming guests, while the candelabrum represents the study of Torah: *For the precept is like a lamp, the teaching like light itself* (Proverbs 6:23). And in such a spiritually furnished home, one can hear the voice of God as in the Tabernacle: *There, from above the cover...I will meet with you and speak with you* (Exodus 25:22). In such a sanctuary, the Divine Presence indeed finds a place to dwell.

THE LUBAVITCHER REBBE

וְכָל־יְתֵדֹתָיו – *All its tent pegs:* Rashi suggests the possibility that the stakes were not actually hammered into the ground, but rather simply held the curtains in place by their weight. Nonetheless, he feels that the evidence indicates that they were indeed imbedded in the ground. If the stakes only acted as weights, the connection between the Tabernacle and the ground it stood on was merely coincidental, but if the stakes were implanted in the ground, it means that the holiness of the Tabernacle actually permeated the ground. The Torah describes later how the ground under the Tabernacle was actually used as part of a religious rite.

פרשת תרומה
PARASHAT TERUMA

THE **BIBLICAL**
IMAGINATION

RABBI SHAI FINKELSTEIN

INDIVIDUAL INITIATIVE

In this *parasha* the Torah describes its vision for the Tabernacle and the utensils that will be used within the compound. Here, for example, is the command to construct the Ark of the Covenant: "Make an Ark of acacia wood, two and a half cubits long, a cubit and a half wide, and a cubit and a half high. Overlay it with pure gold, inside and out, and around it make a gold rim" (25:10–11). Later in the chapter we find the instructions for fashioning a second item: "Make a table of acacia wood, two cubits long, a cubit wide and a cubit and a half high" (25:23).

A reader in the Hebrew might notice a subtle shift in terminology between the two commands, which is impossible to reflect in the English translation. The first instruction, to "make" an Ark, is addressed in the second person plural – *ve'asu* – as if many people were supposed to make it. The second, to "make" a table, is in the second person singular – *ve'asita* – as if it was incumbent only on Moshe to construct the item. This disjunction in the language did not escape the keen eyes of the authors of the Midrash (Shemot Rabba 34), which interprets the plural word as connected with the Ark's symbolism of the Torah, which it housed:

> Why does the Torah use the form *ve'asita* when discussing most of the utensils, whereas *ve'asu* appears in conjunction with the Ark? Rabbi Yehuda son of Rabbi Shalom taught: Said the Holy One, blessed be He, to Moshe: "I desire that all of the Israelites come and contribute to the building of the Ark so that each one will have a share in the Torah that the object represents.

This is a beautiful yet complicated sentiment. For at first glance one would think that the Ark, more than any other feature of the Tabernacle, required the focused attention of the single most skilled artisan. It would have been quite impossible for each Israelite to somehow have a hand in crafting this most sacred object.

Let us suggest a few explanations for the midrash's presentation. Our first approach looks at the commentary *Or Haḥayyim* (Rabbi Ḥayyim Ibn Attar, eighteenth century). That author writes:

> Perhaps the anomaly in our phrase hints that Torah law can only be maintained when the entire population of Israel is devoted to its observance. For there does not exist within the nation any single individual who is capable

of fulfilling all of the Torah's many laws. For example, a priest is exempt from donating the twenty-four gifts that other Israelites are obligated to provide for that caste, nor may he redeem his own firstborn son [as non-priestly fathers must]. On the other hand, common Israelites are not permitted to fulfill the positive commandments of offering sacrifices [duties restricted to the priests] and are therefore barred from the numerous laws which attend to that system of services.

From a purely technical perspective, the full gamut of Torah commandments can only be realized with the participation of every individual, who agrees to fulfill the laws that are applicable to him or to her. The priest works inside the Temple, the Levite sings on his platform, the Israelite supports the service with prayers and the recitation of Psalms. This point is hinted at by the Torah's order that all of Israel contribute to the construction of the Ark – for all the nation's citizens are required for the project that is the Torah.

Furthermore, we could add that by offering this teaching, the Torah emphasizes that the congregation requires not just scholars to maintain the study of God's word, but the assistance of the lay community to provide the needs of the student class. Thus the fourteenth-century commentator Rabbeinu Baḥya ben Asher writes:

The gold of the Ark reflects the anticipation that in the future God will extend a protective shelter over both the students of Torah and those who assist them financially. As the verse states: "For wisdom is a defense, and money is a defense" (Ecclesiastes 7:12), while another verse declares: "It is a tree of life to those who lay hold on it" (Proverbs 3:18). Note that the text says that the Torah is a tree of life not only to those who study her, but even to those who merely support her. And if that is so, certainly people who learn Torah are to be so rewarded.

According to Rabbeinu Baḥya, a sacred partnership exists between those who spend their lives immersed in Torah study and those who make such an endeavor possible. This is another way in which the nation of Israel requires all of its members in order to raise the crown of Torah over the world.

A second possible understanding of the midrash is that God wished to prevent the primary workers in the Tabernacle – that is, the priestly class – from believing that they had exclusive access to the Torah, or that the study and message of the book applied only to them. By inviting the entire nation to join in constructing the Ark, God essentially told the masses that they too own a share in the Torah, even though the tablets would be kept strictly within the priests' domain.

This message could be expressed slightly differently to state that each individual Jew has been granted the ability to study, to teach, to observe and to practice the laws of the Torah. The share that every Israelite has in the communication of God's word is unique to him or her. Such a concept appears only in the Jewish tradition, and it is expressed in the aphorism: "Take care to respect even the impoverished, for they too are teachers of Torah" (Nedarim 81a). Thus we have the responsibility not only to learn Torah but to also ensure that other members of our society have such an opportunity as well.

A final message that we can glean from the collective nature of the Ark's construction has to do with the Jewish national consciousness. The Ark contained two sets of the Tablets of the Law: the pieces of the first broken tablets, and the second whole pair that replaced the initial ones. This combination symbolizes the fact that Israel both endures failure and possesses the ability to recover from their missteps. This concept holds within it the understanding of what it means to cope with tragedy and destruction. The Ark of the Covenant represents the dwelling of God's presence within the community of Israel. And yet it holds both the shattered and the complete tablets. It is jarring to think that Israel would hold on to the fragments of their initial, failed attempt at divine service. Why not bury them forever?

The answer to that question relates to the nature of human beings and our ability to manage experiences of trauma. It is not necessary or indeed wise for a person to banish unpleasant memories, nor to attempt to lead one's life as if the difficult episodes one has undergone never really happened. Suppressing such thoughts might succeed for the short term, but the reality is that such impressions are never addressed in the way they must be. These have a tendency to surface later in life, occasionally in an even more bitter fashion. On the other hand, a healthy approach to emotional wounds, to catastrophe and loss, is to view them in the context of the advancement and progression of life. It is in this light that God wished Israel to remember the debacle of the golden calf and the consequences of that event. This is why the pieces of the original tablets were preserved within the Ark and not shunted aside like the remains of an undesirable relationship.

Now, there are two reasons to remember traumatic events in one's life. Firstly, by recalling the unpleasantness of the past, one is encouraged not to repeat previous mistakes. Secondly, our memories create awareness that in fact, our lives are built on three layers: the past, the present and the future, and that it is impossible to tease these periods apart. Once we realize this, we begin to internalize that our actions have ramifications that reach far beyond the present moment, just as our past activities have shaped who we are today. Our yesterdays and our tomorrows are all strung together and tied as one life by our todays. Rabbi Joseph B. Soloveitchik makes the point in the following paragraphs:

> God endowed man with time awareness. The ability to sense and feel time and the existential stream of selfhood. The time awareness has three basic component parts. First, retrospection: without memory there is no time. Second, the time experience includes exploration of things yet unborn and events not yet in existence. Third is appreciation of the present moment as one's most precious possession. No one is worthy of time-awareness if retrospection is foreign to him. If he is incapable of reliving, recovering, and reproducing past experiences. Past events which are not re-experienced belong not to history, but to archaeology. Archaeology involves past events that occurred once upon a time, disappeared, and while they may be reproduced by memory, are not alive anymore. Memory is not just a storehouse for latent impressions; there is also the living memory which reproduces and re-experiences the past.

The individual and the community must remember and remind themselves of the power of influence that we wield. We must know that the Ark symbolizes the basis for our national existence, and as such we are all participants in the fulfillment of the Torah. This is so not just in a technical sense as expressed above by the *Or Haḥayyim*, and not merely in a qualitative sense that guarantees all Israel equal standing before the law and an equal share in it, but also in the realm governed by our communal and personal memories. Standing in the center of the Tabernacle is the mutual relationship between the individual and the congregation, between the needs, the plans, and the goals of each Israelite and the purpose of the God's nation as a collective. The core of Jewish life must be the fusion of the every single Jew's interests with the grander scheme of the group, and the union of all these disparate directions into a single mission: realizing the will of God.

WHEN GIVING IS TAKING

In Parashat Teruma, the Torah introduces the national project of constructing the Tabernacle. In order to realize God's plan for the structure, the people are asked to donate all the requisite materials. Since the establishment of a sanctuary is presented as a commandment, the reader expects to see an imperative tone from God, demanding that the Israelites supply the goods necessary for the enterprise. However, instead of issuing a statement such as: "Tell the Israelites that they must give an offering to Me," the opening to this section instead declares: "Tell the Israelites to take [*veyikḥu*] an offering for Me" (25:2). While the latter sentence might resemble the former, it seems to express a very different idea. For in God's request that Israel contribute their possessions, He uses the odd verb "take" rather than "give." The commentators have proposed several explanations to explain this choice of term in their exploration of the Jewish concept of charity.

We begin our investigation with the writings of Rabbi Yaakov Tzvi Mecklenburg, of nineteenth-century Germany, whose work on the Torah is titled *Haketav Vehakabbala*. According to Rabbi Mecklenburg, the verse in question teaches us the following lesson:

> When the recipient of a gift is an important person, the status of the donor is raised as a result of his gift. Thus the Talmud maintains (in the first chapter of tractate Kiddushin) that if a woman offers money to an eminent gentleman, and he takes the cash while declaring: "With this gift you are betrothed to me," the woman can be thereby married to the man, even though usually it is the groom who provides something of worth to the bride. In this instance however, the very privilege of having such a distinguished person take something from the woman holds value to her, and it can serve to effect a marriage. This explains why the Torah in the present verse employs the verb "take" and not "give."

Rabbi Mecklenburg thus asserts that the Israelites in the wilderness were not actually givers, but receivers. For they understood the exalted purpose to which their donations were to be put, and they were hence elated at the chance to be a part of the efforts. This explains the presence of the verb "take" – the nation received as much as they supplied.

We move to the approach of a contemporary of Rabbi Mecklenburg – Rabbi Yehuda Aryeh Leib Alter, author of the *Sefat Emet*. This second author offers a completely different perspective, maintaining that the Torah is not focusing here on the benefit gained from the act of giving but rather on the people's willingness to share. The importance of such an interpretation becomes obvious once it occurs to us that the very notion of puny mortals being asked to donate pieces of metal to the Master of the Universe – who not only owns everything already, but Himself *created* all of the gold and the silver – is patently ridiculous. As such, the *Sefat Emet* proposes that the verb "take" should be understood to imply "assuming" a certain generosity of spirit directed at God:

> The most important factor with regard to the fulfillment of all of the commandments and every act of kindness is the state of readiness to perform the will of God. It is that approach to an action which elevates a mere series of motions into a religious experience. Thus does the Torah demand that an individual devote the wholeness of his soul and the totality of his physical resources to reaching the necessary state of devotion to the Almighty. This is the inherent meaning behind the phrase "take an offering for Me." If a person is committed to serving God, the Almighty in turn is eager to assist him in realizing that ambition.

In the act of charity, this generosity must be mirrored in our stance toward those less fortunate than we. People giving charity to needy neighbors or to a noble cause should never open their wallets with feelings of resentment or with a sense of being put upon. How can a benefactor possibly grow in any significant way while harboring the feeling that the money is being taken from him against his will? However, if the donor can somehow empathize with the unfortunate supplicant pleading on his doorstep, the souls of the two individuals can briefly touch while the money changes hands, and the mitzva enriches both parties. Hence it is not only a physical object which a donor is asked to produce, but an emotional and spiritual stance of brotherhood and a willingness to follow the will of the Almighty.

Next we encounter the Malbim, also from the nineteenth century. In this commentator's opinion, the verb in question can only be properly understood when viewed in the context of the verse as a whole. The commandment to Moshe to request money and materials from the Israelites actually comprises several separate conditions which must be examined. Firstly, the clause that contains the problematic verb also includes the term "for Me," whose import is unclear given that everything belongs to God. Commenting on this word, Rashi writes: "'For Me' means 'in My honor.'" The Malbim develops this point and

explains that God here mandates that when the masses fulfill the instruction of collecting for the Tabernacle, they must keep their hearts pure. The people are not to combine their devotion "for God" with any sort of personal feelings of aggrandizement or pride in their generosity. Nor should the Israelites bring their gifts to the Tabernacle project in hopes of being rewarded for their largesse. Rather, the mindset of the nation's donors must be focused on creating a sanctuary for the honor and glorification of God alone. Other acts of charity are similarly at risk of becoming opportunities for affluent people to boast of their wealth, or to bask in the gratitude which the community heaps upon them for their assistance. On these occasions as well, all those capable of giving should view their position as its own gift from God, a freely-given opportunity to join with the Almighty in performing an act of righteousness.

From this starting point, the Malbim proceeds to consider the meaning of the verb "take":

> The verb implies that God's injunction to the Israelites to donate materials had a limitation: nobody was to give everything that he owned to the Tabernacle project, but only some percentage of the family wealth. The Sages construct a similar rule when they state (Ketubbot 50a): When a person hands money over to charity, he may not give more than one fifth of what he owns. The reader should not ignore the remarkable nature of this law – even acts of kindness have boundaries! In this instance our Sages were concerned lest overly good and generous people become destitute themselves. That in turn would require that they too be supported by the community.

What emerges is that the commandment of charity is multifaceted. At the same time that we are enjoined to consider the welfare of others, we are commanded not to ignore our own financial needs and future.

Expanding to the concept of "taking," the Malbim continues to assert that there is a difference between taking a donation from somebody who parts with his money willingly – reflected in the phrasing *kiḥa me'et*, used in our verse – and from a person who is essentially forced into giving up his property (phrased as *kiḥa mimmennu*, which is not used here). Furthermore, the continuation of the verse – "Take My offering from all whose heart moves them to give" – implies that the officers in charge of the donations were not only to seek funds from the wealthy Israelites or from the tribal leaders. It was not only large and impressive gifts which were accepted; any size donation was welcome, and every benefactor acknowledged.

When the Israelites heeded the call to part with their valuables for the sake of God's sanctuary, they did so with an eagerness to participate in the construc-

tion of the Tabernacle. When the people lined up to divest themselves of their possessions, they did so with the willingness to perform an act of national charity. As such, even paltry gifts from the poorest elements of society bore the same spiritual worth as that of the larger donations. For all citizens alike felt the desire for the Divine Presence to dwell within the nation.

The Malbim concludes his commentary to this verse by addressing the proper attitude that people should take toward their possessions:

> Take note of what King David states regarding a person's possessions: "All is from You, and we have given You only what is Yours" (I Chronicles 29:14). Similarly, does God say: "For Mine is the silver and Mine the gold" (Haggai 2:8). Nothing really belongs to human beings. It is only when a person finds himself donating items for the glorification of God that he is really assumed to own these materials. For at that moment, the person takes and acquires the substances that are actually God's possessions, in order to pass them upward. As such the items are briefly considered to belong to the benefactor. This is what the Torah means when it states: "Tell the Israelites to take an offering for Me" – by giving a gift to charity or to the Tabernacle, he for an instant takes that object from God, who is its true master.

As such, through the act of giving, the individual also experiences the experience of receiving. And hence Moshe tells the Israelites to take in order to give.

Rabbinic literature is replete with stories and lessons about the practice of charity. The sheer volume of such discussions indicates how seriously the Sages took this commandment. Judaism has always considered the sharing of wealth and supporting of the destitute to be a central feature of religious and communal life. As such, it was always necessary to encourage the masses to rise above their apathy and donate generously even during difficult times. Perhaps the drive to construct the Tabernacle was the Jewish people's first mass test of charitable giving. In an ideal situation, a benefactor feels not that he or she is being used, but that he has been given the privilege of donating and hence of receiving. Donors of charity do not simply hand over money; they participate in the opportunity to change somebody's life, and they thus become part of something bigger than themselves. And thus the command to the Israelites to supply precious metals and other materials imposed a double responsibility upon the people. Their first task was to join with God in creating an environment that could house the Divine Presence amongst the nation. But the effect of that effort was to train the Hebrews to understand that we are but God's agents who take what belongs to Him, and share it with others for the betterment of the whole world.

THE TABERNACLE – CONTENT AND FORM

In Parashat Teruma we are introduced the process of the construction of the Tabernacle, a compound whose primary function was to house the Divine Presence within the broader camp of the Israelite nation. However, the very idea of physically hosting God raises serious and complex theological problems. Indeed, upon building the permanent structure of the Temple that replaced the Tabernacle, King Shlomo expressed his own astonishment at the entire endeavor by saying: "Will God truly dwell on earth? If the heavens – the highest heavens – cannot contain You, how will this House that I have built?" (I Kings 8:27). What sense does it make then for the essence of God to be contained within four walls and a roof? This is only one initial question for the reader trying to make sense of the earthly relationship that human beings – who are limited by their very nature – strive to build with an infinite deity. The difficulties continue: What is the function or purpose of the sacrificial service? Which is more significant – the building itself or the worship that takes place there? In the absence of a physical means or method to connect to the Almighty, is it still possible to communicate with God?

The Midrash conveys to us the Sages' early attempts to deal with these questions, and it points us on the road toward some answers. Here is a translation of a lengthy passage in Shemot Rabba (33:7):

> The verse states: "Tell the Israelites to take an offering for Me" (Exodus 25:2) We can explicate that command by referring to a later verse at the end of the Torah: "Moshe charged us with the Torah, a heritage of Yaakov's assembly" (Deuteronomy 33:4). Expounding on this verse, Rabbi Simlai taught: 613 commandments were given to the people of Israel, and that is the numerical value [in gematria] of the word *Torah*. Now you might retort that actually the letters in *Torah* add up to only 611. What then are the extra two precepts? The Sages teach that the Israelites heard the two statements "I am the Lord your God who brought you out of Egypt, out of the house of slaves," and "Have no other gods than Me" (Exodus 20:2–3) directly from God Himself. In other words, "Moshe charged us with the Torah," because he conveyed exactly 611 laws to the nation [whereas the other two commandments were transmitted directly from the Almighty]. And when the same verse refers to this corpus as a "heritage," it should be understood that the Torah is an inheritance for Israel and for the entire

> world. Consider the son of a king who is taken captive and carried off to a faraway land as a child. Even though the years may pass the prince remains connected to his heritage and holds his head high, saying: "I shall one day return to the inheritance of my ancestors." Similarly, although a Torah scholar may spend some time away from his studies while he occupies himself with other matters, should he decide years later to once again take up that spiritual pursuit he ought not be embarrassed to do so, saying: "I can always return to the heritage of my ancestors." Another interpretation: Do not read the word "heritage" [*morasha*] as written, but as "betrothed" [*me'orasa*]. As long as a bridegroom has not actually married his fiancée, he remains a guest in his father-in-law's house. But once the wedding has taken place, the bride and her husband are happy to host the in-laws. Such is a metaphor for the relationship between God and the Israelite people. Before God presented the nation with the Torah [likened here to a marriage contract] the text states: "Moshe went up to God" (Exodus 19:3). However, after the Torah was delivered, the Holy One, blessed be He, descended to Moshe: "They shall make Me a Sanctuary and I will dwell in their midst" (25:8). Another interpretation: This teaches that Israel became betrothed, so to speak, to the Torah itself, as the verse states: "I will betroth you to Me forever" (Hosea 2:21).

This midrash connects the opening text of our *parasha* with another verse from the book of Deuteronomy, which at first glance seems to bear no relationship to the command to construct the Tabernacle. Instead, that verse describes the gift of the Torah to the Israelite people. Why is such a verse brought into this discussion at all? The short opening homily of Rabbi Simlai suggests one first connection between the Tabernacle and the Torah – both are vehicles for divine revelation. In this, both serve essentially the same function. But the difference between them is as follows: In the Tabernacle, the glory of God was confined to the inner sanctum, the Holy of Holies, where almost no person could ever set foot. When God introduced the Torah to Israel, however, He spoke to the entire congregation. He addressed the nation publicly and quite visibly. Indeed, the first two of the Ten Commandments, which are cited in the above midrash, and which command us to believe in God and prohibit idolatry, these two ideas were not even presented to the masses through a human intermediary. According to the Sages, they were both spoken by God in all His glory straight to the ears of the assembled people. Perhaps these two commandments are unique because they comprise such critical pillars of Jewish thought that they could not be presented through some human agent.

The midrash moves on to formulate the relationship between God and the nation of Israel in different ways. The first dimension turns on the understanding of the term "heritage" as applied to the Torah – an eternal inheritance that endures and survives through the generations. Thus there is no credence to the claim that God would ever abandon Israel in favor of some other group. Viewed thus, the Torah becomes an inheritance that every Jew can lay a claim too. Even when someone has sinned or strayed from the path of tradition, the way back is always available and within reach. This perspective also reflects on the role of the Tabernacle. The tent that was constantly reassembled, traveling with the Israelites through the wilderness, symbolizes how the Divine Presence will never depart from Israel. God accompanies us and is within reach wherever we go.

Thirdly, the rabbinic text looks at the Torah through a metaphor of betrothal. Here, the conceptual association of the Torah with the Tabernacle is first mentioned explicitly. In the midrash, the Torah is first presented as a fiancée who lives in her father's house, i.e., in God's celestial realm. Because that was where the Torah first resided, Moshe was initially required to climb Mount Sinai and reach up beyond the confines of the earth to reach it. Nevertheless, after the experience of revelation, the people of Israel became the husbands of the Torah. God thus became Israel's father-in-law, so to speak. He then must come to visit whenever He wishes to see His daughter the Torah, who has moved to live with her husband. Viewed in this way, the construction of the Tabernacle is not merely a grand gesture meant to glorify God or provide gainful employment for His priests. Rather, the Tabernacle is established as a point of spiritual communion embedded within the camp of the people. In this telling, the Tabernacle was built as a home for the Torah itself. And indeed, the central architectural focus of the Sanctuary – the contents of the Ark inside the Holy of Holies – was the tablets of the law and the first Torah scroll. The structure itself was secondary in importance to its contents.

The fourth teaching in the midrash restates this betrothal in more abstract terms, quoting a verse from Hosea (2:21): "I will betroth you to Me forever; I will betroth you to Me in righteousness and justice, in kindness and compassion." According to the Malbim's commentary on that verse, the betrothal between God and Israel signifies a future, eternal covenant between the parties:

> This new covenant will differ from the previous agreements, as the prophet declares: "Days are soon coming, declares the LORD, when I will make a new covenant with the House of Israel and the House of Yehuda" (Jeremiah 31:30). The original covenant was temporary, since Israel was destined to sin and nullify its connection with God. However, eventually the nation will cease to sin, and their bond with God will never again be severed. This is

> what the prophet means when he states: "I will betroth you to Me forever," it is *because* "I will betroth you to Me in righteousness and justice, in kindness and compassion." For the perfection of humanity depends on two things: the establishment of healthy relationships among human beings, and the development of a spiritual connection with God. It is concerning the first of these that the verse states: "I will betroth you to Me in righteousness and justice." When these are effected, the nation's betrothed will provide them with the two gifts of "kindness and compassion."

In the Malbim's explication, the betrothal of Israel to God and the Torah represents an ideal closeness that God and Israel will one day achieve. This new human-divine relationship in turn will hinge on how the citizens of the community treat each other. When this idea is reapplied to the Tabernacle, we see God's abode amongst Israel as a symbol of the perfect society. When Jews treat each other justly and with respect, we merit to host God among us. A corrupt society, by contrast, leads inexorably to destruction and exile.

In all four of these readings, the decree given to Israel to construct the Tabernacle was not merely an order to build a physical structure. It was an edict that the Jewish people prepare their hearts for the Divine Presence to dwell among them. The establishment of the Tabernacle symbolize the importance of the Torah – the tablets contained within the space were far more significant than the materials that housed them. The kingdom of God is hence not found within one building or another, but rather in the study and acceptance of the Torah, the fulfillment of the commandments, and the belief in the Almighty. The midrash we have analyzed in this essay teaches that all these basic principles, which define and elevate Judaism, were expressed within the project of the Tabernacle. It was therefore critical for the people to view the Sanctuary not as a goal in and of itself, but as a means to invite the Divine Presence to dwell among the masses. For indeed, God does not truly exist in the Tabernacle so much as inside the hearts of human beings.

THE TABERNACLE AND ITS VESSELS

TABERNACLE IN THE DESERT

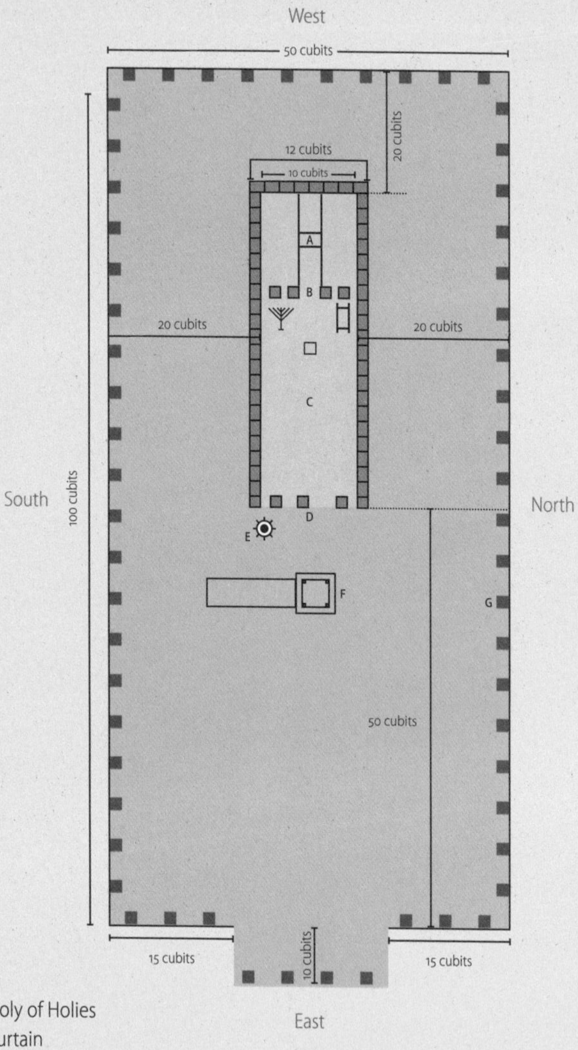

A – Holy of Holies
B – Curtain
C – Sanctuary
D – Screen
E – Laver
F – Sacrificial altar
G – Hangings

INTRODUCTION TO THE TABERNACLE

RABBI MENACHEM MAKOVER

The Torah dedicates five *parashot* to the Tabernacle, from *Parashat Teruma* through *Parashat Pekudei* (Ex. 25:1–40:38). This indicates the significance of the Tabernacle – the location of the revelation of the Divine Presence and the site where sacrifices are offered. In these *parashot*, the Torah describes the structure of the Tabernacle, its vessels, and the priestly vestments in great detail, with regard to both the command to make them and the implementation of the command, as well as their construction.

Notwithstanding this great level of detail, there are numerous opinions among the Sages and the later commentators about many of the specifics. The most significant tannaitic source on this topic is the compendium known as *Baraita deMelekhet HaMishkan*. There are also several extensive discussions in the Talmud. Among the early commentators, Rashi provided the most expansive interpretations of the structure, in his commentary to the Torah. Most of the other commentators based their explanations on Rashi's. Maimonides did not discuss the Tabernacle directly, but in his *Laws of the Chosen Temple* he issued rulings regarding the vessels that often differ from Rashi's interpretations.

In this appendix, we have generally followed Rashi, as he is the primary biblical exegete. In some places we have also mentioned other opinions. There are also several later commentators who expounded upon Rashi's explanations, most significantly the author of *Maaseh Ḥoshev*.

The command to construct the vessels and the Tabernacle itself appears in the Torah in a highly organized manner. *Parashat Teruma* (Ex. 25:1–27:19) begins by discussing the vessels: the Ark, the table, and the candelabrum. After this, it describes the structure of the Tent of Meeting that stood in the center of the Tabernacle courtyard, the sacrificial altar, and the structure of the courtyard. In *Parashat Tetzaveh* (Ex. 27:20–30:10) we learn about the priestly garments, the incense altar, and at its conclusion, about the bronze laver (basin). The commentaries have provided various explanations for this sequence, and in this appendix, we have generally tried to follow it. For the sake of clarity, though, we have deviated from the sequence regarding the incense altar and the bronze laver (basin).

With regard to the boards of the Tabernacle, the Torah uses the expression, "acacia wood, standing." The Sages interpret this homiletically: "Perhaps you will say that their hope is lost, and their chances are gone. For this reason, the verse states, 'Acacia wood, standing' – to teach that they are standing forever" (Yoma 72a). The Tabernacle includes an aspect of eternity, and therefore it is relevant and significant in all generations to study about its structure and vessels.

GENERAL TERMS

HANDBREADTH: This measurement is mentioned in the Torah in the verse describing the frame of the table (Ex. 25:25). According to Rashi and Maimonides, the handbreadth is a measurement equivalent to the width of four fingers held together.

Halakha – A handbreadth is equivalent to 7.6 centimeters according to Maimonides, 8 centimeters according to Rabbi Ḥaim Naeh, and 9.6 centimeters according to the Ḥazon Ish.

CUBIT: This measurement is defined as the length of the forearm, from the elbow to the end of the middle finger. The standard cubit generally referenced by the Sages is equivalent to six handbreadths, and this is the cubit referenced in the biblical passages relating to the Tabernacle. There is also a measurement known as a "minor cubit," which is equivalent to five handbreadths.

Halakha – According to Maimonides, a standard cubit is equivalent to 45.6 centimeters. According to Rabbi Ḥaim Naeh it is 48 centimeters, and according to the Ḥazon Ish it is 57.6 centimeters.

TALENT (*kikar*): The unit of weight called a talent is mentioned in the Torah as the weight of the golden candelabrum (Ex. 25:39) and of the silver sockets (Ex. 38:27). The sacred talent, used in the Tabernacle, was twice the weight of an ordinary talent. According to Maimonides, a desert talent (that was in use at the time of the Tabernacle) is 21.25 kilograms, and thus a sacred talent is equal to 42.5 kilograms.

CRAFTS FOR CONSTRUCTING THE TABERNACLE

SKILLED CRAFTSMANSHIP: According to Rashi's interpretation (Ex. 26:1), this term refers to a type of weaving that produces two different patterns on each of the two sides of the woven material (images of lions on one side and images of eagles on the other). This type of weaving was used for the curtain, the sheets of the Tabernacle, the ephod, and the breast piece.

RAW MATERIALS: In the construction of the Tabernacle, skilled craftsmanship was used only with threads spun of twenty-four strands: six white flax and eighteen dyed wool – six sky blue, six purple, and six scarlet. These were all twisted together into a single thread. In the ephod and the breast piece there were also four threads of gold intertwined with each group of dyed threads that were twisted together.

EMBROIDERED WORK: This term refers to embroidering a single pattern or image onto fabric in a manner that causes it to appear on both sides. This type of embroidery was used in the screen at the entrance to the Tabernacle, the screen at the entrance to the courtyard, and the priests' sashes.

RAW MATERIALS: See above, "Skilled Craftsmanship."

VOVEN WORK: This refers to weaving threads with a loom to roduce fabric. This type of weaving was used for the High Priest's obe and the tunics.

PERFUMERS' BLEND: This refers to the craft of blending a mixture of ground plants and spices. This type of mixture was used in producing the anointing oil and the fragrant incense.

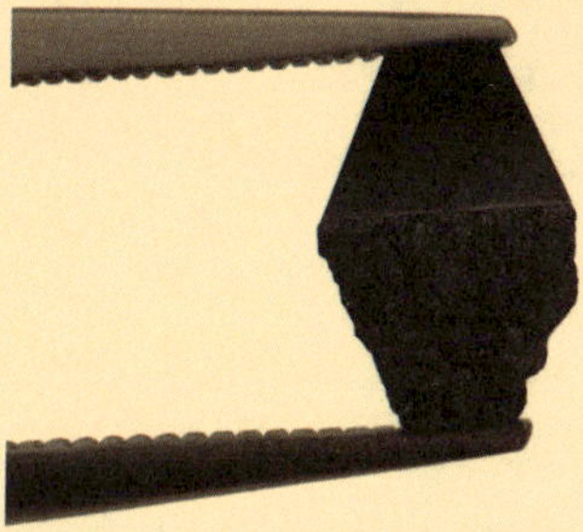

GEM CUTTER'S WORK: This is the craft of carving gemstones from their natural source. This was used in preparing the rock crystal stones for the ephod and the breast piece.

BRAIDED INTO CORDS: This refers to a method of braiding threads for chains. This method was used with the golden threads that attached the ephod to the breast piece.

PROCESSING RAW MATERIALS – WOOD, STONE, AND METAL

Flattened boards of acacia wood

Acacia wood before processing

Polished gemstones

Uncut gemstones

Gold ore

Purified gold

Silver ore

Purified silver

Bronze ore

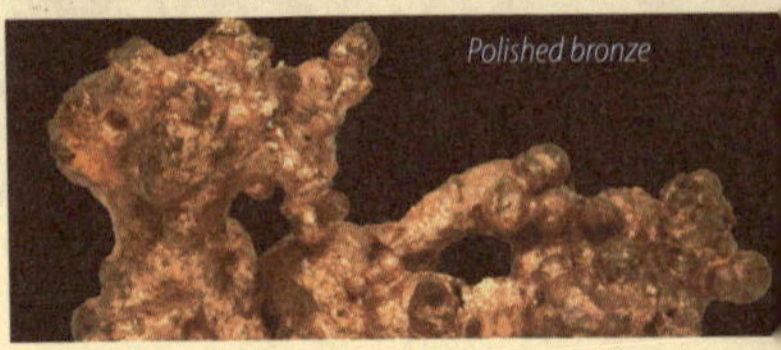

Polished bronze

GOLD PLATING

CROWN

**JAR
OF MANNA**

ARK OF THE COVENANT

Exodus 25:10–22
Exodus 37:1–9

LOCATION: The center of the Holy of Holies.

RAW MATERIALS: Acacia wood and pure gold.

DIMENSIONS: WIDTH: 1.5 cubits (approx. 72 cm).

LENGTH: 2.5 cubits (approx. 1.2 m).

HEIGHT (including cherubim)**:** 1.5 cubits (approx. 72 cm).

STRUCTURE: The Ark was made of three boxes – an inner box made of gold, a middle box made of wood, and an external box made of gold. Outside of the Ark there was a pottery jar containing manna (in the volume of an omer, which according to Maimonides is equivalent to approx. 2.16 l). Later, Aharon's staff that had miraculously blossomed was also placed there. The fragments of the first, broken, tablets of testimony, and the unbroken second tablets of testimony were placed inside the Ark. Later, the original Torah scroll written by Moshe was also inserted into the Ark.

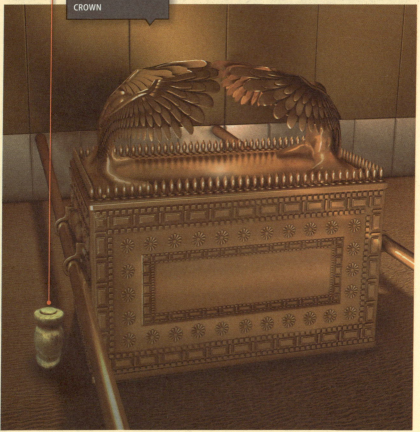

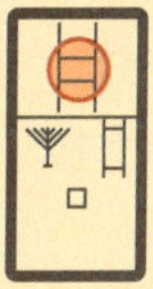

THE TABLE *Exodus 25:23–30, Exodus 37:10–16*

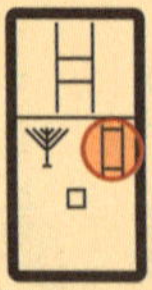

LOCATION: The northern part of the Sanctuary.

RAW MATERIALS: Acacia wood and pure gold.

DIMENSIONS: **WIDTH:** One cubit (approx. 48 cm).
LENGTH: Two cubits (approx. 96 cm).
HEIGHT (without the tubes)**:** 1.5 cubits (approx. 72 cm).

STRUCTURE: The table, and the frame that sat on it, were made of wood and plated with pure gold. At the sides of the frame were four tubes, with supports between them. The twelve loaves of showbread were placed on the supports.

CANDELABRUM

Exodus 25:31–39
Exodus 37:17–24

LOCATION: The southern part of the Sanctuary.

RAW MATERIALS: Pure gold.

DIMENSIONS: HEIGHT: Eighteen handbreadths (approx. 1.73 m).

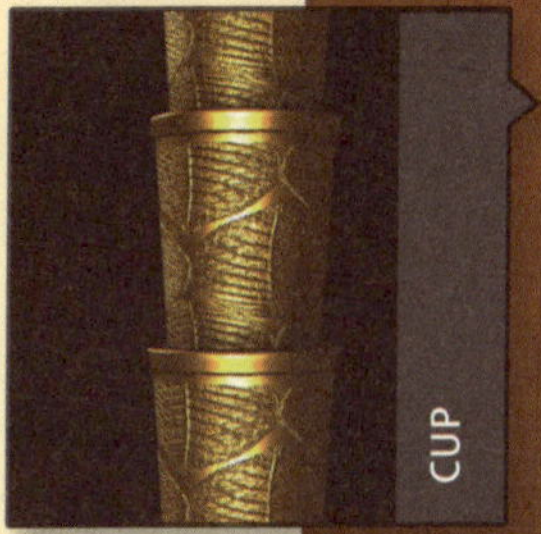

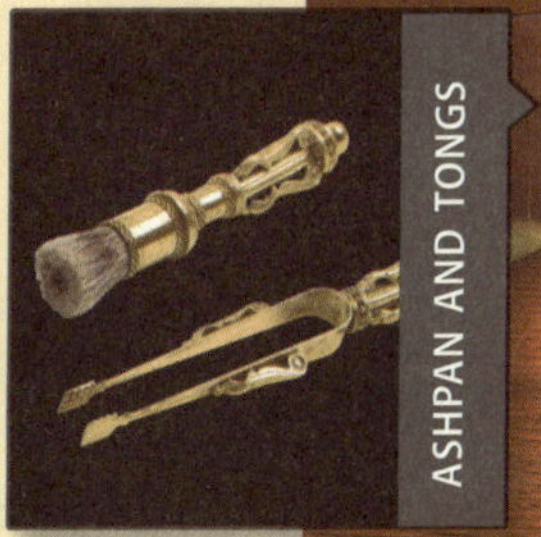

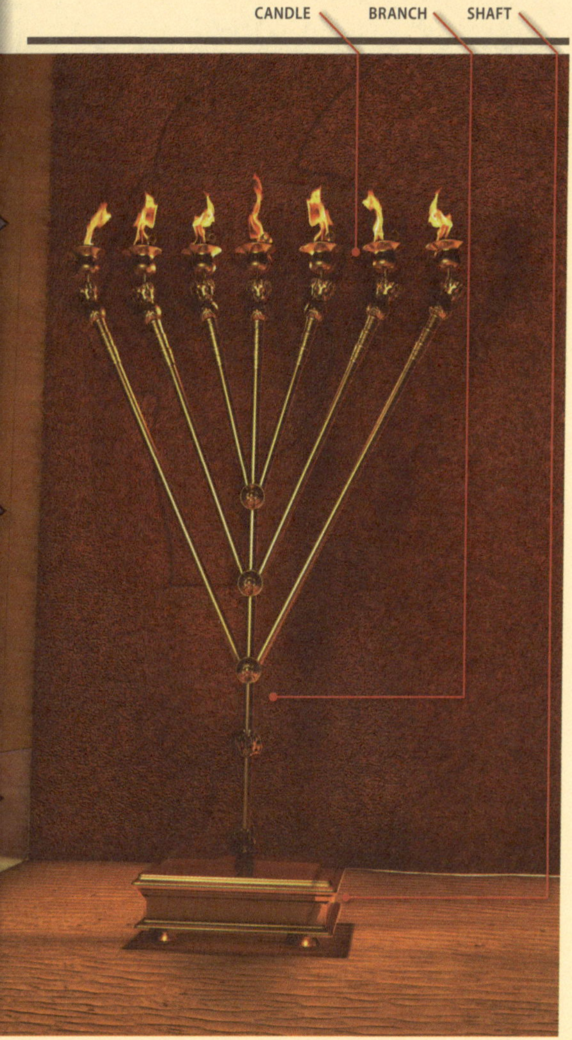

The incense altar *does not appear in the list of the other sacred vessels in* Parashat Teruma *Ex. 25:1–27:19) but only in* Parashat Tetzaveh (Ex. 30:10-27:20) *after the list of the priestly vestments.*

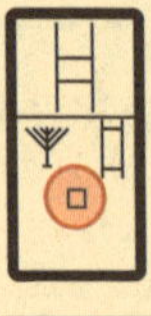

THE INCENSE ALTAR

Exodus 30:1–10
Exodus 37:25–28

LOCATION: The center of the Sanctuary.

RAW MATERIALS: Acacia wood and pure gold.

DIMENSIONS: **WIDTH:** One cubit (approx. 48 cm).
LENGTH: One cubit (approx. 48 cm).
HEIGHT (including horns): Two cubits (approx. 96 cm).

STRUCTURE OF THE TABERNACLE

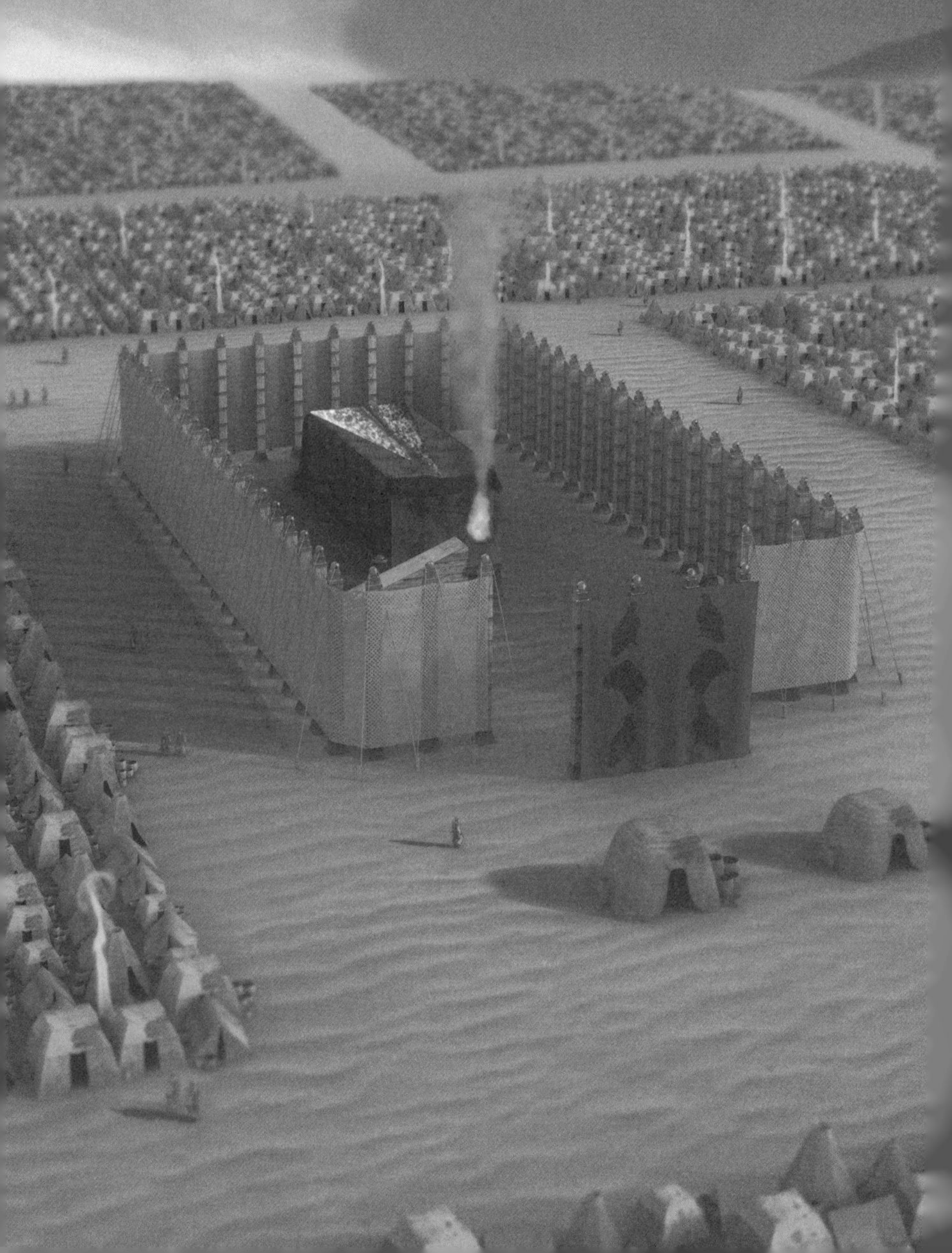

STRUCTURE OF THE TABERNACLE   *Exodus 26:1–14, Exodus 36:8–19*

FUNCTION: The three different sheets were designed to cover the Tent of Meeting.

DESCRIPTION: The bottom sheet, which was laid directly over the Tabernacle's boards, is called the Tabernacle. Above it was placed the goats'-hair sheet, which was longer and wider than the Tabernacle. A person who stood outside the Tent of Meeting was unable to see the Tabernacle, as the goats'-hair sheet concealed it. The goats'-hair sheets hung down an extra two cubits at the facade of the Tabernacle, above the entrance to the tent, and a single cubit extended in the back onto the ground ("the extra overhang"). The goats'-hair sheets were attached with ropes to bronze spikes that were inserted in the ground. Above the goats'-hair sheet was placed the cover of the Tent. This covered only the upper portion of the Tent of Meeting.

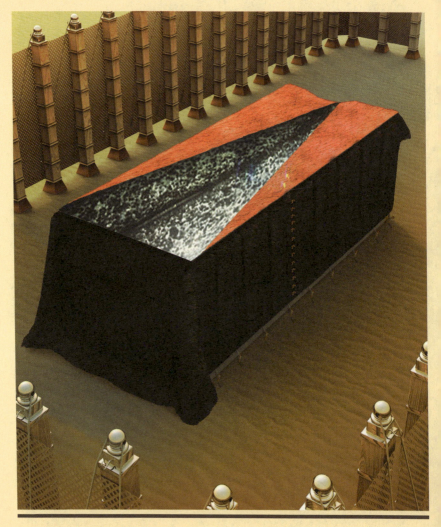

THE TABERNACLE

FUNCTION: To provide a covering for the Tent of Meeting.

RAW MATERIALS: Six strands of white linen, and eighteen strands of colored wool – six sky blue, six purple, and six scarlet red. All the strands were twisted together to form a single thread.

STRUCTURE: Ten sheets, each of which was twenty-eight cubits long and four cubits wide (approx. 13.4 m x 1.92 m).

ATTACHMENT OF THE SHEETS: The ten sheets were sewn together into two separate **couplings**, each of which was composed of five sheets. The two couplings were attached to each other with fifty golden clasps. These clasps were inserted through fifty sky-blue loops that were attached to the edges of the couplings.

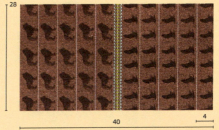

The line of the attachments formed by the golden clasps was positioned directly over the curtain.

GOATS'-HAIR SHEETS

FUNCTION: To provide a tent covering above the sheets of the Tabernacle.

RAW MATERIALS: Goats'-hair.

STRUCTURE: Eleven sheets, each of which was thirty cubits long and four cubits wide (approx. 14.4 m x 1.92 m).

ATTACHMENT OF THE SHEETS: The eleven sheets were combined into two **couplings**, one made from six sheets and the other from five sheets. These two couplings were attached to each other with fifty bronze clasps. These clasps were inserted through fifty loops that were attached to the edges of the couplings.

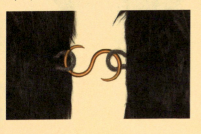
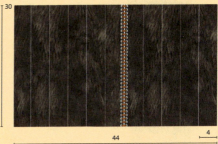

COVER OF THE TENT

FUNCTION: To provide a covering above the goats'-hair sheets.

RAW MATERIALS: Rams' hides dyed red, and *taḥash* skin.

STRUCTURE: A single sheet, half of which was made from rams' hides dyed red, and half from *taḥash* skin. It was thirty cubits long and ten cubits wide (approx. 14.4 m x 4.8 m).

THE TABERNACLE BUILDING *Exodus 26:15–30, Exodus 36:20–34*

FUNCTION: To support the Tabernacle (the bottommost sheet that covers the holy vessels), and contain the holy vessels.

DESCRIPTION: The **boards** were placed within **silver sockets** to form a three-sided structure, with an opening on the fourth side. The boards were attached to one another at the top by **rings**, and the structure was strengthened by the use of **crossbars** on all sides.

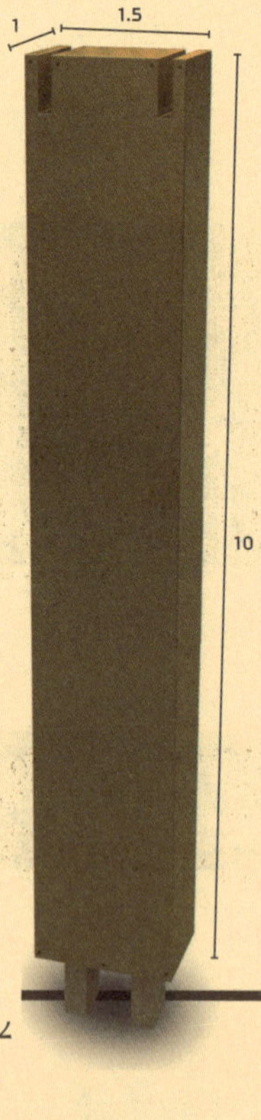

BOARDS

FUNCTION: To support the Tabernacle.

RAW MATERIALS: Acacia wood and gold.

STRUCTURE: The building was assembled from boards: twenty on the northern side, twenty on the southern side, and eight on the western side. At the bottom of each board were two **tenons** (protrusions) that fit into the silver sockets. The boards were covered with gold plates on the sides that faced the interior of the Tabernacle, and on the outside. These plates were attached to the boards with golden nails.

DIMENSIONS: Height: Ten cubits (approx. 4.8 m).

WIDTH (the side facing the interior of the Tabernacle): 1.5 cubits (approx. 72 cm).

DEPTH (the side facing the adjacent board): One cubit (approx. 48 cm).

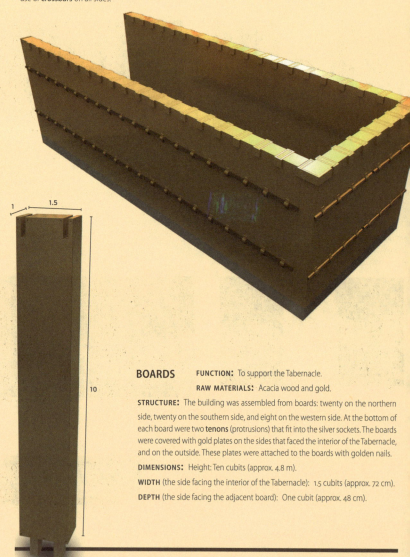

RINGS

FUNCTION: To secure the tops of the boards.

RAW MATERIALS: Gold.

Each of the boards had a groove cut into the top, near the edge of the board. The rings were inserted into these grooves to hold the boards together. At the corners, where two sides of the building met, the ring was inserted on one of the boards, and was designed to fit its width.

DIMENSIONS: Apparently slightly more than one cubit by two fingerbreadths (approx. 50 cm x 4 cm).

SILVER SOCKETS

FUNCTION: To support the boards of the Tabernacle, and protect them.

RAW MATERIALS: Silver.

Each socket had a single impression into which one of the tenons of the board was inserted. In other words, underneath each board there were two sockets; a total of ninety-six sockets on the three sides of the structure.

DIMENSIONS: Height: One cubit (approx. 48 cm).

WIDTH (the side facing the interior of the Tabernacle)**:** Seventy-five cubits (approx. 36 cm).

DEPTH (the side facing the adjacent socket): One cubit (approx. 48 cm).

The impression in each socket measured half a cubit by one-fourth of a cubit (approx. 24 cm x 12 cm).

CROSSBARS

FUNCTION: To hold the boards together and stabilize the walls of the structure.

RAW MATERIALS: Acacia wood and gold.

Each side of the Tabernacle was secured with five round crossbars – two upper crossbars that met in the middle of the wall on the outside, two lower crossbars that met in the middle of the wall on the outside, and a single central crossbar that was inserted into holes that cut through the boards (this crossbar was not visible from the outside). The four external crossbars were attached to the boards by rings. The crossbars and the **rings** were plated with gold.

DIMENSIONS: Thickness: At least one handbreadth (approx. 8 cm).

LENGTH OF THE FOUR EXTERNAL CROSSBARS: On the long walls, fifteen cubits (approx. 7.2 m), and on the short side, six cubits (approx. 2.9 m).

LENGTH OF THE CENTRAL CROSSBAR: On the long walls, thirty cubits (approx. 14.4 m), and on the short side, twelve cubits (approx. 5.8 m).

SCREENS *Exodus 26:31–37, Exodus 36:35–38*

RAW MATERIALS: Six threads of white flax and eighteen threads of colored wool – six sky blue, six purple, and six scarlet.

STRUCTURE: The curtain and the screen were supported by poles. These poles were supported by hooks that were attached to pillars made of acacia wood.

DIMENSIONS OF THE CURTAIN AND THE SCREEN:

HEIGHT: Ten cubits (approx. 4.8 m).

WIDTH: Ten cubits (approx. 4.8 m).

THE CURTAIN

FUNCTION: To separate between the Sanctuary and the Holy of Holies.

METHOD OF WEAVING: Artistic work with the form of cherubim.

LOCATION: Underneath the clasps of the sheets of the Tabernacle, twenty cubits (approx. 9.6 m) from the door of the Tabernacle.

The curtain was supported by four pillars made of gold-plated acacia wood. The pillars were ten cubits (approx. 4.8 m) high and one cubit by one cubit (approx. 48 cm x 48 cm) wide. Each pillar stood on a silver socket.

THE SCREEN AT THE OPENING OF THE TENT OF MEETING

FUNCTION: To serve as the door to the Tent of Meeting.

METHOD OF WEAVING: Woven work.

LOCATION: Entrance to the Sanctuary.

The screen was supported by five pillars made of gold-plated acacia wood, with gold tops and hoops. The pillars were ten cubits (approx. 4.8 m) high and one cubit by one cubit (approx. 48 cm x 48 cm) wide. Each pillar stood on a bronze socket.

PILLAR FOR THE CURTAIN

PILLAR FOR THE SCREEN

THE LAVER AND ITS BASE

Exodus 30:18–21
Exodus 38:8

FUNCTION: To serve as a vessel for the priests for washing their hands and feet prior to the service.

RAW MATERIALS: Bronze from the **mirrors of the assembled women**.

DESCRIPTION: In the lower section of the laver, there were spouts for washing hands and feet. The base of the laver was like a large bronze bowl.

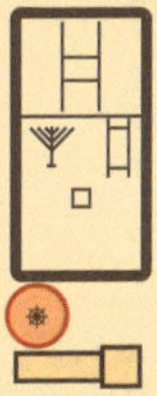

The laver and its base do not appear in Parashat Teruma *(Ex. 25:1-27:19) together with the altar of acacia wood, but only in* Parashat Ki Tisa *(Ex. 30:11-34:35), after the command* ***to collect half shekels.***

THE SACRIFICIAL ALTAR

Exodus 27:1–8
Exodus 38:1–7

LOCATION: The Tabernacle courtyard, opposite the entrance to the Tabernacle.

RAW MATERIALS: Acacia wood and bronze.

DIMENSIONS: **WIDTH:** Five cubits (approx. 2.4 m).

LENGTH: Five cubits (approx. 2.4 m).

HEIGHT (including horns): Ten cubits (approx. 4.8 m).

STRUCTURE: The **foundation** of the altar protruded one cubit outward and was one cubit high. In the center of the altar was the **grate**, which was a bronze net to which were attached four rings for the carrying poles. Above this was the **ledge**, which was a protrusion one cubit wide. At the top of the altar there were **four horns** at the four corners. The altar was hollow, made from boards, meaning that four boards of acacia wood were attached to one another, creating a hollow space between them. Each time the Tabernacle was assembled, this hollow space was filled with dirt, which was visible at the top of the altar. The walls of the altar were plated with bronze, as were the carrying poles (made from acacia wood). It is clear from the text (Ex. 20:23) that there was a ramp leading to the top of the altar.

HORN

LEDGE

GRATE

FOUNDATION

ROOF OF THE ALTAR

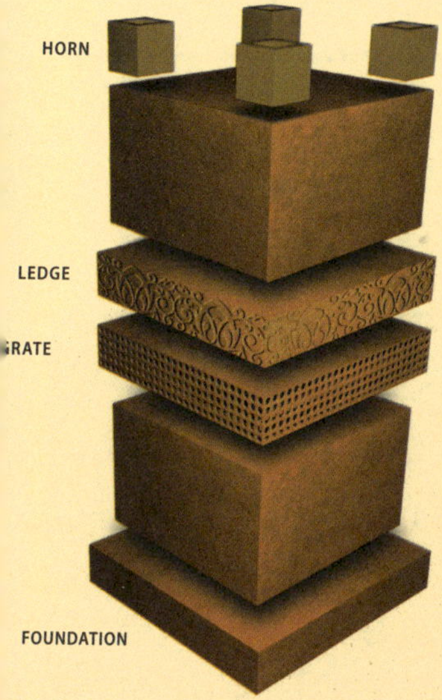

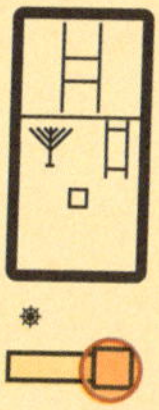

BRONZE VESSELS

FIVE BRONZE VESSELS WERE USED IN THE TABERNACLE SERVICE:

POTS: Bowls for collecting the ashes to remove them from the altar.

SHOVELS: Small rakes for sweeping the ashes into the pots.

BASINS: Cups for collecting the blood of sacrifices and sprinkling it on the altar.

FORKS: Used to turn the sacrificial meat on the altar.

FIRE PANS: Large pans for carrying coals from the bronze altar.

BASIN

FORK

SHOVEL

FIRE PAN

POT

THE TABERNACLE COURTYARD *Exodus 27:9–19, Exodus 38:8–20*

DESCRIPTION: The Tent of Meeting was surrounded on all four sides by partitions called **hangings**. These hangings were supported by **pillars** mounted on **sockets** together with **hooks and loops**. These formed the Tabernacle courtyard. At its entrance was the **courtyard screen.**

DIMENSIONS: **LENGTH:** One hundred cubits (approx. 48 m).
WIDTH: Fifty cubits (approx. 24 m).
HEIGHT (of the pillars)**:** Fifteen cubits (approx. 7.2 m).

HANGINGS

FUNCTION: To enclose the Tabernacle courtyard.

RAW MATERIALS: Six threads of twisted flax.

TYPE OF WEAVING: Twisting.

DIMENSIONS: LENGTH of the edges at the sides of the Tabernacle: One hundred cubits (approx. 48 m).

LENGTH of the edge at the back of the Tabernacle: Fifty cubits (approx. 24 m).

LENGTH of each edge opposite the entrance to the Tabernacle, on each side of the screen: Fifteen cubits (approx. 7.2 m).

At the top, the hangings were attached to small boards. These boards were hung by clips from the tops of each of the pillars. At the bottom, the hangings were attached to cords that were tied to bronze stakes. These stakes pulled the hangings down.

PILLARS

FUNCTION: To support the courtyard hangings.

RAW MATERIALS: Acacia wood (apparently) and silver.

DIMENSIONS OF EACH PILLAR: HEIGHT: Fifteen cubits (approx. 7.2 m).

WIDTH: One cubit (approx. 48 cm).

DEPTH: One cubit (approx. 48 cm).

DESCRIPTION: Each pillar was supported by a bronze socket whose dimensions matched those of the pillar. Silver loops encircled the pillar, and its top was plated with silver. At the top of the pillar, the board that the hangings were hung from was attached. The pillars were attached to the bronze stakes with cords.

THE SCREEN OF THE GATE

FUNCTION: To serve as the entrance gate to the courtyard.

RAW MATERIALS: Six threads of white flax and eighteen threads of colored wool – six sky blue, six purple, and six scarlet.

TYPE OF WEAVING: Embroidery.

LOCATION: At the entrance to the courtyard between two hangings each fifteen cubits high, ten cubits from the courtyard.

DIMENSIONS: LENGTH: Twenty cubits (approx. 9.6 m).

HEIGHT: Fifteen cubits (approx. 7.2 m).

STRUCTURE: The screen of the gate was supported by four pillars (which were identical to the other pillars of the courtyard).

PROCESSING RAW MATERIALS – FLAX, WOOL, AND SKINS

Flax during processing

Processed flax

A strand of spun wool

Wool dyed sky blue

A thread spun from strands of dyed wool, a strand of flax, and a strand of gold

Flax threads

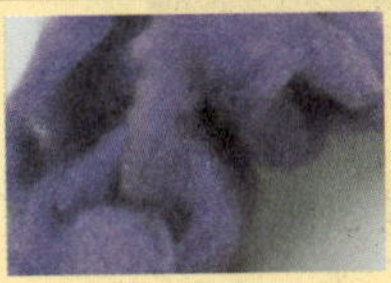
Wool dyed purple

Wool dyed sky blue

An example of woven work

Wool dyed scarlet

Strands of beaten gold

Taḥash skin

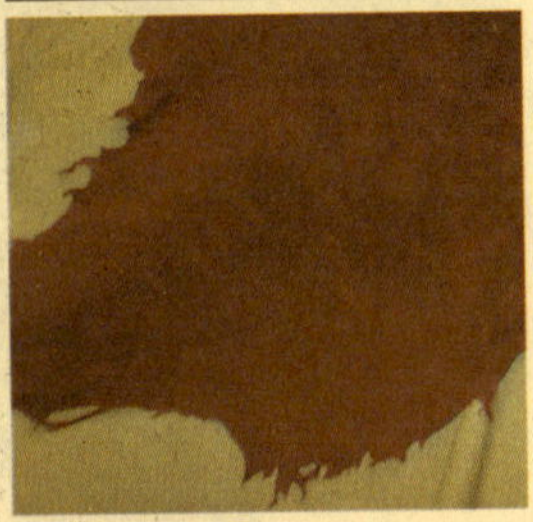
Ram's hide dyed red

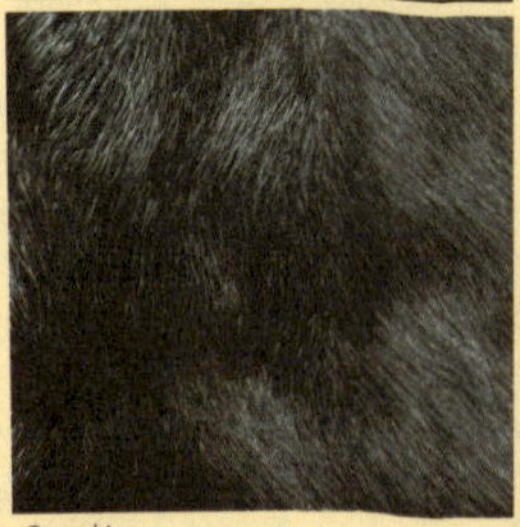
Goatskin

For commentaries and the Biblical Imagination
turn to the left side of this volume.

*For the complete Rashi and haftara
turn to the right side of this volume.*

חומש קורן מקראות הדורות
THE KOREN MIKRAOT HADOROT

פרשת תרומה
PARASHAT TERUMA

קורן ירושלים

THE ROHR FAMILY EDITION

חומש קורן מקראות הדורות
THE KOREN MIKRAOT HADOROT

THE ZAHAVA AND MOSHAEL STRAUS EDITION OF SEFER SHEMOT

פרשת תרומה עם רש״י
PARASHAT TERUMA WITH RASHI

TORAH TRANSLATION BY

Rabbi Lord Jonathan Sacks שליט״א

FROM THE MAGERMAN EDITION OF THE KOREN TANAKH

RASHI'S COMMENTARY TRANSLATED BY

Rabbi Jonathan Mishkin

•

KOREN PUBLISHERS JERUSALEM

The Koren Mikraot HaDorot, The Rohr Edition
Volume 19: Parashat Teruma
First Edition, 2021

Koren Publishers Jerusalem Ltd.
POB 4044, Jerusalem 9104001, ISRAEL
POB 8531, New Milford, CT 06776, USA

www.korenpub.com

The Tanakh translation is excerpted from the Magerman Edition of The Koren Tanakh.

The creation of this work was made possible with the generous support
of the Jewish Book Trust Inc.

Printed in ISRAEL

ISBN 978 965 7760 74 1

KMDTR01

The Rohr Family Edition of
The Koren Mikraot HaDorot
pays tribute to the memory of

Mr. Sami Rohr ז״ל
ר׳ שמואל ב״ר יהושע אליהו ז״ל

who served his Maker with joy
and whose far-reaching vision, warm open hand, love of Torah,
and love for every Jew were catalysts for the revival and growth of
vibrant Jewish life in the former Soviet Union
and in countless communities the world over

and to the memory of his beloved wife

Mrs. Charlotte Rohr (née Kastner) ע״ה
שרה בת ר׳ יקותיאל יהודה ע״ה

who survived the fires of the Shoah to become
the elegant and gracious matriarch,
first in Colombia and later in the United States,
of three generations of a family
nurtured by her love and unstinting devotion.
She found grace in the eyes of all those whose lives she touched.

Together they merited to see all their children
build lives enriched by faithful commitment
to the spreading of Torah and *Ahavat Yisrael*.

Dedicated with love by
The Rohr Family
NEW YORK, USA

עֲטֶרֶת זְקֵנִים בְּנֵי בָנִים

(משלי יז, ו)

Grandchildren
are the crowning glory of the aged
(Proverbs 17:6)

May the learning and traditions of our people be strengthened by our future generations. In honor of our wonderful grandchildren

Zahava and Moshael Straus

CONTENTS

FOR PARASHAT TERUMA WITH COMMENTARIES AND THE BIBLICAL IMAGINATION
TURN TO THE OTHER END OF THIS VOLUME.

PUBLISHER'S PREFACE

The genius of Jewish commentary on the Torah is one of huge and critical import. Jewish life and law for millennia have been directed by our interpretations of the Torah, and each generation has looked to its rabbinic leadership for a deeper understanding of its teachings, its laws, its stories.

For centuries, *Mikraot Gedolot* have been a core part of understanding the Ḥumash; the words of Rashi, Ibn Ezra, Ramban, Rashbam, Ralbag, and other classic commentators illuminate and help us understand the Torah. But traditional editions of *Mikraot Gedolot* present only a slice in time and a small selection of the corpus of Jewish commentators. Almost every generation has produced rabbinic scholars who speak to their times, from Philo and Onkelos two thousand years ago, to Rabbi Joseph B. Soloveitchik, Rabbi Aharon Kotler, the Lubavitcher Rebbe, and Nehama Leibowitz in ours.

The Koren Mikraot HaDorot – Scriptures or Interpretations for the Generations – brings two millennia of Torah commentary into the hands and homes of Jews around the world. Readers will be able to encounter not only the classic commentators, but to gain a much broader sense of the issues that scholars grappled with in their time and the inspiration they drew from the ancient texts. We see, for example, how Philo speaks to an assimilating Greek Jewish audience in first-century Alexandria, and how similar yet different it is from Rabbi Samson Raphael Hirsch's approach to an equally assimilating nineteenth-century German readership; how the perspectives of Rabbi Soloveitchik and Rabbi Kotler differ in a post-Holocaust world; how Rav Se'adya Gaon interpreted the Torah for the Jews of Babylonia. It is an exciting journey through Jewish history via the unchanging words of the Torah.

◀

The text of the Torah features the exceptional new translation of Rabbi Lord Jonathan Sacks, together with the celebrated and meticulously accurate Koren Hebrew text. Of course, with the exception of Rashi – for whom we present an entirely new translation in full – the commentaries are selected. We offer this anthology not to limit our reader's exploration but rather as a gateway for further learning of Torah and its commentaries on a broader and deeper level than space here permits. We discuss below how to use this book.

We must thank **Pamela and George Rohr** of New York, who recognized the unique value of the *Koren Mikraot HaDorot* and its ability to communicate historical breadth and context to the reader. For my colleagues here at Koren, we thank you; for the many generations of users who will find this a continuing source of new learning, we are forever in your debt.

We also are indebted to **Zahava and Moshael Straus**, true leaders of this Jewish generation in so many fields, who have invested not only in *Parashat Teruma* but the entire book of Shemot. Together, we were thus able to launch this innovative and unique project.

We are honored to acknowledge and thank **Debra and David Magerman**, whose support for the Koren Ḥumash with Rabbi Sacks's exemplary translation and commentary laid the foundation for the core English text of this work.

Finally, I must personally thank **Rabbi Marvin Hier**, with whom I had a special breakfast some years ago at the King David Hotel. During the meal, he raised the problem that so few people knew the writings of Rabbi Joseph B. Soloveitchik and Rabbi Aharon Kotler on the Torah; and I, who had just read some of Philo's work, had the same reaction. From that conversation came the seed for this project.

HOW TO USE *THE KOREN MIKRAOT HADOROT*

The Koren Mikraot HaDorot will be a fifty-five-volume edition of the Ḥumash (one for each *parasha* plus a companion volume). Each of the fifty-four volumes of the *parashot* can be read from right to left (Hebrew opening side), and left to right (English opening side).

Opening from the Hebrew side offers:

- the full Torah text, the translation of Rabbi Sacks, and the full commentary of Rashi in both Hebrew and the new English translation

◀

- **all *haftarot* associated with the *parasha* of the volume, including Rosh Ḥodesh and special readings, both in Hebrew and English**

Opening from the English side presents four sections:

- THE TIME OF THE SAGES – **includes commentaries from the Second Temple period and the talmudic period**
- THE CLASSIC COMMENTATORS – **quotes selected explanations by Rashi as well as most of the commentators found in traditional *Mikraot Gedolot***
- CONFRONTING MODERNITY – **selects commentaries from the eighteenth century to the close of the twentieth century**
- THE BIBLICAL IMAGINATION – **features essays surveying some of the broader conceptual ideas as a supplement to the linear, text-based commentary**

The first three of these sections each feature the relevant verses, in Hebrew and English, on the page alongside their respective commentaries, in chronological order, providing the reader with a single window onto the text without excessive page turning.

In addition to being a valuable resource in a Jewish home or synagogue library, we conceived of these volumes as a weekly accompaniment in the synagogue. There is scope for the reader to study each *parasha* on a weekly basis in preparation for the reading on Shabbat. One may select a particular group of commentators for study that week, or perhaps alternate between ancient and modern viewpoints. Some readers may choose to delve into the text through verse-by-verse interpretation, while others may prefer a conceptual perspective on the *parasha* as a whole. The broad array of options for learning means this is a series which can be returned to year after year, always presenting new insights and new approaches to understanding the text.

ACKNOWLEDGMENTS

The creation of this book was possible only thanks to the small but exceptional team here at Koren Jerusalem. We are grateful to:

- Rabbi Tzvi Hersh Weinreb, שליט״א, who conceptualized the structure of the project and provides both moral and halakhic leadership at Koren
- Rabbi Shai Finkelstein, whose encyclopedic knowledge of Torah and its interpreters is equaled only by his community leadership, formerly in Memphis and today in Jerusalem
- Rabbi David Fuchs, whose deep expertise in the midrashim and commentaries built a volume that is both comprehensive and concise

- Rabbi Yedidya Naveh, whose knowledge, organizational skills, and superb leadership brought the disparate elements together
- Rabbi Jonathan Mishkin, translator of Rashi and the other commentaries, who crafted a fluent, accurate, and eloquent English translation

Our design, editing, typesetting, and proofreading staff, including Tani Bayer, Esther Be'er, Tomi Mager, and Carolyn Budow Ben David, enabled an attractive, user-friendly, and accurate edition of these works.

> "One silver basin" (Numbers 7:13) was brought as a symbol of the Torah, which has been likened to wine, as the verse states: "And drink of the wine which I have mingled" (Proverbs 9:5). Because it is customary to drink wine in a basin – as we see in the verse "that drink wine in basins" (Amos 6:6) – he therefore brought a basin. "Of seventy shekels, after the shekel of the sanctuary" (Numbers 7:13). Why? Because just as the numerical value of "wine" [*yayin*] is seventy, so there are seventy modes of expounding the Torah. (Bemidbar Rabba 13:16)

Each generation produces exceptional rabbinic, intellectual leadership. It has been our purpose to enable all Jews to taste the wine of those generations, in the hope of expanding the breadth and depth of their knowledge. Torah is our greatest treasure, and we need the wisdom of those generations to better understand this bountiful gift from God. We hope that we at Koren can deepen that understanding for all who seek it.

Matthew Miller, Publisher
Jerusalem, 5781 (2021)

A NOTE ON THE TRANSLATION OF RASHI

The translation of Rashi's commentary provided here is complete and unabridged, following the meticulously researched Hebrew version of the commentary published by Koren. This version omits some material published in other editions that was found likely to have been added later by Rashi's students and other authors. We have included all of Rashi's numerous grammatical and linguistic discussions, even though these tend to be of less interest to the English-speaking reader, for two reasons: First, we felt it important for the readership to be confident that they are holding a complete version of Rashi's commentary and to know that they are not missing any matter of potential interest it might contain. Second, we wished to impress upon the reader that the elegant Sacks translation of the Torah included in this volume represents only one reading among many possible interpretations. Rashi's inquiries into the meanings of individual words and phrases emphasize the ambiguity of the verses and the potential of any passage to be interpreted in several different ways. This multifaceted nature of the Torah is a central theme of *The Koren Mikraot HaDorot*.

The inclusion of these discussions – often technical and sometimes confusing – bears implications for the translation. Here the translator was often forced to insert himself into the discussion to clearly establish the grammatical difficulty or ambiguity in the Hebrew text that is troubling Rashi. Since these difficulties are not always conveyed in the Sacks verse translation, the reader will find bracketed editorial comments used more aggressively in these discussions. The editor's notes also serve to supply the English-speaking reader with relevant details regarding Hebrew grammar that Rashi assumes to be known to his audience, which are necessary to understanding his point.

◀

Here at the outset, we will provide a very brief overview of the Hebrew system of *binyanim*, or Hebrew verb forms, which is central to so many of Rashi's grammatical arguments.

Hebrew verbs, which are always conjugated by number, person, gender, and tense, are also divided into seven categories of verbs called *binyanim*. Three of these are in the active voice, three passive, and one in a reflexive voice that is neither active nor passive. In theory, any three-letter root (*shoresh*) in Hebrew can be conjugated in any one of these forms, with slightly different meanings in each one, though few roots exist in all forms. Readers who encounter one of Rashi's discourses analyzing to which class a given verb belongs can refer to the following chart to orient themselves.

BINYAN NAME	EXAMPLE (PAST/FUTURE)	VOICE			
Paal (Kal) – פָּעַל (קל)	Katav/Yikhtov – write	Active			
Hifil – הִפְעִיל	Hikdish/Yakdish – consecrate	Active			
Pi'el – פִּעֵל	Giddel/Yegaddel – promote or exalt	Active		Causative	Simple
Hitpael – הִתְפַּעֵל	Hitgaddel/Yitgaddel – become great	Reflexive	Intensive		
Pual – פֻּעַל	Guddal/Yeguddal – be promoted or exalted	Passive			
Hufal – הֻפְעַל	Hukdash/Yukdash – be consecrated	Passive			
Nifal – נִפְעַל	Nikhtav/Yikkatev – be written	Passive			

Each of the three active conjugations pairs with one of the passive ones, as seen in the above chart, such that the seven *binyanim* can be simplified into three more basic forms. The simple form (*paal/nifal*) denotes simple actions. The causative form (*hifil/hufal*) is reserved for actions induced by the subject in the object, e.g., to cause something to become holy (consecrate). The intensive form (*pi'el/pual*) describes a special form of the action, usually more significant or intense. The reflexive form is considered a third subgroup of the intensive form and is used for actions done to oneself. ◀

Rashi's grammatical discussions also focus on the vocalization (*nikkud*, or vowel marks) of the Hebrew text. The reader can review the names of the vowel marks in the following chart, as well as see how these vowels are transliterated in this edition.

VOWEL MARK	NAME	TRANSLITERATION
בְ	*Sheva* (*Ḥataf* when combined with a *segol, pataḥ*, or *kamatz*)	*e* or silent
בֶ	*Segol* (in Rashi's language: *Pataḥ Katan*)	*e*
בַ	*Pataḥ*	*a*
בָ	*Kamatz*	*a* or *o*
בִ	*Ḥirik*	*i*
בֵ	*Tzerei* (in Rashi's language, also: *Kamatz Katan*)	*e* or *ei*
בֹ	*Ḥolam* (in Rashi's language: *Melafum*)	*o*
בֻ	*Kubbutz* (in Rashi's language: *Shuruk*)	*u*
בוּ	*Shuruk*	*u*

For Rashi's terms in Old French, we have been guided by Yisrael Gukovitzky's dictionary *Targum Halaaz* (1985).

Yedidya Naveh, Managing Editor
Jerusalem, 5781 (2021)

פרשת תרומה
PARASHAT TERUMA

חומש עם רש״י
THE ḤUMASH WITH RASHI

25 1/2 The Lord spoke to Moshe, saying, "Tell the Israelites to take
an offering for Me; take My offering from all whose heart
3 moves them to give. These are the offerings you shall receive
4 from them: gold, silver and bronze; sky-blue, purple, and
5 scarlet wool; linen and goats' hair; rams' hides dyed red and
6 fine leather; acacia wood; ▸ oil for the lamps; spices for the

25 2 | **וְיִקְחוּ־לִי תְּרוּמָה** – *Take an offering for Me:* [Although everything belongs to God, the term] "for Me" here means "in My honor."

כה ב| וְיִקְחוּ־לִי תְּרוּמָה. "לִי" – לִשְׁמִי:

תְּרוּמָה – *An offering:* The term *teruma* suggests separation. That is, Israel should set apart donations from their personal property.

תְּרוּמָה. הַפְרָשָׁה, יַפְרִישׁוּ לִי מִמָּמוֹנָם נְדָבָה:

יִדְּבֶנּוּ לִבּוֹ – *Whose heart moves them:* The term *yiddevenu* comes from the word *nedava* [meaning "donation"], and it connotes good will. The Old French term for this would be *present*.

יִדְּבֶנּוּ לִבּוֹ. לְשׁוֹן נְדָבָה, וְהוּא לְשׁוֹן רָצוֹן טוֹב, פרישנ"ט בְּלַעַז:

תִּקְחוּ אֶת־תְּרוּמָתִי – *Take My offering:* [The word "offering" appears three times in verses 2–3.] Our Sages teach that this text refers to three kinds of offerings. The first was the beka of silver donated by each man. These were fashioned into the Tabernacle's sockets as is detailed in Parashat Pekudei (38:26–27). The second offering was for the altar – also a beka from every man. The silver was deposited in chests and used to purchase animals for communal sacrifices. The third offering comprised donations that people volunteered for the construction of the Tabernacle [these had no prescribed amounts]. If you examine the thirteen materials listed in the following verses, you will find that all of them were required to fashion the Tabernacle and the priestly vestments.

תִּקְחוּ אֶת־תְּרוּמָתִי. אָמְרוּ רַבּוֹתֵינוּ, שָׁלֹשׁ תְּרוּמוֹת אֲמוּרוֹת כָּאן: אַחַת תְּרוּמַת בֶּקַע לַגֻּלְגֹּלֶת שֶׁנַּעֲשׂוּ מֵהֶם הָאֲדָנִים, כְּמוֹ שֶׁמְּפֹרָשׁ בְּ'אֵלֶּה פְקוּדֵי' (להלן לח, כו-כז); וְאַחַת תְּרוּמַת הַמִּזְבֵּחַ בֶּקַע לַגֻּלְגֹּלֶת, לַקֻּפּוֹת לִקְנוֹת מֵהֶן קָרְבְּנוֹת צִבּוּר; וְאַחַת תְּרוּמַת הַמִּשְׁכָּן נִדְבַת כָּל אֶחָד וְאֶחָד שֶׁהִתְנַדְּבוּ. שְׁלֹשׁ עֶשְׂרֵה דְּבָרִים הָאֲמוּרִים בָּעִנְיָן כֻּלָּם הֻצְרְכוּ לִמְלֶאכֶת הַמִּשְׁכָּן אוֹ לְבִגְדֵי כְהֻנָּה כְּשֶׁתְּדַקְדֵּק בָּהֶם:

3 | **זָהָב וָכֶסֶף וּנְחֹשֶׁת** – *Gold, silver and bronze:* All of these materials were offered according to the generosity of individual donors, save for the silver. That metal was given in equal amounts by every Israelite man – each was required to give half a shekel's worth of silver. And no additional silver was required for any of the work done in preparing the Tabernacle, as the verses state: *The silver of those recorded in the census… were used for casting the sockets of the Sanctuary, etc.* (38:25–28). Further silver donations were used to craft the utensils employed in the service [see 35:24].

ג| זָהָב וָכֶסֶף וּנְחֹשֶׁת וְגוֹ'. כֻּלָּם בָּאוּ בִּנְדָבָה אִישׁ אִישׁ מַה שֶּׁנְּדָבוֹ לִבּוֹ, חוּץ מִן הַכֶּסֶף שֶׁבָּא בְּשָׁוֶה, מַחֲצִית הַשֶּׁקֶל לְכָל אֶחָד. וְלֹא מָצִינוּ בְּכָל מְלֶאכֶת הַמִּשְׁכָּן שֶׁהֻצְרַךְ שָׁם כֶּסֶף יוֹתֵר, שֶׁנֶּאֱמַר: "וְכֶסֶף פְּקוּדֵי הָעֵדָה וְגוֹ' בֶּקַע לַגֻּלְגֹּלֶת" וְגוֹ' (להלן לח, כה-כו). וּשְׁאָר הַכֶּסֶף הַבָּא שָׁם בִּנְדָבָה (להלן לה, כד) עֲשָׂאוּהוּ לִכְלֵי שָׁרֵת:

◀

כה

וַיְדַבֵּר יְהוָה אֶל־מֹשֶׁה לֵּאמְר: דַּבֵּר אֶל־בְּנֵי יִשְׂרָאֵל ‎ יח

וְיִקְחוּ־לִי תְּרוּמָה מֵאֵת כָּל־אִישׁ אֲשֶׁר יִדְּבֶנּוּ לִבּוֹ

תִּקְחוּ אֶת־תְּרוּמָתִי: וְזֹאת הַתְּרוּמָה אֲשֶׁר תִּקְחוּ ‎ ג

מֵאִתָּם זָהָב וָכֶסֶף וּנְחְשֶׁת: וּתְכֵלֶת וְאַרְגָּמָן וְתוֹלַעַת ‎ ד

שָׁנִי וְשֵׁשׁ וְעִזִּים: וְעֹרֹת אֵילִם מְאָדָּמִים וְעֹרֹת תְּחָשִׁים ‎ ה

וַעֲצֵי שִׁטִּים: • שֶׁמֶן לַמָּאֹר בְּשָׂמִים לְשֶׁמֶן הַמִּשְׁחָה ‎ ו

ד| וּתְכֵלֶת. צֶמֶר צָבוּעַ בְּדַם חִלָּזוֹן, וְצִבְעוֹ יָרֹק:

וְאַרְגָּמָן. צֶמֶר צָבוּעַ מִמִּין צֶבַע שֶׁשְׁמוֹ אַרְגָּמָן:

וְשֵׁשׁ. הוּא פִּשְׁתָּן:

וְעִזִּים. נוֹצָה שֶׁל עִזִּים, לְכָךְ תִּרְגֵּם אוּנְקְלוֹס: "וּמְעַזֵּי", דָּבָר הַבָּא מִן הָעִזִּים וְלֹא עִזִּים עַצְמָן, שֶׁתַּרְגּוּם שֶׁל עִזִּים 'עִזַּיָא':

ה| מְאָדָּמִים. צְבוּעוֹת הָיוּ אָדֹם לְאַחַר עִבּוּדָן:

תְּחָשִׁים. מִין חַיָּה, וְלֹא הָיְתָה אֶלָּא לְשָׁעָה, וְהַרְבֵּה גְּוָנִים הָיוּ לָהּ, לְכָךְ מְתַרְגֵּם "סַסְגּוֹנָא", שֶׁשָּׂשׂ וּמִתְפָּאֵר בִּגְוָנִין שֶׁלּוֹ:

וַעֲצֵי שִׁטִּים. וּמֵאַיִן הָיוּ לָהֶם בַּמִּדְבָּר? פֵּרַשׁ רַבִּי תַּנְחוּמָא, יַעֲקֹב אָבִינוּ צָפָה בְּרוּחַ הַקֹּדֶשׁ שֶׁעֲתִידִין יִשְׂרָאֵל לִבְנוֹת מִשְׁכָּן בַּמִּדְבָּר, וְהֵבִיא אֲרָזִים לְמִצְרַיִם וּנְטָעָם, וְצִוָּה לְבָנָיו לְטַלָּם עִמָּהֶם כְּשֶׁיֵּצְאוּ מִמִּצְרַיִם:

ו| שֶׁמֶן לַמָּאֹר. שֶׁמֶן זַיִת זָךְ לְהַעֲלוֹת נֵר תָּמִיד:

---

4 | וּתְכֵלֶת – *Sky-blue:* This is wool dyed with the greenish-blue blood of a particular snail.

וְאַרְגָּמָן – *Purple:* Wool dyed with a specific stain called *argaman*.

וְשֵׁשׁ – *Linen: Shesh* means "linen."

וְעִזִּים – *And goats' hair:* [Literally, simply, "goats"]: This refers to the hair of the goats. Hence the Targum renders this term *umazei* – meaning a byproduct of goats, not the animals themselves. For the Aramaic word for goats is *izzaya*.

5 | מְאָדָּמִים – *Dyed red:* The hides were dyed red after they were processed.

תְּחָשִׁים – *Fine leather:* [Alternatively, the Hebrew word *tahash* might refer to a species of animal.] The *tahash* was a type of wild beast that only existed in the world for a short time. The beast was multicolored, which is why the Targum refers to it as *sasegona*, for it delighted [*sas*] in its variegated [*gevanin*] fur.

וַעֲצֵי שִׁטִּים – *Acacia wood:* Where did the Israelites find acacia trees in the middle of the wilderness? Rabbi Tanhuma explains: Through divine inspiration, our patriarch Yaakov saw that his descendants were destined to construct a Tabernacle in the desert [and they would require timber to build it]. Hence when he left Canaan Yaakov took trees with him and planted them in Egypt centuries earlier. He then commanded his sons to uproot the trees and take them along when they escaped from Egypt.

6 | שֶׁמֶן לַמָּאֹר – *Oil for the lamps:* The Torah later refers to this substance as *pure oil from crushed olives for light, to kindle the lamp, every night* (27:20).

7 anointing oil and the fragrant incense; and rock crystal together with other precious stones for the ephod and breast piece.
8 They shall make Me a Sanctuary and I will dwell in their
9 midst. Form the Tabernacle and form all of its furnishings fol-
10 lowing the patterns that I show you. ▸ Make an Ark
of acacia wood, two and a half cubits long, a cubit and a half
11 wide, and a cubit and a half high. Overlay it with pure gold,

בְּשָׂמִים לְשֶׁמֶן הַמִּשְׁחָה. שֶׁנַּעֲשָׂה לִמְשֹׁחַ כְּלֵי הַמִּשְׁכָּן וְהַמִּשְׁכָּן לְקַדְּשׁוֹ, וְהֻצְרְכוּ לוֹ בְּשָׂמִים, כְּמוֹ שֶׁמְּפֹרָשׁ בְּ׳כִי תִשָּׂא׳ (להלן ל, כג-כה):

בְּשָׂמִים לְשֶׁמֶן הַמִּשְׁחָה – *Spices for the anointing oil:* Oil was used to consecrate the Tabernacle and its utensils. It contained spices as well, as the Torah specifies in Parashat Ki Tisa (30:23–25).

וְלִקְטֹרֶת הַסַּמִּים. שֶׁהָיוּ מַקְטִירִין בְּכָל בֹּקֶר וָעֶרֶב, כְּמוֹ שֶׁמְּפֹרָשׁ בְּ׳וְאַתָּה תְּצַוֶּה׳ (להלן ל, ז-ח). וּלְשׁוֹן קְטֹרֶת, הַעֲלָאַת קִיטוּר וְתִימְרוֹת עָשָׁן:

וְלִקְטֹרֶת הַסַּמִּים – *And the fragrant incense:* Incense was burned in the mornings and in the evenings, as described in Parashat Tetzaveh (30:7–8). The term *ketoret* derives from the smoke [kitor] that rises from it.

ז| אַבְנֵי־שֹׁהַם. שְׁתַּיִם הֻצְרְכוּ שָׁם לְצֹרֶךְ הָאֵפוֹד הָאָמוּר בְּ׳וְאַתָּה תְּצַוֶּה׳ (שם כח, ט-יב):

7 | **אַבְנֵי־שֹׁהַם** – *Rock crystal:* Two of these, which were used for the ephod as stated in Parashat Tetzaveh (28:9–12).

מִלֻּאִים. עַל שֵׁם שֶׁעוֹשִׂין לָהֶם בַּזָּהָב מוֹשָׁב כְּמִין גּוּמָא וְנוֹתְנִין הָאֶבֶן שָׁם לְמַלְּאוֹת הַגּוּמָא, קְרוּיִים ״אַבְנֵי מִלּוּאִים״, וּמְקוֹם הַמּוֹשָׁב קָרוּי מִשְׁבֶּצֶת:

מִלֻּאִים – *Other:* [Alternatively, "filling."] Settings for these precious stones were made out of gold by carving a sort of cavity in which the gems were fixed. Because the jewels were meant to fill [*lemalot*] the cavity, they were called *miluim* stones. The place where a gem was set was referred to as a *mishbetzet* ["setting"].

לָאֵפֹד וְלַחֹשֶׁן. הַשֹּׁהַם לָאֵפוֹד וְאַבְנֵי הַמִּלּוּאִים לַחֹשֶׁן. וְחֹשֶׁן וְאֵפוֹד מְפֹרָשִׁים בְּ׳וְאַתָּה תְּצַוֶּה׳ (שם כח, ו-ל), וְהֵם מִינֵי תַּכְשִׁיט:

לָאֵפֹד וְלַחֹשֶׁן – *For the ephod and the breast piece:* The rock crystal was reserved for the ephod, while the other precious stones were used for the breast piece. These two vestments – the ephod and the breast piece – were ornaments, and they are described in Parashat Tetzaveh (28:6–30).

ח| וְעָשׂוּ לִי מִקְדָּשׁ. וְעָשׂוּ לִשְׁמִי בֵּית קְדֻשָּׁה:

8 | **וְעָשׂוּ לִי מִקְדָּשׁ** – *They shall make Me a Sanctuary:* [The word *mikdash* usually denotes a permanent Temple. Here, however, the phrase means simply:] They shall make a sacred structure in my Honor.

ט| כְּכֹל אֲשֶׁר אֲנִי מַרְאֶה אוֹתְךָ. כָּאן ״אֵת תַּבְנִית הַמִּשְׁכָּן״. הַמִּקְרָא הַזֶּה מְחֻבָּר לַמִּקְרָא שֶׁלְּמַעְלָה הֵימֶנּוּ: ״וְעָשׂוּ לִי מִקְדָּשׁ... כְּכֹל אֲשֶׁר אֲנִי

9 | **כְּכֹל אֲשֶׁר אֲנִי מַרְאֶה אוֹתְךָ** – *Following the patterns that I show you:* Here [on Mount Sinai] I will show you the plans for the Tabernacle. This verse should be understood in conjunction with the previous verse, and together the message is: "They shall make

◀

ז וְלִקְטֹרֶת הַסַּמִּים: אַבְנֵי־שֹׁהַם וְאַבְנֵי מִלֻּאִים לָאֵפֹד
ח ט וְלַחֹשֶׁן: וְעָשׂוּ לִי מִקְדָּשׁ וְשָׁכַנְתִּי בְּתוֹכָם: כְּכֹל אֲשֶׁר
אֲנִי מַרְאֶה אוֹתְךָ אֵת תַּבְנִית הַמִּשְׁכָּן וְאֵת תַּבְנִית
י כָּל־כֵּלָיו וְכֵן תַּעֲשׂוּ: ◂ וְעָשׂוּ אֲרוֹן עֲצֵי
שִׁטִּים אַמָּתַיִם וָחֵצִי אָרְכּוֹ וְאַמָּה וָחֵצִי רָחְבּוֹ וְאַמָּה
יא וָחֵצִי קֹמָתוֹ: וְצִפִּיתָ אֹתוֹ זָהָב טָהוֹר מִבַּיִת וּמִחוּץ

Me a Sanctuary…following the patterns that I show you for the Tabernacle and all of its furnishings. And so shall you form." [Note that Rashi's understanding of these two verses differs from the translation in this edition.] The enigmatic final clause: "And so shall you form," teaches that all future construction should follow the descriptions I provide. For should an item of furniture ever be lost, or if you later wish to fashion for the permanent Temple more lasting, fixed accoutrements, such as tables, candelabra, washing basins, or the stands that King Shlomo made for those basins, you must follow the plans that I am outlining now for these objects. If this clause were not meant to be linked to the previous one, and instead introduced a new idea, the verse would not have ended with the words *vekhen taasu* ["and so shall you form" – the conjunctive *vav* separates that clause from this one], but simply *ken taasu* ["so shall you form"]. If that were the case, our verse would be referring simply to the construction of the Tabernacle and its utensils [and not to similar items that would be required in the future].

מַרְאֶה אוֹתְךָ... וְכֵן תַּעֲשׂוּ" לְדוֹרוֹת, אִם יֹאבַד אֶחָד מִן הַכֵּלִים, אוֹ כְּשֶׁתַּעֲשׂוּ לִי כְּלֵי בֵּית עוֹלָמִים כְּגוֹן שֻׁלְחָנוֹת וּמְנוֹרוֹת וְכִיּוֹרוֹת וּמְכוֹנוֹת שֶׁעָשָׂה שְׁלֹמֹה, כְּתַבְנִית אֵלּוּ תַּעֲשׂוּ אוֹתָם. וְאִם לֹא הָיָה הַמִּקְרָא מְחֻבָּר לְמַעְלָה הֵימֶנּוּ, לֹא הָיָה לוֹ לִכְתֹּב: "וְכֵן תַּעֲשׂוּ" אֶלָּא "כֵּן תַּעֲשׂוּ", וְהָיָה מְדַבֵּר עַל עֲשִׂיַּת אֹהֶל מוֹעֵד וְכֵלָיו:

10 | **וְעָשׂוּ אֲרוֹן** – *Make an Ark:* A chest made with no legs, shaped like a box called *coffre* in Old French, which sits directly on the floor.

י | וְעָשׂוּ אֲרוֹן. כְּמִין אֲרוֹנוֹת שֶׁעוֹשִׂים בְּלֹא רַגְלַיִם עֲשׂוּיִם כְּמִין אַרְגָּז שֶׁקּוֹרִין אשקרי"ן, יוֹשֵׁב עַל שׁוּלָיו:

11 | **מִבַּיִת וּמִחוּץ תְּצַפֶּנּוּ** – *Overlay it inside and out:* Betzalel [the craftsman, first mentioned by name in chapter 31] fashioned three boxes – two of gold and one of wood. Each box had four walls and a bottom, but was open on the top. The wooden chest fit into the larger gold one, while the smaller gold box slid into the wooden one. Meanwhile the top edges of the wood box were themselves covered in gold, such that the Ark as a whole was completely overlaid with gold inside and out.

יא | מִבַּיִת וּמִחוּץ תְּצַפֶּנּוּ. שְׁלֹשָׁה אֲרוֹנוֹת עָשָׂה בְּצַלְאֵל, שְׁנַיִם שֶׁל זָהָב וְאֶחָד שֶׁל עֵץ, אַרְבָּעָה כְּתָלִים וְשׁוּלַיִם לְכָל אֶחָד, וּפְתוּחִים מִלְמַעְלָה. נָתַן שֶׁל עֵץ בְּתוֹךְ שֶׁל זָהָב, וְשֶׁל זָהָב בְּתוֹךְ שֶׁל עֵץ, וְחִפָּה שְׂפָתוֹ הָעֶלְיוֹנָה בְּזָהָב, נִמְצָא מְצֻפֶּה מִבַּיִת וּמִחוּץ:

◀

12 inside and out, and around it make a gold rim. Cast four gold
rings for it and place them on its four corners, two rings on
13 one side and two on the other. Make staves of acacia wood
14 and overlay them with gold; place these staves in the rings on
15 the sides of the Ark so that the Ark may be carried. The staves
must stay in the rings of the Ark; they must not be removed.
16 Inside the Ark, place the tablets of the Covenant that I will
17 give you. ◂ Make an Ark cover of pure gold, two and a half SHENI
18 cubits long and a cubit and a half wide. Make two cherubim
of beaten gold and place them at the two ends of the cover:

זֵר זָהָב. כְּמִין כֶּתֶר מַקִּיף לוֹ סָבִיב לְמַעְלָה מִשְּׂפָתוֹ, שֶׁעָשָׂה הָאָרוֹן הַחִיצוֹן גָּבוֹהַּ מִן הַפְּנִימִי עַד שֶׁעָלָה לְמוּל עֳבִי הַכַּפֹּרֶת וּלְמַעְלָה הֵימֶנּוּ מַשֶּׁהוּ, וּכְשֶׁהַכַּפֹּרֶת שׁוֹכֵב עַל עֳבִי הַכְּתָלִים עוֹלֶה הַזֵּר לְמַעְלָה מִכָּל עֳבִי הַכַּפֹּרֶת כָּל שֶׁהוּא, וְהוּא סִימָן לְכֶתֶר תּוֹרָה:

זֵר זָהָב – *A gold rim:* A sort of gold crown surrounded the entire Ark [protruding upward from the top edges of the chest]. This mean that the outer box extended to a slightly greater height than the inner box, such that this ornamental band rose just past the thickness of the Ark's cover. Thus when the Ark cover sat on the rim of the Ark, this gold decoration stretched a bit higher than its top. The gold rim symbolized the majesty of the Torah [since the Tablets of the Law were deposited inside the Ark].

יב | **וְיָצַקְתָּ.** לְשׁוֹן הַתָּכָה, כְּתַרְגּוּמוֹ:

12 | **וְיָצַקְתָּ** – *Cast:* The verb means "to cast," as the Targum has it.

פַּעֲמֹתָיו. כְּתַרְגּוּמוֹ: "זָוְיָתֵיהּ". וּבַזָּוִיּוֹת הָעֶלְיוֹנוֹת סָמוּךְ לַכַּפֹּרֶת הָיוּ נְתוּנוֹת, שְׁתַּיִם מִכָּאן וּשְׁתַּיִם מִכָּאן לְרָחְבּוֹ שֶׁל אָרוֹן, וְהַבַּדִּים נְתוּנִים בָּהֶם, וְאָרְכּוֹ שֶׁל אָרוֹן מַפְסִיק בֵּין הַבַּדִּים אַמָּתַיִם וָחֵצִי בֵּין בַּד לְבַד, שֶׁיִּהְיוּ שְׁנֵי בְּנֵי אָדָם הַנּוֹשְׂאִים אֶת הָאָרוֹן מְהַלְּכִין בֵּינֵיהֶם, וְכֵן מְפֹרָשׁ בִּמְנָחוֹת בְּפֶרֶק 'שְׁתֵּי הַלֶּחֶם' (דף צח ע"ב):

פַּעֲמֹתָיו – *Its corners:* The Targum renders this as "corners" [*zaveyatei*]. The rings were situated at the upper corners of the Ark near its cover. They were fastened two on each of the Ark's long sides. Staves were inserted into the rings, with the length of the Ark separating them by a distance of two and a half cubits. This meant that two people carrying the Ark could walk comfortably between the poles. This is all explained in tractate Menaḥot (98b).

וּשְׁתֵּי טַבָּעֹת עַל־צַלְעוֹ הָאֶחָת. הֵן הֵן אַרְבַּע טַבָּעוֹת שֶׁבִּתְחִלַּת הַמִּקְרָא, וּפֵרֵשׁ לְךָ הֵיכָן הָיוּ. וְהַוָּי"ו זוֹ יְתֵרָה הִיא, וּפִתְרוֹנוֹ כְּמוֹ שְׁתֵּי טַבָּעֹת. וְיֵשׁ לְךָ לְיַשְּׁבָהּ כֵּן: וּשְׁתַּיִם מִן הַטַּבָּעוֹת הָאֵלּוּ עַל צַלְעוֹ הָאֶחָת:

וּשְׁתֵּי טַבָּעֹת עַל־צַלְעוֹ הָאֶחָת – *Two rings on one side:* [Literally, "And two rings on one side."] The text here is not introducing additional rings beside the four just mentioned. This clause is merely explaining where those rings were situated on the Ark. The letter *vav* is really unnecessary, and the verse may as well have omitted it. The phrase means: "Two of those rings were on one side."

צַלְעוֹ. צִדּוֹ:

צַלְעוֹ – *Side:* The word *tzal'o* means "its side."

◀

יב תִּצַפֶּ֑נּוּ וְעָשִׂ֧יתָ עָלָ֛יו זֵ֥ר זָהָ֖ב סָבִֽיב׃ וְיָצַ֣קְתָּ לּ֗וֹ אַרְבַּע֙
טַבְּעֹ֣ת זָהָ֔ב וְנָ֣תַתָּ֔ה עַ֖ל אַרְבַּ֣ע פַּעֲמֹתָ֑יו וּשְׁתֵּ֣י טַבָּעֹ֗ת
עַל־צַלְעוֹ֙ הָֽאֶחָ֔ת וּשְׁתֵּי֙ טַבָּעֹ֔ת עַל־צַלְע֖וֹ הַשֵּׁנִֽית׃
יג וְעָשִׂ֥יתָ בַדֵּ֖י עֲצֵ֣י שִׁטִּ֑ים וְצִפִּיתָ֥ אֹתָ֖ם זָהָֽב׃ וְהֵבֵאתָ֤
אֶת־הַבַּדִּים֙ בַּטַּבָּעֹ֔ת עַ֖ל צַלְעֹ֣ת הָאָרֹ֑ן לָשֵׂ֥את
טו אֶת־הָאָרֹ֖ן בָּהֶֽם׃ בְּטַבְּעֹת֙ הָֽאָרֹ֔ן יִהְי֖וּ הַבַּדִּ֑ים לֹ֥א
טז יָסֻ֖רוּ מִמֶּֽנּוּ׃ וְנָתַתָּ֖ אֶל־הָאָרֹ֑ן אֵ֚ת הָעֵדֻ֔ת אֲשֶׁ֥ר אֶתֵּ֖ן
יז אֵלֶֽיךָ׃ • וְעָשִׂ֥יתָ כַפֹּ֖רֶת זָהָ֣ב טָה֑וֹר אַמָּתַ֤יִם וָחֵ֙צִי֙ שני
יח אָרְכָּ֔הּ וְאַמָּ֥ה וָחֵ֖צִי רָחְבָּֽהּ׃ וְעָשִׂ֛יתָ שְׁנַ֥יִם כְּרֻבִ֖ים זָהָ֑ב

13 | **בַּדֵּי** – *Staves:* The word *baddim* means "staves."

יג| בַּדֵּי. מוֹטוֹת:

15 | **לֹא יָסֻרוּ מִמֶּנּוּ** – *They must not be removed:* Ever.

טו| לֹא יָסֻרוּ מִמֶּנּוּ. לְעוֹלָם:

16 | **וְנָתַתָּ אֶל־הָאָרֹן** – *Inside the Ark, place:* [The preposition *el* – literally, "to" – here indicates that the tablets were to be placed] inside the Ark.

טז| וְנָתַתָּ אֶל־הָאָרֹן. כְּמוֹ בָּאָרוֹן:

הָעֵדֻת – *The tablets of the Covenant:* [Literally, simply "the testimony."] This refers to the Torah, which is a testament that God commanded the people to observe the commandments recorded in it.

הָעֵדֻת. הַתּוֹרָה שֶׁהִיא לְעֵדוּת בֵּינִי וּבֵינֵיכֶם שֶׁצִּוִּיתִי אֶתְכֶם מִצְוֹת הַכְּתוּבוֹת בָּהּ:

17 | **כַּפֹּרֶת** – *An Ark cover:* The *kapporet* was a cover placed on top of the Ark, which was itself only an open box. The cover was placed on top of it like a shelf.

יז| כַּפֹּרֶת. כִּסּוּי עַל הָאָרוֹן, שֶׁהָיָה פָּתוּחַ מִלְמַעְלָה וּמַנִּיחוֹ עָלָיו כְּמִין דַּף:

אַמָּתַיִם וָחֵצִי אָרְכָּהּ – *Two and a half cubits long:* Both the length and width of the Ark cover was equal to that of the Ark, which it sealed. The lid rested on the tops of the Ark's four walls. And even though the Torah does not relate the thickness of the Ark cover, our Sages teach us that it was one handbreadth thick [see Sukka 5a].

אַמָּתַיִם וָחֵצִי אָרְכָּהּ. כְּאָרְכּוֹ שֶׁל אָרוֹן, וְרָחְבָּהּ כְּרָחְבּוֹ שֶׁל אָרוֹן, וּמֻנַּחַת עַל עֳבִי הַכְּתָלִים הַרְבַּעְתָּם. וְאַף עַל פִּי שֶׁלֹּא נָתַן שִׁעוּר לְעָבְיָהּ, פֵּרְשׁוּ רַבּוֹתֵינוּ שֶׁהָיָה עָבְיָהּ טֶפַח:

18 | **כְּרֻבִים** – *Cherubim:* The figures had the faces of children.

יח| כְּרֻבִים. דְּמוּת פַּרְצוּף תִּינוֹק לָהֶם:

מִקְשָׁה תַּעֲשֶׂה אֹתָם – *Make them of beaten:* Do not craft separate figures out of gold and then fasten them to the Ark cover, like welders, whose craft is called *souder* ["solder"] in Old French.

מִקְשָׁה תַּעֲשֶׂה אֹתָם. שֶׁלֹּא תַּעֲשֵׂם בִּפְנֵי עַצְמָם וּתְחַבְּרֵם בְּרָאשֵׁי הַכַּפֹּרֶת לְאַחַר עֲשִׂיָּתָם כְּמַעֲשֵׂה

◀

19 one cherub at one end and one at the other; the cherubim
20 shall be made of one piece with the cover. These cherubim
should have wings spread upward, sheltering the cover. They
21 should face one another, and look toward the cover. Place the
cover on top of the Ark, and inside the Ark place the tablets of
22 the Covenant that I will give you. There, from above the cover,
between the two cherubim, above the Ark of the Testimony,

עוֹרְפִים שָׁקוּלִין סוֹלְדְרִי"ן, חֲלֹק
הַטַּל זָהָב הַרְבֵּה פִּתְּחִלַּת עֲשִׂיַּת
הַכַּפֹּרֶת, וְהַכֵּה בְּפַטִּישׁ וּבְקֻרְנָס
בָּאֶמְצַע וְרָאשִׁין בּוֹלְטִין לְמַעְלָה,
וְעַר הַכְּרוּבִים בִּבְלִיטַת קְצוֹתָיו:

מִקְשָׁה. כְּטֵדֵי"ן בְּלַעַז, כְּמוֹ: "דָּא
לְדָא נָקְשָׁן" (דניאל ה, ו):

קְצוֹת הַכַּפֹּרֶת. רָאשֵׁי הַכַּפֹּרֶת:

יט| וְעָשֵׂה כְּרוּב אֶחָד מִקָּצָה. שֶׁלֹּא
תֹּאמַר, שְׁנֵים כְּרוּבִים לְכָל קָצֶה
וְקָצֶה, לְכָךְ הֻצְרַךְ לְפָרֵשׁ: "כְּרוּב
אֶחָד מִקָּצָה מִזֶּה":

מִן הַכַּפֹּרֶת. עַצְמָהּ, "תַּעֲשׂוּ אֵת
הַכְּרֻבִים". זֶהוּ פֵּרוּשׁוֹ שֶׁל "מִקְשָׁה
תַּעֲשֶׂה אֹתָם", שֶׁלֹּא תַעֲשֵׂם בִּפְנֵי
עַצְמָם וּתְחַבְּרֵם לַכַּפֹּרֶת:

כ| פֹּרְשֵׂי כְנָפַיִם. שֶׁלֹּא תַּעֲשֶׂה
כַּנְפֵיהֶם שׁוֹכְבִים, חֲלֹק פְּרוּשִׂים
וּגְבוֹהִים לְמַעְלָה אֵצֶל רָאשֵׁיהֶם,
שֶׁיְּהֵא עֲשָׂרָה טְפָחִים בֶּחָלָל שֶׁבֵּין
הַכְּנָפַיִם לַכַּפֹּרֶת, כִּדְאִיתָא בְּסֻכָּה
(דף ה ע"ב):

כא| וְאֶל הָאָרֹן תִּתֵּן אֶת הָעֵדֻת.
לֹא יָדַעְתִּי לָמָּה נִכְפַּל, שֶׁהֲרֵי
כְּבָר נֶאֱמַר: "וְנָתַתָּ אֶל הָאָרֹן אֵת
הָעֵדֻת" (לעיל פסוק טז)! וְיֵשׁ לוֹמַר,

Rather, begin with a large block of gold and hammer down its middle with a mallet so that material protrudes from its ends. Then fashion these projections into shapes to form the cherubim.

מִקְשָׁה – *Beaten:* [The meaning of the Hebrew word is unclear. Rashi explains:] The Old French term for this is *battu* ["beaten"], as in the verse *And his knees smote [nakeshan] one against the other* (Daniel 5:6).

קְצוֹת הַכַּפֹּרֶת – *Ends of the cover:* [The word *ketzot* means] "ends" of the cover.

19 | וְעָשֵׂה כְּרוּב אֶחָד מִקָּצָה – *One cherub at one end:* This verse teaches that there are not to be two cherubim on each side of the Ark cover [for a total of four]. Rather, our verse emphasizes that there must be *one cherub at one end and one at the other.*

מִן הַכַּפֹּרֶת – *Of one piece with the cover:* The cherubim should be fashioned from the same piece of gold that the cover is made out of. This is what is meant by the clause *Make two cherubim of beaten gold* (25:18) – do not make each figure separately and then attach them to the cover.

20 | פֹּרְשֵׂי כְנָפַיִם – *Wings spread upward:* The wings on these figures should not be folded at their sides. Instead, carve the images so that their wings are raised and spread out high, parallel to their heads. Thus there should be a span of ten handbreadths between the horizontal wings and the lid of the Ark cover, as is described in tractate Sukka (5b).

21 | וְאֶל הָאָרֹן תִּתֵּן אֶת הָעֵדֻת – *And inside the Ark place the tablets of the Covenant:* I do not know why the Torah repeats this command, for it has already been stated above: *Inside the Ark, place the tablets of the Covenant* (20:16). We might

יט מִקְשָׁה תַּעֲשֶׂה אֹתָם מִשְּׁנֵי קְצוֹת הַכַּפֹּרֶת: וַעֲשֵׂה
כְּרוּב אֶחָד מִקָּצָה מִזֶּה וּכְרוּב־אֶחָד מִקָּצָה מִזֶּה
מִן־הַכַּפֹּרֶת תַּעֲשׂוּ אֶת־הַכְּרֻבִים עַל־שְׁנֵי קְצוֹתָיו:
כ וְהָיוּ הַכְּרֻבִים פֹּרְשֵׂי כְנָפַיִם לְמַעְלָה סֹכְכִים בְּכַנְפֵיהֶם
עַל־הַכַּפֹּרֶת וּפְנֵיהֶם אִישׁ אֶל־אָחִיו אֶל־הַכַּפֹּרֶת
כא יִהְיוּ פְּנֵי הַכְּרֻבִים: וְנָתַתָּ אֶת־הַכַּפֹּרֶת עַל־הָאָרֹן
מִלְמָעְלָה וְאֶל־הָאָרֹן תִּתֵּן אֶת־הָעֵדֻת אֲשֶׁר אֶתֵּן
כב אֵלֶיךָ: וְנוֹעַדְתִּי לְךָ שָׁם וְדִבַּרְתִּי אִתְּךָ מֵעַל הַכַּפֹּרֶת

שֶׁבָּא לְלַמֵּד שֶׁבְּעוֹדוֹ אָרוֹן לְבַדּוֹ בְּלֹא כַּפֹּרֶת יִתֵּן תְּחִלָּה הָעֵדוּת לְתוֹכוֹ, וְאַחַר כָּךְ יִתֵּן אֶת הַכַּפֹּרֶת עָלָיו, וְכֵן מָצִינוּ כְּשֶׁהֵקִים אֶת הַמִּשְׁכָּן, נֶאֱמַר: "וַיִּתֵּן אֶת הָעֵדֻת אֶל הָאָרֹן" וְאַחַר כָּךְ: "וַיִּתֵּן אֶת הַכַּפֹּרֶת עַל הָאָרֹן מִלְמָעְלָה" (להלן מ, כ):

suggest that the above verse emphasizes that the tablets of the Covenant were to be placed inside the Ark while it stood uncovered, and that the Ark cover should be positioned on top only afterward. We find this stated explicitly when the Tabernacle was erected: *He took the covenant and put it in the Ark*, and then: *He inserted the carrying staves into the Ark and placed the cover on top of it* (40:20).

כב | **וְנוֹעַדְתִּי.** כְּשֶׁאֶקְבַּע מוֹעֵד לְךָ לְדַבֵּר עִמְּךָ, אוֹתוֹ מָקוֹם אֶקְבַּע לַמּוֹעֵד, שֶׁאָבֹא שָׁם לְדַבֵּר אֵלֶיךָ:

22 | **וְנוֹעַדְתִּי** – *I will meet:* [The word *venoadti* is unfamiliar. Rashi explains:] When I arrange a time [*moed*] to commune with you, I will designate that site to be our regular meeting place. It is there that I will come to address you.

וְדִבַּרְתִּי אִתְּךָ מֵעַל הַכַּפֹּרֶת. וּבְמָקוֹם אַחֵר הוּא אוֹמֵר: "וַיְדַבֵּר ה' אֵלָיו מֵאֹהֶל מוֹעֵד לֵאמֹר" (ויקרא א, א), זֶה הַמִּשְׁכָּן מִחוּץ לַפָּרֹכֶת, נִמְצְאוּ שְׁנֵי כְתוּבִים מַכְחִישִׁים זֶה אֶת זֶה! בָּא הַכָּתוּב הַשְּׁלִישִׁי וְהִכְרִיעַ בֵּינֵיהֶם: "וּבְבֹא מֹשֶׁה אֶל אֹהֶל מוֹעֵד... וַיִּשְׁמַע אֶת הַקּוֹל מִדַּבֵּר אֵלָיו מֵעַל הַכַּפֹּרֶת" וְגוֹ' (במדבר ז, פט), מֹשֶׁה הָיָה נִכְנָס לַמִּשְׁכָּן, וְכֵיוָן שֶׁבָּא כְּתוֹךְ הַפֶּתַח קוֹל יוֹרֵד מִן הַשָּׁמַיִם לְבֵין הַכְּרוּבִים, וּמִשָּׁם יוֹצֵא וְנִשְׁמָע לְמֹשֶׁה בְּאֹהֶל מוֹעֵד:

וְדִבַּרְתִּי אִתְּךָ מֵעַל הַכַּפֹּרֶת – *From above the cover, I will speak with you:* However, a later verse states: *And the* Lord *called to Moshe, and spoke to him out of the Tent of Meeting* (Leviticus 1:1), where the term "Tent of Meeting" refers to the area of the Tabernacle outside of the Holy of Holies. Although these verses seem to contradict each other, we can enlist a third verse to reconcile the difficulty: *And when Moshe had gone into the Tent of Meeting to speak with Him, then he heard the voice speaking to him from off the covering that was upon the Ark of the Testimony, from between the two cherubim* (Numbers 7:89). When Moshe entered the Tabernacle structure, God's voice descended from heaven and emerged from between the two cherubim. Standing on the other side of the curtain, in the Tent of Meeting, Moshe was able to hear God's communication.

I will meet with you and speak with you, and give you all My
commands to the Israelites.
23 Make a table of acacia wood, two cubits long, a cubit wide,
24 and a cubit and a half high. Overlay it with pure gold and
25 around it make a gold rim. Make a frame a handbreadth wide
26 all around, and around the frame also make a gold rim. Make
for it four gold rings, and place the rings on the four corners
27 where the four legs are. The rings should be attached next to
28 the frame as holders for staves to carry the table. Make the
staves of acacia wood and overlay them with gold; by these
29 the table shall be carried. You must also make, out of pure

וְאֵת כָּל־אֲשֶׁר אֲצַוֶּה אוֹתְךָ אֶל־בְּנֵי יִשְׂרָאֵל. הֲרֵי וָי"ו זוֹ יְתֵרָה וּטְפֵלָה. וְכָמוֹהָ הַרְבֵּה בַּמִּקְרָא, וְכֹה תִּפָּתֵר: וַאֲשֶׁר אֲדַבֵּר עִמְּךָ שָׁם "אֵת כָּל אֲשֶׁר אֲצַוֶּה אוֹתְךָ אֶל בְּנֵי יִשְׂרָאֵל" הוּא:

וְאֵת כָּל־אֲשֶׁר אֲצַוֶּה אוֹתְךָ אֶל־בְּנֵי יִשְׂרָאֵל – *All My commands to the Israelites:* [Rashi possessed a variant of the Torah text that had the word *ve'et* rather than *et*. Rashi explains the superfluous letter *vav* in his version:] This *vav* is redundant. Indeed, there are many such instances in Scripture. But sense of the verse is: What I will speak to you there will be *all My commands to the Israelites.*

כג| **קוֹמָתוֹ.** גֹּבַהּ רַגְלָיו עִם עֳבִי הַשֻּׁלְחָן:

23 | **קֹמָתוֹ** – *High:* The table stood a cubit and a half tall including its legs and the thickness of the tabletop itself.

כד| **זֵר זָהָב.** סִימָן לְכֶתֶר מַלְכוּת, שֶׁהַשֻּׁלְחָן שֵׁם עֹשֶׁר וּגְדֻלָּה, כְּמוֹ שֶׁאוֹמְרִים: שֻׁלְחַן מְלָכִים:

24 | **זֵר זָהָב** – *A gold rim:* This gold border symbolizes the crown of the Israelite monarchy, for the table as a whole represents earthly wealth and greatness. Thus do people say: "This food is fit for a king's table!"

כה| **מִסְגֶּרֶת.** כְּתַרְגּוּמוֹ: "גְּדַנְפָא". וְנֶחְלְקוּ חַכְמֵי יִשְׂרָאֵל בַּדָּבָר: יֵשׁ אוֹמְרִים לְמַעְלָה הָיְתָה סָבִיב לַשֻּׁלְחָן, כְּמוֹ לְבִזְבְּזִין שֶׁבִּשְׂפַת שֻׁלְחַן שָׂרִים, וְיֵשׁ אוֹמְרִים לְמַטָּה הָיְתָה תְּקוּעָה מֵרֶגֶל לְרֶגֶל בְּאַרְבַּע רוּחוֹת הַשֻּׁלְחָן, וְדַף הַשֻּׁלְחָן שׁוֹכֵב עַל אוֹתָהּ מִסְגֶּרֶת:

25 | **מִסְגֶּרֶת** – *A frame:* This should be understood as the Targum renders it: a "border" [*gedanefa*]. Now the Sages of Israel debate the position of this frame. According to some, the frame surrounded the table like a vertical ledge found on princes' tables. [That is, it stood upright, projecting above the tabletop like a fence.] Another approach claims that the frame ran beneath the tabletop and stretched from one leg to the next on all four sides. According to this second understanding, the tabletop sat on top of the frame.

וְעָשִׂיתָ זֵר־זָהָב לְמִסְגַּרְתּוֹ. הוּא זֵר הָאָמוּר לְמַעְלָה, וּפֵרֵשׁ לְךָ כָּאן שֶׁעַל הַמִּסְגֶּרֶת הָיָה:

וְעָשִׂיתָ זֵר־זָהָב לְמִסְגַּרְתּוֹ – *And around the frame also make a gold rim:* This is the same rim as that mentioned above [in verse 24; the word "also" is absent from the Hebrew]. Our verse explains that this rim was attached to the frame.

◀

מִבֵּין שְׁנֵי הַכְּרֻבִים אֲשֶׁר עַל־אֲרוֹן הָעֵדֻת אֵת כָּל־
אֲשֶׁר אֲצַוֶּה אוֹתְךָ אֶל־בְּנֵי יִשְׂרָאֵל׃
כג וְעָשִׂיתָ שֻׁלְחָן עֲצֵי שִׁטִּים אַמָּתַיִם אָרְכּוֹ וְאַמָּה רָחְבּוֹ
כד וְאַמָּה וָחֵצִי קֹמָתוֹ׃ וְצִפִּיתָ אֹתוֹ זָהָב טָהוֹר וְעָשִׂיתָ לּוֹ
כה זֵר זָהָב סָבִיב׃ וְעָשִׂיתָ לּוֹ מִסְגֶּרֶת טֹפַח סָבִיב וְעָשִׂיתָ
כו זֵר־זָהָב לְמִסְגַּרְתּוֹ סָבִיב׃ וְעָשִׂיתָ לּוֹ אַרְבַּע טַבְּעֹת
זָהָב וְנָתַתָּ אֶת־הַטַּבָּעֹת עַל אַרְבַּע הַפֵּאֹת אֲשֶׁר
כז לְאַרְבַּע רַגְלָיו׃ לְעֻמַּת הַמִּסְגֶּרֶת תִּהְיֶיןָ הַטַּבָּעֹת
כח לְבָתִּים לְבַדִּים לָשֵׂאת אֶת־הַשֻּׁלְחָן׃ וְעָשִׂיתָ אֶת־
הַבַּדִּים עֲצֵי שִׁטִּים וְצִפִּיתָ אֹתָם זָהָב וְנִשָּׂא־בָם אֶת־
כט הַשֻּׁלְחָן׃ וְעָשִׂיתָ קְּעָרֹתָיו וְכַפֹּתָיו וּקְשׂוֹתָיו וּמְנַקִּיֹּתָיו

27| לְעֻמַּת הַמִּסְגֶּרֶת תִּהְיֶיןָ הַטַּבָּעֹת – *The rings should be attached next to the frame:* The rings were fixed in the legs opposite the ends of the frame.

כז| לְעֻמַּת הַמִּסְגֶּרֶת תִּהְיֶיןָ הַטַּבָּעֹת. בָּרַגְלַיִם תְּקוּעוֹת כְּנֶגֶד רָאשֵׁי הַמִּסְגֶּרֶת:

לְבָתִּים לְבַדִּים – *As holders for staves:* The rings mentioned at the start of the verse had staves inserted in them.

לְבָתִּים לְבַדִּים. אוֹתָן הַטַּבָּעוֹת יִהְיוּ בָּתִּים לְהַכְנִיס בָּהֶן הַבַּדִּים:

לְבָתִּים – *As holders:* [The *lamed* that begins this word does not mean "for" holders, but] "as" holders.

לְבָתִּים. לְצֹרֶךְ בָּתִּים:

לְבַדִּים – *For staves:* The phrase should be understood as the Targum renders it: "as a place for the staves."

לְבַדִּים. כְּתַרְגּוּמוֹ: ״לְאַתְרָא לַאֲרִיחַיָּא״:

28| וְנִשָּׂא־בָם – *By these the table shall be carried:* The verb here is in the passive *nifal* construction, meaning that the table "shall be carried" by its staves.

כח| וְנִשָּׂא־בָם. לְשׁוֹן נִפְעַל, יִהְיֶה נִשָּׂא בָּם אֶת הַשֻּׁלְחָן:

29| וְעָשִׂיתָ קְּעָרֹתָיו וְכַפֹּתָיו – *You must also make its bowls, spoons:* [The meaning of all these terms is unclear. Rashi explains:] The *ke'arot* were pans formed in the shape of the loaves of bread they held. The showbread itself was shaped like an open box with two sides closed and two sides open. It had a bottom and was folded up on opposite sides to create two walls of bread. [That it, is looked like an elongated letter "U"]. The bread

כט| וְעָשִׂיתָ קְּעָרֹתָיו וְכַפֹּתָיו. קְעָרֹתָיו זֶה דְּפוּס, שֶׁהָיָה עָשׂוּי כִּדְפוּס הַלֶּחֶם. וְהַלֶּחֶם הָיָה עָשׂוּי כְּמִין תֵּבָה פְרוּצָה מִשְּׁתֵּי רוּחוֹתֶיהָ, שׁוּלַיִם לוֹ לְמַטָּה, וְקוֹפֵל מִכָּאן וּמִכָּאן כְּלַפֵּי מַעְלָה כְּמִין כְּתָלִים.

gold, its bowls, spoons, pitchers, and jars for pouring liba-
30 tions. On this table the showbread must be placed before Me
at all times.
31 Make a candelabrum of pure gold. Its base and shaft, cups,

וּלְכָךְ קָרוּי לֶחֶם הַפָּנִים, שֶׁיֵּשׁ לוֹ פָּנִים רוֹאִים לְכָאן וּלְכָאן לְצִדֵּי הַבַּיִת מִזֶּה וּמִזֶּה. וְנוֹתֵן אָרְכּוֹ לְרָחְבּוֹ שֶׁל שֻׁלְחָן, וְכָתְלָיו זְקוּפִים כְּנֶגֶד שְׂפַת הַשֻּׁלְחָן. וְהָיָה עָשׂוּי לוֹ דְּפוּס זָהָב וּדְפוּס בַּרְזֶל; בְּשֶׁל בַּרְזֶל הוּא נֶאֱפֶה, וּכְשֶׁמּוֹצִיאוֹ מִן הַתַּנּוּר נוֹתְנוֹ בְּשֶׁל זָהָב עַד לְמָחָר, בְּשַׁבָּת, שֶׁמְּסַדְּרוֹ עַל הַשֻּׁלְחָן, וְאוֹתוֹ דְּפוּס קָרוּי קְעָרָה:

was therefore called *leḥem hapanim* [literally, "bread of faces"], since it had two faces on its sides, facing toward both sides of the Sanctuary. The long side of the loaves was oriented along the width of the table, while the walls of the bread stood upright opposite the edge of the table [and thereby faced the walls of the room]. A copy of this golden pan was made of iron. The bread was baked in the iron mold, but was removed from that when it was taken out of the oven and placed in the gold container. There it sat until the following day, the Sabbath, whereupon all the new loaves were placed on the table. Such a pan was called a *ke'ara*.

וְכַפֹּתָיו. בָּזִיכִין שֶׁנּוֹתְנִין בָּהֶם לְבוֹנָה, שְׁתַּיִם הָיוּ לִשְׁנֵי קָמְצֵי לְבוֹנָה שֶׁנּוֹתְנִין עַל שְׁתֵּי הַמַּעֲרָכוֹת, שֶׁנֶּאֱמַר: "וְנָתַתָּ עַל הַמַּעֲרֶכֶת לְבֹנָה זַכָּה" (ויקרא כד, ז):

וְכַפֹּתָיו – *Its spoons:* The *kappot* were utensils used to hold frankincense. There were two such containers to hold the two handfuls of frankincense, which were positioned on the two rows of bread, as the verse states: *And you shall put pure frankincense upon each row* (Leviticus 24:7).

וּקְשׂוֹתָיו. הֵן כְּמִין חֲצָאֵי קָנִים חֲלוּלִים הַנִּסְדָּקִין לְאָרְכָּן, דֻּגְמָתָן עוֹשֶׂה שֶׁל זָהָב וּמְסַדֵּר שְׁלֹשָׁה עַל רֹאשׁ כָּל לֶחֶם, שֶׁיֵּשֵׁב לֶחֶם הָאֶחָד עַל גַּבֵּי אוֹתָן הַקָּנִים, וּמַבְדִּילִין בֵּין לֶחֶם לְלֶחֶם כְּדֵי שֶׁתִּכָּנֵס הָרוּחַ בֵּינֵיהֶם וְלֹא יִתְעַפְּשׁוּ. וּבְלָשׁוֹן עֲרָבִי כָּל דָּבָר חָלוּל קָרוּי קסו"ה:

וּקְשׂוֹתָיו – *Its pitchers:* The *kesot* looked like halves of hollow canes that have been split along their length. Such forms were made out of gold, and three of them were arranged above each loaf of bread, to separate the loaves from one another. In this way air could circulate between the loaves and prevent mold from forming on them. In Arabic, anything hollow is called *kasweh*.

וּמְנַקִּיֹּתָיו. תַּרְגּוּמוֹ "וּמְכִילָתֵיהּ", הֵן סְנִיפִין כְּמִין יְתֵדוֹת זָהָב עוֹמְדִין בָּאָרֶץ וּגְבוֹהִין עַד לְמַעְלָה מִן הַשֻּׁלְחָן הַרְבֵּה כְּנֶגֶד גֹּבַהּ מַעֲרֶכֶת הַלֶּחֶם, וּמְפֻצָּלִים שִׁשָּׁה פִּצּוּלִים, זֶה לְמַעְלָה מִזֶּה, וְרָאשֵׁי הַקָּנִים שֶׁבֵּין לֶחֶם לְלֶחֶם סְמוּכִין עַל אוֹתָן פִּצּוּלִין, כְּדֵי שֶׁלֹּא יִכְבַּד מַשָּׂא הַלֶּחֶם הָעֶלְיוֹנִים עַל הַתַּחְתּוֹנִים וְיִשָּׁבְרוּ. וּלְשׁוֹן "מְכִילָתֵיהּ" סוֹבְלוֹתָיו,

וּמְנַקִּיֹּתָיו – *Its jars:* The Targum translates this word as *mekhilateih* [meaning "supports" for the tubes described above; see below]. These were fashioned like golden poles that stood on the ground and extended past the height of the table to the level of the loaves themselves. These poles had a series of six holes in them running up their lengths where the ends of the tubes were inserted between the loaves. This was so that the weight of the upper loaves would not overwhelm that of the lower loaves and cause them to break. The Targum's Aramaic term, *mekhilateih*, means "supports," as in the verse

◀

ל אֲשֶׁר יֻסַּךְ בָּהֵן זָהָב טָהוֹר תַּעֲשֶׂה אֹתָם: וְנָתַתָּ עַל־
הַשֻּׁלְחָן לֶחֶם פָּנִים לְפָנַי תָּמִיד:
לא וְעָשִׂיתָ מְנֹרַת זָהָב טָהוֹר מִקְשָׁה תֵּיעָשֶׂה הַמְּנוֹרָה
יְרֵכָהּ וְקָנָהּ גְּבִיעֶיהָ כַּפְתֹּרֶיהָ וּפְרָחֶיהָ מִמֶּנָּה יִהְיוּ:

כְּמוֹ: "נִלְאֵיתִי הָכִיל" (ירמיה ו, יא). אֲבָל לְשׁוֹן 'מְנַקִּיֹּת' אֵינִי יוֹדֵעַ אֵיךְ נוֹפֵל עַל סְנִיפִין. וְיֵשׁ מֵחַכְמֵי יִשְׂרָאֵל אוֹמְרִים, "קְשׂוֹתָיו" אֵלּוּ סְנִיפִין, שֶׁמַּקְשִׁין אוֹתוֹ וּמַחֲזִיקִים אוֹתוֹ שֶׁלֹּא יִשָּׁבֵר, "וּמְנַקִּיֹּתָיו" אֵלּוּ הַקָּנִים, שֶׁמְּנַקִּין אוֹתוֹ שֶׁלֹּא יִתְעַפֵּשׁ. אֲבָל אוּנְקְלוֹס שֶׁתִּרְגֵּם: "וּמְכִילָתֵיהּ" הָיָה שׁוֹנֶה כְּדִבְרֵי הָאוֹמֵר מְנַקִּיּוֹת הֵן סְנִיפִין:

I am weary of holding it in [hakhil] (Jeremiah 6:11). Still, I do not know the connection of the Hebrew word *menakkiyyotav* to such a meaning.

אֲשֶׁר יֻסַּךְ בָּהֵן. אֲשֶׁר יְכֻסֶּה בָּהֶן. וְעַל קְשׂוֹתָיו הוּא אוֹמֵר: "אֲשֶׁר יֻסַּךְ", שֶׁהָיוּ עָלָיו כְּמִין סְכָךְ וְכִסּוּי, וְכֵן בְּמָקוֹם אַחֵר הוּא אוֹמֵר: "וְאֵת קְשׂוֹת הַנָּסֶךְ" (במדבר ד, ז). וְזֶה וָזֶה, 'יֻסַּךְ' וְ'הַנָּסֶךְ', לְשׁוֹן סְכָךְ וְכִסּוּי הֵם:

אֲשֶׁר יֻסַּךְ בָּהֵן – *For pouring libations:* [The word *yussakh* can also mean "be covered." Rashi follows this reading:] The clause means: By which the loaves of bread will be covered. This phrase refers to the tubes [*kesot*], for they sat like a roof [*sekhakh*] or a covering over the bread. Similarly, we read elsewhere: *The covering tubes [kesot hanasekh]* (Numbers 4:7). For both terms – *yussakh* and *nesekh* – are related to the words for roof and covering.

ל| לֶחֶם פָּנִים. שֶׁהָיוּ לוֹ פָּנִים כְּמוֹ שֶׁפֵּרַשְׁתִּי. וּמִנְיַן הַלֶּחֶם וְסֵדֶר מַעַרְכוֹתָיו מְפֹרָשִׁים בְּ'אֱמֹר אֶל הַכֹּהֲנִים' (ויקרא כד, ה-ט):

30 | **לֶחֶם פָּנִים** – *The showbread:* [Literally, "bread of faces."] The bread was so called because it had faces, as I have explained [in comments on the previous verse]. The number of loaves and the way their rows were arranged are detailed in Parashat Emor (Leviticus 24:5–9).

לא| מִקְשָׁה תֵּיעָשֶׂה הַמְּנוֹרָה. שֶׁלֹּא יַעֲשֶׂנָּה חֻלְיוֹת, וְלֹא יַעֲשֶׂה קָנֶיהָ וְנֵרוֹתֶיהָ אֵבָרִים אֵבָרִים וְאַחַר כָּךְ יַדְבִּיקֵם כְּדֶרֶךְ הַצּוֹרְפִים שֶׁקּוֹרִין שולדריי"ן, אֶלָּא כֻּלָּהּ בָּאָה מֵחֲתִיכָה אַחַת, וּמַקִּישׁ בַּקֻּרְנָס וְחוֹתֵךְ בִּכְלֵי הָאֻמָּנוּת וּמַפְרִיד הַקָּנִים אֵילָךְ וְאֵילָךְ. תַּרְגּוּמוֹ שֶׁל "מִקְשָׁה": "נְגִיד",

31 | **מִקְשָׁה תֵּיעָשֶׂה הַמְּנוֹרָה** – *Shall be hammered from a single piece:* You must not fashion the candelabrum out of separate segments. Nor should you create its branches and lamps in different pieces and then join them together like welders whose activity is called *souder* ["solder"] in Old French. Rather, the entire candelabrum is to be crafted from a single block of gold, hammered with a mallet and carved with artisans' chisels to divide the piece into branches on this side and that side. The Targum renders the word *miksha* as *negid*, meaning

32 **knobs, and flowers shall be hammered from a single piece. Six**
branches shall extend from its sides, three on one side, three
33 **on the other. On each branch there shall be three finely craft-**
ed cups, each with a knob and a flower. All six branches ex-
34 **tending from the candelabrum shall be like this. The shaft of**
the candelabrum shall have four finely crafted cups, each with

לְשׁוֹן הַמְשָׁכָה, שֶׁמַּמְשִׁיךְ הָאֵבָרִים מִן הָעֶשֶׁת לְכָאן וּלְכָאן בְּהַקָּשַׁת הַקֻּרְנָס. וּלְשׁוֹן "מִקְשָׁה" מַכַּת קֻרְנָס, בטדי"ן בְּלַעַז:

"to draw out." For the limbs of the candelabrum were formed out of the mass of gold by beating it all over with a mallet. The term *miksha* reflects the striking of the hammer – *battu* ["beating"] in Old French.

תֵּיעָשֶׂה הַמְּנוֹרָה. מֵאֵלֶיהָ, לְפִי שֶׁהָיָה מֹשֶׁה מִתְקַשֶּׁה בָּהּ, אָמַר לוֹ הַקָּדוֹשׁ בָּרוּךְ הוּא: הַשְׁלֵךְ אֶת הַכִּכָּר לָאוּר וְהִיא נַעֲשֵׂית מֵאֵלֶיהָ. לְכָךְ לֹא נִכְתַּב 'תַּעֲשֶׂה':

תֵּיעָשֶׂה הַמְּנוֹרָה – *Shall be hammered:* [Literally, "shall be made."] It shall be made of itself. Because Moshe had difficulty visualizing how the candelabrum was to be fashioned, the Holy One, blessed be He, told him: Cast a talent of gold into the fire and the candelabrum will miraculously create itself. This is why the verse does not use the active case [*taaseh*, but rather the passive *te'aseh*].

יְרֵכָהּ. הוּא הָרֶגֶל שֶׁלְּמַטָּה הֶעָשׂוּי כְּמִין תֵּבָה, וּשְׁלֹשֶׁת הָרַגְלַיִם יוֹצְאִין הֵימֶנָּה מַטָּה:

יְרֵכָהּ – *Its base:* This term refers to the candelabrum's base, at the bottom. This was fashioned like a sort of box, with three feet protruding beneath it.

וְקָנָהּ. הַקָּנֶה הָאֶמְצָעִי שֶׁלָּהּ הָעוֹלֶה בְּאֶמְצַע הַיָּרֵךְ זָקוּף כְּלַפֵּי מַעְלָה, וְעָלָיו נֵר הָאֶמְצָעִי עָשׂוּי כְּמִין בָּזֵךְ לָצוּק הַשֶּׁמֶן לְתוֹכוֹ וְלָתֵת הַפְּתִילָה:

וְקָנָהּ – *And its shaft:* This refers to the central shaft of the candelabrum, which rose from the center of the base and stood upright. The top of this rod held the middle lamp of the candelabrum, which was shaped like a cup. Oil was poured into it, and a wick placed inside the oil.

גְּבִיעֶיהָ. הֵן כְּמִין כּוֹסוֹת שֶׁעוֹשִׂין מִזְּכוּכִית אֲרֻכִּים וּקְצָרִים, וְקוֹרִין לָהֶם מדרינ"ש, וְאֵלּוּ עֲשׂוּיִין שֶׁל זָהָב וּבוֹלְטִין וְיוֹצְאִין מִכָּל קָנֶה וְקָנֶה כַּמִּנְיָן שֶׁנָּתַן בָּהֶם הַכָּתוּב, וְלֹא הָיוּ בָּהּ אֶלָּא לְנוֹי:

גְּבִיעֶיהָ – *Its cups:* These are like long and narrow cups made out of glass, which are referred to in Old French as *madernes*. Those featured on the candelabrum were fashioned out of gold, and they projected out of each of its branches, in amounts enumerated in the text [in verses 33–34]. This feature had an ornamental purpose only.

כַּפְתֹּרֶיהָ. כְּמִין תַּפּוּחִים הָיוּ עֲגֻלִּין סָבִיב, בּוֹלְטִין סְבִיבוֹת הַקָּנֶה הָאֶמְצָעִי, כְּדֶרֶךְ שֶׁעוֹשִׂין לַמְּנוֹרוֹת שֶׁלִּפְנֵי הַשָּׂרִים וְקוֹרִין לָהֶם פומיל"ש, וּמִנְיָן שֶׁלָּהֶם כָּתוּב בַּפָּרָשָׁה, כַּמָּה כַּפְתּוֹרִים בּוֹלְטִין מִמֶּנָּה וְכַמָּה חָלָק בֵּין כַּפְתּוֹר לְכַפְתּוֹר:

כַּפְתֹּרֶיהָ – *Its knobs:* The knobs were spherical like apples. They protruded from the middle shaft of the candelabrum like one can see on candlesticks that are fashioned for princes. In Old French this detail is referred to as *pommettes* ["rounded knobs"]. The text below describes how many knobs appeared on the candelabrum, as well as how much space intervened between each knob.

◀

לב וְשִׁשָּׁה קָנִים יֹצְאִים מִצִּדֶּיהָ שְׁלֹשָׁה ׀ קְנֵי מְנֹרָה
מִצִּדָּהּ הָאֶחָד וּשְׁלֹשָׁה קְנֵי מְנֹרָה מִצִּדָּהּ הַשֵּׁנִי׃
לג שְׁלֹשָׁה גְבִעִים מְשֻׁקָּדִים בַּקָּנֶה הָאֶחָד כַּפְתֹּר וָפֶרַח
וּשְׁלֹשָׁה גְבִעִים מְשֻׁקָּדִים בַּקָּנֶה הָאֶחָד כַּפְתֹּר וָפָרַח
לד כֵּן לְשֵׁשֶׁת הַקָּנִים הַיֹּצְאִים מִן־הַמְּנֹרָה׃ וּבַמְּנֹרָה
אַרְבָּעָה גְבִעִים מְשֻׁקָּדִים כַּפְתֹּרֶיהָ וּפְרָחֶיהָ׃

וּפְרָחֶיהָ – *And its flowers:* Designs were made on the candelabrum that were made to look like flowers.

וּפְרָחֶיהָ. צִיּוּרִין עֲשׂוּיִין בָּהּ כְּמִין פְּרָחִים:

מִמֶּנָּה יִהְיוּ – *From a single piece:* The entire candelabrum was fashioned out of a single mass of gold. The craftsmen were not to form each individual part and then join all the pieces together.

מִמֶּנָּה יִהְיוּ. הַכֹּל מִקְשָׁה יוֹצֵא מִתּוֹךְ חֲתִיכַת הָעֶשֶׁת, וְלֹא יַעֲשֶׂם לְבַדָּם וִידַבְּקֵם:

32 | **יֹצְאִים מִצִּדֶּיהָ** – *Shall extend from its sides:* Three branches extended diagonally upward on one side of the candelabrum, and three branches extended diagonally upward on the other side. These branches rose to the top of the candelabrum, which was the height of middle shaft. The branches emerged from the central shaft one above the other. Hence the lowest two branches were the longest [since they had the farthest to rise to the top], the ones above those were somewhat shorter, while the highest two branches were the shortest. In this way the heights of all the branches' tops were level with that of the middle, seventh branch – the central shaft. The six branches thus extended from the middle shaft.

לב| **יֹצְאִים מִצִּדֶּיהָ.** לְכָאן וּלְכָאן בַּאֲלַכְסוֹן, נִמְשָׁכִים וְעוֹלִין עַד כְּנֶגֶד גָּבְהָהּ שֶׁל מְנוֹרָה שֶׁהוּא קָנֶה הָאֶמְצָעִי, וְיוֹצְאִים מִתּוֹךְ קָנֶה הָאֶמְצָעִי זֶה לְמַעְלָה מִזֶּה, הַתַּחְתּוֹן אָרֹךְ וְשֶׁל מַעְלָה קָצָר הֵימֶנּוּ וְהָעֶלְיוֹן קָצָר הֵימֶנּוּ, לְפִי שֶׁהָיָה גֹּבַהּ רָאשֵׁיהֶן שָׁוֶה לְגָבְהוֹ שֶׁל קָנֶה הָאֶמְצָעִי הַשְּׁבִיעִי שֶׁמִּמֶּנּוּ יוֹצְאִים הַשִּׁשָּׁה:

33 | **מְשֻׁקָּדִים** – *Finely crafted:* The word *meshukkadim* should be understood as the Targum renders it – decorated in the way that gold and silver vessels are. In Old French this is called *nieller* ["filling in engraved designs with color"].

לג| **מְשֻׁקָּדִים.** כְּתַרְגּוּמוֹ, מְצֻיָּרִים הָיוּ כְּדֶרֶךְ שֶׁעוֹשִׂין לִכְלֵי כֶּסֶף וְזָהָב שֶׁקּוֹרִין ניילי״ר:

שְׁלֹשָׁה גְבִעִים – *Three cups:* These cups projected out of each branch of the candelabrum.

שְׁלֹשָׁה גְבִעִים. בּוֹלְטִין מִכָּל קָנֶה וְקָנֶה:

כַּפְתֹּר וָפֶרַח – *A knob and a flower:* [The word "each" is absent from the Hebrew. Rashi explains:] Each branch was decorated with these details.

כַּפְתֹּר וָפֶרַח. הָיָה לְכָל קָנֶה וְקָנֶה:

34 | **וּבַמְּנֹרָה אַרְבָּעָה גְבִעִים** – *The shaft of the candelabrum shall have four cups:* The main shaft of the candelabrum had four

לד| **וּבַמְּנֹרָה אַרְבָּעָה גְבִעִים.** בְּגוּפָהּ שֶׁל מְנוֹרָה הָיוּ אַרְבָּעָה גְבִיעִים,

35 a knob and a flower. For the six branches that extend from the
candelabrum, there must be a knob at the base of each pair of
36 branches. The knobs and their branches shall be of one piece
with it, the whole of it a single, hammered piece of pure gold.
37 Make its seven lamps and mount them so that they light the

cups. One of the cups was situated below all the branches [near the bottom], while the other three were placed above each spot where the branches emerged from its sides.

מְשֻׁקָּדִים כַּפְתֹּרֶיהָ וּפְרָחֶיהָ – *Finely crafted with a knob and a flower:* This clause is one of five in the Torah which cannot be precisely parsed. For the Hebrew phrasing is ambiguous as to whether the term "finely crafted" refers to the cups or to the knobs and flowers.

35 | **וְכַפְתֹּר תַּחַת שְׁנֵי הַקָּנִים** – *There must be a knob at the base of each pair of branches:* The branches that emerged from either side of the central shaft came out of knobs crafted in the middle branch. And these are the dimensions of the candelabrum as taught in Baraita Dimlekhet Hamishkan [a *baraita* appearing in Menahot 28b]: The height of the lamp was eighteen handbreadths, according to the following calculation: The feet that projected from the bottom of the base, together with the base itself, rose to three handbreadths, including the flower just above the base. This is the flower mentioned in the verse *And this was the work of the candlestick: it was of beaten gold, from its shaft, to its flower* (Numbers 8:4). Above that, the central shaft was smooth [unadorned] for two handbreadths, whereupon one handbreadth accounted for one cup out of the structure's four. Then appeared one knob and one flower out of the two that appeared on the main shaft of the candelabrum, as described in the verse *Each with a knob and a flower* (25:34). That verse teaches us that the middle branch held two knobs and two flowers aside from the three knobs at the points where the six branches emerged, which in turn are described by the phrase *A knob at the base of each pair of branches* (25:35). Now, above this ornamentation, were an additional two smooth handbreadths. This was followed by a handbreadth-long knob whence two branches emerged – one on either side. The branches were drawn out and rose to the height of the candelabrum. Above that point was another smooth handbreadth followed by an additional handbreadth with a knob, and two branches emerging from either side of it. Next there was a

אֶחָד בּוֹלֵט בָּהּ לְמַטָּה מִן הַקָּנִים, וְהַשְּׁלֹשָׁה לְמַעְלָה מִן יְצִיאַת הַקָּנִים הַיּוֹצְאִים מִצְּדֶיהָ:

מְשֻׁקָּדִים כַּפְתֹּרֶיהָ וּפְרָחֶיהָ. זֶה אֶחָד מֵחֲמִשָּׁה מִקְרָאוֹת שֶׁאֵין לָהֶם הֶכְרֵעַ, אֵין יָדוּעַ אִם "גְּבִעִים מְשֻׁקָּדִים" אוֹ "מְשֻׁקָּדִים כַּפְתֹּרֶיהָ וּפְרָחֶיהָ":

לה | **וְכַפְתֹּר תַּחַת שְׁנֵי הַקָּנִים.** מִתּוֹךְ הַכַּפְתּוֹר הָיוּ הַקָּנִים נִמְשָׁכִים מִשְּׁנֵי צְדֶיהָ אֵילָךְ וְאֵילָךְ. כָּךְ שָׁנִינוּ בִּמְלֶאכֶת הַמִּשְׁכָּן: גָּבְהָהּ שֶׁל מְנוֹרָה שְׁמוֹנָה עָשָׂר טְפָחִים. הָרַגְלַיִם וְהַפֶּרַח שְׁלֹשָׁה טְפָחִים, הוּא הַפֶּרַח הָאָמוּר בַּיָּרֵךְ שֶׁנֶּאֱמַר: "עַד יְרֵכָהּ עַד פִּרְחָהּ" (במדבר ח, ד), וּטְפָחַיִם חָלָק, וְטֶפַח שֶׁבּוֹ גָּבִיעַ מֵהָאַרְבָּעָה גְּבִיעִים וְכַפְתּוֹר וָפֶרַח מִשְּׁנֵי כַּפְתּוֹרִים וּשְׁנֵי פְרָחִים הָאֲמוּרִים בַּמְּנוֹרָה עַצְמָהּ, שֶׁנֶּאֱמַר: "מְשֻׁקָּדִים כַּפְתֹּרֶיהָ וּפְרָחֶיהָ" (בפסוק הקודם), לָמַדְנוּ שֶׁהָיוּ בַּקָּנֶה שְׁנֵי כַפְתּוֹרִים וּשְׁנֵי פְרָחִים לְבַד מִן הַשְּׁלֹשָׁה כַּפְתּוֹרִים שֶׁהַקָּנִים נִמְשָׁכִין מִתּוֹכָן, שֶׁנֶּאֱמַר: "וְכַפְתֹּר תַּחַת שְׁנֵי הַקָּנִים" וְגוֹ', וּטְפָחַיִם חָלָק, וְטֶפַח כַּפְתּוֹר, וּשְׁנֵי קָנִים יוֹצְאִים מִמֶּנּוּ אֵילָךְ וְאֵילָךְ נִמְשָׁכִים וְעוֹלִים כְּנֶגֶד גָּבְהָהּ שֶׁל מְנוֹרָה, וְטֶפַח חָלָק, וְטֶפַח כַּפְתּוֹר, וּשְׁנֵי קָנִים יוֹצְאִים מִמֶּנּוּ, וְטֶפַח חָלָק, וְטֶפַח כַּפְתּוֹר, וּשְׁנֵי קָנִים יוֹצְאִים מִמֶּנּוּ,

לה וְכַפְתֹּר תַּחַת שְׁנֵי הַקָּנִים מִמֶּנָּה וְכַפְתֹּר תַּחַת שְׁנֵי
הַקָּנִים מִמֶּנָּה וְכַפְתֹּר תַּחַת־שְׁנֵי הַקָּנִים מִמֶּנָּה
לו לְשֵׁשֶׁת הַקָּנִים הַיֹּצְאִים מִן־הַמְּנֹרָה׃ כַּפְתֹּרֵיהֶם
וּקְנֹתָם מִמֶּנָּה יִהְיוּ כֻּלָּהּ מִקְשָׁה אַחַת זָהָב טָהוֹר׃
לז וְעָשִׂיתָ אֶת־נֵרֹתֶיהָ שִׁבְעָה וְהֶעֱלָה אֶת־נֵרֹתֶיהָ

וּטְפָחַיִם חָלָק, נִשְׁתַּיְּרוּ שָׁם שְׁלֹשָׁה טְפָחִים, שֶׁבָּהֶם שְׁלֹשָׁה גְּבִיעִים וְכַפְתּוֹר וָפֶרַח. נִמְצְאוּ גְּבִיעִים שְׁנַיִם וְעֶשְׂרִים, שְׁמוֹנָה עָשָׂר לְשִׁשָּׁה קָנִים שְׁלֹשָׁה לְכָל אֶחָד וְאֶחָד, וְאַרְבָּעָה בְּגוּפָהּ שֶׁל מְנוֹרָה; וְאַחַד עָשָׂר כַּפְתּוֹרִים, שִׁשָּׁה בְּשֵׁשֶׁת הַקָּנִים, וּשְׁלֹשָׁה בְּגוּפָהּ שֶׁל מְנוֹרָה שֶׁהַקָּנִים יוֹצְאִים מֵהֶם, וּשְׁנַיִם עוֹד בַּמְּנוֹרָה שֶׁנֶּאֱמַר: "מְשֻׁקָּדִים כַּפְתֹּרֶיהָ" וּמִעוּט כַּפְתּוֹרִים שְׁנַיִם, הָאֶחָד לְמַטָּה אֵצֶל הַיָּרֵךְ וְהָאֶחָד בִּשְׁלֹשָׁה טְפָחִים הָעֶלְיוֹנִים עִם הַשְּׁלֹשָׁה גְּבִיעִים. וְתִשְׁעָה פְּרָחִים הָיוּ לָהּ, שִׁשָּׁה לְשֵׁשֶׁת הַקָּנִים, שֶׁנֶּאֱמַר: "בַּקָּנֶה הָאֶחָד כַּפְתֹּר וָפֶרַח" (לעיל פסוק לג), וּשְׁלֹשָׁה לַמְּנוֹרָה, שֶׁנֶּאֱמַר: "מְשֻׁקָּדִים כַּפְתֹּרֶיהָ וּפְרָחֶיהָ" (בפסוק הקודם) וּמִעוּט פְּרָחִים שְׁנַיִם, וְאֶחָד הָאָמוּר בְּפָרָשַׁת 'בְּהַעֲלֹתְךָ' (במדבר ח, ד) "עַד יְרֵכָהּ עַד פִּרְחָהּ". וְאִם תְּדַקְדֵּק בְּמִשְׁנָה זוֹ הַכְּתוּבָה לְמַעְלָה תִּמְצָאֵם כְּמִנְיָנָם אִישׁ אִישׁ בִּמְקוֹמוֹ׃

third smooth handbreadth before the third handbreadth-long knob. From that knob emerged the final two branches of the candelabrum to rise to the lamp's full height. Following that there were two smooth handbreadths. [At this point we have climbed fifteen handbreadths up the middle shaft]. This leaves three handbreadths which held three cups [out of the four on the central branch], and the second knob and flower set [of two on the central branch]. Altogether, the candelabrum held twenty-two cups: eighteen on the six outer branches – three on each branch – and an additional four on the central shaft. The number of knobs totaled eleven, with one on each of the six branches, three on the body of the middle shaft where the branches emerged, and an additional two knobs on the central shaft, as the verse states: *Finely-crafted knobs* (25:34). [Although the verse does not specify how many additional knobs should be crafted there, it uses a plural noun,] and the minimum plural is two. One of these appeared low on the central shaft near the base, with the other within the top three handbreadths of the structure with the three cups that were fashioned there. The total number of flowers on the candelabrum was nine. Each of the six branches had one flower, as the verse states: *On each branch there shall be...a flower* (25:33), and the central shaft had three flowers of its own, as the verse states: *Finely-crafted... flowers* (25:34). [Again the text does not give a number for how many flowers are to be fashioned on the central rod, but] the minimum plural is two, and we add to those two a third flower mentioned in Parashat Behaalotekha: *From its base to its flower* (Numbers 8:4). [Rashi concludes:] If you study the *baraita* cited above you will find all the components of the candelabrum according to their number and position.

לז| **אֶת־נֵרֹתֶיהָ.** כְּמִין בָּזִיכִין שֶׁנּוֹתְנִין בְּתוֹכָם הַשֶּׁמֶן וְהַפְּתִילוֹת׃

37 | **אֶת־נֵרֹתֶיהָ** – *Its seven lamps:* The lamps were formed as receptacles to hold oil that was poured into them, and wicks which were placed there.

◀

38 39 space in front of it. Make its tongs and pans of pure gold. All
40 these items shall be made from a talent of pure gold. Take care
to make them according to that design that is shown to you
26 1 on the mountain. As for the Tabernacle itself, make SHELISHI
it with ten sheets of finely spun linen and sky-blue, purple, and
scarlet wool, with a design of cherubim worked into them.

וְהֵאִיר עַל־עֵבֶר פָּנֶיהָ. עֲשֵׂה פִּי שֵׁשֶׁת הַנֵּרוֹת שֶׁבְּרָאשֵׁי הַקָּנִים הַיּוֹצְאִים מִצִּדֶּיהָ מְסֻבִּים כְּלַפֵּי הָאֶמְצָעִי, כְּדֵי שֶׁיִּהְיוּ הַנֵּרוֹת כְּשֶׁתַּדְלִיקֵם מְאִירִים "אֶל עֵבֶר פָּנֶיהָ", מוּסָב אוֹרָם אֶל צַד פְּנֵי הַקָּנֶה הָאֶמְצָעִי שֶׁהוּא גּוּף הַמְּנוֹרָה:

וְהֵאִיר עַל־עֵבֶר פָּנֶיהָ – *So that they light the space in front of it:* [Alternatively, "so that they light toward it."] Fashion the six lamps at the tops of the six branches so that they point toward the middle shaft. In this way, when the lamps are lit, they will "light toward it," that is, in the direction of the central branch, which forms the body of the candelabrum.

לח | **וּמַלְקָחֶיהָ.** הֵם הַצְּבָתִים הָעֲשׂוּיִין לִקַּח בָּהֶם הַפְּתִילוֹת מִתּוֹךְ הַשֶּׁמֶן לְיַשְּׁבָן וּלְמָשְׁכָן בְּפִי הַנֵּרוֹת, וְעַל שֵׁם שֶׁלּוֹקְחִים בָּהֶם קְרוּיִים מֶלְקָחַיִם, וְ"צֵיבְתָהָא" שֶׁתִּרְגֵּם אוּנְקְלוֹס, לְשׁוֹן צְבַת, טנייל"ש בְּלַעַז:

38 | **וּמַלְקָחֶיהָ** – *Its tongs:* The term *malkaḥeha* refers to tongs that were made to remove the wicks from the oil, to position the wicks within the lamps, and to draw them toward the mouths of the lamps. Because they were used to take [*lakaḥat*] the wicks out, these tools were called *melkaḥayim*. Onkelos employs the word *tzeivetaha*, which derives from the term *tzevat* – which in Old French is *tenailles* ["tongs"].

וּמַחְתֹּתֶיהָ. הֵם כְּמִין בָּזִיכִין קְטַנִּים שֶׁחוֹתֶה בָּהֶן אֶת הָאֵפֶר שֶׁבַּנֵּר בְּכָל בֹּקֶר, כְּשֶׁהוּא מֵטִיב אֶת הַנֵּרוֹת מֵאֵפֶר הַפְּתִילוֹת שֶׁדָּלְקוּ הַלַּיְלָה וְכָבוּ. וּלְשׁוֹן מַחְתָּה פושיידור"א בְּלַעַז, כְּמוֹ: "לַחְתּוֹת אֵשׁ מִיָּקוּד" (ישעיה ל, יד):

וּמַחְתֹּתֶיהָ – *And its pans:* These were small vessels into which the priest would rake the ashes from the lamps every morning when he prepared the candelabrum. This involved removing the ashes from the wicks that had burned through the night and had gone out. The word *maḥta* translates into Old French as *poseydure* ["fireplace shovel"]. The root also appears in the verse *A shred sufficient for taking fire [laḥtot] from the hearth* (Isaiah 30:14).

לט | **כִּכָּר זָהָב טָהוֹר.** שֶׁלֹּא יִהְיֶה מִשְׁקָלָהּ עִם כָּל כֵּלֶיהָ אֶלָּא כִּכָּר, לֹא פָּחוֹת וְלֹא יוֹתֵר. וְהַכִּכָּר שֶׁל חוֹל שִׁשִּׁים מָנֶה, וְשֶׁל קֹדֶשׁ הָיָה כָּפוּל, מֵאָה וְעֶשְׂרִים מָנֶה, וְהַמָּנֶה הוּא לִיטְרָא שֶׁשּׁוֹקְלִין בָּהּ כֶּסֶף לְמִשְׁקַל קוֹלוֹנְיָא, וְהֵם מֵאָה זְהוּבִים, עֶשְׂרִים וַחֲמִשָּׁה סְלָעִים, וְהַסֶּלַע אַרְבָּעָה זְהוּבִים:

39 | **כִּכַּר זָהָב טָהוֹר** – *A talent of pure gold:* The weight of the candelabrum together with its accoutrements [the tongs and pans] must weigh exactly a talent – no more and no less. Now although an ordinary talent weighed sixty minas, the weight of a sacred talent was twice that, and stood at one hundred and twenty minas. A mina is equal to a litra used to weigh silver according to the weight of Cologne. It is equivalent to one hundred dinars or twenty-five selas, since a sela is equal to four dinars.

מ | **וּרְאֵה וַעֲשֵׂה.** רְאֵה כָּאן בָּהָר תַּבְנִית שֶׁאֲנִי מַרְאֶה אוֹתְךָ, מַגִּיד

40 | **וּרְאֵה וַעֲשֵׂה** – *Take care to make them:* [Literally, "see and make them."] God instructed Moshe to look at a diagram of

לח וְהֵאִיר עַל־עֵבֶר פָּנֶיהָ: וּמַלְקָחֶיהָ וּמַחְתֹּתֶיהָ זָהָב
לט טָהוֹר: כִּכָּר זָהָב טָהוֹר יַעֲשֶׂה אֹתָהּ אֵת כָּל־הַכֵּלִים
מ הָאֵלֶּה: וּרְאֵה וַעֲשֵׂה בְּתַבְנִיתָם אֲשֶׁר־אַתָּה מָרְאֶה
כו א בָּהָר: וְאֶת־הַמִּשְׁכָּן תַּעֲשֶׂה עֶשֶׂר יְרִיעֹת יט שלישי
שֵׁשׁ מָשְׁזָר וּתְכֵלֶת וְאַרְגָּמָן וְתֹלַעַת שָׁנִי כְּרֻבִים

שֶׁנִּתְקַשָּׁה מֹשֶׁה בְּמַעֲשֵׂה הַמְּנוֹרָה עַד שֶׁהֶרְאָה לוֹ הַקָּדוֹשׁ בָּרוּךְ הוּא מְנוֹרָה שֶׁל אֵשׁ:

the candelabrum that He showed him on the mountain. This tells us that Moshe had difficulty understanding how to construct this item, and only grasped its design once God Himself showed him a candelabrum of fire.

אֲשֶׁר־אַתָּה מָרְאֶה. כְּתַרְגּוּמוֹ: "דְּאַתְּ מִתַּחְזֵי בְּטוּרָא". אִלּוּ הָיָה נָקוּד 'מַרְאֶה' בְּפַתָּח, הָיָה פִּתְרוֹנוֹ, אַתָּה מַרְאֶה לַאֲחֵרִים, עַכְשָׁיו שֶׁנָּקוּד חֲטַף קָמָץ, פִּתְרוֹנוֹ 'דְּאַתְּ מִתַּחְזֵי', שֶׁאֲחֵרִים מַרְאִים לְךָ:

אֲשֶׁר־אַתָּה מָרְאֶה – *That is shown to you:* [The word *mor'eh* – "is shown" – is unusual.] This clause should be understood as the Targum renders it: "That is shown to you on the mountain." Had the first letter of the word *mor'eh* been vocalized with a *pataḥ* [making the word *mar'eh*, an active *hifil* form], the verse would have meant that Moshe was meant to show others. However, since the *mem* appears instead with a *kamatz katan*, the word [in a passive *hufal* form] means: That which you "are shown" by others.

כו א | **וְאֶת־הַמִּשְׁכָּן תַּעֲשֶׂה עֶשֶׂר יְרִיעֹת.** לִהְיוֹת לוֹ לְגַג וְלִמְחִיצוֹת מִחוּץ לַקְּרָשִׁים, שֶׁהַיְרִיעוֹת תְּלוּיוֹת מֵאֲחוֹרֵיהֶן לְכַסּוֹתָן:

26 1 | **וְאֶת־הַמִּשְׁכָּן תַּעֲשֶׂה עֶשֶׂר יְרִיעֹת** – *As for the Tabernacle itself, make it with ten sheets:* These ten sheets would serve as a roof for the Tabernacle structure, as well as for coverings outside the boards [that formed the walls of the Tabernacle]. For the sheets were hung over the boards to cover them.

שֵׁשׁ מָשְׁזָר וּתְכֵלֶת וְאַרְגָּמָן וְתֹלַעַת שָׁנִי. הֲרֵי אַרְבָּעָה מִינִין בְּכָל חוּט וְחוּט, אֶחָד שֶׁל פִּשְׁתִּים וּשְׁלֹשָׁה שֶׁל צֶמֶר, וְכָל מִין וּמִין חוּטוֹ כָּפוּל שִׁשָּׁה, הֲרֵי אַרְבָּעָה מִינִין כְּשֶׁהֵן שְׁזוּרִין יַחַד עֶשְׂרִים וְאַרְבָּעָה כְּפָלִים לַחוּט:

שֵׁשׁ מָשְׁזָר וּתְכֵלֶת וְאַרְגָּמָן וְתֹלַעַת שָׁנִי – *Finely spun linen and sky-blue, purple, and scarlet wool:* One strand of each of these four materials, one linen and three wool, was spun into each thread, which in turn was twisted six fold. Thus when twisted together the four different materials made a thread of twenty-four strands.

כְּרֻבִים מַעֲשֵׂה חשֵׁב. כְּרוּבִים הָיוּ מְצֻיָּרִין בָּהֶם בַּאֲרִיגָתָן, וְלֹא בִּרְקִימָה שֶׁהוּא מַעֲשֵׂה מַחַט, אֶלָּא בַּאֲרִיגָה בִּשְׁנֵי כְּתָלִים, פַּרְצוּף אֶחָד מִכָּאן וּפַרְצוּף אֶחָד מִכָּאן, אֲרִי מִצַּד זֶה וְנֶשֶׁר מִצַּד זֶה, כְּמוֹ

כְּרֻבִים מַעֲשֵׂה חשֵׁב – *With a design of cherubim worked into them:* Images of cherubim were worked into the curtains as they were being woven. These were not embroidered through needlework [sewn on after the sheets were woven]; rather the cherubim were woven into the two sides of the curtain as they were being prepared. There were two different faces for the cherubim on either side of the sheet – on one side the figures'

◄

2 **Each sheet shall be twenty-eight cubits long and four cubits**
3 **wide; all the sheets should be the same size. Five of the sheets**
4 **should be sewn together; the other five likewise. Make loops**
of sky-blue wool on the upper edge of the end sheet in the first
set, and likewise on the upper edge of the outermost sheet in
5 **the second set. Make fifty loops on each sheet on one side**
and fifty on the upper edge of the corresponding sheets in the

שֶׁאוֹרְגִין חֲגוֹרוֹת שֶׁל מֶשִׁי שֶׁקּוֹרִין בְּלַעַז פיישי״ש:

faces resembled lions; and on the other side the faces on the figures looked like eagles. In this manner are silk sashes woven, an art called *faisses* in Old French.

ג| תִּהְיֶיןָ חֹבְרֹת. תּוֹפְרָן בְּמַחַט זוֹ בְּצַד זוֹ, חָמֵשׁ לְבַד וְחָמֵשׁ לְבַד:

3 | **תִּהְיֶיןָ חֹבְרֹת** – *Should be sewn together:* Five sheets were sewn end-to-end with a needle, and the other five were sewn into a second set.

אִשָּׁה אֶל־אֲחֹתָהּ. כָּךְ דֶּרֶךְ הַמִּקְרָא לְדַבֵּר בְּדָבָר שֶׁהוּא לְשׁוֹן נְקֵבָה; וּבְדָבָר שֶׁהוּא לְשׁוֹן זָכָר אוֹמֵר: ׳אִישׁ אֶל אָחִיו׳, כְּמוֹ שֶׁנֶּאֱמַר בַּכְּרוּבִים: ״וּפְנֵיהֶם אִישׁ אֶל אָחִיו״ (לעיל כה, כ):

אִשָּׁה אֶל־אֲחֹתָהּ – *One to another:* [Literally, "a woman to her sister."] When Scripture refers to pairs of objects with a feminine gender, it describes one item as "a woman" and the next as "her sister." [In Hebrew all nouns are classified as feminine or masculine.] When the objects are masculine, the language used is "a man and his brother." Thus the verse states about the cherubim: *They should face one another* [literally, "a man toward his brother"] (25:20).

ד| לֻלָאֹת. לַצו״ל בְּלַעַז, וְכֵן תִּרְגֵּם אוּנְקְלוֹס: ״עֲנוּבִין״, לְשׁוֹן עֲנִיבָה:

4 | **לֻלָאֹת** – *Loops:* The term *lule'ot* translates as *lacels* ["loops"] in Old French. Similarly, Onkelos refers to this feature of the curtains as *anubin* ["bows" or "loops"].

מִקָּצָה בַּחֹבָרֶת. בְּאוֹתָהּ יְרִיעָה שֶׁבְּסוֹף הַחִבּוּר, קְבוּצַת חֲמֵשֶׁת הַיְרִיעוֹת קְרוּיָה חֹבֶרֶת:

מִקָּצָה בַּחֹבָרֶת – *Of the end sheet in the first set:* The loops were fashioned on the border of the last [fifth] sheet of the set. Each set of five sheets that were joined together were referred to as a *ḥoveret* ["joining" or "set"].

וְכֵן תַּעֲשֶׂה בִּשְׂפַת הַיְרִיעָה הַקִּיצוֹנָה בַּמַּחְבֶּרֶת הַשֵּׁנִית. בְּאוֹתָהּ יְרִיעָה שֶׁהִיא קִיצוֹנָה, לְשׁוֹן קָצֶה, כְּלוֹמַר לְסוֹף הַחוֹבֶרֶת:

וְכֵן תַּעֲשֶׂה בִּשְׂפַת הַיְרִיעָה הַקִּיצוֹנָה בַּמַּחְבֶּרֶת הַשֵּׁנִית – *And likewise on the upper edge of the outermost sheet in the second set:* Another group of fifty loops was fashioned on the outer edge of the second *ḥoveret*. The term *kitzona* ["outermost"] is derived from *katzehi* ["edge"], that is, the loops were positioned at the end of the set of five sheets.

ה| מַקְבִּילֹת הַלֻּלָאֹת אִשָּׁה אֶל־אֲחֹתָהּ. שְׁמֹר שֶׁתַּעֲשֶׂה הַלּוּלָאוֹת מְכֻוָּנוֹת בְּמִדָּה אַחַת הַבְדָּלָתָן זוֹ מִזּוֹ, וּכְמִדָּתָן בִּירִיעָה זוֹ כֵּן יְהֵא

5 | **מַקְבִּילֹת הַלֻּלָאֹת אִשָּׁה אֶל־אֲחֹתָהּ** – *With the loops opposite one another:* Take care to fashion the loops with identical measurements such that the distance between them is uniform across the sheets. The distance between the loops on one

◀

ב מַעֲשֵׂה חֹשֵׁב תַּעֲשֶׂה אֹתָם׃ אֹרֶךְ ׀ הַיְרִיעָה הָאַחַת
שְׁמֹנֶה וְעֶשְׂרִים בָּאַמָּה וְרֹחַב אַרְבַּע בָּאַמָּה הַיְרִיעָה
ג הָאֶחָת מִדָּה אַחַת לְכָל־הַיְרִיעֹת׃ חֲמֵשׁ הַיְרִיעֹת
תִּהְיֶיןָ חֹבְרֹת אִשָּׁה אֶל־אֲחֹתָהּ וְחָמֵשׁ יְרִיעֹת חֹבְרֹת
ד אִשָּׁה אֶל־אֲחֹתָהּ׃ וְעָשִׂיתָ לֻלְאֹת תְּכֵלֶת עַל שְׂפַת
הַיְרִיעָה הָאֶחָת מִקָּצָה בַּחֹבָרֶת וְכֵן תַּעֲשֶׂה בִּשְׂפַת
ה הַיְרִיעָה הַקִּיצוֹנָה בַּמַּחְבֶּרֶת הַשֵּׁנִית׃ חֲמִשִּׁים לֻלָאֹת
תַּעֲשֶׂה בַּיְרִיעָה הָאֶחָת וַחֲמִשִּׁים לֻלָאֹת תַּעֲשֶׂה

sheet should match the spacing between the loops on the second sheet. Thus when you lay out one set of five sheets next to the second set of five sheets, the loops on one sheet will fall directly opposite the other row of loops on the second sheet. This is what the Torah meant when it described the loops as "opposite" [*makbilot*] each other. Indeed, the Targum's translation of the word *keneged* ["opposite"] is *lakavel* [related to *makbilot*]. Now each of the ten sheets was twenty-eight cubits long and four cubits wide, which meant that when five of these curtains were combined into a single set, they had a combined width of twenty cubits. The second set of course had the same dimensions. The Tabernacle structure itself [which was to be covered by the two sets of sheets] stood thirty cubits long from east to west. For the verse states: *Make twenty boards for the southern side of the Tabernacle* (26:18), while an additional twenty boards comprised the structure's northern side [see 26:20], and each board was one and a half cubits wide, for a total of thirty cubits from the Tabernacle's east end to its west. Meanwhile, the width of the Tabernacle from the north side to the south side was ten cubits, for the verse states: *Make six boards for the west side of the Tabernacle* (26:22), *and two additional boards for the Tabernacle's rear corners* (26:23). Altogether these eight boards on the far west side spanned ten cubits, as I will explain later. [Each of the eight boards was also a cubit and a half wide for a total of twelve cubits. However, only ten cubits faced the inside of

בַּחֲבֶרְתָּהּ, כְּשֶׁתִּפְרֹשׂ חוֹבֶרֶת אֵצֶל חוֹבֶרֶת יִהְיוּ הַלּוּלָאוֹת שֶׁל יְרִיעָה זוֹ מְכֻוָּנוֹת כְּנֶגֶד לוּלָאוֹת שֶׁל זוֹ. וְזֶהוּ לְשׁוֹן 'מַקְבִּילֹת', זוֹ כְּנֶגֶד זוֹ, תַּרְגּוּמוֹ שֶׁל 'נֶגֶד' (לעיל י, י) – 'לָקֳבֵל'. הַיְרִיעוֹת אָרְכָּן עֶשְׂרִים וּשְׁמוֹנֶה וְרָחְבָּן אַרְבַּע, וּכְשֶׁחִבֵּר חָמֵשׁ יְרִיעוֹת יַחַד נִמְצָא רָחְבָּן עֶשְׂרִים, וְכֵן הַחוֹבֶרֶת הַשֵּׁנִית. וְהַמִּשְׁכָּן אָרְכּוֹ שְׁלֹשִׁים מִן הַמִּזְרָח לַמַּעֲרָב, שֶׁנֶּאֱמַר: "עֶשְׂרִים קְרָשִׁים לִפְאַת נֶגֶב תֵּימָנָה" (להלן לו, כג; כעין זה להלן פסוק יח), וְכֵן לַצָּפוֹן (להלן פסוק כ), וְכָל קֶרֶשׁ אַמָּה וַחֲצִי הָאַמָּה (להלן פסוק טז), הֲרֵי שְׁלֹשִׁים מִן הַמִּזְרָח לַמַּעֲרָב. רֹחַב הַמִּשְׁכָּן מִן הַצָּפוֹן לַדָּרוֹם עֶשֶׂר אַמּוֹת, שֶׁנֶּאֱמַר: "וּלְיַרְכְּתֵי הַמִּשְׁכָּן יָמָּה וְגוֹ' וּשְׁנֵי קְרָשִׁים... לִמְקֻצְעֹת" (להלן פסוקים כב-כג) הֲרֵי עֶשֶׂר, וּבִמְקוֹמָם אֲפָרְשֵׁם לְמִקְרָאוֹת הַלָּלוּ. נוֹתֵן הַיְרִיעוֹת אָרְכָּן לְרָחְבּוֹ שֶׁל מִשְׁכָּן, עֶשֶׂר אַמּוֹת הָאֶמְצָעִיּוֹת לְגַג חֲלַל רֹחַב

◄

6 other set, with the loops opposite one another. And make fifty
gold clasps. With the clasps, join the sheets together so that
7 the Tabernacle becomes one whole. Make sheets of goats'
hair as a tent over the Tabernacle; make eleven of these sheets.
8 Each sheet shall be thirty cubits long and four cubits wide, all

הַמִּשְׁכָּן, וְאַמָּה מִכָּאן וְאַמָּה מִכָּאן לְעָבִי רָאשֵׁי הַקְּרָשִׁים, שֶׁעָבְיָן אַמָּה, נִשְׁתַּיְּרוּ שֵׁשׁ עֶשְׂרֵה אַמָּה, שְׁמוֹנֶה לַצָּפוֹן וּשְׁמוֹנֶה לַדָּרוֹם, מְכַסּוֹת קוֹמַת הַקְּרָשִׁים שֶׁגָּבְהָן עֶשֶׂר, נִמְצְאוּ שְׁתֵּי אַמּוֹת הַתַּחְתּוֹנוֹת מְגֻלּוֹת. רָחְבָּן שֶׁל יְרִיעוֹת אַרְבָּעִים אַמָּה כְּשֶׁהֵן מְחֻבָּרוֹת, עֶשְׂרִים אַמָּה לְחוֹבֶרֶת. שְׁלֹשִׁים מֵהֶן לְגַג חֲלַל הַמִּשְׁכָּן לְאָרְכּוֹ, וְאַמָּה כְּנֶגֶד עֳבִי רָאשֵׁי הַקְּרָשִׁים שֶׁבַּמַּעֲרָב, וְאַמָּה לְכַסּוֹת עֳבִי הָעַמּוּדִים שֶׁבַּמִּזְרָח, שֶׁלֹּא הָיוּ קְרָשִׁים בַּמִּזְרָח אֶלָּא אַרְבָּעָה עַמּוּדִים שֶׁהַמָּסָךְ פָּרוּשׂ וְתָלוּי בַּוָּוִין שֶׁבָּהֶן כְּמִין וִילוֹן, נִשְׁתַּיְּרוּ שְׁמוֹנֶה אַמּוֹת הַתְּלוּיִין עַל אֲחוֹרֵי הַמִּשְׁכָּן שֶׁבַּמַּעֲרָב, וּשְׁתֵּי אַמּוֹת הַתַּחְתּוֹנוֹת מְגֻלּוֹת. זוֹ מָצָאתִי בַּבָּרַיְתָא דְּאַרְבָּעִים וָתֵשַׁע מִדּוֹת. אֲבָל בְּמַסֶּכֶת שַׁבָּת (דף צח ע״ב) אֵין הַיְרִיעוֹת מְכַסּוֹת אֶת עַמּוּדֵי הַמִּזְרָח, וְתֵשַׁע אַמּוֹת תְּלוּיוֹת אֲחוֹרֵי הַמִּשְׁכָּן, וְהַכָּתוּב מְסַיְּעֵנוּ: "וְנָתַתָּה אֶת הַפָּרֹכֶת תַּחַת הַקְּרָסִים" (להלן פסוק לג), וְאִם כְּדִבְרֵי הַבָּרַיְתָא הַזֹּאת, נִמְצֵאת פָּרֹכֶת מְשׁוּכָה מִן הַקְּרָסִים וְלַמַּעֲרָב אַמָּה:

the Tabernacle because one cubit on either end was blocked by the last board in the walls running west-east.] The sheets were placed such that their length [of twenty-eight cubits] lay across the width of the Tabernacle structure, such that only the middle ten cubits of the sheets sat atop the space of the Tabernacle as its roof. [This left eighteen cubits of material, of which] one cubit covered the width of the board on the north side of the structure's wall, and one cubit covered the width of the board on the south side. This left sixteen cubits of curtains, eight of which hung down and covered the northern wall of the Tabernacle, and eight of which hung down and covered its southern side. However, since these walls stood ten cubits high, the lower two cubits of the Tabernacle walls remained exposed [and uncovered by the sheets. Measuring now from east to west,] when all the sheets were joined together [in two sets] the total width of the curtains stretched for forty cubits – each of the two sets contributing twenty cubits of material. Thirty cubits of the curtains covered the inner space of the structure and formed the roof down the length of the Tabernacle. One cubit [of the remaining ten] sat upon the width of the boards on the far western side of the building, while an additional single cubit sat upon the width of the columns on the near eastern side of the structure. For there were no boards making an eastern wall, only four columns across which a screen was spread and hung using hooks like a veil. This left eight cubits [out of the original forty] and these hung down the back of the Tabernacle on the west side. [And since the walls of the Tabernacle were all ten cubits high,] the bottom two cubits remained exposed. The above description follows what I have discovered in the *baraita* referred to as *Arba'im Vatesha Middot*. However, a discussion in tractate Shabbat (98b) claims that the sheets did not sit upon the eastern columns at all [that is, they stopped short just west of them]. This means that a remainder of nine cubits was available to cover the western end of the structure [leaving just a single cubit of those boards exposed]. Indeed, the language

◄

בִּקְצֵה הַיְרִיעָה אֲשֶׁר בַּמַּחְבֶּרֶת הַשֵּׁנִית מַקְבִּילֹת
ו הַלֻּלָאֹת אִשָּׁה אֶל־אֲחֹתָהּ: וְעָשִׂיתָ חֲמִשִּׁים קַרְסֵי
זָהָב וְחִבַּרְתָּ אֶת־הַיְרִיעֹת אִשָּׁה אֶל־אֲחֹתָהּ בַּקְּרָסִים
ז וְהָיָה הַמִּשְׁכָּן אֶחָד: וְעָשִׂיתָ יְרִיעֹת עִזִּים לְאֹהֶל עַל־
ח הַמִּשְׁכָּן עַשְׁתֵּי־עֶשְׂרֵה יְרִיעֹת תַּעֲשֶׂה אֹתָם: אֹרֶךְ ׀
הַיְרִיעָה הָאַחַת שְׁלֹשִׁים בָּאַמָּה וְרֹחַב אַרְבַּע בָּאַמָּה
הַיְרִיעָה הָאֶחָת מִדָּה אַחַת לְעַשְׁתֵּי עֶשְׂרֵה יְרִיעֹת:

of our passage supports this reading, for the verse states: *Hang the curtain under the clasps and bring the Ark of the Testimony behind it* [26:33. The cited verse refers to the clasps described in verse 6, which were used to connect the two sets of sheets. Since each set combined five curtains of four cubits each, there were exactly twenty cubits on either side of the row of clasps. Verse 33 indicates that this row also marked the boundary between the structure's two chambers, since the larger, outer chamber was twenty cubits long, and the smaller one which held the Ark was ten]. According to the *baraita* however, the veil that divided the two chambers would have been one cubit to the west of the row of clasps [since an extra cubit of material was required to cover the columns at the eastern edge of the structure].

ו| קַרְסֵי זָהָב. פירמיל"ש בְּלַעַז, וּמַכְנִיסִין רֹאשָׁן אֶחָד בַּלּוּלָאוֹת שֶׁבְּחוֹבֶרֶת זוֹ וְרֹאשָׁן אֶחָד בַּלּוּלָאוֹת שֶׁבְּחוֹבֶרֶת זוֹ וּמְחַבְּרָן בָּהֶן:

6 | **קַרְסֵי זָהָב** – *Gold clasps:* The term translates as *fermails* ["hooks"] in Old French. One end of the clasp was inserted into a loop on the edge of one set of curtains, and the other end of the clasp was inserted into a loop on the edge of the other set of curtains, thereby connecting the sets.

ז| יְרִיעֹת עִזִּים. מִנּוֹצָה שֶׁל עִזִּים:

7 | **יְרִיעֹת עִזִּים** – *Sheets of goats' hair:* [Literally, "sheets of goats." Rashi explains:] These were made from the fleece of goats.

לְאֹהֶל עַל־הַמִּשְׁכָּן. לִפְרֹשׂ אוֹתָן עַל הַיְרִיעוֹת הַתַּחְתּוֹנוֹת:

לְאֹהֶל עַל־הַמִּשְׁכָּן – *As a tent over the Tabernacle:* These secondary sheets were to be spread over the inner layer of curtains [described above].

ח| שְׁלֹשִׁים בָּאַמָּה. שֶׁכְּשֶׁנּוֹתֵן אָרְכָּן לְרֹחַב הַמִּשְׁכָּן כְּמוֹ שֶׁנָּתַן אֶת הָרִאשׁוֹנוֹת, נִמְצְאוּ אֵלּוּ עוֹדְפוֹת אַמָּה מִכָּאן וְאַמָּה מִכָּאן, לְכַסּוֹת

8 | **שְׁלֹשִׁים בָּאַמָּה** – *Thirty cubits long:* When the width of the goat-hair curtains was laid across the Tabernacle like the first layer of curtains was, the remainder of the curtains hanging vertically surpassed that of the first sets by a cubit on either

◀

9 eleven sheets the same size. Join five of the sheets by themselves, and the other six by themselves. Fold the sixth sheet
10 over the front of the Tent. Make fifty loops on the edge of the
end sheet of one set, and fifty on the edge of the end sheet
11 of the other. Make, also, fifty bronze clasps. Put the clasps
through the loops, joining the tent together so that it becomes
12 one whole. As for the additional length of the tent sheets, the
extra half sheet is to hang down at the rear of the Tabernacle.
13 The extra cubit at either end of each of the tent sheets should
hang over the sides of the Tabernacle to cover it on both sides.

side. [The inner sets of curtains were twenty-eight cubits wide. However, the second layer made of goats' hair were thirty cubits wide.] This second layer was therefore able to cover up the uppermost of the two exposed cubits of boards at the bottom of either side. Meanwhile the final cubit of board which stood uncovered by curtains consisted of tenons that were inserted into the holes of the sockets [bases for the boards described in verse 19]. For the height of each socket was itself a cubit.

אַחַת מֵהַשְּׁתַּיִם אַמּוֹת שֶׁנִּשְׁאֲרוּ מְגֻלּוֹת בַּקְּרָשִׁים. וְהָאַמָּה הַתַּחְתּוֹנָה שֶׁל קֶרֶשׁ שֶׁאֵין הַיְרִיעָה מְכַסָּה אוֹתוֹ, הִיא הָאַמָּה הַתְּחוּבָה בְּנֶקֶב הָאֶדֶן, שֶׁהָאֲדָנִים גָּבְהָן אַמָּה:

9 | **וְכָפַלְתָּ אֶת־הַיְרִיעָה הַשִּׁשִּׁית** – *Fold the sixth sheet:* The verse refers to the extra sheet of goats' hair compared to the number of inner sheets. [The inner layer had ten sheets sewn into two sets of five each; the outer layer of goats' hair sheets comprised a set of five sheets and a set of six.]

ט | **וְכָפַלְתָּ אֶת־הַיְרִיעָה הַשִּׁשִּׁית.** שֶׁעוֹדֶפֶת בְּאֵלּוּ הָעֶלְיוֹנוֹת יוֹתֵר מִן הַתַּחְתּוֹנוֹת:

אֶל־מוּל פְּנֵי הָאֹהֶל – *Over the front of the tent:* Half of the extra sheet's width was folded down over the screen that stood at the eastern entrance to the Tabernacle. [Since each sheet was four cubits wide, this meant that two cubits overlapped the end of the structure.] This additional material evoked the modesty of a bride who covers her face with a veil.

אֶל־מוּל פְּנֵי הָאֹהֶל. חֲצִי רָחְבָּהּ הָיָה תָּלוּי וְכָפוּל עַל הַמָּסָךְ שֶׁבַּמִּזְרָח כְּנֶגֶד הַפֶּתַח, דּוֹמֶה לְכַלָּה צְנוּעָה הַמְכֻסָּה בְּצָעִיף עַל פָּנֶיהָ:

12–13 | **וְסֶרַח הָעֹדֵף בִּירִיעֹת הָאֹהֶל** – *As for the additional length of the tent sheets:* This refers to the extra material that exceeded the length of the lower layer of Tabernacle sheets. The term "curtains of the tent" refers to the upper layer of goats' hair sheets, called the "tent" in a later verse that states: *He made sheets of goats' hair for a tent over the Tabernacle* (36:14). The word "tent" connotes a roof, and it applies to these sheets because they formed a shelter and a covering over the lower layer of sheets. Now this second layer exceeded the length of the lower sheets on the west side by half a sheet-width [that is, by two cubits]. For one half of the additional, eleventh sheet

יב–יג | **וְסֶרַח הָעֹדֵף בִּירִיעֹת הָאֹהֶל.** עַל יְרִיעוֹת הַמִּשְׁכָּן. 'יְרִיעֹת הָאֹהֶל' הֵן הָעֶלְיוֹנוֹת שֶׁל עִזִּים שֶׁקְּרוּיִם אֹהֶל, כְּמוֹ שֶׁאָמוּר בָּהֶן: "לְאֹהֶל עַל הַמִּשְׁכָּן" (לעיל פסוק ז), וְכָל אֹהֶל הָאָמוּר בָּהֶן אֵינוֹ אֶלָּא לְשׁוֹן גַּג, שֶׁמַּאֲהִילוֹת וּמְסַכְּכוֹת עַל הַתַּחְתּוֹנוֹת. וְהֵן הָיוּ עוֹדְפוֹת עַל הַתַּחְתּוֹנוֹת חֲצִי הַיְרִיעָה לַמַּעֲרָב, שֶׁהַחֲצִי שֶׁל יְרִיעָה אַחַת עֶשְׂרֵה

◀

ט וְחִבַּרְתָּ אֶת־חֲמֵשׁ הַיְרִיעֹת לְבָד וְאֶת־שֵׁשׁ הַיְרִיעֹת
לְבָד וְכָפַלְתָּ אֶת־הַיְרִיעָה הַשִּׁשִּׁית אֶל־מוּל פְּנֵי
י הָאֹהֶל: וְעָשִׂיתָ חֲמִשִּׁים לֻלָאֹת עַל שְׂפַת הַיְרִיעָה
הָאֶחָת הַקִּיצֹנָה בַּחֹבָרֶת וַחֲמִשִּׁים לֻלָאֹת עַל שְׂפַת
יא הַיְרִיעָה הַחֹבֶרֶת הַשֵּׁנִית: וְעָשִׂיתָ קַרְסֵי נְחֹשֶׁת
חֲמִשִּׁים וְהֵבֵאתָ אֶת־הַקְּרָסִים בַּלֻּלָאֹת וְחִבַּרְתָּ אֶת־
יב הָאֹהֶל וְהָיָה אֶחָד: וְסֶרַח הָעֹדֵף בִּירִיעֹת הָאֹהֶל חֲצִי
יג הַיְרִיעָה הָעֹדֶפֶת תִּסְרַח עַל אֲחֹרֵי הַמִּשְׁכָּן: וְהָאַמָּה
מִזֶּה וְהָאַמָּה מִזֶּה בָּעֹדֵף בְּאֹרֶךְ יְרִיעֹת הָאֹהֶל יִהְיֶה

overlapped the front of the Tabernacle [on the eastern side as mentioned in verse 9], and that left an excess of two cubits more than the lower layer, equal to half the width of a single sheet, which hung down in the west.

תִּסְרַח עַל אֲחֹרֵי הַמִּשְׁכָּן – *Is to hang down at the rear of the Tabernacle:* This additional material covered up the two cubits of boards left exposed [by the shorter inner layer of sheets].

וְהָאַמָּה מִזֶּה וְהָאַמָּה מִזֶּה – *The extra cubit at either end:* [The goats' hair sheets ran an extra cubit] down the north side and down the south side.

בָּעֹדֵף בְּאֹרֶךְ יְרִיעֹת הָאֹהֶל – *At either end of each of the tent sheets:* The goats' hair sheets were each longer than those of the original layer by two cubits. [The sheets of this layer were thirty cubits long; the lower layer, twenty-eight cubits.]

יִהְיֶה סָרוּחַ עַל־צִדֵּי הַמִּשְׁכָּן – *Should hang over the sides of the Tabernacle:* These hung down the northern and southern sides [completely covering the Tabernacle's walls] as I have explained above. The Torah thereby teaches us proper etiquette: One should always shelter and protect something precious.

אֲחֹרֵי הַמִּשְׁכָּן – *At the rear of the Tabernacle:* The Torah calls the western side of the structure its back, because the opening to the Tabernacle stood in the east, and hence represented its front. The northern and southern walls were the Tabernacle's sides on the right and on the left.

הַיְתֵרָה הָיָה נִכְפָּל אֶל מוּל פְּנֵי הָאֹהֶל, נִשְׁאֲרוּ שְׁתֵּי אַמּוֹת רֹחַב חֶצְיָהּ עוֹדֵף עַל רֹחַב הַתַּחְתּוֹנוֹת:

תִּסְרַח עַל אֲחֹרֵי הַמִּשְׁכָּן. לְכַסּוֹת שְׁתֵּי אַמּוֹת שֶׁהָיוּ מְגֻלּוֹת בַּקְּרָשִׁים:

וְהָאַמָּה מִזֶּה וְהָאַמָּה מִזֶּה. לַצָּפוֹן וְלַדָּרוֹם:

בָּעֹדֵף בְּאֹרֶךְ יְרִיעֹת הָאֹהֶל. שֶׁהֵן עוֹדְפוֹת עַל אֹרֶךְ יְרִיעוֹת הַמִּשְׁכָּן שְׁתֵּי אַמּוֹת:

יִהְיֶה סָרוּחַ עַל־צִדֵּי הַמִּשְׁכָּן. לַצָּפוֹן וְלַדָּרוֹם, כְּמוֹ שֶׁפֵּרַשְׁתִּי לְמַעְלָה. לִמְּדָה תּוֹרָה דֶּרֶךְ אֶרֶץ, שֶׁיְּהֵא אָדָם חָס עַל הַיָּפֶה:

אֲחֹרֵי הַמִּשְׁכָּן. הוּא צַד הַמַּעֲרָב, לְפִי שֶׁהַפֶּתַח בַּמִּזְרָח שֶׁהֵן פָּנָיו, וְצָפוֹן וְדָרוֹם קְרוּיִין צְדָדִין לַיָּמִין וְלַשְּׂמֹאל:

14 Make a covering for the tent from rams' hides dyed red. Above
it make a covering of fine leather.
15 Make the upright boards for the Tabernacle of acacia wood. REVI'I
16 Each board shall be ten cubits long and one and a half cubits
17 wide. Each board should have two matching tenons; all the

יד| מִכְסֶה לָאֹהֶל. לְאוֹתוֹ גַּג שֶׁל יְרִיעוֹת עִזִּים, עֲשֵׂה עוֹד מִכְסֶה אֶחָד שֶׁל "עֹרֹת אֵילִם מְאָדָּמִים", וְעוֹד לְמַעְלָה מִמֶּנּוּ "מִכְסֵה עֹרֹת תְּחָשִׁים", וְאוֹתָן מִכְסָאוֹת לֹא הָיוּ מְכַסִּין אֶלָּא אֶת הַגַּג, אָרְכָּן שְׁלֹשִׁים וְרָחְבָּן עֶשֶׂר, אֵלּוּ דִּבְרֵי רַבִּי נְחֶמְיָה. וּלְדִבְרֵי רַבִּי יְהוּדָה מִכְסֶה אֶחָד הָיָה, חֶצְיוֹ שֶׁל עוֹרוֹת אֵילִים מְאָדָּמִים וְחֶצְיוֹ שֶׁל עוֹרוֹת תְּחָשִׁים:

14 | מִכְסֶה לָאֹהֶל – *A covering for the tent:* The Torah now commands the fashioning of a cover for the goats' hair tent. Thus an additional covering was to be made, this one *from rams' hides dyed red.* On top of that would be another *covering of fine leather.* These curtains only covered the roof [and were not draped over the Tabernacle's walls], since they were only thirty cubits long and ten cubits wide. Such is the opinion of Rabbi Neḥemya [as expressed in Shabbat 28a], whereas Rabbi Yehuda maintains that our verse describes a single covering, half of which comprised *rams' hides dyed red* and half of which was *a covering of fine leather.*

טו| וְעָשִׂיתָ אֶת־הַקְּרָשִׁים. הָיָה לוֹ לוֹמַר: 'וְעָשִׂיתָ קְרָשִׁים', כְּמוֹ שֶׁנֶּאֱמַר בְּכָל דָּבָר וְדָבָר. מַהוּ "הַקְּרָשִׁים"? מֵאוֹתָן הָעוֹמְדִין וּמְיֻחָדִין לְכָךְ; יַעֲקֹב אָבִינוּ נָטַע אֲרָזִים בְּמִצְרַיִם, וּכְשֶׁמֵּת צִוָּה לְבָנָיו לְהַעֲלוֹתָם עִמָּהֶם כְּשֶׁיֵּצְאוּ מִמִּצְרַיִם, וְאָמַר לָהֶם שֶׁעָתִיד הַקָּדוֹשׁ בָּרוּךְ הוּא לְצַוּוֹת אוֹתָן לַעֲשׂוֹת מִשְׁכָּן בַּמִּדְבָּר מֵעֲצֵי שִׁטִּים, רְאוּ שֶׁיִּהְיוּ מְזֻמָּנִים בְּיֶדְכֶם. הוּא שֶׁיִּסַּד הַבַּבְלִי בַּפִּיּוּט שֶׁלּוֹ: "טָס מַטַּע מְזֹרָזִים, קוֹרוֹת בָּתֵּינוּ אֲרָזִים" (יוצר ליום ראשון של פסח), שֶׁנִּזְדָּרְזוּ לִהְיוֹת מוּכָנִים בְּיָדָם מִקֹּדֶם לָכֵן:

15 | וְעָשִׂיתָ אֶת־הַקְּרָשִׁים – *Make the boards:* It seems that the verse should have omitted the definite article and said merely "make upright boards." After all, such is the style used throughout this passage. [For example in verse 25:23, the Torah states: *Make a table,* not: "Make the table."] Why then does the text refer to the Tabernacle's boards as something already known? The Torah thereby teaches that the craftsmen were to fashion the walls out of wood that had already been designated for such usage. For our patriarch Yaakov planted trees in Egypt and on his deathbed instructed his sons to make sure to cut down the timber and transport it with them upon their departure from the country. Yaakov explained that the Holy One, blessed be He, would eventually command them to construct a Tabernacle in the wilderness out of acacia wood, and therefore it would behoove Israel to maintain a supply of that material for the project. This is what Shlomo Habavli [a tenth-century Italian Jewish liturgist] referred to in his poem [a *yotzer* for the morning of Passover] when he wrote: "He hurried to plant for the zealous, the cedar walls of our house [the Tabernacle]" – Israel eagerly prepared the materials for the structure long in advance.

עֲצֵי שִׁטִּים עֹמְדִים. אישטנטיב"ש בְּלַעַז, שֶׁיְּהֵא אֹרֶךְ הַקְּרָשִׁים זָקוּף לְמַעְלָה בְּקִירוֹת הַמִּשְׁכָּן, וְלֹא תַּעֲשֶׂה הַכְּתָלִים בִּקְרָשִׁים שׁוֹכְבִים לִהְיוֹת רֹחַב הַקְּרָשִׁים לְגֹבַהּ

עֲצֵי שִׁטִּים עֹמְדִים – *Upright boards of acacia wood:* The Old French term for this position is *estantivs* ["upright"], meaning that the length of the boards must be arranged vertically to form the walls of the Tabernacle. Do not construct the walls by piling the boards on top of each other horizontally

◀

יד סָרוּחַ עַל־צִדֵּי הַמִּשְׁכָּן מִזֶּה וּמִזֶּה לְכַסֹּתוֹ: וְעָשִׂיתָ
מִכְסֶה לָאֹהֶל עֹרֹת אֵילִם מְאָדָּמִים וּמִכְסֵה עֹרֹת
תְּחָשִׁים מִלְמָעְלָה:
טו וְעָשִׂיתָ אֶת־הַקְּרָשִׁים לַמִּשְׁכָּן עֲצֵי שִׁטִּים עֹמְדִים: רביעי
טז עֶשֶׂר אַמּוֹת אֹרֶךְ הַקָּרֶשׁ וְאַמָּה וַחֲצִי הָאַמָּה רֹחַב
יז הַקֶּרֶשׁ הָאֶחָד: שְׁתֵּי יָדוֹת לַקֶּרֶשׁ הָאֶחָד מְשֻׁלָּבֹת
אִשָּׁה אֶל־אֲחֹתָהּ כֵּן תַּעֲשֶׂה לְכֹל קַרְשֵׁי הַמִּשְׁכָּן:

הַכְּתָלִים קֶרֶשׁ עַל קֶרֶשׁ:

such that the widths of the boards comprise the structure's height.

טז| עֶשֶׂר אַמּוֹת אֹרֶךְ הַקָּרֶשׁ. לָמַדְנוּ גָּבְהוֹ שֶׁל מִשְׁכָּן עֶשֶׂר אַמּוֹת:

16 | עֶשֶׂר אַמּוֹת אֹרֶךְ הַקָּרֶשׁ – *Each board shall be ten cubits long:* We learn from this that the height of the Tabernacle was ten cubits.

וְאַמָּה וַחֲצִי הָאַמָּה רֹחַב. לָמַדְנוּ אָרְכּוֹ שֶׁל מִשְׁכָּן לְעֶשְׂרִים קְרָשִׁים שֶׁהָיוּ בַּצָּפוֹן וּבַדָּרוֹם מִן הַמִּזְרָח לַמַּעֲרָב, שְׁלֹשִׁים אַמָּה:

וְאַמָּה וַחֲצִי הָאַמָּה רֹחַב – *And one and a half cubits wide:* Since we know the width of each board, and that there were twenty boards running along the north and south walls [as stated in verses 18 and 20], we can calculate that there were thirty cubits from the east side of the Tabernacle to its west side.

יז| שְׁתֵּי יָדוֹת לַקֶּרֶשׁ הָאֶחָד. הָיָה חוֹרֵץ אֶת הַקֶּרֶשׁ מִלְּמַטָּה בְּאֶמְצָעוֹ בְּגֹבַהּ אַמָּה, מַנִּיחַ רְבִיעַ רָחְבּוֹ מִכָּאן וּרְבִיעַ רָחְבּוֹ מִכָּאן וְהֵן הֵן הַיָּדוֹת, וְהֶחָרִיץ חֲצִי רֹחַב הַקֶּרֶשׁ בָּאֶמְצַע. וְאוֹתָן הַיָּדוֹת מַכְנִיס בָּאֲדָנִים שֶׁהָיוּ חֲלוּלִים, וְהָאֲדָנִים גָּבְהָן אַמָּה וְיוֹשְׁבִים רְצוּפִים אַרְבָּעִים זֶה אֵצֶל זֶה. וִידוֹת הַקֶּרֶשׁ הַנִּכְנָסוֹת בַּחֲלַל הָאֲדָנִים חֲרוּצוֹת מִשְּׁלֹשֶׁת צִדֵּיהֶן, רֹחַב הֶחָרִיץ כָּעֳבִי שְׂפַת הָאֶדֶן, שֶׁיְּכַסֶּה הַקֶּרֶשׁ אֶת כָּל רֹאשׁ הָאֶדֶן, שֶׁאִם לֹא כֵן נִמְצָא רֶוַח בֵּין קֶרֶשׁ לְקֶרֶשׁ כָּעֳבִי שְׂפַת שְׁנֵי הָאֲדָנִים שֶׁיַּפְסִיקוּ בֵּינֵיהֶם, וְזֶהוּ שֶׁנֶּאֱמַר: "וְיִהְיוּ תֹאֲמִם מִלְּמַטָּה" (להלן פסוק כד), שֶׁיַּחֲרֹץ אֶת צִדֵּי הַיָּדוֹת כְּדֵי שֶׁיִּתְחַבְּרוּ הַקְּרָשִׁים זֶה אֵצֶל זֶה:

17 | שְׁתֵּי יָדוֹת לַקֶּרֶשׁ הָאֶחָד – *Each board should have two tenons:* The carpenter cut a groove down the middle of the bottom of each board to a height of a cubit, leaving a quarter [of the total width] intact on one side and a quarter intact on the other side. These two pins formed the tenons that our verse introduces. The groove between the tenons occupied half the width of the board, and it was situated precisely in the middle. The two tenons on each board were inserted into two hollow sockets, each one cubit long. Forty sockets [on each wall] were thus positioned one next to the other. Now the tenons themselves were chiseled on three sides before being inserted into their sockets, to a width equal to that of the sockets so that the board would cover the entire upper surface of the socket. For if shoulders were not carved around the tenons, the outside widths of the sockets of neighboring boards would create a space between adjoining planks. This is the meaning of the phrase *These should adjoin each other at the bottom* (26:24) – the thickness of each tenon should be pared down so that the boards could be positioned right next to each other.

◀

18 Tabernacle's boards should be made in this way. Make twenty
19 boards for the southern side of the Tabernacle, and forty silver sockets under the twenty boards, two sockets under the
20 first board for its two tenons, and two under the next. For the
second side of the Tabernacle, the northern side, there should
21 be twenty boards, along with their forty silver sockets, two
22 under the first board and two under each of the others. Make
23 six boards for the west side of the Tabernacle, and two addi-
24 tional boards for the Tabernacle's rear corners. These should
adjoin each other at the bottom, and be joined together at
the top by a ring. So it should be for both sides; they shall

מְשֻׁלָּבֹת – *Matching:* The tenons were fashioned to look like rungs [*shelivot*] on a ladder, which have space in between them. Furthermore, the ends of the tenons were beveled to facilitate their insertion into the hollows of the socket, like a rung fits into a hole on the side of a ladder.

מְשֻׁלָּבֹת. עֲשׂוּיוֹת כְּמִין שְׁלִיבוֹת סֻלָּם מֻבְדָּלוֹת זוֹ מִזּוֹ, וּמְשֻׁפִּין רָאשֵׁיהֶם לִכָּנֵס בְּתוֹךְ חֲלַל הָאֶדֶן כִּשְׁלִיבָה הַנִּכְנֶסֶת בְּנֶקֶב עַמּוּדֵי הַסֻּלָּם:

אִשָּׁה אֶל־אֲחֹתָהּ – *Matching:* The two tenons on the end of each board were mirror images of each other, such that the shoulders around them were of identical dimensions. In other words, the stock removed from around one tenon could not be so great that that tenon would be situated closer to the middle of the board, while the other had less material carved away, thereby positioning it closer to the edge of the board. Rather, the shoulders should be of equal size across the handbreadth of the board, and the tenons would stand parallel to each other. The Targum renders the term *yadot* ["tenons"] as *tzirin* ["hinges"] since they resemble door hinges that fit into sockets in the doorframe.

אִשָּׁה אֶל אֲחֹתָהּ. מְכֻוָּנוֹת זוֹ כְּנֶגֶד זוֹ, שֶׁיִּהְיוּ חֲרִיצֵיהֶם שָׁוִים זוֹ כְּמִדַּת זוֹ, כְּדֵי שֶׁלֹּא יִהְיוּ שְׁתֵּי יָדוֹת זוֹ מְשׁוּכָה לְצַד פְּנִים וְזוֹ מְשׁוּכָה לְצַד חוּץ בָּעֳבִי הַקֶּרֶשׁ שֶׁהוּא אַמָּה. וְתַרְגּוּם שֶׁל ״יָדוֹת״ – ״צִירִין״, לְפִי שֶׁדּוֹמוֹת לְצִירֵי הַדֶּלֶת הַנִּכְנָסִים בְּחוֹרֵי הַמִּפְתָּן:

18 | **לִפְאַת נֶגְבָּה תֵימָנָה** – *For the southern side:* The term *pe'ah* here does not connote a corner, rather the entire side is referred to as a *pe'ah*. Similarly, the Targum renders this phrase "All along the southern side" [*leruaḥ* ever *daroma*].

יח| לִפְאַת נֶגְבָּה תֵּימָנָה. אֵין ׳פֵּאָה׳ זוֹ לְשׁוֹן מִקְצוֹעַ, אֶלָּא כָּל הָרוּחַ קְרוּיָה פֵּאָה. כְּתַרְגּוּמוֹ: ״לְרוּחַ עֵבֶר דָּרוֹמָא״:

22 | **וּלְיַרְכְּתֵי** – *Side:* The term *yarketei* means "end" [*sof*] as the Targum translates it – *seyafei*. Because the opening to the Tabernacle stood on the east side, that side was referred to as the front of the structure, while the west side was called the rear, or "end." For the front is considered a thing's beginning.

כב| וּלְיַרְכְּתֵי. לְשׁוֹן סוֹף, כְּתַרְגּוּמוֹ: ״וְלִסְיָפֵי״. וּלְפִי שֶׁהַפֶּתַח בַּמִּזְרָח, קָרוּי מִזְרָח פָּנִים וְהַמַּעֲרָב אֲחוֹרַיִם, וְזֶהוּ סוֹף, שֶׁהַפָּנִים הֵן הָרֹאשׁ:

◀

יח וְעָשִׂ֥יתָ אֶת־הַקְּרָשִׁ֖ים לַמִּשְׁכָּ֑ן עֶשְׂרִ֣ים קֶ֔רֶשׁ
יט לִפְאַ֖ת נֶ֥גְבָּה תֵימָֽנָה׃ וְאַרְבָּעִים֙ אַדְנֵי־כֶ֔סֶף תַּעֲשֶׂ֕ה
תַּ֖חַת עֶשְׂרִ֣ים הַקָּ֑רֶשׁ שְׁנֵ֨י אֲדָנִ֜ים תַּֽחַת־הַקֶּ֤רֶשׁ
הָאֶחָד֙ לִשְׁתֵּ֣י יְדֹתָ֔יו וּשְׁנֵ֧י אֲדָנִ֛ים תַּֽחַת־הַקֶּ֥רֶשׁ
כ הָאֶחָ֖ד לִשְׁתֵּ֥י יְדֹתָֽיו׃ וּלְצֶ֧לַע הַמִּשְׁכָּ֛ן הַשֵּׁנִ֖ית לִפְאַ֣ת
כא צָפ֑וֹן עֶשְׂרִ֖ים קָֽרֶשׁ׃ וְאַרְבָּעִ֥ים אַדְנֵיהֶ֖ם כָּ֑סֶף שְׁנֵ֣י
אֲדָנִ֗ים תַּ֚חַת הַקֶּ֣רֶשׁ הָאֶחָ֔ד וּשְׁנֵ֣י אֲדָנִ֔ים תַּ֖חַת
כב הַקֶּ֥רֶשׁ הָאֶחָֽד׃ וּֽלְיַרְכְּתֵ֥י הַמִּשְׁכָּ֖ן יָ֑מָּה תַּעֲשֶׂ֖ה שִׁשָּׁ֥ה
כג קְרָשִֽׁים׃ וּשְׁנֵ֤י קְרָשִׁים֙ תַּעֲשֶׂ֔ה לִמְקֻצְעֹ֖ת הַמִּשְׁכָּ֑ן
כד בַּיַּרְכָתָֽיִם׃ וְיִהְי֣וּ תֹאֲמִם֮ מִלְּמַטָּה֒ וְיַחְדָּ֗ו יִהְי֤וּ תַמִּים֙
עַל־רֹאשׁ֔וֹ אֶל־הַטַּבַּ֖עַת הָאֶחָ֑ת כֵּ֚ן יִהְיֶ֣ה לִשְׁנֵיהֶ֔ם

תַּעֲשֶׂה שִׁשָּׁה קְרָשִׁים – *Make six boards:* [Since each board was one and a half cubits wide] the entire width of the western side was nine cubits.

תַּעֲשֶׂה שִׁשָּׁה קְרָשִׁים. הֲרֵי תֵּשַׁע אַמּוֹת רֹחַב:

23 | **וּשְׁנֵי קְרָשִׁים תַּעֲשֶׂה לִמְקֻצְעֹת** – *And two additional boards for the rear corners:* One of these two additional boards was situated at the northwest corner of the Tabernacle, and the other was at the southwest corner. Thus all eight boards comprising the western wall of the Tabernacle stood in a straight row. However the widths of the corner boards could not be seen entirely from the interior of the structure – only half a cubit of each would have been visible inside the smaller chamber. These two halves combined with the nine cubits of the six western wall boards to create a total width of ten cubits for the inside of the Tabernacle. Meanwhile, the remaining cubit of each corner board was covered by the cubit-thick boards comprising the northern and southern walls of the structure. In this way the corners where two walls met in the northwest and southwest were perfect right angles.

כג| וּשְׁנֵי קְרָשִׁים תַּעֲשֶׂה לִמְקֻצְעֹת. אֶחָד לְמִקְצוֹעַ צְפוֹנִית מַעֲרָבִית וְאֶחָד לְמַעֲרָבִית דְּרוֹמִית. כָּל שְׁמוֹנָה קְרָשִׁים בְּסֵדֶר אֶחָד הֵן, אֶלָּא שֶׁאֵלּוּ הַשְּׁתַּיִם אֵינָן בַּחֲלַל הַמִּשְׁכָּן, אֶלָּא חֲצִי אַמָּה מִזּוֹ וַחֲצִי אַמָּה מִזּוֹ נִרְאוֹת בֶּחָלָל, לְהַשְׁלִים רָחְבּוֹ לְעֶשֶׂר, וְהָאַמָּה מִזֶּה וְהָאַמָּה מִזֶּה בָּאוֹת כְּנֶגֶד אַמַּת עֳבִי קַרְשֵׁי הַמִּשְׁכָּן הַצָּפוֹן וְהַדָּרוֹם, כְּדֵי שֶׁיְּהֵא הַמִּקְצוֹעַ מִבַּחוּץ שָׁוֶה:

24 | **וְיִהְיוּ** – *These should:* All of the boards should be positioned next to each other at their bases; that is, the thickness of the sockets should not push them apart in the slightest, as I have

כד| וְיִהְיוּ. כָּל הַקְּרָשִׁים ״תֹאֲמִם״ זֶה לָזֶה ״מִלְּמַטָּה״, שֶׁלֹּא יַפְסִיק עֳבִי שְׂפַת שְׁנֵי הָאֲדָנִים בֵּינֵיהֶם

◄

25 **form the two corners. So there should be eight boards and**
26 **sixteen silver sockets, two sockets under each board. Make**
crossbars, too, of acacia wood, five for the boards of the first

explained above. For this to be so, the shoulders of the tenons had to be carved out around them. This would leave the width of the boards extending farther out than the tenons, covering up the width of the sides of the sockets beneath the boards. The neighboring board would be prepared in the identical manner, which means that all of the boards would be adjacent. Now the thickness of the corner boards situated at the [north and south ends of the] western side was carved out along its width parallel to the grooves of the end boards of the north and south walls. In this way the sockets would not prevent the corner boards from touching the north and south walls. [That is, like the boards that stood next to each other on any of the three walls, boards that were perpendicular to each other also had to have shoulders carved on the surfaces that met each other. This meant that a corner board had to have its thickness carved before it was juxtaposed to the width of the north or south board.]

לְהַרְחִיקָם זוֹ מִזּוֹ. זֶהוּ שֶׁפֵּרַשְׁתִּי שֶׁיִּהְיוּ צִדֵּי הַיָּדוֹת חֲרוּצִים מִצִּדֵּיהֶן, שֶׁיְּהֵא רֹחַב הַקֶּרֶשׁ בּוֹלֵט לְצִדָּיו חוּץ לִידֵי הַקֶּרֶשׁ לְכַסּוֹת אֶת שְׂפַת הָאֶדֶן, וְכֵן הַקֶּרֶשׁ שֶׁאֶצְלוֹ, וְנִמְצְאוּ תּוֹאֲמִים זֶה לָזֶה. וְקֶרֶשׁ הַמִּקְצוֹעַ שֶׁבְּסֵדֶר הַמַּעֲרָב חָרוּץ לְרָחְבּוֹ בְּעָבְיוֹ, כְּנֶגֶד חָרִיץ שֶׁל צַד קֶרֶשׁ הַצְּפוֹנִי וְהַדְּרוֹמִי, כְּדֵי שֶׁלֹּא יַפְרִידוּ הָאֲדָנִים בֵּינֵיהֶם:

וְיַחְדָּו יִהְיוּ תַמִּים – *And be joined together:* The term *tamim* has the same meaning as *te'omim* [at the start of the verse, meaning "closely joined"].

וְיַחְדָּו יִהְיוּ תַמִּים. כְּמוֹ "תֹאֲמִם":

עַל־רֹאשׁוֹ – *At the top:* Of each board.

עַל־רֹאשׁוֹ. שֶׁל קֶרֶשׁ:

אֶל־הַטַּבַּעַת הָאֶחָת – *By a ring:* Two slits were cut across the width of the boards on either side [near the edge of the board]. The width of these slits was equal to the thickness of the rings that would be placed in them. A ring [like a bracket] was thus placed through the slits of two neighboring boards, holding them together. I do not know whether these rings were placed on the boards permanently or whether they were movable. Meanwhile the corner boards had a ring that encompassed both the thickness of the southern or northern wall board and the top of the adjacent corner board on the western side, thus joining the perpendicular walls.

אֶל־הַטַּבַּעַת הָאֶחָת. כָּל קֶרֶשׁ וָקֶרֶשׁ הָיָה חָרוּץ לְמַעְלָה בְּרָחְבּוֹ שְׁנֵי חֲרִיצִין בִּשְׁנֵי צִדָּיו כְּדֵי עֳבִי טַבַּעַת, וּמַכְנִיסוֹ בְּטַבַּעַת אַחַת, נִמְצָא מַתְאִים לַקֶּרֶשׁ שֶׁאֶצְלוֹ. אֲבָל אוֹתָן טַבָּעוֹת לֹא יָדַעְתִּי אִם קְבוּעוֹת הֵן אִם מְטֻלְטָלוֹת. וּבַקֶּרֶשׁ שֶׁבַּמִּקְצוֹעַ הָיָה טַבַּעַת בְּעֳבִי הַקֶּרֶשׁ הַדְּרוֹמִי וְהַצְּפוֹנִי וְרֹאשׁ קֶרֶשׁ הַמִּקְצוֹעַ שֶׁבְּסֵדֶר מַעֲרָב נִכְנָס לְתוֹכוֹ, נִמְצְאוּ שְׁנֵי הַכְּתָלִים מְחֻבָּרִים:

כֵּן יִהְיֶה לִשְׁנֵיהֶם – *So it should be for both sides:* [The word "sides" is absent from the Hebrew. Literally the whole phrase means: "So shall it be for the two of them; it shall be for the two corners." Rashi explains the repetitive phrasing:] So it was for the

כֵּן יִהְיֶה לִשְׁנֵיהֶם. הַקְּרָשִׁים שֶׁבַּמִּקְצוֹעַ, לַקֶּרֶשׁ שֶׁבְּסוֹף צָפוֹן וְלַקֶּרֶשׁ הַמַּעֲרָבִי. וְכֵן "לִשְׁנֵי הַמִּקְצֹעֹת":

◀

כה לִשְׁנֵי הַמִּקְצֹעֹת יִהְיוּ: וְהָיוּ שְׁמֹנָה קְרָשִׁים וְאַדְנֵיהֶם
כֶּסֶף שִׁשָּׁה עָשָׂר אֲדָנִים שְׁנֵי אֲדָנִים תַּחַת הַקֶּרֶשׁ
כו הָאֶחָד וּשְׁנֵי אֲדָנִים תַּחַת הַקֶּרֶשׁ הָאֶחָד: וְעָשִׂיתָ
בְרִיחִם עֲצֵי שִׁטִּים חֲמִשָּׁה לְקַרְשֵׁי צֶלַע־הַמִּשְׁכָּן

כה | **וְהָיוּ שְׁמֹנָה קְרָשִׁים.** הֵן הָאֲמוּרוֹת לְמַעְלָה: "תַּעֲשֶׂה שִׁשָּׁה קְרָשִׁים וּשְׁנֵי קְרָשִׁים תַּעֲשֶׂה לִמְקֻצְעֹת" (לעיל פסוקים כב-כג), נִמְצְאוּ שְׁמֹנָה קְרָשִׁים בַּסֵּדֶר מַעֲרָבִי. כָּךְ שְׁנוּיָה בִּמְשְׁנַת מַעֲשֵׂה סֵדֶר הַקְּרָשִׁים בִּמְלֶאכֶת הַמִּשְׁכָּן (ברייתא דמלאכת המשכן, פרק א): הָיָה עוֹשֶׂה אֶת הָאֲדָנִים חֲלוּלִים, וְחוֹרֵץ אֶת הַקֶּרֶשׁ מִלְּמַטָּה רְבִיעַ מִכָּאן וּרְבִיעַ מִכָּאן וְהֶחָרִיץ חֶצְיוֹ בָּאֶמְצַע, וְעָשָׂה לוֹ שְׁתֵּי יָדוֹת כְּמִין שְׁנֵי חֲמוּקִין, וְלִי נִרְאֶה שֶׁהַגִּרְסָא: כְּמִין שְׁנֵי חֲוָקִין, כְּמִין שְׁתֵּי שְׁלִיבוֹת סֻלָּם הַמֻּבְדָּלוֹת זוֹ מִזּוֹ, וּמְשֻׁפּוֹת לִכָּנֵס בַּחֲלַל הָאֹדֶן כִּשְׁלִיבָה הַנִּכְנֶסֶת בְּנֶקֶב עַמּוּד הַסֻּלָּם, וְהוּא לְשׁוֹן "מְשֻׁלָּבֹת", עֲשׂוּיוֹת כְּמִין שְׁלִיבָה. וּמַכְנִיסָן לְתוֹךְ שְׁנֵי אֲדָנִים, שֶׁנֶּאֱמַר: "שְׁנֵי אֲדָנִים... וּשְׁנֵי אֲדָנִים" (לעיל פסוק יט). וְחוֹרֵץ אֶת הַקֶּרֶשׁ מִלְּמַעְלָה אֶצְבַּע מִכָּאן וְאֶצְבַּע מִכָּאן וְנוֹתֵן לְתוֹךְ טַבַּעַת אַחַת שֶׁל זָהָב, כְּדֵי שֶׁלֹּא יִהְיוּ נִפְרָדִים זֶה מִזֶּה, שֶׁנֶּאֱמַר: "וְיִהְיוּ תֹאֲמִם מִלְּמַטָּה" וְגוֹ' (לעיל פסוק כד). כָּךְ הָיְתָה הַמִּשְׁנָה, וְהַפֵּרוּשׁ שֶׁלָּהּ הִנַּחְתִּי לְמַעְלָה בְּסֵדֶר הַמִּקְרָאוֹת:

כו | **בְּרִיחִם.** כְּתַרְגּוּמוֹ "עָבְרִין", וּבְלַעַז אשפרי"ש:

two boards that met in the corner, i.e., the end board in the northern wall and the western board standing at a right angle to it. [These were held together by a rectangular ring.] And so it was for "the two corners."

25 | **וְהָיוּ שְׁמֹנָה קְרָשִׁים** – *So there should be eight boards:* These are the eight boards mentioned above: *Make six boards for the west side of the Tabernacle, and two additional boards for the Tabernacle's rear corners* (26:22–23). This yields eight boards total to comprise the western wall. Now the following description of the boards' arrangement appears in the Baraita Dimlekhet Hamishkan (chapter 1): "The sockets were made as hollow fixtures. Tenons were carved out of the bottoms of the boards, each with a width of one quarter of the board's entire width, while the groove itself accounted for half of the board's width. The space between the tenons was situated directly in the middle of the bottom surface. Thus were created the tenons, which were like two legs [*ḥamukin*] for the boards. (It seems to me that that word should really be *ḥavakin*, which implies rungs like those on a ladder.) These were separated from each other and beveled to fit easily into their sockets, like a ladder's rung is inserted snugly into the holes of a ladder's sides. This is the sense of the term *meshulavot* ["matching," in verse 17] – each one was fashioned like a rung [*sheliva*]. The two tenons were slid into their corresponding sockets, as the verse states: *So there were... silver sockets, two under each board* (36:30). On the top of the boards, slits were sliced across the width on either side, creating two wedges of wood, each the width of a finger. A ring made out of gold was placed around the wedges of adjacent boards to keep them from shifting apart, as the Torah states: *These should adjoin each other at the bottom* (26:24)." This is the description appearing in that *baraita*, and I have consulted that text in explicating the above verses.

26 | **בְּרִיחִם** – *Crossbars:* The term *beriḥim* should be understood as the Targum has it: *averin* ["bars"], while the Old French word would be *espares* ["crossbars"].

◄

27 side of the Tabernacle, five for the boards of the second side
of the Tabernacle, and five for the boards of the western side
28 of the Tabernacle at the rear. The central crossbar should go
through the middle of the boards from one end to the other.
29 Overlay the boards with gold, and make gold rings for the
crossbars. The crossbars too should be overlaid with gold.

חֲמִשָּׁה לְקַרְשֵׁי צֶלַע־הַמִּשְׁכָּן – *Five for the boards of the first side of the Tabernacle:* The five crossbars mentioned in this verse were actually only three, for both the top bar and the bottom bar on each side of the structure were composed of two separate pieces. The first piece [of the upper and lower horizontal crossbars] stretched the length of half the wall it was supporting, while a second piece held together the second half of the wall. In other words, one piece was inserted in the ring from one side of the structure until it reached the halfway mark of the wall, while a second piece was inserted from the other direction meeting its partner in the middle. Thus the upper crossbar and the lower crossbar were really two sections each, for a total of four pieces. However, the middle crossbar was a single long piece that stretched the whole length of the wall it was supporting. It passed clear through from one end of the wall to the other, as the verse states: *The central crossbar should go through the middle of the boards from one end to the other* (26:28). The upper and lower crossbars were held in place by a series of rings, two of which were fastened to each of the boards [one near the top the upper crossbar, and a lower ring near the base for the bottom crossbar]. The ten cubits of the boards' height were thereby divided into four equal sections. The space from the upper ring to the top of the board was the first, and the space between the lower ring to the bottom was the last. Each of these spaces took up one quarter of the board's length. The space between those two rings was further divided into two additional sections [by the middle crossbar]. Following this arrangement, all of the rings were evenly placed in straight rows next to each other. The middle crossbar, however, had no rings, because the boards were bored through the middle of the boards themselves. The holes were perfectly aligned, allowing that crossbar to pass directly from one board to the next. This is what the verse means when it states: *The central crossbar should go through the middle of the boards* (26:28). Now the lengths of the four upper and lower crossbars,

חֲמִשָּׁה לְקַרְשֵׁי צֶלַע־הַמִּשְׁכָּן. אֵלּוּ חֲמִשָּׁה שְׁלֹשָׁה הֵן, אֶלָּא שֶׁהַבְּרִיחַ הָעֶלְיוֹן וְהַתַּחְתּוֹן עָשׂוּי מִשְּׁתֵּי חֲתִיכוֹת, זֶה מַבְרִיחַ עַד חֲצִי הַכֹּתֶל וְזֶה מַבְרִיחַ עַד חֲצִי הַכֹּתֶל, זֶה נִכְנָס בַּטַּבַּעַת מִצַּד זֶה וְזֶה נִכְנָס בַּטַּבַּעַת מִצַּד זֶה עַד שֶׁמַּגִּיעִין זֶה לָזֶה, נִמְצְאוּ הָעֶלְיוֹן וְהַתַּחְתּוֹן שְׁנַיִם שֶׁהֵן אַרְבָּעָה. אֲבָל הָאֶמְצָעִי אָרְכּוֹ כְּנֶגֶד כָּל הַכֹּתֶל, וּמַבְרִיחַ מִקָּצֶה הַכֹּתֶל וְעַד קָצֵהוּ, שֶׁנֶּאֱמַר: "וְהַבְּרִיחַ הַתִּיכֹן וְגוֹ' מַבְרִחַ מִן הַקָּצֶה אֶל הַקָּצֶה" (להלן פסוק כח). שֶׁהָעֶלְיוֹנִים וְהַתַּחְתּוֹנִים הָיוּ לָהֶן טַבָּעוֹת בַּקְּרָשִׁים לִכָּנֵס לְתוֹכָן, שְׁתֵּי טַבָּעוֹת לְכָל קֶרֶשׁ, מְשֻׁלָּשִׁים בְּתוֹךְ עֶשֶׂר אַמּוֹת שֶׁל גֹּבַהּ הַקֶּרֶשׁ, חֵלֶק אֶחָד מִן הַטַּבַּעַת הָעֶלְיוֹנָה וּלְמַעְלָה וְחֵלֶק אֶחָד מִן הַתַּחְתּוֹנָה וּלְמַטָּה, וְכָל חֵלֶק הוּא רְבִיעַ אֹרֶךְ הַקֶּרֶשׁ, וּשְׁנֵי חֲלָקִים בֵּין טַבַּעַת לְטַבַּעַת, כְּדֵי שֶׁיִּהְיוּ כָּל הַטַּבָּעוֹת מְכֻוָּנִין זֶה כְּנֶגֶד זֶה. אֲבָל לַבְּרִיחַ הַתִּיכוֹן אֵין טַבָּעוֹת, אֶלָּא הַקְּרָשִׁים נְקוּבִין בְּעָבְיָן, וְהוּא נִכְנָס בָּהֶם דֶּרֶךְ הַנְּקָבִים שֶׁהֵם מְכֻוָּנִין זֶה מוּל זֶה, וְזֶהוּ שֶׁנֶּאֱמַר: "בְּתוֹךְ הַקְּרָשִׁים" (שם). הַבְּרִיחִים הָעֶלְיוֹנִים וְהַתַּחְתּוֹנִים שֶׁבַּצָּפוֹן וְשֶׁבַּדָּרוֹם אֹרֶךְ כָּל אֶחָד חָמֵשׁ עֶשְׂרֵה אַמָּה, וְהַתִּיכוֹן אָרְכּוֹ שְׁלֹשִׁים אַמָּה, וְזֶהוּ "מִן הַקָּצֶה אֶל הַקָּצֶה" (שם),

◀

כז הָאֶחָד: וַחֲמִשָּׁה בְרִיחִם לְקַרְשֵׁי צֶלַע־הַמִּשְׁכָּן
הַשֵּׁנִית וַחֲמִשָּׁה בְרִיחִם לְקַרְשֵׁי צֶלַע הַמִּשְׁכָּן
כח לַיַּרְכָתַיִם יָמָּה: וְהַבְּרִיחַ הַתִּיכֹן בְּתוֹךְ הַקְּרָשִׁים
כט מַבְרִחַ מִן־הַקָּצֶה אֶל־הַקָּצֶה: וְאֶת־הַקְּרָשִׁים תְּצַפֶּה
זָהָב וְאֶת־טַבְּעֹתֵיהֶם תַּעֲשֶׂה זָהָב בָּתִּים לַבְּרִיחִם

which were oriented along the north and south walls of the Tabernacle, were each fifteen cubits long [half the total length of the structure], whereas the length of the middle crossbar stretched the full thirty cubits, as the verse states: *From one end to the other*, i.e., from the east wall to the west wall. With regard to the five crossbars that supported the west wall, the upper and the lower crossbars were each six cubits long [so that the two upper crossbars together and the two lower crossbars together covered the twelve-cubit width of the Tabernacle], while the middle crossbar [running through the wall's center] ran the full length of twelve cubits that comprised the total of the eight boards on this side. This description follows Baraita Dimlekhet Hamishkan.

מִן הַמִּזְרָח וְעַד הַמַּעֲרָב. וַחֲמִשָּׁה בְרִיחִים שֶׁבַּמַּעֲרָב, אֹרֶךְ הָעֶלְיוֹנִים וְהַתַּחְתּוֹנִים שֵׁשׁ אַמּוֹת, וְהַתִּיכוֹן אָרְכּוֹ שְׁתֵּים עֶשְׂרֵה, כְּנֶגֶד רֹחַב שְׁמוֹנָה קְרָשִׁים. כָּךְ הִיא מְפֹרֶשֶׁת בִּמְלֶאכֶת הַמִּשְׁכָּן:

29 | בָּתִּים לַבְּרִיחִם – *Rings for the crossbars:* The rings that you fasten to the boards will serve as holders for the crossbars after you insert them.

כט | בָּתִּים לַבְּרִיחִם. הַטַּבָּעוֹת שֶׁתַּעֲשֶׂה בָּהֶן יִהְיוּ בָּתִּים לִכָּנֵס בָּהֶן הַבְּרִיחִים:

וְצִפִּיתָ אֶת־הַבְּרִיחִם זָהָב – *The crossbars too should be overlaid with gold:* The poles that comprised the crossbars were not themselves actually overlaid with gold; they had no covering at all. Rather, the rings held gold tubes that served as sheaths for the crossbars like hollow reeds. These pieces extended on either side of the ring such that they spanned the width of the boards from the ring [in the middle of each board] to either edge. The crossbars entered the opening of one holder and extended from it to the opening of the next sheath at the next ring. Thus the crossbars truly were wrapped in gold when they were fastened to the boards. Note that the crossbars supported the walls from the outside of the Tabernacle, such that they projected on the exterior side of the walls and were not visible on the inside, just as the rings and tubes were also not apparent from the structure's interior. The insides of the walls were completely smooth [with nothing protruding from them].

וְצִפִּיתָ אֶת הַבְּרִיחִם זָהָב. לֹא שֶׁהָיָה הַזָּהָב מְדֻבָּק עַל הַבְּרִיחִים, שֶׁאֵין עֲלֵיהֶם שׁוּם צִפּוּי, אֶלָּא בַּקֶּרֶשׁ הָיָה קוֹבֵעַ כְּמִין שְׁנֵי פִּיפִיּוֹת שֶׁל זָהָב כְּמִין שְׁנֵי סִדְקֵי קָנֶה חָלוּק, וְקוֹבְעָן אֵצֶל הַטַּבָּעוֹת לְכָאן וּלְכָאן, אָרְכָּן מְמַלֵּא אֶת רֹחַב הַקֶּרֶשׁ מִן הַטַּבַּעַת לְכָאן וּמִמֶּנָּה לְכָאן, וְהַבְּרִיחַ נִכְנָס לְתוֹכוֹ וּמִמֶּנּוּ לַטַּבַּעַת וּמִן הַטַּבַּעַת לַפֶּה הַשֵּׁנִי, נִמְצְאוּ הַבְּרִיחִים מְצֻפִּים זָהָב כְּשֶׁהֵן תְּחוּבִין בַּקְּרָשִׁים. וְהַבְּרִיחִים הַלָּלוּ מִבַּחוּץ הָיוּ; בְּלִיטַת הַטַּבָּעוֹת וְהַפִּיפִיּוֹת לֹא הָיְתָה נִרְאֵית בְּתוֹךְ הַמִּשְׁכָּן, אֶלָּא כָּל הַכֹּתֶל חָלָק מִבִּפְנִים:

◄

30 So shall you set up the Tabernacle, according to the plan you
31 were shown on the mountain. Make a curtain ḤAMISHI
of sky-blue, purple, and scarlet wool, and finely spun linen
32 with a design of cherubim worked into it. Hang it on four
gold-covered posts of acacia wood with gold hooks, set on
33 four sockets of silver. Hang the curtain under the clasps and
bring the Ark of the Testimony behind it, so that the curtain
34 separates the holy place from the Holy of Holies. Put the cover
35 on the Ark of the Testimony in the Holy of Holies. The table
shall be placed on the north side of the Tabernacle outside
the curtain, and the candelabrum on the south side, opposite

ל| וַהֲקֵמֹתָ אֶת־הַמִּשְׁכָּן. לְאַחַר שֶׁיִּגָּמֵר הֲקִימֵהוּ:

30 | וַהֲקֵמֹתָ אֶת־הַמִּשְׁכָּן – *So shall you set up the Tabernacle:* Set up the Tabernacle after all the components have been produced.

הָרְאֵיתָ בָּהָר. קֹדֶם לָכֵן, שֶׁאֲנִי עָתִיד לְלַמֶּדְךָ וּלְהַרְאוֹתְךָ סֵדֶר הֲקָמָתוֹ:

הָרְאֵיתָ בָּהָר – *You were shown on the mountain:* As you will be shown prior to assembling the Tabernacle, for I will demonstrate to you the sequence of setting up the structure. [A more fitting translation according to Rashi would be "you will have been shown."]

לא| פָּרֹכֶת. לְשׁוֹן מְחִצָּה הוּא, וּבִלְשׁוֹן חֲכָמִים: פַּרְגּוֹד, דָּבָר הַמַּבְדִּיל בֵּין הַמֶּלֶךְ וּבֵין הָעָם:

31 | פָּרֹכֶת – *A curtain:* The term *parokhet* connotes a partition. The Sages refer to this as a *pargod*: a barrier that separates a king from the people.

תְּכֵלֶת וְאַרְגָּמָן. כָּל מִין וּמִין הָיָה כָּפוּל, בְּכָל חוּט וְחוּט שִׁשָּׁה חוּטִין:

תְּכֵלֶת וְאַרְגָּמָן – *Sky-blue and purple:* Each material mentioned here was twined with six strands in each thread.

מַעֲשֵׂה חֹשֵׁב. כְּבָר פֵּרַשְׁתִּי שֶׁזּוֹ הִיא אֲרִיגָה שֶׁל שְׁתֵּי קִירוֹת, וְהַצִּיּוּרִין שֶׁמִּשְּׁנֵי עֲבָרֶיהָ אֵינָן דּוֹמִין זֶה לָזֶה:

מַעֲשֵׂה חֹשֵׁב – *With a design:* I have already explained [in comments to 26:1] that the design was woven into both sides of the curtain, with different figures displayed on either side of the tapestry.

כְּרֻבִים. צִיּוּרִין שֶׁל בְּרִיּוֹת יַעֲשֶׂה בָּהּ:

כְּרֻבִים – *Cherubim:* He shall make images of creatures upon it.

לב| אַרְבָּעָה עַמּוּדִים תְּקוּעִים בְּתוֹךְ אַרְבָּעָה אֲדָנִים, וְאֻנְקְלָיוֹת קְבוּעִין בָּהֶן עֲקוּמִין לְמַעְלָה, לְהוֹשִׁיב עֲלֵיהֶן כְּלוֹנָס שֶׁרֹאשׁ הַפָּרֹכֶת כָּרוּךְ בָּהּ; וְהָאֻנְקְלָיוֹת הֵן הַוָּוִין, שֶׁהֲרֵי כְּמִין וָוִין הֵן עֲשׂוּיִים. וְהַפָּרֹכֶת אָרְכָּהּ עֶשֶׂר אַמּוֹת לְרָחְבּוֹ

32 | Four posts were inserted into four sockets, and hooks were hung at the top of these posts. The ends of the hooks were bent so that a rod could be rested on them; these are the gold hooks that our verse refers to. They are called *vavim* because they resemble the [hook-shaped] letter *vav*. The top of the curtain was wound around the rod that lay across the hooks. The curtain itself was ten cubits long, stretching the width of the Tabernacle. Its width [height] was also ten cubits to match

◀

ל וְצִפִּיתָ אֶת־הַבְּרִיחִם זָהָב׃ וַהֲקֵמֹתָ אֶת־הַמִּשְׁכָּן
לא כְּמִשְׁפָּטוֹ אֲשֶׁר הָרְאֵיתָ בָּהָר׃ וְעָשִׂיתָ כ חמישי
פָרֹכֶת תְּכֵלֶת וְאַרְגָּמָן וְתוֹלַעַת שָׁנִי וְשֵׁשׁ מָשְׁזָר
לב מַעֲשֵׂה חֹשֵׁב יַעֲשֶׂה אֹתָהּ כְּרֻבִים׃ וְנָתַתָּה אֹתָהּ
עַל־אַרְבָּעָה עַמּוּדֵי שִׁטִּים מְצֻפִּים זָהָב וָוֵיהֶם זָהָב
לג עַל־אַרְבָּעָה אַדְנֵי־כָסֶף׃ וְנָתַתָּה אֶת־הַפָּרֹכֶת תַּחַת
הַקְּרָסִים וְהֵבֵאתָ שָׁמָּה מִבֵּית לַפָּרֹכֶת אֵת אֲרוֹן
הָעֵדוּת וְהִבְדִּילָה הַפָּרֹכֶת לָכֶם בֵּין הַקֹּדֶשׁ וּבֵין
לד קֹדֶשׁ הַקֳּדָשִׁים׃ וְנָתַתָּ אֶת־הַכַּפֹּרֶת עַל אֲרוֹן הָעֵדֻת
לה בְּקֹדֶשׁ הַקֳּדָשִׁים׃ וְשַׂמְתָּ אֶת־הַשֻּׁלְחָן מִחוּץ לַפָּרֹכֶת
וְאֶת־הַמְּנֹרָה נֹכַח הַשֻּׁלְחָן עַל צֶלַע הַמִּשְׁכָּן תֵּימָנָה

the height of the structure's boards. The curtain hung at a third of the length of the Tabernacle [from the western wall] such that the chamber created by the barrier contained a space of ten cubits. The room on the outside of the curtain was twenty cubits long. Thus the Holy of Holies measured ten cubits by ten cubits. For the verse states, *Hang the curtain under the clasps and bring the Ark of the Testimony behind it* (26:33) – and the clasps mentioned here are those that connected one set of sheets [that covered the Tabernacle] to the second set of sheets [above in 26:6]. Since we know that each set of sheets was twenty cubits wide, when the sets were spread over the top of the structure starting from its opening [at the eastern end] toward the west wall, the first set of sheets ended two thirds of the way down the Tabernacle. [Therefore, the curtain, which hung directly beneath the seam of the two sets of curtains, must have been situated twenty cubits from the eastern wall and ten cubits from the western one]. The second set of sheets covered the rear third of the Tabernacle and hung down the back of the structure to conceal the boards.

שֶׁל מִשְׁכָּן, וְרָחְבָּהּ עֶשֶׂר אַמּוֹת כְּגָבְהָן שֶׁל קְרָשִׁים, פְּרוּסָה בִּשְׁלִישׁוֹ שֶׁל מִשְׁכָּן, שֶׁיְּהֵא הֵימֶנָּה וְלִפְנִים עֶשֶׂר אַמּוֹת וְהֵימֶנָּה וְלַחוּץ עֶשְׂרִים אַמָּה. נִמְצָא בֵּית קָדְשֵׁי הַקֳּדָשִׁים עֶשֶׂר עַל עֶשֶׂר, שֶׁנֶּאֱמַר: "וְנָתַתָּה אֶת הַפָּרֹכֶת תַּחַת הַקְּרָסִים" (להלן פסוק לג) הַמְחַבְּרִים אֶת שְׁתֵּי חוֹבְרוֹת שֶׁל יְרִיעוֹת הַמִּשְׁכָּן; רֹחַב הַחוֹבֶרֶת עֶשְׂרִים אַמָּה, וּכְשֶׁפְּרָשָׂהּ עַל גַּג הַמִּשְׁכָּן מִן הַפֶּתַח לַמַּעֲרָב, כָּלְתָה בִּשְׁנֵי שְׁלִישֵׁי הַמִּשְׁכָּן, וְהַחוֹבֶרֶת הַשֵּׁנִית כִּסְּתָה שְׁלִישׁוֹ שֶׁל מִשְׁכָּן, וְהַמּוֹתָר תָּלוּי לַאֲחוֹרָיו לְכַסּוֹת אֶת הַקְּרָשִׁים:

35 | וְשַׂמְתָּ אֶת־הַשֻּׁלְחָן – *The table shall be placed:* The table [described in chapter 25] sat on the north side of the Tabernacle room, two and a half cubits from the northern wall. The ◄

לה | **וְשַׂמְתָּ אֶת־הַשֻּׁלְחָן.** שֻׁלְחָן בַּצָּפוֹן מָשׁוּךְ מִן הַכֹּתֶל הַצְּפוֹנִי שְׁתֵּי אַמּוֹת וּמֶחֱצָה, וּמְנוֹרָה בַּדָּרוֹם מְשׁוּכָה מִן

36 the table. Make a screen for the entrance to the Tent, embroidered with sky-blue, purple, and scarlet wool and finely spun
37 linen. Make five posts of acacia wood for the screen and overlay them with gold; their hooks, also, shall be of gold. Cast for
27 1 them, too, five sockets of bronze. Make the altar SHISHI
from acacia wood. It should be square, five cubits long, five
2 cubits wide, and three cubits high. Make horns for it on its
four corners, the horns being of one piece with it, and over-
3 lay it with bronze. Make pots for removing its ashes, together with shovels, basins, forks, and pans. Make all of these of

הַכֹּתֶל הַדְּרוֹמִי שְׁתֵּי אַמּוֹת וּמֶחֱצָה, וּמִזְבַּח הַזָּהָב נָתוּן כְּנֶגֶד חֲוִיר שֶׁבֵּין שֻׁלְחָן לַמְּנוֹרָה מָשׁוּךְ קִמְעָא כְּלַפֵּי הַמִּזְרָח, וְכֻלָּם נְתוּנִים מִן חֲצִי הַמִּשְׁכָּן וְלִפְנִים. כֵּיצַד? אֹרֶךְ הַמִּשְׁכָּן מִן הַפֶּתַח לַפָּרֹכֶת עֶשְׂרִים אַמָּה, הַמִּזְבֵּחַ וְהַשֻּׁלְחָן וְהַמְּנוֹרָה מְשׁוּכִים מִן הַפֶּתַח לְצַד מַעֲרָב עֶשֶׂר אַמּוֹת:

candelabrum opposite it stood two and a half cubits from the southern wall. The golden incense altar was situated in the space between the table and the candelabrum, but it was positioned closer to the east opening [than the other furniture]. But all three items stood past the halfway mark of the chamber. How was that? There were twenty cubits from the opening of the Tabernacle to the curtain separating the first room from the Holy of Holies, and the altar, the table, and the candelabrum were all placed in the western half of that space.

לו | וְעָשִׂיתָ מָסָךְ. וִילוֹן שֶׁהוּא מֵסֵךְ כְּנֶגֶד הַפֶּתַח, כְּמוֹ: "שַׂכְתָּ בַעֲדוֹ" (איוב א, י), לְשׁוֹן מָגֵן:

36 | **וְעָשִׂיתָ מָסָךְ** – *A screen:* The Torah now describes a curtain hung in front of the Tabernacle's entrance. We find a similar term denoting a protective covering in the verse *Have you not sheltered [sakhta] him?* (Job 1:10).

מַעֲשֵׂה רֹקֵם. הַצּוּרוֹת עֲשׂוּיוֹת בּוֹ מַעֲשֵׂה מַחַט, כְּפַרְצוּף שֶׁל עֵבֶר זֶה כָּךְ פַּרְצוּף שֶׁל עֵבֶר זֶה:

מַעֲשֵׂה רֹקֵם – *Embroidered:* The designs on this curtain were added to the material by needlework. The figures were identical on both sides of the curtain.

רֹקֵם. שֵׁם הָאֻמָּן וְלֹא שֵׁם הָאֻמָּנוּת, וְתַרְגּוּמוֹ: "עוֹבָד צַיָּר" וְלֹא 'עוֹבָד צִיּוּר'. מִדַּת הַמָּסָךְ כְּמִדַּת הַפָּרֹכֶת, עֶשֶׂר אַמּוֹת עַל עֶשֶׂר אַמּוֹת:

רֹקֵם – *Embroidered:* [Literally, "the work of an embroiderer."] The term *rokem* here refers to the craftsman and not to the art. Hence the Targum renders this "the work of an embroider [*tzayyar*]," and not "a work of embroidery [*tziyyur*]." The dimensions of this screen were the same as the curtain – ten cubits by ten cubits.

כז א | וְעָשִׂיתָ אֶת־הַמִּזְבֵּחַ וְגוֹ' וְשָׁלֹשׁ אַמּוֹת קֹמָתוֹ. דְּבָרִים כִּכְתָבָן, דִּבְרֵי רַבִּי יְהוּדָה. רַבִּי יוֹסֵי אוֹמֵר: נֶאֱמַר כָּאן "רָבוּעַ" וְנֶאֱמַר בַּפְּנִימִי "רָבוּעַ"

27 1 | **וְעָשִׂיתָ אֶת־הַמִּזְבֵּחַ... וְשָׁלֹשׁ אַמּוֹת קֹמָתוֹ** – *Make the altar... three cubits high:* According to Rabbi Yehuda, the verse should be understood simply. Rabbi Yosei, on the other hand, compares the term "square" appearing here with another instance of the term in a later passage describing the inner

לו וְהַשֻּׁלְחָן תִּתֵּן עַל־צֶלַע צָפוֹן: וְעָשִׂיתָ מָסָךְ לְפֶתַח
הָאֹהֶל תְּכֵלֶת וְאַרְגָּמָן וְתוֹלַעַת שָׁנִי וְשֵׁשׁ מָשְׁזָר
לז מַעֲשֵׂה רֹקֵם: וְעָשִׂיתָ לַמָּסָךְ חֲמִשָּׁה עַמּוּדֵי שִׁטִּים
וְצִפִּיתָ אֹתָם זָהָב וָוֵיהֶם זָהָב וְיָצַקְתָּ לָהֶם חֲמִשָּׁה
כז א אַדְנֵי נְחֹשֶׁת: וְעָשִׂיתָ אֶת־הַמִּזְבֵּחַ עֲצֵי ששי
שִׁטִּים חָמֵשׁ אַמּוֹת אֹרֶךְ וְחָמֵשׁ אַמּוֹת רֹחַב רָבוּעַ
ב יִהְיֶה הַמִּזְבֵּחַ וְשָׁלֹשׁ אַמּוֹת קֹמָתוֹ: וְעָשִׂיתָ קַרְנֹתָיו
עַל אַרְבַּע פִּנֹּתָיו מִמֶּנּוּ תִּהְיֶיןָ קַרְנֹתָיו וְצִפִּיתָ אֹתוֹ
ג נְחֹשֶׁת: וְעָשִׂיתָ סִּירֹתָיו לְדַשְּׁנוֹ וְיָעָיו וּמִזְרְקֹתָיו
וּמִזְלְגֹתָיו וּמַחְתֹּתָיו לְכָל־כֵּלָיו תַּעֲשֶׂה נְחֹשֶׁת:

(להלן ל, ח), מַה לְהַלָּן גָּבְהוֹ פִּי שְׁנַיִם כְּאָרְכּוֹ, אַף כָּאן גָּבְהוֹ פִּי שְׁנַיִם כְּאָרְכּוֹ; וּמָה אֲנִי מְקַיֵּם "וְשָׁלֹשׁ אַמּוֹת קֹמָתוֹ"? מִשְּׂפַת סוֹבֵב וּלְמַעְלָה:

altar: *It shall be square, a cubit long, a cubit wide and two cubits high* (30:2). Just as there the altar had a height that was twice its length, so too this altar must have had a height that was twice its length. [And since the length of the outer altar was five cubits, the structure must have been ten cubits high.] How then should we understand the phrase *three cubits high*? There were three cubits from the top edge of the ledge [surrounding the altar] to its top. [Rashi refers to the grate introduced in verse 4, as a bronze protrusion from the altar.]

ב| מִמֶּנּוּ תִּהְיֶיןָ קַרְנֹתָיו. שֶׁלֹּא יַעֲשֵׂם לְבַדָּם וִיחַבְּרֵם בּוֹ:

2 | מִמֶּנּוּ תִּהְיֶיןָ קַרְנֹתָיו – *The horns being of one piece with it:* Do not fashion the horns as a separate pieces and then attach them to the altar. [The horns were vertical projections from each of the altar top's four corners.]

וְצִפִּיתָ אֹתוֹ נְחֹשֶׁת. לְכַפֵּר עַל עַזּוּת מֵצַח, שֶׁנֶּאֱמַר: "וּמִצְחֲךָ נְחוּשָׁה" (ישעיה מח, ד):

וְצִפִּיתָ אֹתוֹ נְחֹשֶׁת – *And overlay it with bronze:* This material signified atonement for insolence, which the prophet associates with it in the verse *Because I know that you are obstinate, and your neck is an iron sinew, and your forehead bronze* (Isaiah 48:4).

ג| סִירֹתָיו. כְּמִין יוֹרוֹת:

3 | סִירֹתָיו – *Pots:* The word *sir* denotes a type of pot.

לְדַשְּׁנוֹ. לְהָסִיר דִּשְׁנוֹ לְתוֹכָם; וְהוּא שֶׁתִּרְגֵּם אוּנְקְלוֹס: "לְמִסְפֵּי קִטְמֵיהּ", לִסְפּוֹת הַדֶּשֶׁן לְתוֹכָם. כִּי יֵשׁ מִלּוֹת בִּלְשׁוֹן עִבְרִית מִלָּה

לְדַשְּׁנוֹ – *For removing its ashes:* The ashes from the top of the altar were swept into these pots. Thus Onkelos translates the phrase as "to remove the ashes into them." [The word *ledashen*, which literally seems to mean "to ash," thus actually means "to remove

4 bronze. Make a grate of bronze mesh for it, and on the mesh
5 make four bronze rings at its four corners. The grate should
be set below, under the ledge of the altar, so that the mesh
6 reaches the middle of the altar. And make staves of acacia

אַחַת מִתְחַלֶּפֶת בַּפִּתְרוֹן לְשַׁמֵּשׁ בִּנְיָן וּסְתִירָה, כְּמוֹ "וַתַּשְׁרֵשׁ שָׁרָשֶׁיהָ" (תהלים פ, י), "אֱוִיל מַשְׁרִישׁ" (איוב ה, ג), וְחִלּוּפוֹ: "וּבְכָל תְּבוּאָתִי תְשָׁרֵשׁ" (שם לא, יב). וְכָמוֹהוּ: "בִּסְעִפֶיהָ פֹּרִיָּה" (ישעיה יז, ו), וְחִלּוּפוֹ: "מְסָעֵף פֻּארָה" (שם י, לג), מְפַסֵּחַ סְעִיפֶיהָ. וְכָמוֹהוּ: "וְזֶה הָאַחֲרוֹן עִצְּמוֹ" (ירמיה נ, יז), שִׁבֵּר עַצְמוֹתָיו. וְכָמוֹהוּ: "וַיִּסְקְלֻהוּ בָאֲבָנִים" (מלכים א' כא, יג), וְחִלּוּפוֹ: "סַקְּלוּ מֵאֶבֶן" (ישעיה סב, י), הָסִירוּ אֲבָנֶיהָ, וְכֵן: "וַיְעַזְּקֵהוּ וַיְסַקְּלֵהוּ" (שם ה, ב). אַף כָּאן "לְדַשְּׁנוֹ" לְהָסִיר דִּשְׁנוֹ, וּבְלַעַז אשנדרי"ר:

ash."] For there are certain words in the Hebrew language that can express opposite meanings, denoting both construction and destruction. For example, we read in one verse: *You did cause it to take deep root [vatashresh]* (Psalms 80:10), and similarly, *I have seen the foolish taking root [mashrish]* (Job 5:3). But the same term appears with the opposite meaning in the verse, *would root out [tesharesh] all my increase* (Job 31:12). In a second example, we find the verse *Four or five in its fruitful branches [bis'ifeha]* [Isaiah 17:6, that is, the branches shall thrive], whereas a second verse employs the same term in an opposite manner: *The Lord of Hosts, shall lop the bough [mesa'ef] with terror* (Isaiah 10:33), meaning "He shall cut off its branches." In a third instance we read: *And last this Nevukhadretzar has broken his bones [itzmo]* [Jeremiah 50:17; here the word *etzem* means simply "bone," but the verb formed from it denotes breaking bones]. Finally, we find the verse *And stoned him [vayiskeluhu] with stones, that he died* (I Kings 21:13), but the term is used in the opposite sense in the verse *Clear [sakkelu] the stones; lift up a standard for the people* (Isaiah 62:10) meaning that the stones were to be removed [as opposed to piled on]. A similar usage appears in the verse *He dug it, and cleared away [vaysakkelehu] its stones* (Isaiah 5:2). In our verse as well, the term *ledasheno* actually means "to clear away the ashes." In Old French the translation for the verb would be *escendrer* ["to remove ash"].

וְיָעָיו. כְּתַרְגּוּמוֹ, מַגְרֵפוֹת שֶׁנּוֹטֵל בָּהֶם הַדֶּשֶׁן, וְהֵן כְּמִין כִּסּוּי קְדֵרָה, וְהוּא שֶׁל מַתֶּכֶת דַּק וְלוֹ בֵּית יָד, וּבְלַעַז וודי"ל:

וְיָעָיו – *Shovels:* This should be understood as the Targum renders the term: shovels used to remove the ashes. These resembled a thin pot cover with a handle. The Old French word for this would be *vadil* ["shovel"].

וּמִזְרְקֹתָיו. לְקַבֵּל בָּהֶם דַּם הַזְּבָחִים:

וּמִזְרְקֹתָיו – *Basins:* These utensils would be used to collect the blood from the sacrificial animals.

וּמִזְלְגֹתָיו. כְּמִין אֻנְקְלִיּוֹת כְּפוּפִין, וּמַכֶּה בָּהֶן בַּבָּשָׂר וְנִתְחָבִין בּוֹ, וּמְהַפְּכָן בָּהֶן עַל גַּחֲלֵי הַמַּעֲרָכָה שֶׁיְּהֵא מְמַהֵר שְׂרֵפָתָן, וּבְלַעַז קרוצי"ש, וּבִלְשׁוֹן חֲכָמִים: צִנּוֹרִיּוֹת:

וּמִזְלְגֹתָיו – *Forks:* These were fashioned like hooks which were stuck into the flesh of the sacrifice to turn the meat over on top of the wood coals. This action would expedite the burning of the sacrifice. The word for this utensil in Old French is *croces* ["hooks"], whereas the Sages refer to these items as *tzinoriyot* ["fleshhooks"].

ד וְעָשִׂיתָ לּוֹ מִכְבָּר מַעֲשֵׂה רֶשֶׁת נְחֹשֶׁת וְעָשִׂיתָ עַל־
הָרֶשֶׁת אַרְבַּע טַבְּעֹת נְחֹשֶׁת עַל אַרְבַּע קְצוֹתָיו׃
ה וְנָתַתָּה אֹתָהּ תַּחַת כַּרְכֹּב הַמִּזְבֵּחַ מִלְּמָטָּה וְהָיְתָה
ו הָרֶשֶׁת עַד חֲצִי הַמִּזְבֵּחַ׃ וְעָשִׂיתָ בַדִּים לַמִּזְבֵּחַ

וּמַחְתֹּתָיו – *Pans:* These were receptacles used to carry coals from the outer altar to the inner altar where they were employed to burn the incense. The objects were referred to as *maḥtot* because of the raking [*ḥatiyya*] done with them. We find a similar usage of the term in the verse *Taking fire [laḥtot] from the hearth* (Isaiah 30:14), where the term means "drawing fire from its place." Another instance of the root appears in the verse *Can a man take [hayaḥteh] fire in his bosom, and his clothes not be burned?* (Proverbs 6:27).

וּמַחְתֹּתָיו. בֵּית קִבּוּל יֵשׁ לָהֶם לִטֹּל בָּהֶן גֶּחָלִים מִן הַמִּזְבֵּחַ לְשֵׂאתָם עַל מִזְבֵּחַ הַפְּנִימִי לַקְּטֹרֶת. וְעַל שֵׁם חֲתִיָּתָן קְרוּיִים מַחְתּוֹת, כְּמוֹ: "לַחְתּוֹת אֵשׁ מִיָּקוּד" (ישעיה ל, יד), לְשׁוֹן שְׁאִיבַת אֵשׁ מִמְּקוֹמָהּ, וְכֵן: "הֲיַחְתֶּה אִישׁ אֵשׁ בְּחֵיקוֹ" (משלי ו, כז):

לְכָל־כֵּלָיו – *Make all of these:* [Literally, "make for all of these."] This should be understood as if the verse said simply: "Make all of these utensils of bronze" [without the preposition "for"].

לְכָל־כֵּלָיו. כְּמוֹ כָּל כֵּלָיו:

4 | **מִכְבָּר** – *A grate:* The term *mikhbar* here is related to the Hebrew word for a sieve – *kevara* – called *cruvel* in Old French. This item was fashioned as sort of a garment for the altar, and it was perforated with holes like a net. The wording of the verse is inverted, and what it really means is: "Make a bronze grate of mesh," rather than "Make a grate of bronze mesh."

ד| מִכְבָּר. לְשׁוֹן כְּבָרָה שֶׁקּוֹרִין קריב"ל, כְּמִין לְבוּשׁ עָשׂוּ לוֹ לַמִּזְבֵּחַ, עָשׂוּי חוֹרִין חוֹרִין כְּמִין רֶשֶׁת. וּמִקְרָא זֶה מְסֹרָס וְכָךְ פִּתְרוֹנוֹ: וְעָשִׂיתָ לוֹ מִכְבַּר נְחֹשֶׁת מַעֲשֵׂה רֶשֶׁת:

5 | **כַּרְכֹּב הַמִּזְבֵּחַ** – *The ledge of the altar:* The *karkov* mentioned in this verse is also known [in the Talmud] as the *sovev* [literally, "that which encircles"], for anything that surrounds something else is called a *karkov*. Thus we learn in tractate Ḥullin (25a): "The following are considered unfinished wood utensils [but are still serviceable]: Whatever still needs to be polished and to be hollowed out [*ulkharkev*]." For a vessel is hollowed out in the same way that round ornamental grooves are carved in the walls of chests and wooden benches. Now on the altar as well, a groove was made all around its walls for decorative purposes. This feature appeared six cubits off the ground, according to the approach that the total height of the altar was twice its length [i.e., ten cubits]. And how does that interpretation explain the Torah's command that the altar be only *three cubits high* (27:1)? There were three cubits from the top edge

ה| כַּרְכֹּב הַמִּזְבֵּחַ. סוֹבֵב. כָּל דָּבָר הַמַּקִּיף סָבִיב בְּעִגּוּל קָרוּי כַּרְכֹּב, כְּמוֹ שֶׁשָּׁנִינוּ בְּהֵיכַל שׁוֹחֲטִין: "אֵלּוּ הֵן גְּלָמֵי כְלֵי עֵץ, כָּל שֶׁעָתִיד לָשׁוּף וּלְכַרְכֵּב" (חולין כה ע"א), וְהוּא שֶׁעוֹשִׂין חֲרִיצִין עֲגֻלִּין בְּקַרְשֵׁי דַּפְנֵי הַתֵּבוֹת וְסַפְסְלֵי הָעֵץ, אַף לַמִּזְבֵּחַ עָשָׂה חָרִיץ סְבִיבוֹ בְּדָפְנוֹ לְנוֹי, וְהוּא לְסוֹף שֵׁשׁ אַמּוֹת שֶׁל גָּבְהוֹ כְּדִבְרֵי הָאוֹמֵר (זבחים נט ע"ב – ס ע"א) מָה אֲנִי מְקַיֵּם "וְשָׁלֹשׁ אַמּוֹת קֹמָתוֹ"? מִשְּׂפַת סוֹבֵב וּלְמַעְלָה. אֲבָל סוֹבֵב לְהִלּוּךְ הַכֹּהֲנִים לֹא הָיָה לַמִּזְבֵּחַ

◀

7 wood for the altar, and overlay them with bronze. Place the
poles in the rings, so that the poles will be on the two sides of
8 the altar when it is carried. Make it hollow, with planks; make
9 it as it was shown to you on the mountain. Make SHEVI'I
the courtyard of the Tabernacle thus: on the south side there
should be hangings a hundred cubits long of finely spun linen,

הַנְּחֹשֶׁת אֶלָּא עַל רֹאשׁוֹ לִפְנִים מִקַּרְנוֹתָיו. וְכֵן שָׁנִינוּ בִּזְבָחִים (דף סב ע"א): אֵיזֶהוּ כַּרְכֹּב? בֵּין קֶרֶן לְקֶרֶן, וְלִפְנִים מֵהֶן אַמָּה שֶׁל הִלּוּךְ רַגְלֵי הַכֹּהֲנִים, שְׁתֵּי אַמּוֹת הַלָּלוּ קְרוּיִים כַּרְכֹּב. וְדִקְדַּקְנוּ שָׁם: וְהָכְתִיב: "תַּחַת כַּרְכֻּבּוֹ מִלְּמַטָּה" (להלן לח, ד), לָמַדְנוּ שֶׁהַכַּרְכֹּב בְּדָפְנוֹ הוּא וּלְבוּשׁ הַמִּכְבָּר תַּחְתָּיו! וְתֵרֵץ הַמְתָרֵץ: תְּרֵי הֲווֹ, חַד לְנוֹי וְחַד לַכֹּהֲנִים דְּלֹא נִשְׁתָּרְקוּ; זֶה שֶׁבַּדֹּפֶן לְנוֹי הָיָה, וּמִתַּחְתָּיו הִלְבִּישׁוּ הַמִּכְבָּר, וְהִגִּיעַ רָחְבּוֹ עַד חֲצִי הַמִּזְבֵּחַ, וְהוּא הָיָה סִימָן לַחֲצִי גָּבְהוֹ לְהַבְדִּיל בֵּין דָּמִים הָעֶלְיוֹנִים לְדָמִים הַתַּחְתּוֹנִים, וּכְנֶגְדּוֹ עָשׂוּ לְמִזְבַּח בֵּית עוֹלָמִים חֲגוֹרַת חוּט הַסִּקְרָא בְּאֶמְצָעוֹ (מדות ג, א). וְכֶבֶשׁ שֶׁהָיוּ עוֹלִין בּוֹ, אַף עַל פִּי שֶׁלֹּא פֵּרְשׁוֹ בְּעִנְיָן זֶה, כְּבָר שָׁמַעְנוּ בְּפָרָשַׁת 'מִזְבַּח אֲדָמָה תַּעֲשֶׂה לִּי': "וְלֹא תַעֲלֶה בְמַעֲלֹת" (לעיל כ, כב), לֹא תַעֲשֶׂה לוֹ מַעֲלוֹת בַּכֶּבֶשׁ שֶׁלּוֹ, אֶלָּא כֶּבֶשׁ חָלָק, לָמַדְנוּ שֶׁהָיָה לוֹ כֶּבֶשׁ. כָּךְ שָׁנִינוּ בַּמְּכִילְתָּא (בחדש פרשה יא). וּ'מִזְבַּח אֲדָמָה' הוּא מִזְבַּח הַנְּחֹשֶׁת, שֶׁהָיוּ מְמַלְּאִין חֲלָלוֹ אֲדָמָה בִּמְקוֹם חֲנִיָּתָן. וְהַכֶּבֶשׁ הָיָה בִּדְרוֹם הַמִּזְבֵּחַ מֻבְדָּל מִן הַמִּזְבֵּחַ מְלֹא חוּט הַשַּׂעֲרָה, וְרַגְלָיו מַגִּיעִין עַד אַמָּה סָמוּךְ לְקַלְעֵי הֶחָצֵר שֶׁבַּדָּרוֹם, כְּדִבְרֵי הָאוֹמֵר עֶשֶׂר

of the *sovev* to the top of the altar. [The *sovev* described here was merely ornamental. However on the altar in the Temple of Jerusalem there was a second] *sovev* upon which the priests walked, which did not feature in the brass altar [employed in the Tabernacle]. That additional *sovev* was located on the top of the altar and ran between the structure's corners. As we read in tractate Zevaḥim (62a): "What was the *karkov*? This was an area the width of a cubit that led from corner to corner. Within that cubit circumference was an additional cubit-wide path where the priests were able to walk. These two cubit-wide rings combined to form the *karkov*." The Gemara continues to challenge that interpretation: "Doesn't the Torah state that the grate was *beneath the ledge, extending downward?* (38:4)" For that verse implies that the *karkov* was an object situated ["downward," i.e.,] on the wall of the altar, and the grate was placed beneath it. The Gemara answers: "There were in fact two features of the altar both called *karkov*: one ornamental, and one to protect the priests from slipping on the altar." The *karkov* that was attached to the altar's walls was put there for decorative purposes, and the grate was fastened below it. The bottom of the grate sat at the midpoint of the altar [five cubits from the ground], and it served to identify the exact middle of the altar's height and thereby separate between the blood [of certain sacrifices] that had to be applied to the altar's upper half and that [of others] which had to be sprinkled on the lower half. Later, the Temple's altar would sport a red painted line running around its midpoint as a replacement for the grate on this altar. A ramp led up to the top of the altar, and even though it is not described in the current passage, the Torah alludes to that structure when it introduces the altar of earth, stating: *Do not ascend to My altar with steps* (20:23). What this means is that stairs should not be carved into the ramp, and it should rather be left smooth. From this we infer that the altar had a ramp for access. This is explained in the Mekhilta. Indeed, the "altar of earth" (20:21) mentioned in that

◀

ז בַּדֵּי עֲצֵי שִׁטִּים וְצִפִּיתָ אֹתָם נְחֹשֶׁת׃ וְהוּבָא אֶת־
בַּדָּיו בַּטַּבָּעֹת וְהָיוּ הַבַּדִּים עַל־שְׁתֵּי צַלְעֹת הַמִּזְבֵּחַ
ח בִּשְׂאֵת אֹתוֹ׃ נְבוּב לֻחֹת תַּעֲשֶׂה אֹתוֹ כַּאֲשֶׁר הֶרְאָה
ט אֹתְךָ בָּהָר כֵּן יַעֲשׂוּ׃ וְעָשִׂיתָ אֵת חֲצַר שביעי
הַמִּשְׁכָּן לִפְאַת נֶגֶב־תֵּימָנָה קְלָעִים לֶחָצֵר שֵׁשׁ מָשְׁזָר

passage is the same as the bronze altar being discussed here. The Torah initially refers to this altar as being made of earth because its hollow was filled with soil whenever Israel made camp. The ramp stood on the south side of the altar, but it was separated from the altar itself by a hair's breadth of empty space. The bottom of the ramp ended one cubit away from the hangings surrounding the southern side of the courtyard. Such is the description of the ramp according to the opinion that the altar reached a height of ten cubits. However, based on the alternative approach which argues that verse 1 should be understood as written and that the altar was in fact three cubits high, the ramp was only ten cubits long [and thus ended some distance from the wall of the courtyard]. This is the explanation I discovered in a work called *Arba'im Vatesha Middot*. As for the detail that the ramp was separated from the altar by a hair's breadth, the Talmud in tractate Zevaḥim (62b) derives it through analysis of the Torah text.

אַמּוֹת קוֹמָתוֹ; וּלְדִבְרֵי הָאוֹמֵר דְּבָרִים כִּכְתָבָן ״שָׁלֹשׁ אַמּוֹת קֹמָתוֹ״ (זבחים נט ע״ב), לֹא הָיָה אֹרֶךְ הַכֶּבֶשׁ אֶלָּא עֶשֶׂר אַמּוֹת. כָּךְ מָצָאתִי בִּמִשְׁנַת אַרְבָּעִים וְתֵשַׁע מִדּוֹת. וְזֶה שֶׁהוּא מֻבְדָּל מִן הַמִּזְבֵּחַ מְלֹא הַחוּט, בְּמַסֶּכֶת זְבָחִים (דף סב ע״ב) לְמֵדוּהָ מִן הַמִּקְרָא:

7 | **בַּטַּבָּעֹת** – *In the rings:* That is, the four rings fashioned for the grate.

ז| **בַּטַּבָּעֹת.** בְּאַרְבַּע טַבָּעוֹת שֶׁנַּעֲשׂוּ לַמִּכְבָּר:

8 | **נְבוּב לֻחֹת** – *Hollow with planks:* This phrase should be understood as the Targum renders it: "hollow with planks" [*ḥalil luḥin*]. The altar must be constructed with acacia wood boards on each of its four sides and kept hollow in the middle. It should not be fashioned out of a single piece of wood five cubits wide and five cubits deep like a butcher's block.

ח| **נְבוּב לֻחֹת.** כְּתַרְגּוּמוֹ: ״חֲלִיל לוּחִין״, לוּחוֹת עֲצֵי שִׁטִּים מִכָּל צַד וְהֶחָלָל בָּאֶמְצַע, וְלֹא יְהֵא כֻּלּוֹ עֵץ אֶחָד שֶׁיְּהֵא עָבְיוֹ חָמֵשׁ אַמּוֹת עַל חָמֵשׁ אַמּוֹת כְּמִין סַדָּן:

9 | **קְלָעִים** – *Hangings:* These curtains were fashioned like the sails of a ship, but perforated with holes [to permit the wind to flow through]. They were plaited not woven, as the Targum's translation of the word *kela'im* – *seradin* ["network"] – suggests. Onkelos similarly renders the term *mikhbar* ["grate," in verse 4] as *serada*, because that piece was perforated like a sieve.

ט| **קְלָעִים.** עֲשׂוּיִין כְּמִין קַלְעֵי סְפִינָה נְקָבִים נְקָבִים, מַעֲשֵׂה קְלִיעָה וְלֹא מַעֲשֵׂה אוֹרֵג. וְתַרְגּוּמוֹ: ״סְרָדִין״, כְּתַרְגּוּמוֹ שֶׁל ״מִכְבָּר״ (לעיל פסוק ד) הַמְתֻרְגָּם: ״סְרָדָא״, לְפִי שֶׁהֵן מְנֻקָּבִין כִּכְבָרָה:

◀

10 all the length of the courtyard on that side, with twenty posts
and their twenty bronze sockets. The hooks and bands of the
11 posts shall be of silver. Likewise on the north side; the hangings shall be a hundred cubits long, with twenty posts and
their twenty corresponding bronze sockets, with hooks and
12 bands of silver. The width of the hangings at the western end
of the courtyard shall be fifty cubits, and it should have ten
13 posts and their ten corresponding sockets. The width of the
14 courtyard at the front, facing east, shall be fifty cubits: fifteen
cubits of hangings with three posts and three sockets on one

לַפֵּאָה הָאֶחָת – *On that side:* Each side of the Tabernacle is referred to as a *pe'ah* [which can also mean a "corner" or "fringe"].

לַפֵּאָה הָאֶחָת. כָּל הָרוּחַ קָרוּי פֵּאָה:

10 | **וְעַמֻּדָיו עֶשְׂרִים** – *With twenty posts:* The posts surrounding the courtyard should be placed five cubits apart.

י׀ וְעַמֻּדָיו עֶשְׂרִים. חָמֵשׁ אַמּוֹת בֵּין עַמּוּד לְעַמּוּד:

וְאַדְנֵיהֶם – *And their sockets:* The posts were inserted into bronze sockets that sat directly on the ground. There were also shafts, six handbreadths long by three handbreadths wide, which were affixed to the posts. These are referred to in Old French as *pals* ["posts"]. Bronze rings were welded to the center of these attachments. Now the hems of the hangings were wound around these shafts with cords at every post, and the rings in turn were looped onto matching hooks situated at the top of the posts. The hooks themselves looked like the letter *vav*, with their long ends bored into the posts, and their short ends bent upward to to hold the rings. This is similar to the instruments made to keep doors upright, which are called *gouns* ["hinge-pins"] in Old French. The width [height] of the hangings hung below the hooks, and that represented the height of the courtyard's partitions.

וְאַדְנֵיהֶם. שֶׁל הָעַמּוּדִים "נְחֹשֶׁת". הָאֲדָנִים יוֹשְׁבִין עַל הָאָרֶץ וְהָעַמּוּדִים תְּקוּעִים לְתוֹכָן. וְהָיָה עוֹשֶׂה כְּמִין קֻנְדָּסִין שֶׁקּוֹרִין פלא"ש אָרְכָּן שִׁשָּׁה טְפָחִים וְרָחְבָּן שְׁלֹשָׁה, וְטַבַּעַת נְחֹשֶׁת קְבוּעָה בּוֹ בְּאֶמְצָעוֹ, וְכוֹרֵךְ שְׂפַת הַקֶּלַע סְבִיבָיו בְּמֵיתָרִים כְּנֶגֶד כָּל עַמּוּד וְעַמּוּד, וְתוֹלֶה הַקֻּנְדָּס דֶּרֶךְ טַבַּעְתּוֹ בָּאֻנְקְלִי שֶׁבָּעַמּוּד, הֶעָשׂוּי כְּמִין וָי"ו, רֹאשׁוֹ זָקוּף לְמַעְלָה וְרֹאשׁוֹ אֶחָד תָּקוּעַ בָּעַמּוּד, כְּאוֹתָן שֶׁעוֹשִׂין לְהַצִּיב דְּלָתוֹת שֶׁקּוֹרִין גונזי"ש, וְרֹחַב הַקֶּלַע תָּלוּי מִלְמַטָּה וְהִיא קוֹמַת מְחִצּוֹת הֶחָצֵר:

וָוֵי הָעַמֻּדִים – *The hooks:* This refers to the hooks set in the tops of the posts.

וָוֵי הָעַמֻּדִים. הֵם הָאֻנְקְלִיּוֹת:

וַחֲשֻׁקֵיהֶם – *And bands:* The courtyard posts were filleted with bands of silver. But I do not know whether these pieces covered the entire surface of the posts, or whether they were wrapped around the posts' tops or middles. However, I do know that the term *ḥishuk* connotes a girdle, for we find the word employed in the story of the concubine from Giva, as

וַחֲשֻׁקֵיהֶם. מֻקָּפִין הָיוּ הָעַמּוּדִים בְּחוּטֵי כֶּסֶף סָבִיב. וְאֵינִי יוֹדֵעַ אִם עַל פְּנֵי כֻלָּם אִם בְּרָאשָׁם אִם בְּאֶמְצָעָם, אַךְ יוֹדֵעַ אֲנִי שֶׁ"חִשּׁוּק" לְשׁוֹן חֲגוֹרָה, שֶׁכֵּן מָצִינוּ בְּפִילֶגֶשׁ בַּגִּבְעָה: "וְעִמּוֹ

◀

י מֵאָה בָּאַמָּה אֹרֶךְ לַפֵּאָה הָאֶחָת: וְעַמֻּדָיו עֶשְׂרִים
וְאַדְנֵיהֶם עֶשְׂרִים נְחֹשֶׁת וָוֵי הָעַמֻּדִים וַחֲשֻׁקֵיהֶם
יא כָּסֶף: וְכֵן לִפְאַת צָפוֹן בָּאֹרֶךְ קְלָעִים מֵאָה אֹרֶךְ
וְעַמֻּדָו עֶשְׂרִים וְאַדְנֵיהֶם עֶשְׂרִים נְחֹשֶׁת וָוֵי הָעַמֻּדִים
יב וַחֲשֻׁקֵיהֶם כָּסֶף: וְרֹחַב הֶחָצֵר לִפְאַת־יָם קְלָעִים
חֲמִשִּׁים אַמָּה עַמֻּדֵיהֶם עֲשָׂרָה וְאַדְנֵיהֶם עֲשָׂרָה:
יג וְרֹחַב הֶחָצֵר לִפְאַת קֵדְמָה מִזְרָחָה חֲמִשִּׁים אַמָּה:
יד וַחֲמֵשׁ עֶשְׂרֵה אַמָּה קְלָעִים לַכָּתֵף עַמֻּדֵיהֶם שְׁלֹשָׁה

the verse states, *and there were with him two donkeys saddled [ḥavushim]* (Judges 19:10), and the Targum renders *ḥavushim* as *ḥashikim*.

צֶמֶד חֲמוֹרִים חֲבוּשִׁים" (שופטים יט, י), תַּרְגּוּמוֹ: 'חֲשִׁיקִין':

13 | **לִפְאַת קֵדְמָה מִזְרָחָה** – *At the front, facing east:* The term *kedem* connotes the front of something, while the word *aḥor* refers to its back. This is why the eastern direction is called *kedem* – it is in the front [of the world, where the sun rises], and the western direction is called *aḥor* – it is in the back. Hence the term *hayam haaḥaron* [literally, "hindmost sea," in Deuteronomy 11:24] is translated by Onkelos as "the western sea."

יג | **לִפְאַת קֵדְמָה מִזְרָחָה.** פְּנֵי הַמִּזְרָח קָרוּי 'קֶדֶם', לְשׁוֹן פָּנִים, 'אָחוֹר' לְשׁוֹן אֲחוֹרַיִם. לְפִיכָךְ מִזְרָח קָרוּי קֶדֶם שֶׁהוּא פָּנִים, וּמַעֲרָב קָרוּי אָחוֹר, כְּמָה דְּאַתְּ אָמַר: "הַיָּם הָאַחֲרוֹן" (דברים יא, כד) – "יַמָּא מַעַרְבָאָה" (אונקלוס שם):

חֲמִשִּׁים אַמָּה – *Fifty cubits:* The fifty cubits that spanned the width of the courtyard were not entirely blocked by hangings, since the entrance to the compound had to be left open on the eastern side. Rather, the barrier was hung fifteen cubits on each side of the entrance, leaving a space of twenty empty cubits in the middle. Thus the verse that states: *And for the gate of the courtyard there shall be an embroidered screen of twenty cubits* (27:16), describes a curtain twenty cubits long that defined the entrance, in front of the described open space. [This supplementary hanging was situated ten cubits eastward from the courtyard, allowing people to walk behind it to enter the compound.]

חֲמִשִּׁים אַמָּה. אוֹתָן חֲמִשִּׁים אַמָּה לֹא הָיוּ סְתוּמִים כֻּלָּם בִּקְלָעִים, לְפִי שֶׁשָּׁם הַפֶּתַח, אֶלָּא חֲמֵשׁ עֶשְׂרֵה אַמָּה קְלָעִים לְכָתֵף הַפֶּתַח מִכָּאן וְכֵן לַכָּתֵף הַשֵּׁנִית, נִשְׁאַר רֹחַב חֲלַל הַפֶּתַח בֵּינְתַיִם עֶשְׂרִים אַמָּה, וְזֶהוּ שֶׁנֶּאֱמַר: "וּלְשַׁעַר הֶחָצֵר מָסָךְ עֶשְׂרִים אַמָּה" (להלן פסוק טז), וִילוֹן לְהָסֵךְ כְּנֶגֶד הַפֶּתַח עֶשְׂרִים אַמָּה אֹרֶךְ, כְּרֹחַב הַפֶּתַח:

14 | **עַמֻּדֵיהֶם שְׁלֹשָׁה** – *With three posts:* There were five cubits between each of these three posts. That is, a post [not counted as one of the three, but rather as the final post on the southern side] stood in the south-east corner, and five cubits removed

יד | **עַמֻּדֵיהֶם שְׁלֹשָׁה.** חָמֵשׁ אַמּוֹת בֵּין עַמּוּד לְעַמּוּד, בֵּין עַמּוּד שֶׁבְּרֹאשׁ הַדָּרוֹם הָעוֹמֵד בְּמִקְצוֹעַ דְּרוֹמִית מִזְרָחִית עַד עַמּוּד שֶׁהוּא מִן

15 side, and fifteen cubits of hangings with three posts and three
16 sockets on the other, and for the gate of the courtyard there
shall be an embroidered screen of twenty cubits of sky-blue,
purple, and scarlet wool and finely spun linen, with four posts
17 and four sockets. All the posts around the courtyard should MAFTIR
be banded with silver. Their hooks shall be of silver, and their
18 sockets of bronze. The courtyard shall be a hundred cubits
long, fifty cubits wide, and five cubits high, with hangings of
19 finely spun linen and sockets of bronze. All the Tabernacle

from that corner pole on the east side stood the first eastern side post. A second post was situated five cubits farther, with the third post a further five cubits down that side. A similar set-up of three posts was erected on the other side of the courtyard entrance. Meanwhile the screen that stood opposite the entrance was supported by four posts which were also spaced at intervals of five cubits. Hence there were ten posts altogether on the east side of the compound, corresponding to the ten posts that held the hangings along the western side.

הַשְּׁלֹשָׁה שֶׁבַּמִּזְרָח חָמֵשׁ אַמּוֹת, וּמִמֶּנּוּ לַשֵּׁנִי חָמֵשׁ אַמּוֹת, וּמִן הַשֵּׁנִי לַשְּׁלִישִׁי חָמֵשׁ אַמּוֹת, וְכֵן לַכָּתֵף הַשֵּׁנִית, וְהָאַרְבָּעָה עַמּוּדִים לַמָּסָךְ. הֲרֵי עֲשָׂרָה עַמּוּדִים לַמִּזְרָח כְּנֶגֶד עֲשָׂרָה לַמַּעֲרָב:

17 | **כָּל־עַמּוּדֵי הֶחָצֵר סָבִיב** – *All the posts around the courtyard:* [This would seem to have already been conveyed in verses 10–11. Rashi explains:] Earlier, the text only specified that the posts on the northern and southern sides should be equipped with silver hooks and bands and bronze sockets. But the Torah has not yet stated that the posts standing on the eastern and western sides should similarly be fashioned. Our verse now clarifies that indeed all the courtyard posts were outfitted identically.

יז| כָּל־עַמּוּדֵי הֶחָצֵר סָבִיב וְגוֹ׳. לְפִי שֶׁלֹּא פֵּרֵשׁ וָוִין וַחֲשׁוּקִים וְאַדְנֵי נְחֹשֶׁת אֶלָּא לַצָּפוֹן וְלַדָּרוֹם, אֲבָל לַמִּזְרָח וְלַמַּעֲרָב לֹא נֶאֱמַר וָוִין וַחֲשׁוּקִים וְאַדְנֵי נְחֹשֶׁת, לְכָךְ בָּא וְלִמֵּד כָּאן:

18 | **אֹרֶךְ הֶחָצֵר** – *The length of the courtyard:* This refers to the northern and southern sides, which ran east to west. Each of those sides was one hundred cubits long.

יח| אֹרֶךְ הֶחָצֵר. הַצָּפוֹן וְהַדָּרוֹם שֶׁמִּן הַמִּזְרָח לַמַּעֲרָב "מֵאָה בָאַמָּה":

וְרֹחַב חֲמִשִּׁים בַּחֲמִשִּׁים – *Fifty cubits wide:* [Literally, "fifty by fifty cubits wide."] That is, the eastern area of the courtyard [situated in front of the Tabernacle structure] was a square space fifty cubits on each side. For the Tabernacle itself was thirty cubits long [running west to east] and ten cubits wide [north to south]. Its entrance in the east was set back fifty cubits from the front of the courtyard. What emerges is that the Tabernacle stood entirely within the innermost [western] fifty cubits of the courtyard's length, with its own length culminating thirty

וְרֹחַב חֲמִשִּׁים בַּחֲמִשִּׁים. חָצֵר שֶׁבַּמִּזְרָח הָיְתָה מְרֻבַּעַת חֲמִשִּׁים עַל חֲמִשִּׁים, שֶׁהַמִּשְׁכָּן אָרְכּוֹ שְׁלֹשִׁים וְרָחְבּוֹ עֶשֶׂר, הֶעֱמִיד מִזְרַח פִּתְחוֹ בִּשְׂפַת חֲמִשִּׁים הַחִיצוֹנִים שֶׁל אֹרֶךְ הֶחָצֵר, נִמְצָא כֻּלּוֹ בַּחֲמִשִּׁים הַפְּנִימִיִּים, וְכָלָה אָרְכּוֹ לְסוֹף שְׁלֹשִׁים, נִמְצְאוּ עֶשְׂרִים אַמָּה רֶוַח

◀

טו וְאַדְנֵיהֶם שְׁלֹשָׁה: וְלַכָּתֵף הַשֵּׁנִית חֲמֵשׁ עֶשְׂרֵה
טז קְלָעִים עַמֻּדֵיהֶם שְׁלֹשָׁה וְאַדְנֵיהֶם שְׁלֹשָׁה: וּלְשַׁעַר
הֶחָצֵר מָסָךְ ׀ עֶשְׂרִים אַמָּה תְּכֵלֶת וְאַרְגָּמָן וְתוֹלַעַת
שָׁנִי וְשֵׁשׁ מָשְׁזָר מַעֲשֵׂה רֹקֵם עַמֻּדֵיהֶם אַרְבָּעָה
יז וְאַדְנֵיהֶם אַרְבָּעָה: כָּל־עַמּוּדֵי הֶחָצֵר סָבִיב מְחֻשָּׁקִים מפטיר
יח כֶּסֶף וָוֵיהֶם כָּסֶף וְאַדְנֵיהֶם נְחֹשֶׁת: אֹרֶךְ הֶחָצֵר
מֵאָה בָאַמָּה וְרֹחַב ׀ חֲמִשִּׁים בַּחֲמִשִּׁים וְקֹמָה
יט חָמֵשׁ אַמּוֹת שֵׁשׁ מָשְׁזָר וְאַדְנֵיהֶם נְחֹשֶׁת: לְכֹל כְּלֵי

לַאֲחוֹרָיו בֵּין הַקְּלָעִים שֶׁבַּמַּעֲרָב לִירִיעוֹת שֶׁל אֲחוֹרֵי הַמִּשְׁכָּן. וְרֹחַב הַמִּשְׁכָּן עֶשֶׂר אַמּוֹת בְּאֶמְצַע רֹחַב הֶחָצֵר, נִמְצְאוּ לוֹ עֶשְׂרִים אַמָּה רֶוַח לַצָּפוֹן וְלַדָּרוֹם מִן קַלְעֵי הֶחָצֵר לִירִיעוֹת הַמִּשְׁכָּן, וְכֵן לַמַּעֲרָב, וַחֲמִשִּׁים עַל חֲמִשִּׁים חָצֵר לְפָנָיו:

cubits into that area. This means that there were twenty cubits of empty space behind the sheets of the Tabernacle's western wall, separating them from the western edge of the courtyard hangings. Now the width of the Tabernacle was ten cubits, and the structure was positioned directly in the middle of the courtyard's width [of fifty cubits]. Hence there were twenty cubits of unused space between the sheets covering the northern wall of the structure and the courtyard's edge, and an additional twenty cubits of space between the southern wall and the southern border's hangings. These twenty-cubit areas matched the space of twenty open cubits on the building's western side.

וְקֹמָה חָמֵשׁ אַמּוֹת. גֹּבַהּ מְחִצּוֹת הֶחָצֵר, וְהוּא רֹחַב הַקְּלָעִים:

וְקֹמָה חָמֵשׁ אַמּוֹת – *And five cubits high:* The partitions of the courtyard were five cubits high, such that the width [height] of the hangings was five cubits high.

וְאַדְנֵיהֶם נְחֹשֶׁת. לְהָבִיא אַדְנֵי הַמָּסָךְ, שֶׁלֹּא תֹּאמַר, לֹא נֶאֶמְרוּ אַדְנֵי נְחֹשֶׁת אֶלָּא לְעַמּוּדֵי הַקְּלָעִים, אֲבָל אַדְנֵי הַמָּסָךְ שֶׁל מִין אַחֵר. כָּךְ נִרְאֶה בְּעֵינַי שֶׁלְּכָךְ חָזַר וּשְׁנָאָן:

וְאַדְנֵיהֶם נְחֹשֶׁת – *And their sockets of bronze:* [The repetition of this detail, which was already mentioned in verse 17,] teaches that this applies even to the sockets of the screen standing opposite the entrance. For we might have argued that since the Torah has only specified that the posts supporting the hangings should be inserted into bronze sockets, the sockets for the screen could be fashioned out of some other material. It seems to me that this is why the text now repeats this particular.

יט | לְכֹל כְּלֵי הַמִּשְׁכָּן. שֶׁהָיוּ צְרִיכִין לַהֲקָמָתוֹ וּלְהוֹרָדָתוֹ, כְּגוֹן מַקָּבוֹת לִתְקֹעַ יְתֵדוֹת וְעַמּוּדִים:

19 | **לְכֹל כְּלֵי הַמִּשְׁכָּן** – *All the Tabernacle utensils:* This clause refers to the tools that were needed to assemble and disassemble the Tabernacle. For example, the mallets that were

utensils, for every use, as well as all its tent pegs and the tent pegs of the courtyard, shall be of bronze.

יְתֵדֹת. כְּמִין נַגְרֵי נְחֹשֶׁת עֲשׂוּיִין לִירִיעוֹת הָאֹהֶל וּלְקַלְעֵי הֶחָצֵר קְשׁוּרִים בְּמֵיתָרִים סָבִיב סָבִיב בְּשִׁפּוּלֵיהֶן כְּדֵי שֶׁלֹּא תְהֵא הָרוּחַ מַגְבִּיהָתָן. וְאֵינִי יוֹדֵעַ אִם תְּחוּבִין

used to strike the pegs and posts were also fashioned out of bronze.

יְתֵדֹת – *Tent pegs:* These were bronze pins whose purpose was to secure the sheets covering the Tabernacle and the hangings surrounding the courtyard. Ropes tied to the hems of those materials were wound around the bottom of these dowels to prevent the wind from lifting them up. Now I do not know whether the pegs were pounded into the ground, or whether

◀

הַמִּשְׁכָּן בְּכֹל עֲבֹדָתוֹ וְכָל־יְתֵדֹתָיו וְכָל־יִתְדֹת הֶחָצֵר נְחֹשֶׁת:

בָּאָרֶץ, אוֹ קְשׁוּרִין וּתְלוּיִין וְכָבְדָּן מַכְבִּיד שִׁפּוּלֵי הַיְרִיעוֹת שֶׁלֹּא יָנוּעוּ בָּרוּחַ. וְאוֹמֵר אֲנִי שֶׁשְּׁמָן מוֹכִיחַ עֲלֵיהֶם שֶׁהֵם תְּקוּעִים בָּאָרֶץ, לְכָךְ נִקְרְאוּ ׳יְתֵדוֹת׳, וּמִקְרָא זֶה מְסַיְּעֵנִי: ״אֹהֶל בַּל יִצְעָן בַּל יִסַּע יְתֵדֹתָיו לָנֶצַח״ (ישעיה לג, כ):

these fixtures were merely tied to the sheets and the hangings and left loose, with their sheer weight preventing the bottom edges from flapping around in the wind. However, it seems to me that the name of this tool proves that the pegs were in fact driven into the desert floor. For the name *yated* suggests that usage, and a biblical text supports me: *Your eyes shall see Jerusalem a quiet habitation, a tent that shall not be taken down; its pegs [yetedotav] shall not be removed for ever* [Isaiah 33:20, implying that such pegs fasten the tent firmly to the ground].

◀

HAFTARAT TERUMA

On the Shabbat of Parashat Shekalim, even if it is also Rosh Ḥodesh or erev Rosh Ḥodesh Adar, read the maftir and haftara on page 55.

On the Shabbat of Parashat Zakhor read the maftir and haftara on page 59.

On Rosh Ḥodesh Adar Rishon, read the maftir and haftara on page 51.

5 26 The Lord had endowed Shlomo with wisdom, as He had promised I KINGS
him. There was peace between Ḥiram and Shlomo, and the two of them
27 formed an alliance. King Shlomo began to levy forced labor upon all of
28 Israel; the levy was thirty thousand men. He had ten thousand men sent
to Lebanon every month, in shifts; they would spend a month in Lebanon and two months at home. Adoniram was in charge of the forced
29 labor. And Shlomo had seventy thousand porters and eight
30 thousand quarriers in the mountains, besides Shlomo's three thousand
and three hundred prefect officers in charge of the labor, who super-
31 vised the people who performed the labor. At the king's command, they
quarried enormous blocks of prime stone so that the foundations of the
32 House would be laid with hewn stone. And Shlomo's builders, together
with Ḥiram's builders and the Gevalites, carved the wood and the stone
6 1 in preparation for the construction of the House. In the four
hundred and eightieth year after the Israelites left Egypt, in the month of
Ziv – the second month – of the fourth year of Shlomo's reign over Israel,
2 he began to build the House for the Lord. The House that King Shlomo
built for the Lord was sixty cubits long, twenty cubits wide, and thirty
3 cubits high. The Hall leading up to the Sanctuary of the House was twenty
cubits long along the width of the House, and ten cubits wide leading up
4 5 to the House. He made recessed, paned windows for the House. Around
the outer wall of the House – the outer walls around the Sanctuary and
Inner Sanctuary – he built a tiered structure and made side chambers all
6 around. The lowest tier was five cubits wide, the middle tier was six cubits
wide, and the third tier was seven cubits wide, as he had designed recesses
around the outside of the House to avoid making grooves in the walls of
7 the House. The House was entirely built of finished stones that had been
cut at the quarry; no hammer, ax, or iron tool was heard in the House
8 during its construction. There was an entrance through the central alcove
on the southern side of the House; a winding staircase led to the middle
9 tier and from the middle tier to the third one. When he finished building

הפטרת תרומה

בשבת פרשת שקלים, גם אם חל בה ראש חודש או ערב ראש חודש אדר, קוראים את המפטיר וההפטרה בעמ' 55.
בשבת פרשת זכור קוראים את המפטיר וההפטרה בעמ' 59.
בראש חודש אדר א' קוראים את המפטיר וההפטרה בעמ' 51.

ה כו וַיהוָה נָתַן חָכְמָה לִשְׁלֹמֹה כַּאֲשֶׁר דִּבֶּר־לוֹ וַיְהִי שָׁלֹם בֵּין חִירָם מלכים א
כז וּבֵין שְׁלֹמֹה וַיִּכְרְתוּ בְרִית שְׁנֵיהֶם: וַיַּעַל הַמֶּלֶךְ שְׁלֹמֹה מַס מִכָּל־
כח יִשְׂרָאֵל וַיְהִי הַמַּס שְׁלֹשִׁים אֶלֶף אִישׁ: וַיִּשְׁלָחֵם לְבָנוֹנָה עֲשֶׂרֶת
אֲלָפִים בַּחֹדֶשׁ חֲלִיפוֹת חֹדֶשׁ יִהְיוּ בַלְּבָנוֹן שְׁנַיִם חֳדָשִׁים בְּבֵיתוֹ
כט וַאֲדֹנִירָם עַל־הַמַּס: וַיְהִי לִשְׁלֹמֹה שִׁבְעִים אֶלֶף נֹשֵׂא
ל סַבָּל וּשְׁמֹנִים אֶלֶף חֹצֵב בָּהָר: לְבַד מִשָּׂרֵי הַנִּצָּבִים לִשְׁלֹמֹה אֲשֶׁר
עַל־הַמְּלָאכָה שְׁלֹשֶׁת אֲלָפִים וּשְׁלֹשׁ מֵאוֹת הָרֹדִים בָּעָם הָעֹשִׂים
לא בַּמְּלָאכָה: וַיְצַו הַמֶּלֶךְ וַיַּסִּעוּ אֲבָנִים גְּדֹלוֹת אֲבָנִים יְקָרוֹת לְיַסֵּד
לב הַבָּיִת אַבְנֵי גָזִית: וַיִּפְסְלוּ בֹּנֵי שְׁלֹמֹה וּבֹנֵי חִירוֹם וְהַגִּבְלִים וַיָּכִינוּ
ו א הָעֵצִים וְהָאֲבָנִים לִבְנוֹת הַבָּיִת: וַיְהִי בִשְׁמוֹנִים
שָׁנָה וְאַרְבַּע מֵאוֹת שָׁנָה לְצֵאת בְּנֵי־יִשְׂרָאֵל מֵאֶרֶץ־מִצְרַיִם
בַּשָּׁנָה הָרְבִיעִית בְּחֹדֶשׁ זִו הוּא הַחֹדֶשׁ הַשֵּׁנִי לִמְלֹךְ שְׁלֹמֹה
ב עַל־יִשְׂרָאֵל וַיִּבֶן הַבַּיִת לַיהוָה: וְהַבַּיִת אֲשֶׁר בָּנָה הַמֶּלֶךְ שְׁלֹמֹה
לַיהוָה שִׁשִּׁים־אַמָּה אָרְכּוֹ וְעֶשְׂרִים רָחְבּוֹ וּשְׁלֹשִׁים אַמָּה קוֹמָתוֹ:
ג וְהָאוּלָם עַל־פְּנֵי הֵיכַל הַבַּיִת עֶשְׂרִים אַמָּה אָרְכּוֹ עַל־פְּנֵי רֹחַב
ד הַבָּיִת עֶשֶׂר בָּאַמָּה רָחְבּוֹ עַל־פְּנֵי הַבָּיִת: וַיַּעַשׂ לַבָּיִת חַלּוֹנֵי
ה שְׁקֻפִים אֲטֻמִים: וַיִּבֶן עַל־קִיר הַבַּיִת יצוע סָבִיב אֶת־קִירוֹת הַבַּיִת יָצִיעַ
ו סָבִיב לַהֵיכָל וְלַדְּבִיר וַיַּעַשׂ צְלָעוֹת סָבִיב: היצוע הַתַּחְתֹּנָה חָמֵשׁ הַיָּצִיעַ
בָּאַמָּה רָחְבָּהּ וְהַתִּיכֹנָה שֵׁשׁ בָּאַמָּה רָחְבָּהּ וְהַשְּׁלִישִׁית שֶׁבַע
בָּאַמָּה רָחְבָּהּ כִּי מִגְרָעוֹת נָתַן לַבַּיִת סָבִיב חוּצָה לְבִלְתִּי אֲחֹז
ז בְּקִירוֹת הַבָּיִת: וְהַבַּיִת בְּהִבָּנֹתוֹ אֶבֶן־שְׁלֵמָה מַסָּע נִבְנָה וּמַקָּבוֹת
ח וְהַגַּרְזֶן כָּל־כְּלִי בַרְזֶל לֹא־נִשְׁמַע בַּבַּיִת בְּהִבָּנֹתוֹ: פֶּתַח הַצֵּלָע
הַתִּיכֹנָה אֶל־כֶּתֶף הַבַּיִת הַיְמָנִית וּבְלוּלִּים יַעֲלוּ עַל־הַתִּיכֹנָה וּמִן־
ט הַתִּיכֹנָה אֶל־הַשְּׁלִשִׁים: וַיִּבֶן אֶת־הַבַּיִת וַיְכַלֵּהוּ וַיִּסְפֹּן אֶת־הַבַּיִת

10 the House, he paneled the House with beams and planks of cedar. He built the tiered structure against the whole house, each story five cubits

11 high, so that the House was encased with cedarwood.   And the

12 word of the LORD came to Shlomo: "Concerning this House that you are building: if you follow My laws and uphold My rulings and keep all My commandments by following them, then I will fulfill My promise through

13 you, the promise that I made to your father David. I will dwell in the midst of the Israelites, and I will never abandon My people Israel."

MAFTIR FOR SHABBAT ROSH ḤODESH

9 On the Sabbath day: two yearling sheep without blemish and two-tenths NUMBERS

10 of fine flour as a grain offering, mixed with oil, and its libation. This is the burnt offering for every Sabbath, in addition to the regular daily burnt offering and its libation.

11 On your new moons you shall present a burnt offering to the LORD: two

12 young bulls, one ram, and seven yearling sheep, all without blemish. With each bull, there shall be a grain offering of three-tenths of fine flour mixed with oil, a grain offering of two-tenths of fine flour mixed with oil for each

13 ram, and a grain offering of one-tenth of fine flour mixed with oil for each lamb. This shall be a burnt offering of pleasing aroma, a fire offering to

14 the Lord. Their libations shall be half a hin of wine for a bull, a third of a hin of wine for a ram, and a quarter of a hin of wine for a lamb. This is

15 the monthly burnt offering for each new moon of the year. There shall be one male goat as a sin offering to the Lord in addition to the regular burnt offering and its libation.

HAFTARA FOR SHABBAT ROSH ḤODESH

1 Thus speaks the LORD: The heavens are My throne, the world, My foot- ISAIAH stool. What House, then, would You build for Me, where could I rest?

2 My own hands made all this, all these are Mine, so says the LORD. And these are the ones I look toward: the poor, of humbled spirit, trembling to

3 heed My words. While he, killing his ox is like a murderer of men, the one who offers up a lamb, might so well behead a dog, the offering brought may just as well be pigs' blood; and his remembrance incense is a blessing

י גֵּבִים וּשְׂדֵרֹת בָּאֲרָזִים: וַיִּבֶן אֶת־הַיָּצִיעַ עַל־כָּל־הַבַּיִת חָמֵשׁ   הַיָּצִיעַ
יא אַמּוֹת קוֹמָתוֹ וַיֶּאֱחֹז אֶת־הַבַּיִת בַּעֲצֵי אֲרָזִים: וַיְהִי
יב דְּבַר־יְהוָה אֶל־שְׁלֹמֹה לֵאמֹר: הַבַּיִת הַזֶּה אֲשֶׁר־אַתָּה בֹנֶה אִם־
תֵּלֵךְ בְּחֻקֹּתַי וְאֶת־מִשְׁפָּטַי תַּעֲשֶׂה וְשָׁמַרְתָּ אֶת־כָּל־מִצְוֹתַי לָלֶכֶת
בָּהֶם וַהֲקִמֹתִי אֶת־דְּבָרִי אִתָּךְ אֲשֶׁר דִּבַּרְתִּי אֶל־דָּוִד אָבִיךָ:
יג וְשָׁכַנְתִּי בְּתוֹךְ בְּנֵי יִשְׂרָאֵל וְלֹא אֶעֱזֹב אֶת־עַמִּי יִשְׂרָאֵל:

מפטיר לשבת ראש חודש

כח ט וּבְיוֹם הַשַּׁבָּת שְׁנֵי־כְבָשִׂים בְּנֵי־שָׁנָה תְּמִימִם וּשְׁנֵי עֶשְׂרֹנִים סֹלֶת   במדבר
י מִנְחָה בְּלוּלָה בַשֶּׁמֶן וְנִסְכּוֹ: עֹלַת שַׁבַּת בְּשַׁבַּתּוֹ עַל־עֹלַת הַתָּמִיד
וְנִסְכָּהּ:
יא וּבְרָאשֵׁי חָדְשֵׁיכֶם תַּקְרִיבוּ עֹלָה לַיהוָה פָּרִים בְּנֵי־בָקָר שְׁנַיִם
יב וְאַיִל אֶחָד כְּבָשִׂים בְּנֵי־שָׁנָה שִׁבְעָה תְּמִימִם: וּשְׁלֹשָׁה עֶשְׂרֹנִים
סֹלֶת מִנְחָה בְּלוּלָה בַשֶּׁמֶן לַפָּר הָאֶחָד וּשְׁנֵי עֶשְׂרֹנִים סֹלֶת מִנְחָה
יג בְּלוּלָה בַשֶּׁמֶן לָאַיִל הָאֶחָד: וְעִשָּׂרֹן עִשָּׂרוֹן סֹלֶת מִנְחָה בְּלוּלָה
יד בַשֶּׁמֶן לַכֶּבֶשׂ הָאֶחָד עֹלָה רֵיחַ נִיחֹחַ אִשֶּׁה לַיהוָה: וְנִסְכֵּיהֶם
חֲצִי הַהִין יִהְיֶה לַפָּר וּשְׁלִישִׁת הַהִין לָאַיִל וּרְבִיעִת הַהִין לַכֶּבֶשׂ
טו יָיִן זֹאת עֹלַת חֹדֶשׁ בְּחָדְשׁוֹ לְחָדְשֵׁי הַשָּׁנָה: וּשְׂעִיר עִזִּים אֶחָד
לְחַטָּאת לַיהוָה עַל־עֹלַת הַתָּמִיד יֵעָשֶׂה וְנִסְכּוֹ:

הפטרת שבת ראש חודש

סו א כֹּה אָמַר יְהוָה הַשָּׁמַיִם כִּסְאִי וְהָאָרֶץ הֲדֹם רַגְלָי אֵי־זֶה בַיִת אֲשֶׁר   ישעיה
ב תִּבְנוּ־לִי וְאֵי־זֶה מָקוֹם מְנוּחָתִי: וְאֶת־כָּל־אֵלֶּה יָדִי עָשָׂתָה וַיִּהְיוּ
כָל־אֵלֶּה נְאֻם־יְהוָה וְאֶל־זֶה אַבִּיט אֶל־עָנִי וּנְכֵה־רוּחַ וְחָרֵד
ג עַל־דְּבָרִי: שׁוֹחֵט הַשּׁוֹר מַכֵּה־אִישׁ זוֹבֵחַ הַשֶּׂה עֹרֵף כֶּלֶב מַעֲלֵה
מִנְחָה דַּם־חֲזִיר מַזְכִּיר לְבֹנָה מְבָרֵךְ אָוֶן גַּם־הֵמָּה בָּחֲרוּ בְּדַרְכֵיהֶם

of sin. These men, they choose their paths, their souls desire disgusting
4 things, and so I too will choose – will choose their torments, and bring
to them what they most fear; for I called out – no one answered, I spoke;
but none was listening. They did what was evil in My sight, and chose
5 what I never desired. You who tremble at His word – listen to
the Lord's word: Your brothers said; the ones who hated you, who cast
you out because of My name, "Let us see, then, your joy –" they will be
6 shamefaced. A voice roaring out from the city – a voice, from the Sanctu-
7 ary – a voice – it is the Lord's – as He repays His enemies. Before she
had writhed in labor she gave birth; before the agonies took her she had
8 delivered a boy. Who ever heard of anything like this? Who ever saw anything like this? Can the land give birth in a day? Can a nation be born at
9 a single step? Yet Zion has labored, and has birthed her children. "Would
I bring on the labor and not deliver?" So the Lord speaks. "Would I who
10 fathered, close the womb?" So your God speaks. Bring Jerusalem joy, exult in her, all of you who love her; celebrate her joy with
11 her, all of you who mourned her; That you may suck your fill from the
bosom of her comforting; may suckle, take delight in the brilliance of her
12 glory. For thus says the Lord: See Me make peace flow to her
like a river, the wealth of nations like a rushing brook, and you shall suckle.
13 You will be borne on hips, playing upon loving laps – as a man is consoled
by his mother, just so shall I comfort you, and in Jerusalem, you shall be
14 consoled. You shall look on, your heart rejoicing, while your bones grow
vigorous, like grass, and the hand of the Lord becomes known to His
15 servants, and His rage known to all His enemies. For see: the Lord is
coming in fire, His chariots like a storm-wind, to slake His fury in rage,
16 His rebuke in flames of fire. For in fire, the Lord comes to judgment,
and by the sword, to all flesh, and many are those the Lord will execute.
17 Those in the gardens, sanctifying and purifying themselves, one after the
other in the midst of it, while eating the flesh of pigs and pests and mice,
18 they will all be gathered in together: so the Lord has spoken. For I know
their works, their thoughts; and time will come, to gather all nations and
19 tongues, and they will come, and look upon My glory. I shall place a sign
among them, send out survivors from them to all nations, to Tarshish,
Pul and Lud, to the great archers, Tuval, Yavan, to the distant coastlands
where none ever heard tell of Me or saw My glory, and they will tell of My
20 glory to the nations. And they will bring back all your brothers from in
among all nations, an offering to the Lord, on horseback and on chariot,
on camels, mules and dromedaries, to My holy mount, Jerusalem: so says
the Lord – just as the children of Israel would bring up their offerings

ד וּבְשִׁקּוּצֵיהֶם נַפְשָׁם חָפֵצָה׃ גַּם־אֲנִי אֶבְחַר בְּתַעֲלֻלֵיהֶם וּמְגוּרֹתָם
אָבִיא לָהֶם יַעַן קָרָאתִי וְאֵין עוֹנֶה דִּבַּרְתִּי וְלֹא שָׁמֵעוּ וַיַּעֲשׂוּ הָרַע
ה בְּעֵינַי וּבַאֲשֶׁר לֹא־חָפַצְתִּי בָּחָרוּ׃ שִׁמְעוּ דְּבַר־
יְהוָה הַחֲרֵדִים אֶל־דְּבָרוֹ אָמְרוּ אֲחֵיכֶם שֹׂנְאֵיכֶם מְנַדֵּיכֶם לְמַעַן
ו שְׁמִי יִכְבַּד יְהוָה וְנִרְאֶה בְשִׂמְחַתְכֶם וְהֵם יֵבֹשׁוּ׃ קוֹל שָׁאוֹן מֵעִיר
ז קוֹל מֵהֵיכָל קוֹל יְהוָה מְשַׁלֵּם גְּמוּל לְאֹיְבָיו׃ בְּטֶרֶם תָּחִיל יָלָדָה
ח בְּטֶרֶם יָבוֹא חֵבֶל לָהּ וְהִמְלִיטָה זָכָר׃ מִי־שָׁמַע כָּזֹאת מִי רָאָה
כָּאֵלֶּה הֲיוּחַל אֶרֶץ בְּיוֹם אֶחָד אִם־יִוָּלֵד גּוֹי פַּעַם אֶחָת כִּי־חָלָה
ט גַּם־יָלְדָה צִיּוֹן אֶת־בָּנֶיהָ׃ הַאֲנִי אַשְׁבִּיר וְלֹא אוֹלִיד יֹאמַר יְהוָה אִם־
י אֲנִי הַמּוֹלִיד וְעָצַרְתִּי אָמַר אֱלֹהָיִךְ׃ שִׂמְחוּ אֶת־יְרוּשָׁלִַם
וְגִילוּ בָהּ כָּל־אֹהֲבֶיהָ שִׂישׂוּ אִתָּהּ מָשׂוֹשׂ כָּל־הַמִּתְאַבְּלִים עָלֶיהָ׃
יא לְמַעַן תִּינְקוּ וּשְׂבַעְתֶּם מִשֹּׁד תַּנְחֻמֶיהָ לְמַעַן תָּמֹצּוּ וְהִתְעַנַּגְתֶּם
יב מִזִּיז כְּבוֹדָהּ׃ כִּי־כֹה ׀ אָמַר יְהוָה הִנְנִי נֹטֶה־אֵלֶיהָ כְּנָהָר
שָׁלוֹם וּכְנַחַל שׁוֹטֵף כְּבוֹד גּוֹיִם וִינַקְתֶּם עַל־צַד תִּנָּשֵׂאוּ וְעַל־בִּרְכַּיִם
יג תְּשָׁעֳשָׁעוּ׃ כְּאִישׁ אֲשֶׁר אִמּוֹ תְּנַחֲמֶנּוּ כֵּן אָנֹכִי אֲנַחֶמְכֶם וּבִירוּשָׁלִַם
יד תְּנֻחָמוּ׃ וּרְאִיתֶם וְשָׂשׂ לִבְּכֶם וְעַצְמוֹתֵיכֶם כַּדֶּשֶׁא תִפְרַחְנָה וְנוֹדְעָה
טו יַד־יְהוָה אֶת־עֲבָדָיו וְזָעַם אֶת־אֹיְבָיו׃ כִּי־הִנֵּה יְהוָה בָּאֵשׁ יָבוֹא
וְכַסּוּפָה מַרְכְּבֹתָיו לְהָשִׁיב בְּחֵמָה אַפּוֹ וְגַעֲרָתוֹ בְּלַהֲבֵי־אֵשׁ׃
טז כִּי בָאֵשׁ יְהוָה נִשְׁפָּט וּבְחַרְבּוֹ אֶת־כָּל־בָּשָׂר וְרַבּוּ חַלְלֵי יְהוָה׃
יז הַמִּתְקַדְּשִׁים וְהַמִּטַּהֲרִים אֶל־הַגַּנּוֹת אַחַר אחד בַּתָּוֶךְ אֹכְלֵי בְּשַׂר אַחַת
יח הַחֲזִיר וְהַשֶּׁקֶץ וְהָעַכְבָּר יַחְדָּו יָסֻפוּ נְאֻם־יְהוָה׃ וְאָנֹכִי מַעֲשֵׂיהֶם
וּמַחְשְׁבֹתֵיהֶם בָּאָה לְקַבֵּץ אֶת־כָּל־הַגּוֹיִם וְהַלְּשֹׁנוֹת וּבָאוּ וְרָאוּ
יט אֶת־כְּבוֹדִי׃ וְשַׂמְתִּי בָהֶם אוֹת וְשִׁלַּחְתִּי מֵהֶם ׀ פְּלֵיטִים אֶל־הַגּוֹיִם
תַּרְשִׁישׁ פּוּל וְלוּד מֹשְׁכֵי קֶשֶׁת תֻּבַל וְיָוָן הָאִיִּים הָרְחֹקִים אֲשֶׁר
לֹא־שָׁמְעוּ אֶת־שִׁמְעִי וְלֹא־רָאוּ אֶת־כְּבוֹדִי וְהִגִּידוּ אֶת־כְּבוֹדִי
כ בַּגּוֹיִם׃ וְהֵבִיאוּ אֶת־כָּל־אֲחֵיכֶם ׀ מִכָּל־הַגּוֹיִם ׀ מִנְחָה ׀ לַיהוָה
בַּסּוּסִים וּבָרֶכֶב וּבַצַּבִּים וּבַפְּרָדִים וּבַכִּרְכָּרוֹת עַל הַר קָדְשִׁי יְרוּשָׁלִַם
אָמַר יְהוָה כַּאֲשֶׁר יָבִיאוּ בְנֵי יִשְׂרָאֵל אֶת־הַמִּנְחָה בִּכְלִי טָהוֹר

21 in pure vessels, to the LORD's House – and from among them also I shall
22 take priests and Levites: so says the LORD. For as just as the new heavens,
the new earth that I am now forming, will stand forever before Me, so says
23 the LORD, so will stand your children, your name. And it shall be – every
new moon, every Sabbath – all flesh will come to worship Me: so says the
24 LORD. Going out, they will see the bodies of those people who sinned
against Me, for the worms will not die nor the fire be quenched, and they
will be repugnant to all flesh.

And it shall be – every new moon, every Sabbath, all flesh will come to worship Me: so says the LORD.

MAFTIR PARASHAT SHEKALIM

11 12 The LORD said to Moshe, "When you take the census of the Israelites, EXODUS
as you count, each must give ransom for his life to the LORD, so that no
13 plague strikes them when you count them. Everyone numbered in the
census shall give half a shekel according to the sanctuary weight, where
the shekel is twenty gerah. This half shekel is an offering to the LORD.
14 Every male over twenty is to be included in the census and must give the
15 LORD's offering. The rich shall not give more, and the poor shall not give
less, than this half shekel. It is an offering to the LORD to redeem your
16 lives. Take this redemption money from the Israelites and assign it for the
service of the Tent of Meeting. It shall be a remembrance for the Israelites
before the LORD, to redeem your lives."

HAFTARAT PARASHAT SHEKALIM

17 Then Yehoyada reinstated the covenant between the LORD, the king, II KINGS
and the people, to be the LORD's people; and between the king and the *Sepharadim*
18 people. All the people of the land came to the temple of Baal and tore it *begin*
down and shattered its altars and images through and through, and killed *here*
Matan, the priest of Baal, in front of the altars. The priest set watchmen
19 over the House of the LORD, and he had the officers of the hundreds,
the Keretites, the sentry, and all the people of the land escort the king
down from the House of the LORD. They came in through the sentry gate of the royal palace, and he took his seat upon the royal throne.
20 All the people of the land rejoiced, and calm settled over the city.

כא בֵּית יהוה: וְגַם־מֵהֶם אֶקַּח לַכֹּהֲנִים לַלְוִיִּם אָמַר יהוה: כִּי כַאֲשֶׁר
הַשָּׁמַיִם הַחֲדָשִׁים וְהָאָרֶץ הַחֲדָשָׁה אֲשֶׁר אֲנִי עֹשֶׂה עֹמְדִים לְפָנַי
כג נְאֻם־יהוה כֵּן יַעֲמֹד זַרְעֲכֶם וְשִׁמְכֶם: וְהָיָה מִדֵּי־חֹדֶשׁ בְּחָדְשׁוֹ וּמִדֵּי
כד שַׁבָּת בְּשַׁבַּתּוֹ יָבוֹא כָל־בָּשָׂר לְהִשְׁתַּחֲוֺת לְפָנַי אָמַר יהוה: וְיָצְאוּ
וְרָאוּ בְּפִגְרֵי הָאֲנָשִׁים הַפֹּשְׁעִים בִּי כִּי תוֹלַעְתָּם לֹא תָמוּת וְאִשָּׁם
לֹא תִכְבֶּה וְהָיוּ דֵרָאוֹן לְכָל־בָּשָׂר:

וְהָיָה מִדֵּי־חֹדֶשׁ בְּחָדְשׁוֹ וּמִדֵּי שַׁבָּת בְּשַׁבַּתּוֹ יָבוֹא כָל־בָּשָׂר
לְהִשְׁתַּחֲוֺת לְפָנַי אָמַר יהוה:

מפטיר פרשת שקלים

שמות

ל יא יב וַיְדַבֵּר יהוה אֶל־מֹשֶׁה לֵּאמֹר: כִּי תִשָּׂא אֶת־רֹאשׁ בְּנֵי־יִשְׂרָאֵל
לִפְקֻדֵיהֶם וְנָתְנוּ אִישׁ כֹּפֶר נַפְשׁוֹ לַיהוה בִּפְקֹד אֹתָם וְלֹא־יִהְיֶה
יג בָהֶם נֶגֶף בִּפְקֹד אֹתָם: זֶה | יִתְּנוּ כָּל־הָעֹבֵר עַל־הַפְּקֻדִים מַחֲצִית
הַשֶּׁקֶל בְּשֶׁקֶל הַקֹּדֶשׁ עֶשְׂרִים גֵּרָה הַשֶּׁקֶל מַחֲצִית הַשֶּׁקֶל תְּרוּמָה
יד לַיהוה: כֹּל הָעֹבֵר עַל־הַפְּקֻדִים מִבֶּן עֶשְׂרִים שָׁנָה וָמָעְלָה יִתֵּן
טו תְּרוּמַת יהוה: הֶעָשִׁיר לֹא־יַרְבֶּה וְהַדַּל לֹא יַמְעִיט מִמַּחֲצִית
טז הַשָּׁקֶל לָתֵת אֶת־תְּרוּמַת יהוה לְכַפֵּר עַל־נַפְשֹׁתֵיכֶם: וְלָקַחְתָּ
אֶת־כֶּסֶף הַכִּפֻּרִים מֵאֵת בְּנֵי יִשְׂרָאֵל וְנָתַתָּ אֹתוֹ עַל־עֲבֹדַת אֹהֶל
מוֹעֵד וְהָיָה לִבְנֵי יִשְׂרָאֵל לְזִכָּרוֹן לִפְנֵי יהוה לְכַפֵּר עַל־נַפְשֹׁתֵיכֶם:

הפטרת פרשת שקלים

מלכים ב
הספרדים מתחילים כאן

יא יז וַיִּכְרֹת יְהוֹיָדָע אֶת־הַבְּרִית בֵּין יהוה וּבֵין הַמֶּלֶךְ וּבֵין הָעָם
יח לִהְיוֹת לְעָם לַיהוה וּבֵין הַמֶּלֶךְ וּבֵין הָעָם: וַיָּבֹאוּ כָל־עַם הָאָרֶץ
בֵּית־הַבַּעַל וַיִּתְּצֻהוּ אֶת־מִזְבְּחֹתָו וְאֶת־צְלָמָיו שִׁבְּרוּ הֵיטֵב וְאֵת
מַתָּן כֹּהֵן הַבַּעַל הָרְגוּ לִפְנֵי הַמִּזְבְּחוֹת וַיָּשֶׂם הַכֹּהֵן פְּקֻדֹּת עַל־
יט בֵּית יהוה: וַיִּקַּח אֶת־שָׂרֵי הַמֵּאוֹת וְאֶת־הַכָּרִי וְאֶת־הָרָצִים
וְאֵת | כָּל־עַם הָאָרֶץ וַיֹּרִידוּ אֶת־הַמֶּלֶךְ מִבֵּית יהוה וַיָּבוֹאוּ דֶּרֶךְ־
כ שַׁעַר הָרָצִים בֵּית הַמֶּלֶךְ וַיֵּשֶׁב עַל־כִּסֵּא הַמְּלָכִים: וַיִּשְׂמַח כָּל־

As for Atalya, they had put her to death by sword in the royal pal-
12 1 2 ace. Yehoash was seven years old when he became king; Yehoash *Ashkenazim and Yemenites begin here*
became king in the seventh year of Yehu, and for forty years, he reigned
3 in Jerusalem. His mother's name was Tzivya, of Be'er Sheva. Yehoash did
what was right in the eyes of the LORD all his days, as the priest Yehoyada
4 had taught him. Yet the high shrines were not removed; the people still
5 offered sacrifices and incense at the high shrines. Yehoash said to the
priests, "All the dedicated money brought to the House of the LORD – the
money from the census, the money equivalent to a person's worth, or any
6 money that a person is moved to bring to the House of the LORD – let the
priests accept it, each from his donor, and they will see to the repair of the
7 House wherever damage may be found." But by the twenty-third
year of King Yehoash, the priests had not seen to the repair of the House,
8 and King Yehoash summoned the priest Yehoyada and the priests. "Why
have you not kept the House in repair?" he said to them. "From now on,
do not take any money from your donors; rather, you must donate it to-
9 ward the repair of the House." The priests agreed that they would neither
10 take money from the people nor see to the House's repair. So the priest
Yehoyada took a chest, made a hole in its lid, and placed it to the right of
the altar, where people entered the House of the LORD. There, the priestly
guardians of the threshold placed all the money that was brought to the
11 House of the LORD. Whenever they saw that there was a considerable
amount of money in the chest, the royal scribe and the High Priest would
come up, tie it into a bundle, and count the money found in the House
12 of the LORD. They then gave the weighed out money to the foremen in
charge of the House of the LORD, who would use it to pay the carpenters
13 and the builders who worked in the House of the LORD, and the masons
and stonecutters, and to purchase timber and quarry stones to keep the
House of the LORD in repair, and for any other expenses for maintenance
14 of the House. However, no silver bowls, shears, basins, or trumpets – or
any golden or silver vessels – were made from the money that was brought
15 to the House of the LORD, as it was given to the overseers, who used it to
16 keep the House of the LORD in repair. They did not need to keep track
of the men who received the money to pay out to the workers, for they
17 dealt honestly. Money from guilt offerings and money from purification
offerings was not brought to the House of the LORD; it belonged to the
priests.

עַם־הָאָרֶץ וְהָעִיר שָׁקָטָה וְאֶת־עֲתַלְיָהוּ הֵמִיתוּ בַחֶרֶב בֵּית
יב א ב מֶלֶךְ: *בֶּן־שֶׁבַע שָׁנִים יְהוֹאָשׁ בְּמָלְכוֹ: בִּשְׁנַת־שֶׁבַע הַמֶּלֶךְ האשכנזים והתימנים מתחילים כאן
לְיֵהוּא מָלַךְ יְהוֹאָשׁ וְאַרְבָּעִים שָׁנָה מָלַךְ בִּירוּשָׁלָם וְשֵׁם אִמּוֹ
ג צִבְיָה מִבְּאֵר שָׁבַע: וַיַּעַשׂ יְהוֹאָשׁ הַיָּשָׁר בְּעֵינֵי יְהוָה כָּל־יָמָיו אֲשֶׁר
ד הוֹרָהוּ יְהוֹיָדָע הַכֹּהֵן: רַק הַבָּמוֹת לֹא־סָרוּ עוֹד הָעָם מְזַבְּחִים
ה וּמְקַטְּרִים בַּבָּמוֹת: וַיֹּאמֶר יְהוֹאָשׁ אֶל־הַכֹּהֲנִים כֹּל כֶּסֶף הַקֳּדָשִׁים
אֲשֶׁר יוּבָא בֵית־יְהוָה כֶּסֶף עוֹבֵר אִישׁ כֶּסֶף נַפְשׁוֹת עֶרְכּוֹ כָּל־כֶּסֶף
ו אֲשֶׁר יַעֲלֶה עַל לֶב־אִישׁ לְהָבִיא בֵּית יְהוָה: יִקְחוּ לָהֶם הַכֹּהֲנִים
אִישׁ מֵאֵת מַכָּרוֹ וְהֵם יְחַזְּקוּ אֶת־בֶּדֶק הַבַּיִת לְכֹל אֲשֶׁר־יִמָּצֵא
ז שָׁם בָּדֶק: וַיְהִי בִּשְׁנַת עֶשְׂרִים וְשָׁלֹשׁ שָׁנָה לַמֶּלֶךְ
ח יְהוֹאָשׁ לֹא־חִזְּקוּ הַכֹּהֲנִים אֶת־בֶּדֶק הַבָּיִת: וַיִּקְרָא הַמֶּלֶךְ יְהוֹאָשׁ
לִיהוֹיָדָע הַכֹּהֵן וְלַכֹּהֲנִים וַיֹּאמֶר אֲלֵהֶם מַדּוּעַ אֵינְכֶם מְחַזְּקִים
אֶת־בֶּדֶק הַבָּיִת וְעַתָּה אַל־תִּקְחוּ־כֶסֶף מֵאֵת מַכָּרֵיכֶם כִּי־לְבֶדֶק
ט הַבַּיִת תִּתְּנֻהוּ: וַיֵּאֹתוּ הַכֹּהֲנִים לְבִלְתִּי קְחַת־כֶּסֶף מֵאֵת הָעָם
י וּלְבִלְתִּי חַזֵּק אֶת־בֶּדֶק הַבָּיִת: וַיִּקַּח יְהוֹיָדָע הַכֹּהֵן אֲרוֹן אֶחָד
וַיִּקֹּב חֹר בְּדַלְתּוֹ וַיִּתֵּן אֹתוֹ אֵצֶל הַמִּזְבֵּחַ בימין בְּבוֹא־אִישׁ בֵּית מִיָּמִין
יְהוָה וְנָתְנוּ־שָׁמָּה הַכֹּהֲנִים שֹׁמְרֵי הַסַּף אֶת־כָּל־הַכֶּסֶף הַמּוּבָא
יא בֵית־יְהוָה: וַיְהִי כִּרְאוֹתָם כִּי־רַב הַכֶּסֶף בָּאָרוֹן וַיַּעַל סֹפֵר הַמֶּלֶךְ
יב וְהַכֹּהֵן הַגָּדוֹל וַיָּצֻרוּ וַיִּמְנוּ אֶת־הַכֶּסֶף הַנִּמְצָא בֵית־יְהוָה: וְנָתְנוּ
אֶת־הַכֶּסֶף הַמְתֻכָּן עַל־יַד עֹשֵׂי הַמְּלָאכָה הפקדים בֵּית יְהוָה הַמֻּפְקָדִים
יג וַיּוֹצִיאֻהוּ לְחָרָשֵׁי הָעֵץ וְלַבֹּנִים הָעֹשִׂים בֵּית יְהוָה: וְלַגֹּדְרִים
וּלְחֹצְבֵי הָאֶבֶן וְלִקְנוֹת עֵצִים וְאַבְנֵי מַחְצֵב לְחַזֵּק אֶת־בֶּדֶק בֵּית־
יד יְהוָה וּלְכֹל אֲשֶׁר־יֵצֵא עַל־הַבַּיִת לְחָזְקָה: אַךְ לֹא יֵעָשֶׂה בֵּית
יְהוָה סִפּוֹת כֶּסֶף מְזַמְּרוֹת מִזְרָקוֹת חֲצֹצְרוֹת כָּל־כְּלִי זָהָב וּכְלִי־
טו כָסֶף מִן־הַכֶּסֶף הַמּוּבָא בֵית־יְהוָה: כִּי־לְעֹשֵׂי הַמְּלָאכָה יִתְּנֻהוּ
טז וְחִזְּקוּ־בוֹ אֶת־בֵּית יְהוָה: וְלֹא יְחַשְּׁבוּ אֶת־הָאֲנָשִׁים אֲשֶׁר יִתְּנוּ
אֶת־הַכֶּסֶף עַל־יָדָם לָתֵת לְעֹשֵׂי הַמְּלָאכָה כִּי בֶאֱמֻנָה הֵם עֹשִׂים:
יז כֶּסֶף אָשָׁם וְכֶסֶף חַטָּאוֹת לֹא יוּבָא בֵּית יְהוָה לַכֹּהֲנִים יִהְיוּ:

MAFTIR PARASHAT ZAKHOR

25 ¹⁷₁₈ Remember what Amalek did to you on your way as you left Egypt, how DEUTERONOMY
he attacked you on the way, when you were tired and exhausted, striking
19 down all the stragglers in your rear, with no fear of God. And so, when
the LORD your God gives you rest from all the enemies around you in the
land that the LORD your God is giving you as an inheritance to possess,
you shall blot out the memory of Amalek from beneath the sky. Do not
forget.

HAFTARAT PARASHAT ZAKHOR

I SAMUEL

14 52 There was fierce war against the Philistines all the days of Sha'ul, and *Yemenites*
whenever Sha'ul saw any strong man or valiant warrior, he would recruit *begin here*
15 1 him.   Shmuel said to Sha'ul, "It was I whom the LORD sent to *Sepharadim*
anoint you as king over His people, over Israel; now, heed the words of *begin here*
2 the LORD.   Thus says the LORD of Hosts: I have taken note of *Ashkenazim*
what Amalek did to Israel; how they set upon them on the way as they *begin here*
3 came out of Egypt. Now, go and strike down Amalek; you must utterly
destroy all that is theirs – spare nothing. You must slay man and woman;
4 child and infant; ox and sheep; camel and donkey." Sha'ul summoned the men and mustered them at Telaim; two hundred thousand in-
5 fantrymen and ten thousand men from Yehuda. Sha'ul reached the city of
6 Amalek and lay in wait in the wadi. And Sha'ul said to the Kenites, "Leave;
turn and withdraw from among the Amalekites lest I destroy you together
with them; you dealt loyally with all the Israelites when they left Egypt,"
7 and the Kenites departed from Amalek. Then Sha'ul struck down Amalek
8 from Ḥavila up to Shur, which is east of Egypt. He captured King Agag
of Amalek alive and utterly destroyed the entire people by the sword.
9 But Sha'ul and the men spared Agag and the best of the sheep, cattle, fat
calves, and lambs – the very best of everything; they were not willing to
destroy them. As for all the spurned, worthless property – that, they ut-
10 terly destroyed.   Then the word of the LORD reached Shmuel:

מפטיר פרשת זכור

דברים

כה יז זָכ֗וֹר אֵ֤ת אֲשֶׁר־עָשָׂ֥ה לְךָ֖ עֲמָלֵ֑ק בַּדֶּ֖רֶךְ בְּצֵאתְכֶ֥ם מִמִּצְרָֽיִם: אֲשֶׁ֨ר
קָֽרְךָ֜ בַּדֶּ֗רֶךְ וַיְזַנֵּ֤ב בְּךָ֙ כָּל־הַנֶּחֱשָׁלִ֣ים אַֽחֲרֶ֔יךָ וְאַתָּ֖ה עָיֵ֣ף וְיָגֵ֑עַ וְלֹ֥א
יט יָרֵ֖א אֱלֹהִֽים: וְהָיָ֡ה בְּהָנִ֣יחַ יְהוָ֣ה אֱלֹהֶ֣יךָ ׀ לְ֠ךָ מִכָּל־אֹֽיְבֶ֜יךָ מִסָּבִ֗יב
בָּאָ֨רֶץ֙ אֲשֶׁר֩ יְהוָ֨ה אֱלֹהֶ֜יךָ נֹתֵ֤ן לְךָ֙ נַֽחֲלָה֙ לְרִשְׁתָּ֔הּ תִּמְחֶה֙ אֶת־
זֵ֣כֶר עֲמָלֵ֔ק מִתַּ֖חַת הַשָּׁמָ֑יִם לֹ֖א תִּשְׁכָּֽח:

הפטרת פרשת זכור

שמואל א
התימנים
מתחילים כאן
* הספרדים
מתחילים כאן

יד נב וַתְּהִ֤י הַמִּלְחָמָה֙ חֲזָקָ֣ה עַל־פְּלִשְׁתִּ֔ים כֹּ֖ל יְמֵ֣י שָׁא֑וּל וְרָאָ֨ה שָׁא֜וּל
טו א כָּל־אִ֤ישׁ גִּבּוֹר֙ וְכָל־בֶּן־חַ֔יִל וַיַּֽאַסְפֵ֖הוּ אֵלָֽיו: *וַיֹּ֣אמֶר
שְׁמוּאֵל֮ אֶל־שָׁאוּל֒ אֹתִ֨י שָׁלַ֤ח יְהוָה֙ לִמְשָׁחֲךָ֣ לְמֶ֔לֶךְ עַל־עַמּ֖וֹ
ב עַל־יִשְׂרָאֵ֑ל וְעַתָּ֣ה שְׁמַ֔ע לְק֖וֹל דִּבְרֵ֥י יְהוָֽה: כֹּ֤ה
אָמַר֙ יְהוָ֣ה צְבָא֔וֹת פָּקַ֕דְתִּי אֵ֛ת אֲשֶׁר־עָשָׂ֥ה עֲמָלֵ֖ק לְיִשְׂרָאֵ֑ל
ג אֲשֶׁר־שָׂ֥ם לוֹ֙ בַּדֶּ֔רֶךְ בַּֽעֲלֹת֖וֹ מִמִּצְרָֽיִם: עַתָּה֩ לֵ֨ךְ וְהִכִּיתָ֜ה אֶת־
עֲמָלֵ֗ק וְהַֽחֲרַמְתֶּם֙ אֶת־כָּל־אֲשֶׁר־ל֔וֹ וְלֹ֥א תַחְמֹ֖ל עָלָ֑יו וְהֵֽמַתָּ֞ה
מֵאִ֣ישׁ עַד־אִשָּׁ֗ה מֵֽעֹלֵל֙ וְעַד־יוֹנֵ֔ק מִשּׁ֣וֹר וְעַד־שֶׂ֔ה מִגָּמָ֖ל וְעַד־
ד חֲמֽוֹר: וַיְשַׁמַּ֤ע שָׁאוּל֙ אֶת־הָעָ֔ם וַֽיִּפְקְדֵם֙ בַּטְּלָאִ֔ים מָאתַ֖יִם
ה אֶ֤לֶף רַגְלִי֙ וַֽעֲשֶׂ֣רֶת אֲלָפִ֔ים אֶת־אִ֖ישׁ יְהוּדָֽה: וַיָּבֹ֥א שָׁא֖וּל עַד־עִ֣יר
ו עֲמָלֵ֑ק וַיָּ֖רֶב בַּנָּֽחַל: וַיֹּ֣אמֶר שָׁא֣וּל אֶל־הַקֵּינִ֡י לְכוּ֩ סֻּ֨רוּ רְד֜וּ מִתּ֣וֹךְ
עֲמָֽלֵקִ֗י פֶּן־אֹֽסִפְךָ֙ עִמּ֔וֹ וְאַתָּ֞ה עָשִׂ֤יתָה חֶ֨סֶד֙ עִם־כָּל־בְּנֵ֣י יִשְׂרָאֵ֔ל
ז בַּֽעֲלוֹתָ֖ם מִמִּצְרָ֑יִם וַיָּ֥סַר קֵינִ֖י מִתּ֥וֹךְ עֲמָלֵֽק: וַיַּ֥ךְ שָׁא֖וּל אֶת־
ח עֲמָלֵ֑ק מֵֽחֲוִילָ֥ה בּֽוֹאֲךָ֛ שׁ֖וּר אֲשֶׁ֥ר עַל־פְּנֵ֥י מִצְרָֽיִם: וַיִּתְפֹּ֛שׂ אֶת־אֲגַ֥ג
ט מֶֽלֶךְ־עֲמָלֵ֖ק חָ֑י וְאֶת־כָּל־הָעָ֖ם הֶֽחֱרִ֥ים לְפִי־חָֽרֶב: וַיַּחְמֹל֩ שָׁא֨וּל
וְהָעָ֜ם עַל־אֲגָ֗ג וְעַל־מֵיטַ֣ב הַצֹּאן֩ וְהַבָּקָ֨ר וְהַמִּשְׁנִ֤ים וְעַל־הַכָּרִים֙
וְעַל־כָּל־הַטּ֔וֹב וְלֹ֥א אָב֖וּ הַֽחֲרִימָ֑ם וְכָל־הַמְּלָאכָ֛ה נְמִבְזָ֥ה וְנָמֵ֖ס
י אֹתָ֥הּ הֶֽחֱרִֽימוּ: וַֽיְהִי֙ דְּבַר־יְהוָ֔ה אֶל־שְׁמוּאֵ֖ל לֵאמֹֽר:

11 "I regret that I crowned Sha'ul as king, for he has turned away from following Me and he has failed to fulfill My words." This enraged Shmuel, and
12 he cried out to the LORD all night long. And Shmuel set out early in the
morning toward Sha'ul, and Shmuel was told, "Sha'ul has gone to Carmel,
where he set up a monument for himself; then he turned off and made
13 his way down to Gilgal." When Shmuel reached Sha'ul, Sha'ul said to him,
14 "Blessed are you to the LORD! I have fulfilled the LORD's word." "Then
what is this bleating of sheep in my ears," said Shmuel, "and the lowing of
15 cattle that I hear?" "They brought them from the Amalekites," said Sha'ul,
"for the men spared the best of the sheep and cattle for sacrificing to the
16 LORD, your God – but we utterly destroyed the rest." "Stop," said
Shmuel, "and let me tell you what the LORD told me last night." "Speak,"
17 he said to him. And Shmuel said, "Though you may seem small
in your own eyes, you are the head of the tribes of Israel, and the LORD
18 anointed you as king over Israel. The LORD sent you on a mission, bid-
ding, 'Go and utterly destroy the offenders – Amalek – and fight them
19 until you have destroyed them.' But why did you fail to heed the voice
of the LORD, pouncing on the spoil and doing evil in the eyes of the
20 LORD?" "But I did heed the voice of the LORD," Sha'ul said to
Shmuel. "I set out on the mission the LORD assigned me, and I brought
21 Agag, king of Amalek, and utterly destroyed Amalek. And the men took
of the spoil – the choicest sheep and cattle from what was banned – to
22 sacrifice to the LORD, your God, at Gilgal." And Shmuel said,
"Does the LORD delight in burnt offerings and sacrifices as much as obedience to the LORD's voice? Behold – obedience is better than sacrifice,
23 and compliance than the fat of rams. For rebellion is as bad as the sin of
divination, and presumption as corruption and idolatry. Because you
24 rejected the word of the LORD, He has rejected you as king." "I
have sinned," Sha'ul said to Shmuel, "for I violated the LORD's command
25 and your word, because I feared the people and heeded their voice. But
now, please forgive my sin and return with me, so I may worship before
26 the LORD." "I will not return with you," Shmuel said to Sha'ul, "for you
have rejected the word of the LORD – and the LORD has rejected you from
27 being king over Israel." And Shmuel turned to go, but Sha'ul grabbed the
28 corner of his robe, and it tore. "The LORD has torn the kingship of Israel
away from you today," Shmuel said to him, "and has granted it to your

יא נִחַמְתִּי כִּי־הִמְלַכְתִּי אֶת־שָׁאוּל לְמֶלֶךְ כִּי־שָׁב מֵאַחֲרַי וְאֶת־
דְּבָרַי לֹא הֵקִים וַיִּחַר לִשְׁמוּאֵל וַיִּזְעַק אֶל־יְהֹוָה כָּל־הַלָּיְלָה׃
יב וַיַּשְׁכֵּם שְׁמוּאֵל לִקְרַאת שָׁאוּל בַּבֹּקֶר וַיֻּגַּד לִשְׁמוּאֵל לֵאמֹר
בָּא־שָׁאוּל הַכַּרְמֶלָה וְהִנֵּה מַצִּיב לוֹ יָד וַיִּסֹּב וַיַּעֲבֹר וַיֵּרֶד הַגִּלְגָּל׃
יג וַיָּבֹא שְׁמוּאֵל אֶל־שָׁאוּל וַיֹּאמֶר לוֹ שָׁאוּל בָּרוּךְ אַתָּה לַיהֹוָה
יד הֲקִימֹתִי אֶת־דְּבַר יְהֹוָה׃ וַיֹּאמֶר שְׁמוּאֵל וּמֶה קוֹל־הַצֹּאן הַזֶּה
טו בְּאָזְנָי וְקוֹל הַבָּקָר אֲשֶׁר אָנֹכִי שֹׁמֵעַ׃ וַיֹּאמֶר שָׁאוּל מֵעֲמָלֵקִי
הֱבִיאוּם אֲשֶׁר חָמַל הָעָם עַל־מֵיטַב הַצֹּאן וְהַבָּקָר לְמַעַן זְבֹחַ
טז לַיהֹוָה אֱלֹהֶיךָ וְאֶת־הַיּוֹתֵר הֶחֱרַמְנוּ׃ וַיֹּאמֶר שְׁמוּאֵל
אֶל־שָׁאוּל הֶרֶף וְאַגִּידָה לְּךָ אֵת אֲשֶׁר דִּבֶּר יְהֹוָה אֵלַי הַלָּיְלָה
יז וַיֹּאמְרוּ לוֹ דַּבֵּר׃ וַיֹּאמֶר שְׁמוּאֵל הֲלוֹא אִם־קָטֹן וַיֹּאמֶר
אַתָּה בְּעֵינֶיךָ רֹאשׁ שִׁבְטֵי יִשְׂרָאֵל אָתָּה וַיִּמְשָׁחֲךָ יְהֹוָה לְמֶלֶךְ
יח עַל־יִשְׂרָאֵל׃ וַיִּשְׁלָחֲךָ יְהֹוָה בְּדָרֶךְ וַיֹּאמֶר לֵךְ וְהַחֲרַמְתָּה אֶת־
יט הַחַטָּאִים אֶת־עֲמָלֵק וְנִלְחַמְתָּ בוֹ עַד־כַּלּוֹתָם אֹתָם׃ וְלָמָּה
לֹא־שָׁמַעְתָּ בְּקוֹל יְהֹוָה וַתַּעַט אֶל־הַשָּׁלָל וַתַּעַשׂ הָרַע בְּעֵינֵי
כ יְהֹוָה׃ וַיֹּאמֶר שָׁאוּל אֶל־שְׁמוּאֵל אֲשֶׁר שָׁמַעְתִּי
בְּקוֹל יְהֹוָה וָאֵלֵךְ בַּדֶּרֶךְ אֲשֶׁר־שְׁלָחַנִי יְהֹוָה וָאָבִיא אֶת־אֲגַג מֶלֶךְ
כא עֲמָלֵק וְאֶת־עֲמָלֵק הֶחֱרַמְתִּי׃ וַיִּקַּח הָעָם מֵהַשָּׁלָל צֹאן וּבָקָר
כב רֵאשִׁית הַחֵרֶם לִזְבֹּחַ לַיהֹוָה אֱלֹהֶיךָ בַּגִּלְגָּל׃ וַיֹּאמֶר
שְׁמוּאֵל הַחֵפֶץ לַיהֹוָה בְּעֹלוֹת וּזְבָחִים כִּשְׁמֹעַ בְּקוֹל יְהֹוָה הִנֵּה
כג שְׁמֹעַ מִזֶּבַח טוֹב לְהַקְשִׁיב מֵחֵלֶב אֵילִים׃ כִּי חַטַּאת־קֶסֶם
מֶרִי וְאָוֶן וּתְרָפִים הַפְצַר יַעַן מָאַסְתָּ אֶת־דְּבַר יְהֹוָה וַיִּמְאָסְךָ
כד מִמֶּלֶךְ׃ וַיֹּאמֶר שָׁאוּל אֶל־שְׁמוּאֵל חָטָאתִי כִּי־עָבַרְתִּי
אֶת־פִּי־יְהֹוָה וְאֶת־דְּבָרֶיךָ כִּי יָרֵאתִי אֶת־הָעָם וָאֶשְׁמַע בְּקוֹלָם׃
כה כו וְעַתָּה שָׂא נָא אֶת־חַטָּאתִי וְשׁוּב עִמִּי וְאֶשְׁתַּחֲוֶה לַיהֹוָה׃ וַיֹּאמֶר
שְׁמוּאֵל אֶל־שָׁאוּל לֹא אָשׁוּב עִמָּךְ כִּי מָאַסְתָּה אֶת־דְּבַר יְהֹוָה
כז וַיִּמְאָסְךָ יְהֹוָה מִהְיוֹת מֶלֶךְ עַל־יִשְׂרָאֵל׃ וַיִּסֹּב שְׁמוּאֵל לָלֶכֶת
כח וַיַּחֲזֵק בִּכְנַף־מְעִילוֹ וַיִּקָּרַע׃ וַיֹּאמֶר אֵלָיו שְׁמוּאֵל קָרַע יְהֹוָה

29 peer, who is better than you. What is more, Israel's Eternal will not betray
30 or waver, for He is not a mere wavering human." "I have sinned," he said.
"Now please honor me in front of the elders of my people and in front of
31 Israel; return with me and I will worship the LORD your God." So Shmuel
32 followed Sha'ul back, and Sha'ul worshipped the LORD. Shmuel
then gave the order, "Bring Agag, king of Amalek, to me." Agag walked up
to him with stately steps. "So," said Agag, "the bitterness of death is upon
33 me." And Shmuel said, "As your sword has made women childless, so your
mother shall be childless among women!" And Shmuel hacked Agag to
34 pieces before the LORD at Gilgal. Then Shmuel went to Rama
while Sha'ul made his way up to his home in Givat Sha'ul.

Yemenites end here

Ashkenazim and Sepharadim end here

אֶת־מַמְלְכ֧וּת יִשְׂרָאֵ֛ל מֵעָלֶ֖יךָ הַיּ֑וֹם וּנְתָנָ֕הּ לְרֵעֲךָ֖ הַטּ֥וֹב מִמֶּֽךָּ׃
כט וְגַם֙ נֵ֣צַח יִשְׂרָאֵ֔ל לֹ֥א יְשַׁקֵּ֖ר וְלֹ֣א יִנָּחֵ֑ם כִּ֣י לֹ֥א אָדָ֛ם ה֖וּא לְהִנָּחֵֽם׃
ל וַיֹּ֣אמֶר חָטָ֔אתִי עַתָּ֗ה כַּבְּדֵ֥נִי נָ֛א נֶ֥גֶד זִקְנֵֽי־עַמִּ֖י וְנֶ֣גֶד יִשְׂרָאֵ֑ל
לא וְשׁ֣וּב עִמִּ֔י וְהִֽשְׁתַּחֲוֵ֖יתִי לַיהוָ֥ה אֱלֹהֶֽיךָ׃ וַיָּ֥שָׁב שְׁמוּאֵ֖ל אַחֲרֵ֣י
לב שָׁא֑וּל וַיִּשְׁתַּ֥חוּ שָׁא֖וּל לַֽיהוָֽה׃ וַיֹּ֣אמֶר שְׁמוּאֵ֗ל הַגִּ֤ישׁוּ
אֵלַי֙ אֶת־אֲגַג֙ מֶ֣לֶךְ עֲמָלֵ֔ק וַיֵּ֣לֶךְ אֵלָ֔יו אֲגַ֖ג מַעֲדַנֹּ֑ת וַיֹּ֣אמֶר אֲגָ֔ג
לג אָכֵ֖ן סָ֥ר מַר־הַמָּֽוֶת׃ וַיֹּ֣אמֶר שְׁמוּאֵ֔ל כַּאֲשֶׁ֨ר שִׁכְּלָ֤ה נָשִׁים֙ חַרְבֶּ֔ךָ
כֵּן־תִּשְׁכַּ֥ל מִנָּשִׁ֖ים אִמֶּ֑ךָ וַיְשַׁסֵּ֨ף שְׁמוּאֵ֧ל אֶת־אֲגָ֛ג לִפְנֵ֥י יְהוָ֖ה
לד בַּגִּלְגָּֽל׃* וַיֵּ֥לֶךְ שְׁמוּאֵ֖ל הָרָמָ֑תָה וְשָׁא֗וּל עָלָ֛ה אֶל־
בֵּית֖וֹ גִּבְעַ֥ת שָׁאֽוּל׃

* התימנים מסיימים כאן

אשכנזים וספרדים מסיימים כאן